NATIONAL
IDENTITY
AND
DEMOCRATIC
PROSPECTS
IN
SOCIALIST
CHINA

"*National Identity and Democratic Prospects in Socialist China* is a challenging contribution to the debate about democratic prospects in China which vividly captures the contradictory cultural forces that have emerged with the crisis of national identity in the reform era."

—Frank Dikötter,
School of Oriental and Africa Studies,
University of London

"This engaging collection of essays by Edward Friedman pursues the closely related themes that have defined his scholarship in recent years: democracy, the debilities of Leninism, the demise of the cultural mythology of a single Han people. Friedman has a keen sense of history, acute enough to forsake prophecy, but to read carefully the powerful trends that interrogate the destiny of China. Can an indispensable democratization create a new political order which accommodates competing narratives of China's origins and cultural essence? Only the future will reveal the answer, but these insightful essays raise the key questions."

—M. Crawford Young,
University of Wisconsin, Madison

NATIONAL IDENTITY
AND
DEMOCRATIC
PROSPECTS
IN
SOCIALIST
CHINA

Edward Friedman

An East Gate Book

M.E. Sharpe
Armonk, New York
London, England

An East Gate Book

Library of Congress Cataloging-in-Publication Data

Friedman, Edward.
National identity and democratic prospects in socialist China /
Edward Friedman.
p.   cm.
Includes bibliographical references and index.
ISBN 1-56324-433-0. — ISBN 1-56324-434-9 (pbk.)
1. China—Politics and government—1076– . I. Title.
DS779.26.F75   1995
951.05—dc20   94-42257
CIP

Printed in the United States of America

The paper used in this publication meets the minimum requirements of
American National Standard for Information Sciences—
Permanence of Paper for Printed Library Materials,
ANSI Z 39.48-1984.

BM (c)   10   9   8   7   6   5   4   3   2   1
BM (p)   10   9   8   7   6   5   4   3   2   1

For

Helen Marcus Friedman, Anne Thompson Stanford,
Susan Stanford Friedman,
Ruth Jennifer Friedman, Joanna Stanford Friedman

Contents

Part Four: Democratic Prospects

Part Five: Conclusion

Preface

In the post-Mao era of deep involvement with the world economy, and in an era when Mao's legitimation of the People's Republic in terms of militarized, anti-imperialist self-reliance makes no sense to the Chinese people, is there a glue of common values or goals or a worldview that holds the Chinese people together as one nation? If not, how long can that dictatorial, overly centralized regime survive? If not long, what is likely to replace it?

These crucial questions have informed my research agenda since 1987–88. This book offers tentative answers to these vital questions, answers that challenged the conventional wisdom of 1988 that did not grapple with socialist China's deepening crisis of national identity and thereby obscured important forces of division, chaos, or civil war, or perhaps confederation, federation, or democracy.

In addition to identifying forces and dynamics that could take China in the twenty-first century on a political path of democracy, this book tries to contribute to the ongoing debate among analysts of nationalism, especially by adding to the discussion about what makes for a democratic national identity. In the early 1990s, ever more theorists found wisdom in deep structural approaches that located distant turning points at which the possibility for democracy was won or defeated ever further back in time. In contrast, this study stresses the centrality of political creativity at reappearing, albeit not continuous or numerous, moments of political opportunity.

In the wisdom of a deep structuralist, on the other hand, China's loss of democratic possibility can be located half a millennia ago, when the early-modern military revolution in all "the East" failed to produce a democratic potential that allegedly developed uniquely in "the West." In the East, "instead, we have found powerful central states unencumbered by estates, legal necessities or local centers of power."[1]

In sharp contrast, this study is based on the fact that all societies are capable of a politics of successful democratization. This is obviously so in "the East," where Japan, South Korea, Taiwan, and Mongolia have already democratized. A serious comparative political sociology would show that these Asian societies have long had at least as much cultural and social potential for democracy as "the West."[2]

Still, this book accepts a central premise of the cultural structuralists, that is, that the cultural construction of a national identity compatible with democracy is indeed crucial to democratic consolidation. This study details the construction of a democratic national identity in China. Thus, in contrast to the conventional wisdom that distinguishes East and West as two absolutely opposed worlds, this analysis is premised on the finding that what is decisive in any society is a politics of democratization in which contested national identities vie as projects of diverse political coalitions. In other words, constitution making alone will be a weak reed against hurricane-force antidemocratic gales unless key strata stand firmly with that constitution and can construct a political edifice of democratic inertia where the larger purpose of a solid and broad-based democratic politics prevents the toppling of democracy because the constitutional order is at one with a deeply rooted popular democratic nationalism.[3] This work tries to capture the cultural construction of that democratic nationalism in late-twentieth-century China.[4] Much scholarship already details how in the Taisho era in Japan, as in the May Fourth era in China, crucial groups have promoted democracy in opposition to despised tyrannies. Indeed, once the institutional realities of building democracy were known, it was inevitable that key strata and interests would embrace democracy to discredit despotism. The promotion of a democratic project in China therefore was to be expected.

The beginning of the twenty-first century will be marked by the rise of East Asia; it is therefore extraordinary how much scholarly work is still premised on a long-discredited Eurocentric "othering" that distinguishes the good West from all the bad rest, with "western nationalism as relatively benign and nice, and the eastern kind as nasty, and doomed to nastiness by the conditions which gave rise to it."[5] In line with the influential writings of Harvard University professor Samuel Huntington, the profound structural inquiry of *Nationalism: Five Roads to Modernity* once again has found democratic potential only in Anglo-American Christian democracy. For the United States, from this parochial and Anglophile perspective, the English settlers of the seventeenth century had already institutionalized democratic nationalism in America.[6]

In contrast, this study, as do the numerous brilliant works that take seriously Abraham Lincoln's concern about free government and whether "this nation or any nation so conceived and so dedicated can long endure," ponders the fate of a fragile and threatened liberty in the United States in the era of its Civil War[7] and, like those works, finds that democracy is always but one national potential, one that is challengeable and that could be lost depending on a series of political struggles at continually arising crucial historical points. Thus this study rejects the unistranded monist structuralism that finds that by the mid-nineteenth century Germany was already on an irreversible antiliberal course that would treat the West as evil incarnate, with "the role of the savior of mankind . . . to be played by the anti-West."[8] In opposition to structuralism, this book highlights contingency, conjuncture, creativity, and politics.

This study assumes that post–World War II German democracy has built on democratic potentials that were viable but temporarily defeated not only in the late nineteenth century but also in the Weimar Republic, only later to win in decisive struggles shaped by contingent, conjunctural, and political factors after World War II. If the punitive Versailles Treaty and subsequent global depression are internationally contingent events that helped defeat democracy, then the defeat of Nazism in World War II and the subsequent Allied intervention are internationally contingent events that helped democrats win. Politics is decisive.

What is truly remarkable is how, despite even prolonged power by despotic states, all human societies find ways to struggle for democratic human dignity, such that all people can construct and manage viable notions of their national community at one with democratic nationalism and can challenge antidemocratic notions of nation. This is certainly true of the people of China.

This creative and liberating work in China of building a democratic national identity, the subject of this study, has been succeeding despite a monopoly of the media and all national cultural institutions by militant antidemocrats. Those who feel an affinity for democracy nonetheless reimagine their history in support of democratization. To watch Chinese society culturally construct a democratic national identity is to see what is usually hidden when one presumes that state power in the hands of authoritarian patriots precludes alternative notions of nation. To comprehend the construction of this potential democratic identity in China is to understand the general error in presupposing that democracy is a unique and ancient emanation of peculiarly English cultural institutions, an almost racist notion that was used by the purported proponents of Anglo-American Christian democracy in the United States in the Ku Klux Klan to practice a terrorist politics that would deny democratic participation to various Catholic Americans, African Americans, and Jewish Americans. One better understands the struggle for democracy in China, or anywhere, when one sees how protracted, bloody, and frustrating was the actual struggle for meaningful democracy for all Americans in the United States, a struggle that was stubbornly opposed by purported heirs of Anglo-American Christian democracy in policies of immigration and voting exclusions, as well as other racist and coercive antidemocratic efforts.

This book, then, is not premised on the optimistic notion that democratization in China or anywhere else will be easy. No such happy view is possible—for any culture. Democratization is never a simple matter of preordained victory for a democratic national identity that wins once and forever. Nonetheless, this study

happily accepts, warmly embraces, and gladly builds on the important structuralist insight that a democratic political outcome is made more likely by the cultural
creation of a democratic national identity. Much thus can be illuminated by
analyzing the politics of this cultural work in China. It is therefore worth exploring *National Identity and Democratic Prospects in Socialist China.*[9]

Notes

1. Brian Downing, *The Military Revolution and Political Change: Origins of Democracy and Autocracy in Early Modern Europe* (Princeton: Princeton University Press,
1992), p. 53.
2. Edward Friedman, ed., *The Politics of Democratization: Generalizing East Asian
Experiences* (Boulder, CO: Westview Press, 1994).
3. E. Spencer Wellhofer, " 'Men Make Their Own History, But . . .': The New Institu-
tionalism and the Fate of Liberal Democracy in Inter-War Europe," *Democratization* 1.2
(Summer 1994), pp. 323–42.
4. On cultural construction, see Benedict Anderson, *Imagined Communities* (London:
Verso, 1991 [1983]).
5. Ernest Gellner, *Nations and Nationalism* (Ithaca: Cornell University Press, 1983),
p. 99.
6. Liah Greenfield, *Nationalism: Five Roads to Modernity* (Cambridge, MA: Harvard
University Press, 1992).
7. Barrington Moore, Jr., *Social Origins of Dictatorship and Democracy* (Boston:
Beacon Press, 1966); James McPherson, *Abraham Lincoln and the Second American
Revolution* (New York: Oxford University Press, 1991).
8. Greenfield, *Nationalism*, p. 394.
9. Chapters in this book previously published are so acknowledged at the start of a
chapter. After writing the first two chapters separately, the overall idea of the book took
shape and guided the writing of the rest of the chapters, some of which were published in
journals only after the book's manuscript was complete and accepted for publication.
Changes have been made only on matters such as tense, style, and grammar.

Part One

Introduction

Chapter 1

Contending
National Projects

In 1988, a few years after having worked for almost three years on the staff of the United States House of Representatives Committee on Foreign Affairs, I traveled from north to south in China lecturing on the role of the American Congress in Chinese-American relations.[1] I discovered on that early-1988 trip that China's south seemed, in comparison to China's north, another country. On returning to the United States, I learned that anthropologist Dru Gladney was investigating the crisis of Han national identity,[2] that Lowell Dittmer and Samuel Kim were editing a volume on the new problematique of national identity in China,[3] that anthropologist Helen Siu was detailing the changes in southern identity,[4] and that Edward Gargan, a *New York Times* correspondent who had been trained in Chinese studies at the University of California at Berkeley, was sketching this north–south clash in a book.

The Beijing regime, Gargan noted, was popularly blamed for almost destroying China's great cuisines, which survived and were revived in the south. In the south, home to most schools of Chinese geomancy, that practice could be credited with keeping places in the south "untouched by the happenings in the distant north." Asked why a 1987 campaign for political orthodoxy was ignored in the south, a Cantonese explained, "That's Beijing. We do things differently down here." The reporter found "the habits of one region of China are not those of another." Or, as a southern official put it, "north and south cannot mix." Foreigners could move freely on southern roads, not northern ones. In contrast to the staid north, young lovers in the south found public places for intimate sharing and caring. The south took pride in new and more open cultural identities—color, foreign music, individuality—while the north seemed locked in old-fashioned, outmoded identities.[5] In all these matters where the south was ahead, the north would eventually follow the lead of the south.

In diverse writings, Geremie Barmé, a specialist in Chinese literature and culture, detailed how pop songs from the Chinese diaspora moved through Canton in China's south to conquer the rest of the mainland (whose music seemed behind the times), that the south was becoming the publishing center for dangerous ideas, that a dictionary was published explaining new phrases both from the diaspora and Canton, and that increasing numbers of fashionable northerners and businesspeople were accepting Cantonese expressions and Taiwanese turns of phrase in their everyday speech.

I found that northerners, even in rural areas, in the Cantonese way, increasingly drummed two fingers as a thank-you to a pouring of tea and repeated a tale of its origins to an incognito visit of the Qian Long emperor to the south. The public popularity of this southern custom in the north, a custom previously decried by northerners as crude, seems a safe but open way of distancing oneself from the anti-imperialist, northern regime. In addition, southern food grew popular in the north. Indeed southern cuisine is described as modern, healthy, and scientific, based on vegetables, rice, fish, and lean meat, while northern cuisine is defined as behind the times, deadly, and unscientific in its preference for fats and red meat.

Yet when I sketched my first thoughts on this most palpable phenomenon of a rising southern political culture that was subverting a northern nationalist identity, my political science colleagues responded dismissively and derisively, arguing that Chinese were patriots and that nationalism in China required a strong authoritarian center: "Democracy [is] not suited to China. . . . In China, an authoritarian system . . . produce[s] the greatest happiness of the greatest number."[6] In contrast, my first talk on the topic of this volume to Chinese in Hong Kong who regularly traveled in China's south was well received.

Few Hong Kong residents or Chinese anywhere in the southern diaspora identify with the regime in Beijing. The future seems to be with the south, not the hinterland north China plain. A Hawaii conference on these explosive changes sought to develop an understanding of the national significance of the south's Guangdong province's growing interaction with Hong Kong.[7] University of Hawaii professor Roger Ames suggested the possibility of a south China nation, similar to the southern Song Dynasty of a millennium past, or a coastal federation—linked to "Hong Kong and Taiwan . . . the two largest investors in mainland China, with sinic Korea ranking third."

University of Hong Kong history professor Ming Chan imagined a new southern-based nationalism that might conquer the whole country and give life to the cliché, "Shenzhen is Hong Kong–ized, Guangdong is Shenzhen-ized, and the whole country is Guangdong-ized." He projected a continuation of a century-and-a-half process in which Canton and Ningbo business spread throughout China. Ningbo and Shanghai capital had temporarily fled from chaos in China to the Hong Kong area during the Mao era, but that dynamic force had returned in the post-Mao era to envelop south China and challenge all of China.

A national market has grown in which merchandise from the south is prized in the north and the government in the north depends on the foreign exchange earnings from the south, as well as on ties to the Chinese (largely Cantonese and Fujianese) diaspora. Pacific Lutheran University anthropology professor Greg Guldin noted that in the north, from beauty parlors to clothing stores, Chinese sought a product made by skilled southerners that carried the outside world into the rest of China, not as foreign pollutants, as anti-imperialist elders in the north anxiously claimed, but as products already made Chinese in their passage through the south. Apparently, what was invisible to political realists in America, who perhaps were too fixated on the declarations of continuity and unity by rulers in the northern city of Beijing, the national capital, was obvious to students of the culture, whether anthropologists, analysts of popular literature, or journalists, who paid less attention to the official story. The south was rising.

But that only partially explains why the findings of Gladney, Siu, Gargan, Barmé, and the Hawaii conference, as well as of two more scholars who are drawn on later in this chapter, Anita Chan and Ann-ping Chin, that the forces for a great rupture in national identity had already piled up in China, were at first ridiculed or shunned as one might mock a lone protester in front of the White House carrying a placard announcing the end of the world for tomorrow at noon. Tocqueville long ago pointed out that revolutions always come as a surprise and appear afterward as inevitable. No one predicted the rupture of the Soviet Union.[8]

Realism makes it seem that the best guide to tomorrow is today.[9] Continuity, misleadingly, appears as reality. Hence major ruptures are seldom predicted in advance. Since all the realists, or pseudorealists, tend to be wrong together when a rupture explodes, they do not explore the reasons for their error; instead, they explain it away. Eventually they do not even notice how misleading their paradigms of continuity had been. In the China studies field, almost no one foresaw the Moscow–Beijing split or that Mao would be open to normalizing relations with the United States. The conventional wisdom projected a long-term Sino-Soviet alliance and no hope for an improvement in Beijing–Washington relations until after the anti-imperialist leader Mao died. After the fact, it was China that was blamed for being surprising.

It is important, if one is not to be surprised yet again, to open up to the prospects for rupture in China today. Continuity is not the only realistic possibility. Indeed, it is most unrealistic to be mesmerized by the pseudorealism of continuity theories.

By the 1990s, some analysts of China were at last noting "that 'China' really consists of many Chinas: the linguistically distinct provinces, the ethnically and linguistically distinct regions . . . and the racially, ethnically and culturally distinct portions . . . such as Sichuan or Guangdong."[10] Even ruling groups recognized "the danger of the country's disintegration."[11]

Yet most analysts still find, in stark contrast, that the Chinese people have long been and remain "a single nation and [a]re aware of being a single ethnos, with certain common moral laws and a single historical destiny."[12] Actually, the concept of "ethnos" does not even exist in the language of Beijing. This presupposition of organic continuity misunderstands how the Mao-era story of a long, one-dimensional history of antiforeign, especially anti-Japanese, nationalism is a most recent construction. Back at the turn of the twentieth century, in fact, Chinese ruling groups found they had to emulate Meiji Japan and implement similar institutional changes in order for China to hold together. That was the rationale for China's 1898 reform movement. Chinese also looked to Japanese police reforms, with "police" (jingcha) a neologism taken from Japan, whose centralized police model was borrowed from continental Europe. The Chinese sent police trainees to Japan and brought in police trainers from Japan.[13] Chinese political writers imagined Asians joining to repel a European danger. Japan was not China's enemy.

However much Chinese nationalists would have preferred to march hand in hand with the rapidly strengthening Japanese, an aggressive Japanese military intervention in China eventually made that impossible, as described in this book in chapters on the China–Japan relationship and a chapter on China's anti-imperialist foreign policy. To build a new China, Chinese in the 1930s had to build a new national identity, one not premised on racial-political oneness with the Japanese.

Part of what Chinese students of everything from art[14] to armaments had brought back from Japan was a belief that only a potent nationalism could save China. But it was not obvious what it meant to identify with the Chinese nation. By the 1930s that patriotic anti-imperialism ironically targeted Japan, whose military presence on Chinese soil was threatening to conquer all of China. Mao's Communist-led anti-imperialist soldiers imagined themselves as heirs to a China that had long maintained its independence by fighting to keep out invaders. The new worldview that independence meant keeping foreigners out was expressed in the anthem of the new People's Republic, "Arise! Refuse to be enslaved! We'll use our flesh and blood to build a new Great Wall." Mao's Communist-led peasant Red Army was presented as the latest avatar of the savior of the Chinese people, a strong fist that united the people and maintained a defensive order, as muddleheaded anachronistic Confucians or anarchical liberals never could. The narrative of anti-imperialist Leninist socialism seemed, in the context of sacrificing anything and everything to expel Japanese invaders, to express a necessary truth. Even non-Communist Ma Yinqu found in 1935 that for China "there is no way of survival . . . besides collectivism . . . [because] the extremity of individualism would only lead to anarchism. China's weakness is derived from the laxity of, and lack of control over, her citizens."[15]

Maoist nationalist identity, with its critique of individual freedom as a force splitting the nation, seemed such a true embodiment of China's historical essence that its mythos even shaped the historiography of deservedly renowned senior foreign historians such as C. P. Fitzgerald and John King Fairbank. A Maoist narrative of Chinese national history became so presuppositional that it infused the best textbooks and popular works on China. A 1992 textbook summarized this understanding of a northern national center defending China with walls to keep out foreigners. According to the textbook, the Yellow River served as

"the cradle of Chinese civilization". . . around 3,000 BCE. . . . [S]ettlements spread . . . towards the natural barriers that were to establish their relative isolation from more distant lands. . . . King Zheng [of Qin] . . . by 221 BCE . . . united the former Zhou kingdoms and . . . set the character of Chinese Dynasties. . . .

To the north the nomadic Xiongnu empire was rising on the Eurasian steppe. . . . In response, the First Emperor [of Qin] developed fortifications that were to be extended and rebuilt . . . as the Great Wall.

[The] southern area has been physically distinct from the rest of China. . . . Minority groups are the norm here because the Han Chinese only arrived in large numbers in the twelfth century.[16]

This paean to the armed might of north China found little to praise in the softer virtues of a common Confucian culture, which was instead damned for locking China into feudal obscurantism. The narrative was silent on how much of China (for example, rice, cotton, and indigo dark-blue dyes for cotton peasant clothing) came from the south or from without, or on how much commerce united and enhanced the life of all Chinese people. Instead, the mythos made Mao's Communist Party dictatorship the natural and necessary heir of a tough despotism that kept foreigners out. As one able American researcher condensed this seemingly presuppositional national narrative that legitimated Mao's despotism:

The state has always governed dictatorially . . . and hence there is a legitimacy to dictatorship and a willingness to comply. . . . [I]ngrained subservience . . . begins in childhood . . . [with] every individual dependent upon and subordinate to the dictates of the state. . . . Each sphere [heaven, earth, or the netherworld] [i]s governed by a supreme leader who on earth, by whatever name . . . others might . . . label him, [i]s the emperor. . . . So Chairman Mao, the modern-day emperor. . . . Qin Shi Huangdi [first emperor of Qin] had begun the dynastic tradition that was to continue almost uninterrupted for more than 2,000 years.

Deep in the Chinese psyche is the belief that only recognized authority stands between order and chaos, that . . . when leadership has failed, *luan*— chaos—the situation most feared by Chinese has followed, [with] the society . . . disintegrating into . . . violent, bloody, and terrifying civil war.[17]

Mao's anti-imperialist dictatorship seemed so obviously a natural emergence of a deep Chinese essence that outside observers concluded that "legitimacy and authority" had been made permanent for China's Communist rulers through popular mobilization that achieved "national integration."[18] The consensus of knowledgeable observers of Maoist anti-imperialism was that China's choices were either a strong dictatorship or anarchical disorder. "Ever since Chinese civilization began some 4,000 years ago along the Yellow River, the state has been either autocratic or 'impotent.' "[19] So it was at the end of the twentieth century in this Maoist narrative:

> If the center continues to flounder, the regions will ... pursue their own agendas. Apart from ... secession in Tibet ... [and] problems in Xinjiang and possibly Inner Mongolia, there is now the growing *defacto* economic independence of Guangdong and the coastal areas.... [R]egionalism will become ... stronger.... [T]o develop a more democratic China is to allow ... decentralization ... within a federalist structure.... However, two thousand years of striving towards centralized rule warns against thinking that such an option will be easy to achieve.[20]

By the 1980s, however, even if most foreign observers remained mesmerized by that now discredited narrative of inevitably imperative centralized dictatorship, Chinese increasingly saw little that seemed natural or authoritative in the ancient despotic system or its legitimating history supposedly going back in a tightly woven historical network of meaning at least to the first emperor of Qin, and often much further back in time. Chinese, by the 1980s, instead focused on how over the millennia they had actually lived without strong central rule for longer than with it. They redirected their focus to the benefits of freedom and federalism and openness to foreign forces of scientific, technological, and economic progress. Suddenly the open Tang Dynasty, with its international commerce and welcoming of Buddhism from abroad, seemed central to understanding what it meant to be Chinese. People entirely reimagined China's history, as described especially in chapter 6, "Reconstructing China's National Identity."

As with other desiccating Leninist states, the anti-imperialist glue of China's Leninist anti-imperialism turned out not to hold a people together. Peoples reimagined their history to identify with an open project of beneficial cross-fertilization.

The general crisis of Leninism, which is analyzed in chapters 2 and 3 of this book, made possible the privileging of openness and the peripheralizing of anti-imperialist nationalism analyzed throughout the book. If the Leninist ruling groups conserved their ever more shaky monopoly of state power, they consequently would have to reroot their legitimacy in something other than the now palpably alien and alienating worldview of Leninist anti-imperialism. Such a rupture, creating a Leninist regime crisis opening up new political possibilities, including democracy, is explored in Part 4 of this volume. History, culture, and national identity became matters of fierce contestation. The individual subject, an agency of self-creation, potentially a force for democratic construction, became central to the Chinese debate.[21]

In 1994, foreign observers finally focused on these extraordinary possibilities. A Hong Kong correspondent noted that

> provincial and even county leaders are simply ignoring Beijing's directives. Last year . . . Guangdong authorities, faced with orders from Beijing to limit oil consumption, simply contracted for tankers to deliver foreign oil. . . . Local banks also largely ignored Executive Vice Premier Zhu Rongji's order to cease making speculative loans. The central government . . . now routinely revise[s] them [its edicts] into weaker measures when confronted with regional opposition.[22]

Professor Emeritus Robert Scalapino asked, "Can authority be properly allocated among center, region, province and locality? No issue is more critical. . . . [T]he most profound revolution lies ahead."[23] The editor of the *Pacific Review* noted that China faced "an identity crisis" and a "struggle between southern China and Beijing" such that the "basic question over China's future revolves around the degree to which Beijing's authority will give way to the centrifugal pull of China's increasingly dynamic periphery." With such powerful fissiparous tendencies, "China stands on the brink of redefinition."[24]

Professor Cheng Li remarked from Shanghai:

> No one seems to doubt that the old political system has to go. But there the consensus ends. . . .
> A crucial question . . . is: *if Communism will not hold China together, what will?* The country needs a new vision, a new direction, and a new sense of purpose.[25]

That potential for something new and different, even for democracy, should have been obvious long before. It seemed obvious to me in 1981 that it was dangerously misleading to conceive of China as totalitarian because that notion hid democratic potentials from our view:[26] [the following quote ends at the top of page 13]

Let us pause to remember what the Reagan administration means by totalitarian, authoritarian, and democratic kinds of governments and then see if these meanings even come close to describing what we all know has been happening in the world for the last quarter century or more. We will take our authoritative meanings from two of Mr. Reagan's foreign policy spokespeople, Alexander Haig, the former Secretary of State, and Jeane Kirkpatrick, the U.S. emissary to the United Nations. Mr. Haig, in arguing against the Carter administration's human rights policies, declared:

> It neither serves the purposes of social justice nor the vital interests of America to pursue policies under the rubric of human rights which have the practical consequences of driving authoritarian regimes friendly to the west into totalitarian models where they will remain in a state of permanent animosity to the American people and our interests.[27]

The nub of the matter in this distinction between totalitarianism and authoritarianism is the notion of a "permanent" state. A totalitarian dictatorship is just that, total. Once you are in it, you can never get out. That is why it is an ultimate moral imperative, from this perspective, to keep totalitarians from winning victory.

Mr. Haig clarified this view in a March 31, 1981, speech:

> We should distinguish between the so-called totalitarian and authoritarian regimes. The totalitarian model unfortunately draws upon the resources of modern technology to impose its will on *all* aspects of a citizen's behavior. The totalitarian regimes tend to be . . . ideologically *resistant* to political *change*.

Mr. Haig continued, contrasting authoritarian regimes with totalitarian ones that never change:

> The *authoritarian* regime usually stems from a lack of political or economic development and customarily reserves for itself absolute authority in only a few politically sensitive areas. . . . I am making the case that such regimes are more likely to *change* than their totalitarian counterparts. It should be our objective . . . to help the evolution of authoritarian government toward a more democratic form.

Hence it is almost natural for an authoritarian regime to evolve, since only the lack of material development precluded success for democracy. Mr. Haig summed up his position in this way:

> We should oppose the establishment of totalitarian regimes; we should encourage the evolution of authoritarian regimes toward a more humane society.[28]

Ms. Kirkpatrick drew out the policy implications. The Carter administration should have supported to the end the Shah in Iran and Somoza in Nicaragua, "moderate autocrats friendly to American interests."[29]

By now you can see that what is at stake is defending the Reagan administration's military policies in places such as El Salvador.[30] Surely facts are not the issue. Whatever one thinks of the complicated politics of Khomeini's Iran, for example, it certainly is not a Communist totalitarian state.

Yet in Iran, traditional authoritarianism is contrasted with modern totalitarianism.[31] Kirkpatrick disciples state:

> The first [totalitarian states] are not only repressive but create political structures that *eliminate all possibilities for the development of freedom*. The second [authoritarian states] are often heavily repressive, but are designed to perpetuate the rule of a single individual or group, rather than to establish a *durable system* that will *withstand* any and all *initiatives for change*.[32]

Again, the permanent evil is contrasted with the mutable evil. Yet something central seems left out in the Reagan–Haig–Kirkpatrick categorizations: the murderous, torturing, brutally barbaric secret-police practices of the Shah's Savak or of Argentina under military dictatorship.[33] *Washington Star* cartoonist Dan Wasserman caught this omission in a caricature of Kirkpatrick in which he has her say:

> What is the difference between totalitarian and authoritarian? Well, a totalitarian government arrests, tortures and murders. An authoritarian government on the other hand . . . leaves many of these functions to the private sector.

What our attention is being called to is something else now, not kinds of governments but kinds of states. We live in a world where the state is capable of great autonomy above and against society, almost isolated from its own people. Terror states like Idi Amin's in Uganda or Duvalier's in Haiti or the endless tyranny in Paraguay do not necessarily fall of their own weight or easily evolve into democracies. In fact, the defense of authoritarianism by the Reagan administration not only was taken as a green light by some terror states, but in Spain it may almost have sparked or facilitated a military coup away from democracy, something that deeply upsets many Spaniards.[34]

Calling attention to this problem of terror states, one history professor wrote in 1981 that the authoritarian-totalitarian dichotomy does not tell us

> whether or not fear and terror are used as instruments of power. If in present-day [1981] Poland dissent can be expressed, but the same dissent in Guatemala would lead to murder or torture, then what is the meaning of that much touted distinction?[35]

This suggests that it may not be useful to think of Poland as an unchanging totalitarian state. In fact a whole host of very conservative people, including Herman Kahn, now [1981] insist that even the Soviet Union has evolved into an authoritarian society.[36] But if even a supporter of Reagan's El Salvador policy can discuss "the prospect of Poland's transformation from totalitarianism to democracy,"[37] then what is the meaning of totalitarianism, of this tripartite division of governments? Remember that a totalitarian state was supposed to be total, permanent, unchanging. Yet here we find totalitarianism evolving into authoritarian [in the Soviet Union] or even a democratic state form [in Poland]. Then totalitarianism does not exist. After all, the whole point of the totalitarian category was that precisely that kind of total state was supposed to be incapable of evolution into democracy or authoritarianism.

This is not the place for a debate on the nature of the Soviet system. Among professional students of the topic such a prolonged debate exists.[38] People argue positions ranging from the USSR as a rationalized totalitarian state to the USSR as an authoritarian, interest-based, industrialized state. The question obviously is not, Is the USSR a democratic, pacifist state? But just as obviously transformations from Stalinist "totalitarianism" seem real. It is no longer the terror state it once was.

But we have seen these transformations before, and in far larger and more significant measure. They have been among the most earth-shaking, heroic events.

They deserve our attention and our support. How can we think and act when the Reagan administration's categories deny the possibility of this core reality of our era? In 1956 the Hungarian people successfully overthrew their terror state and were, magnificently, democratizing it—until Soviet bloc troops stormed in and crushed them. In 1968 the Czechoslovak people were reforming their suffocating tyranny into "communism with a human face," until once again Soviet bloc troops smashed that more decent prospect. And in 1980–81 we all admired the Polish people as their great union movement known as Solidarity began to democratize that distant, privileged state structure. At the same time, we all held our breath and pondered if there were ways this time to keep the Soviet empire from cruelly imposing its despotic will.

What is striking in all these cases is that left to their own will, the people and democracy would defeat a dictatorial, one-party, Leninist system that utilized modern technology and a powerful secret-police system. Thus, what is called totalitarianism by the Reagan administration hardly seems a permanent and unchanging system.

Not surprisingly, similar forces are at work in the People's Republic of China.

This democracy is not a gift. Therefore it is struggled against [in China] by many state power holders;[39] antidemocratic Leninists, military people, and entrenched, privileged administrators opposed the breadth of free speech of 1979–80 and pushed back some of the democratic gains. The antidemocrats again in 1980, after the freedom of the media was expanded, pushed that away from its greatest gains. And in 1981, when local elections, a union movement, campaign speeches, and strikes and organizations similar to Solidarity all moved forward, the antidemocrats once more pressed back against the democratic surge. Thus, victory for the democrats is far from guaranteed. The struggle to democratize the state is usually long and often has its martyrs.

To advance the cause of democracy requires liberating ourselves from a crusade against something mislabeled as totalitarianism.[40] Of course, if you believe instead that China is essentially totalitarian and therefore cannot evolve into any better kind of state, then you cannot even see the point of what I am arguing. But surely Hungary, Czechoslovakia, and Poland are weighty examples that prove how dangerously misleading is the Reagan administration's notion of a permanent system called totalitarianism. In fact, privileged Leninist ruling parties become isolated, lose legitimacy, and are targets of powerful democratic forces that can and will hit their mark. These distant, privileged statist elites live a life that so palpably contradicts the ethic of service to the poor that they preach that they regularly delegitimize themselves. We should have more faith in how human it is to resist the suffocating hypocritical state and we should welcome the popularity of self-determination inherent in democracy.

While the above comments from 1981 should now be beyond dispute,[41] nonetheless Leninist power holders do not invariably meekly surrender to democrats. By 1984 the rulers in China sought safety and support in ancient authoritarian Confucianism. As discussed in chapter 9, they made studying Confucianism "a key state project in the Five-Year Plan (1986–90)."[42] They promoted a Confucian society and restored Confucius's birthplace. There they re-created or created the supposed rituals of ancient times that Confucius so admired. Music, song, and dance were combined in praise of the ancient tribal leader Shun, who united all the tribes with their various totems, subsuming all under one central, powerful, masculine authority, "gradually forming a national psychology."[43] Acknowledging by the 1980s that people lacked "patriotic zeal" and dismissed the Leninist, one-party, dictatorial state system as a feudal dictatorship that embodied the old-fashioned, ancient evils of China, China's ruling Central Committee launched a campaign to build a so-called socialist spiritual civilization, that is, to "revive Chinese culture."[44]

The Mao-era policy of cultural desecration of Confucianism was criticized. A new appeal was made by officialdom to ancient notions of hierarchical legitimacy in which everyone knew his or her place and the entire people benefited. This appeal was ethically attractive to many older people frightened by post-Mao market-oriented reforms and rapid change in which the young, who might not be filial or ethical enough to care for the elderly, had their own worldview, one that supposedly borrowed much evil from abroad, from a West where, conservatives claimed, the young abandoned their parents to old-age homes and lost all sense of shame, becoming juvenile delinquents and drug addicts, and even catching and spreading AIDS.[45] Consequently, there "awakened a new nationalism and respect for tradition among some young writers, leading them to reevaluate the anti-nationalism [actually, anti-imperialist nationalism] of the May Fourth Movement."[46] The anti-Confucian effort of the World War I era and after was reconceived as a great error that subverted China's moral strength.

One response of democrats to this attempt to cover and legitimate the tattered Leninist despotism with rewoven Confucian garb condemns Confucianism as suffocating the vitality of people and instead praises pre-Confucian tribalism as full of vital energies. The crisis of national identity in socialist China has led to an extraordinary debate over China's future and China's past and how they are linked. Leninist dictators, however, stick to their antidemocratic perspective. But, ever more Chinese increasingly look away from that authoritarian worldview.

Just as fifty years ago Mao's movement rode high on Chinese and international tides of anti-imperialism, so also at the end of the twentieth century the federated, open ecumene seems an embodiment of deep historical forces both in

China and elsewhere. It helps shape the glass that images national identity such that histories as divergent as the Czech's and the Chinese are both imagined in a similar brain optic and reflected back from seemingly real and unique pasts that, in reality, are visions and reflections of the same world-historical mirror and a similar political project.

The persuasiveness of a post-Leninist national project will, in part, reflect its congruence with the happier dynamics of the end of the twentieth century. Dictators in Beijing are responding to the popularity of a new national vision that subverts their authoritarian appeals. This subversive history of a nation as open ecumene, with its feeling of inevitability and naturalness, is similarly reflected elsewhere than in China. The challenge to tyranny and to closed doors is worldwide. For the Czech Republic, Vaclav Havel, its first president, finds:

> We are what history has made us. We live in the very center of Central Europe, in a place that from the beginning of time has been the main European crossroads of every possible interest, invasion and influence. . . . [A]ll of these overlapped . . . combining to form our national and cultural consciousness. . . .
>
> [W]e are like a sponge that has gradually absorbed and digested all kinds of intellectual and cultural impulses. . . . Many European initiatives were born or first formulated here. . . .
>
> [W]e are on the threshold of an era of globality, an era of open society, an era in which ideologies will be replaced by ideas.[47]

In contrast, one of the continuing attractions of the old, northern narrative for China's Leninist dictators is that that authoritarian mythos, even in Confucian guise, discredits the new Chinese national vision of democracy by equating only strong dictatorship with national unity. In his elegant debunking of that northern myth in *The Great Wall of China: From History to Myth*, Arthur Waldron finds that new " 'nationalistic' ideas can fundamentally change the nature of politics."[48] When one recognizes that the narrative that legitimated walling out imperialist influences through a militaristic, mobilizational despotism is a human construction, one then can review Chinese society, culture, and history and discover democratic shoots as "a basic and enduring feature of Chinese politics."[49] Although Chinese nationals do not read Waldron, they do see the world in similar ways that legitimate a more pluralist politics for China.

Social science data suggest that in this struggle over China's future national culture, young Chinese are embracing the southern-oriented open identity and rejecting the new Confucian nationalism. These studies of childhood socialization, as with the previously mentioned cultural analyses that likewise highlight the rise of a south-oriented national identity, were similarly not recognized by the professional pseudorealists fixated on continuity, not appreciated by analysts whose conventional wisdom kept them from comprehending the great achievements of scholarship that found a rupture in Chinese political culture.

Evidence of a reimagination of the nation pervades recent socialization studies. In her wise study of youth socialization in China, Anita Chan found that "post-industrial" societies decrease the saliency of parents and increase that of "authority surrogates from the peer group and mass culture." While schools in China taught students "to perceive the world in Manichean terms," a student disenchanted with Mao's anti-imperialist story "simply reverses the labels." Rejecting Mao's walled-in nativist nationalism led to reading "a lot of novels, including foreign novels." It meant, instead of facing north and bowing to where Mao and gerontocratic officials resided, as southern Chinese actually were compelled to do in the Cultural Revolution, youngsters rather concluded that "to contribute anything to China, I *must* venture out." If you look at China's history of the last hundred years, "the new thinking all came from the outside." When one now found repression in "the countryside in the north" that the official story insisted was revolutionary, then one looked for solutions that would not "strangle individual personality development." Youngsters valued and imagined an open future that was anathema to the repressive, collectivist northern dictatorship. Finding the walled-in northern nationalism devalued, Dr. Chan concluded that "modern China's history . . . cannot be resurrected. . . . [T]he children of Deng are not the children of Mao."[50] A real rupture had already occurred in the political culture of China's young.

Wesleyan University professor Ann-ping Chin, who interviewed a couple of dozen Chinese youngsters in depth in 1979 and again in 1984 in order to learn how school and family and other influences shaped children's values, likewise found that their desire for independence and autonomy was strong, as was their resistance to autocratic parents. Youngsters even spoke for "constitutional rights" and opposed the imposed propaganda of "political classes."[51]

Professor Chin's data are congruent with the hypothesis of a failed project of northern monist nationalism and a new awareness of rich pluralities in a southern project. There is a striking conflict between the northern orientation into which the state long tried to socialize the children and the political identities that youngsters have recently embraced. Socialization by the rulers failed to persuade youth to embrace the promise of a continuous civilization that rose in the north China plain.

Instead, the children revealed a strong north–south differentiation, with the north viewed as poor and backward. One nine-year-old Beijing boy declared that his southern grandmother "lives in [richer] Jiangsu Province. She is not used to the [harsher] lifestyle of the North, and so she never comes here." A girl in Hangzhou in the south reported, "my parents didn't let me go to a school in the North. . . . [L]ife was a little harder there." In Shanghai in the south, where preferred-quality rice is the staple, a student reported of the north, "my father told me that I wouldn't get used to the food there. They eat noodles all the time and things made from flour."

In contrast, reflecting the anti-imperialist, northern perspective, a girl who moved into Canton in the south, whose parents "don't speak" Cantonese, who "thought about the revolutionary martyrs who sacrificed their lives so that we could have the good life we have today," thought that the Cantonese of the south were "very crafty." She continued, "Usually they don't care about anyone else other than themselves."

No one identified as a Han. A boy from Beijing complained that he needed an interpreter in Shanghai in the south. He could not even "go shopping by myself." But the south was the future. A boy in Chongqing in Sichuan in China's southwest expected hopefully that "eventually Chongqing will be like Shenzhen," the Special Economic Zone abutting Hong Kong on the southeast coast.

Whereas northerners long praised women who stayed close to home, youngsters now took pride in Chinese women supposedly being more liberated than Japanese women who "stay home [and] are no good." In gender equality, China supposedly was "superior to other countries." This matter of identifying the fate of young women with the prospect of a democratic China is explored in chapter 9.

The youngsters did not take pride in a northern narrative of furthering a magnificent Chinese past. "China has a long history and thousands of years of culture. . . . This long feudal history has made us ignorant." And, "Most kids today are only concerned with the future." What stood between them and the past was "quite a large gap" between "the rest of the thousands of years of Chinese history."

The youngsters did not find the China of the Mao era a success either. Actually, China was backward. The youngsters believed that Deng Xiaoping's study abroad made him a better leader than Mao. And they criticized the customary view of envy that wished that higher people fell to one's level; they now preferred "the Western type—if you are good, then I will be just as good." They sought open horizons and craved foreign literature. They experienced a generation gap in which their parents were the past and they, open to the world of foreign music, colorful clothes, and autonomy, were the future. They knew the regime's line on Confucius and Mencius, but "I don't like Confucius and Mencius at all. . . . [T]hey are pretentious and preachy. They are so self-righteous." Because of popular skepticism about Confucian repression, it would not be easy for China's authoritarian rulers, as chapter 9 details, to relegitimate their dictatorships through the repression of young women.

The youngsters were grateful to teachers who confirmed their understanding of the official story as a fraud but also caringly warned them to be cautious about their utterances in public. They were conscious of the difference between "what the books tell us and what we say to our friends, classmates and colleagues." In short, the anti-imperialist mythos of Mao that praised a continuous civilization going back to a hinterland Yellow River origin of defending against foreign forces was embraced by no interviewee. Virtually all tended, instead, toward a national project that looked outward toward the future through China's successful south.[52] Both socialization studies reflect a transvaluation of values that discredits Mao's closed nationalism and instead legitimates the open national project of the south. Villagers in the south were imagined in terms of Buddhist vitality that could help energize the rest of the nation, which had long been rendered too cautious and conservative by Confucian northern socialization.

China's rulers, in the last decade of the twentieth century, nevertheless continue to seek ways to legitimate their despotism as a kind of Confucian Chinese nationalism. They do this in economic and great-power terms. They have explained the economic rise of East Asia as the success of a Confucian cultural region. Whereas Mao took Japan as the imperialist enemy, his heirs treat it as a historical model. Meiji Japan, in their view, had risen because Japan had absorbed Chinese Confucian values of frugality, loyalty, hard work, education, respect for elders, etc. China's future greatness was assured because China was returning to its Confucian roots, the purported source of East Asia's great authoritarian modernization.[53] Consequently, the issue of Japan, including the purported authoritarian premise of Confucian economic development, is central to the Chinese debate and is analyzed in Part 2 of this book. Here again the dictators were caught in a conundrum. Could they relegitimate themselves by identifying with Japan when opposition to Japanese exploitation had long been the emotional core of Mao-era Chinese nationalism?

To Confucian Leninists, to the red–brown alliance of fascist socialism, foreign ideas such as freedom and democracy would subvert that Confucian authoritarian source of growth embodied in the Japanese model of development and thereby keep China poor and backward. That weakening of China was said to be the real purpose of sinister and alien promoters of so-called human rights. Democratization supposedly would subvert China's authoritarian hope for a return to greatness. If Chinese would instead be true to their magnificent Confucian hierarchical heritage, China then would rise again to become the leader of Asia, the world's most dynamic region. Chinese would, as explained in Part 3, again be able to take pride in China's leading role among all humankind. And China's successful and relegitimated conservative dictatorship could, of course, hold on to power. Thus a close examination of the evidence reveals an ongoing struggle over China's national identity in the era after the delegitimation of anti-imperialism. As detailed in chapter 10, China has not successfully transitted out of command economy trammels.

In 1985, in opposition to the overoptimistic, pseudorealist conventional wisdom that a pragmatic reform group led by Deng Xiaoping would move from success to success as authoritarianism evolved toward democracy, it seemed obvious in the south rather that[54] the initiative was not in the hands of the reformers, let alone their democratic faction. The Western press coverage of China's September [1985] Party Congress, which interpreted the promotion of younger people and the retirement of older people as a victory for the reformers, was misleading. Even conservatives age and retire. Chinese journals in Hong Kong did not see the rapid promotion of Li Peng—who had been raised by Zhou Enlai, eventually perhaps to become prime minister—as a victory for the reformers. The Chinese journals focused on Li's technical education in the Soviet Union and his ties to the children of other leaders such as Chen Yun. This combination was said to make Li and his friends absolutely opposed to the economic irrationalities of Maoism but also strongly committed to a rationalized, Soviet-style, so-called planned economy and vanguard government, leaving little room for the emergence of genuine pluralism based on the self-representation of social forces. Centralization and political education were the legitimate themes of 1985, whereas the reformers inveigh against overcentralization and argue for delegating power and liberating the mind, code words that mean negating the Stalinist politico-economic system.[55] The point, however, is not that Chen Yun and the conservatives have won but that their entrenched power in the post-Mao era puts grave limits on the reformers and guarantees a continuation of a fierce struggle at the apex of state power.

This nativistic conservative nationalism, which actually had much in common with authoritarian Leninist anti-imperialism—a fascist socialism uniting browns and reds—was presented by its leaders as China's salvation, the only alternative to disintegration, chaos, and weakness. It would be an error to believe that such chauvinism lacks attractiveness to nationalistic Chinese. After all, it has been appealing to diverse peoples throughout the world. In fact, it tends to flourish in most Leninist or post-Leninist territories. The reformers are scapegoated as alien lovers of foreigners.

Yet the regime is so illegitimate that Chinese find popular ways to turn the regime's categories against the discredited rulers. Popular gossip has it that foreign, third-world scholarship students are pampered, while their own children suffer in poverty. The old Leninist regime is experienced as antinational because it worried about South African blacks, while the mistreatment of "our" people at home or in the neighboring county was accepted. As anti-African outbursts in China indicate, racist nativism can be most popular.

Tough chauvinism to right proforeign wrongs seems legitimate. Consequently, people close ranks in a "bunker mentality" against hypostatized alien rulers and a suicidal internationalism experienced as previously keeping "us" poor and backward. Liberalism and Cultural Revolution–era Leninism, as detailed in chapter 5, are conflated and condemned as alien impositions. People seek tough measures on behalf of "us," "an ethnic-genealogical concept 'the nation,' complete with built-in racial hierarchies."[56] This tough, mean, racialist alternative to democracy that bubbles up in all transitions out of Leninism is discussed throughout this volume but was overlooked in the overoptimistic 1980s analyses of pseudo-realists, who imagined Chinese totalitarianism as having naturally evolved into an ever softer authoritarianism.

Consequently, if more open-minded people are to win out in China, they will have to legitimate a national project of liberty or democracy or openness or federalism in a way that would be more patriotically appealing than both the Mao-era anti-imperialist nationalism sketched at the outset of this introduction and also more appealing than the post-Mao, conservative, Confucian chauvinist nativism just described. Such diverse projects already exist and are, as suggested above, quite popular with the young. They contend for national allegiance. These alternative projects of national identity are analyzed in this book, which in prob- ing the prospects for democracy also explores potent antidemocratic chauvinist forces strongly contending for national legitimacy.

This volume thus probes the origins, vicissitudes, and potential of alternative projects in an anti-imperialist Leninist regime facing a profound crisis of legiti- mation. It is difficult to exaggerate the remarkable—yet seldom remarked upon —transformation of consciousness that has come to equate the Communist Party as much an enemy of the people as alien invaders. A 1989 group of democratic activists in Hunan province "comprised partly of PLA officers" distributed a flyer declaring:

> The Mongols of the Yuan Dynasty ran rampant all over Eurasia. But when they advanced on Changsha, Hunan Province, "people heard the northerners cry: the walls of Tanzhou are iron-clad." The brutes of the Eight Banners of the Manchus could not have entered Changsha had they not bribed. . . . The Japanese invaders . . . lost 40,000 crack troops. . . . Everyone knows what hap- pened to the Taiping Heavenly Kingdom and to the Communist Party.[57]

From the regional perspective, Mao's Communists were as alien as the Japa- nese. That point is repeated in the Chinese film *Bawang Bie Jie* (Farewell My Concubine). This enemy is also cruel. The founder of the Ming, Mao's avatar, Li Zicheng, instead of being celebrated as a great peasant rebel was reimagined and condemned as someone who murdered the deserving as soon as he became Emperor Dashun in 1644, just as Mao would do after he conquered state power.[58] For the people not to suffer, leaders must be checked and balanced. National identity is profoundly contested in China in ways that open democratic possibilities.

Unless a new and open national identity is embraced by Chinese, any prospect for democratic progress is likely to be quite tenuous. There are intimate logical, psychological, and political linkages contained in *National Identity and Demo- cratic Prospects in Socialist China* as elsewhere in the post-Leninist world. Based on six years of research, this book tries to understand just how strong these links are and whether they are likely to hold the possibility of forging a Chinese democratic nation. The alternatives, in an era when national identity is rapidly changing, are extraordinarily broad, including federalist democracy, con- servative despotism, and splintering disintegration, and embody deep regional communalist identities and angers with a potential for bloody civil strife. The chapters in this volume explore the political and experiential factors that either enhance or squelch the political prospects of these contending national projects as solutions to the legitimation crisis in socialist China, which appears popularly as a crisis of national identity.[59]

Notes

1. Wang Xi, ed., *The Role of the U.S. Congress in the American Foreign Policy Process* (in Chinese) (Shanghai: Fudan University Press, 1990), pp. 36–43.
2. Gladney, *Muslim Chinese* (Cambridge, MA: Harvard Council on East Asian Studies, 1991).
3. Dittmer and Kim, eds., *China's Quest for National Identity* (Ithaca: Cornell University Press, 1993). I was an early reader of the manuscript for the press.
4. Siu, *Agents and Victims in South China* (New Haven: Yale University Press, 1989).
5. Edward Gargan, *China's Fate* (New York: Doubleday, 1990), pp. 78, 79, 121, 233, 129, 91, 140, 186.
6. Suisheng Zhao, "A Tragedy of History: The Chinese Search for Democracy in the Twentieth Century," *The Journal of Contemporary China*, No. 3 (Summer 1993), p. 19, citing a senior American historian.
7. R. Yin-wang Kwok and Alvin Y. So, eds., *Historical Changes in Hong Kong and South China* (Manoa, HI: School of Hawaiian, Asian and Pacific Studies, 1991).
8. As the Soviet Union disintegrated, specialists on nationalities in the Soviet Union went to press explaining why disintegration was impossible. See *World Politics* 44.1 (October 1991), "Liberalization and Democratization in the Soviet Union and Eastern Europe."
9. An author in the December 1992 issue of the flagship journal of the China studies profession, *The China Quarterly*, averred, "The Chinese political power structure will, for the foreseeable future, be based on an uneasy alliance between reformers and conservatives. . . . The most likely scenario, therefore, is that . . . China will experience gradual peaceful evolution" (p. 972).
10. Robert W. McGee and Danny Kin-Kong Lam, "Hong Kong's Option to Secede," *Harvard International Law Journal* 33.2 (Spring 1992), p. 438. "The greater economic independence of the south and the restlessness of the ethnic minorities threatened to undermine the Chinese state." (Michael Williams, "China, Hong Kong and Taiwan," Ditchley Conference Report, No. D92/6 [May 1992], p. 3.)
11. Grigory Sukharchuk, "A Weak People, A Strong State," *Far Eastern Affairs* (Moscow), No. 5 (1991), p. 65.
12. Ibid., p. 56.
13. Oura Kenetake, "The Police of Japan," in Okume Shigenobu, comp., *Fifty Years of New Japan* (New York: Dutton, 1909), Vol. 1, pp. 281–95. The source was called to my attention by Frederic Wakeman.
14. Ralph Crozier, *Art and Revolution in Modern China* (Berkeley: University of California Press, 1988).
15. Translated in Sun Lung-kee, "Ma Yin-qu and the Problem of Socialist Transition in China," *Bulletin of Concerned Asian Scholars* 9.2 (April–June 1977), p. 63.
16. Mark Bothwick, *Pacific Century* (Boulder, CO: Westview Press, 1992), pp. 4, 17, 18, 5.
17. Anne Thurston, *A Chinese Odyssey* (New York: Scribners, 1991), pp. xiv, 22, 104, 202, 191–92. For subtle explications of this appreciation of Chinese political culture, see the work of Lucien Pye and Richard Solomon.
18. Robert Bedeski, "The Formation of National Society in Communist China," *The Review of Politics* 33.4 (October 1971), pp. 484, 488.
19. Brantly Womack, "In Search of Democracy," in B. Womack, ed., *Contemporary Chinese Politics in Historical Perspective* (New York: Cambridge University Press, 1991), p. 85.
20. Tony Saich, "The Reform Decade in China," in Marta Dassu and Tony Saich, eds., *The Reform Decade in China* (London: Kegan Paul International, 1992), p. 64.

21. For an analysis of how philosopher Li Zehou's ideas on individual subjectivity became the premises of reform and modernization, see Lin Min, "Chinese Intellectual Discourse and Society, 1978–88," *The China Quarterly*, No. 132 (December 1992), pp. 969–98.

22. Dave Lindorff, "China's Economic Miracle Runs Out," *The Nation*, March 30, 1994, p. 743.

23. Scalapino, "Back to the Future," *Far Eastern Economic Review*, May 26, 1994, p. 38.

24. Gerald Segal, "China's Changing Shape," *Foreign Affairs*, May–June 1994, pp. 44, 48, 43, 56.

25. Cheng Li, "Political Forecast: A Little Knowledge Is a Dangerous Thing," *Institute of Current World Affairs*, CL–5 (1994), pp. 15, 16.

26. What follows is excerpted from Edward Friedman, "Totalitarian Communism as Enemy of Democracy in Asia," in Mark Kann, ed., *The Future of American Democracy* (Philadelphia: Temple University Press, 1983), pp. 297, 298, 299, 300, 301, 303, 304.

27. Quoted in *The Nation*, January 3–10, 1981, p. 1.

28. *New York Times*, April 21, 1981, p. 6.

29. Cited in *The Nation*, January 3–10, 1981, p. 1.

30. On El Salvador, see Alan Riding, "The Sword and the Cross," *New York Review of Books*, May 28, 1981, pp. 3–8.

31. In fact, in many areas the Shah was more the modernizer, Khomeini more the traditionalist.

32. Cited by Shaul Bakhash in "Who Lost Iran?" *New York Review of Books*, May 14, 1981, p. 19 (emphasis added).

33. Anthony Lewis, "Accomplice to Terror," *New York Times*, March 22, 1981, p. 19.

34. James Markham, "Comment by Haig Draws Fire in Spain," *New York Times*, March 12, 1981.

35. Gabor Vermes, "Can't Tell a Nation by Its Label," *New York Times*, May 3, 1981, letter to the editor.

36. "U.S. Pullout from ROK Unthinkable: Kahn," *Korean Newsletter* 3.7 (November–December 1980), p. 2. This is not to suggest that the Soviet Union was not a militarily expansionist power.

37. Arch Puddington, "Crisis in the East," *Commentary*, May 1981, p. 91.

38. Cf. Rolf H. W. Theen, "The Soviet Political System Since Stalin," *Problems of Communism*, January–February 1981, pp. 74–77.

39. A very similar struggle continues in Taiwan. For an argument that it has already failed in China, see James Seymour, "The Abortive Attempt to Democratize China's Political System," in *The Limits of Reform in China* (Washington, DC: The Wilson Center, 1982), pp. 139–55.

40. For the opposite view, see Norman Podhoretz, "The Future Danger," *Commentary*, April 1981, pp. 29–47.

41. Robert Scalapino concludes a study of Asian Leninist states by reminding readers that the "defect" of "the term 'totalitarianism' . . . was that it assumed a degree of reach and control that no government ever attained" (Scalapino, *The Last Leninists* [Washington, DC: Center for Strategic and International Studies, 1992], p. 89).

42. Xi Mi, "Confucianism Confused in Contemporary China," *China Daily*, July 3, 1993, p. 4.

43. Guo Anding, "Dancing to the Tune of Confucius," *China Today*, April 1991, pp. 50–54.

44. Hu Qiaomu, September 1986 speech; reprinted in *Zhongguo Jiaoyu bao*, February 7, 1987, p. 1.

45. In this manner, John Fairbank argued, and Michel Oksenberg agreed, that "until

we can set an example by properly curbing media violence and the drug and gun industries, we can hardly urge China to be more [democratic] like us" (Oksenberg, "Brahmen in the China Shop: Late Doyen of U.S. Sinologists Sings His Swan Song," *Far Eastern Economic Review*, October 8, 1992, p. 45).

46. Yeh Chih-ying, "The Reassessment of Confucianism in Contemporary Chinese Fiction," *Issues and Studies*, June 1990, p. 1214.

47. Havel, *Summer Meditations* (New York: Vintage, 1993), pp. 125–26.

48. Waldron, *The Great Wall of China* (Cambridge: Cambridge University Press, 1991).

49. Waldron, *Great Wall of China*.

50. Chan, *Children of Mao* (Seattle: University of Washington Press, 1988), pp. 212, 211, 199, 200, 194, 193, 192, 224, 225.

51. Chin, *Children of China* (Ithaca: Cornell University Press, 1988), p. 139.

52. Ibid., pp. 52, 214, 216, 83, 84, 87, 52, 135, 217, 170, 123, 281, 257, 201, 210, 211, 268, 231, 226, 181, 139, 113, 138, 236, 263.

53. Chinese democrats responded, calling the restoration of Confucianism reactionary and anachronistic and arguing that "One reason for the success of Japan's industrialization has been . . . its limiting of Confucianism to the field of ethics" (Xi Mi, "Confucianism Confused"). They criticized Confucianism for its preoccupation with harmony (see John Wu, "Chinese Legal and Political Philosophy," in Charles Moore, ed., *The Chinese Mind* [Honolulu: East–West Center Press, 1967], pp. 213–27), which produced a "tendency to conform to, instead of transcend reality" (Xi Mi, "Confuciansim Confused"), echoing the great writer Lu Xun's May Fourth–era rejoinder to Bertrand Russell's praise of Chinese love for harmony that fostered "gentle, peaceful, contemplative qualities." Lu Xun wanted Chinese to stop "eating bitterness" and instead to end the institutional causes of bitterness. Lu Xun commented that "Russell . . . praises Chinese after seeing smiling porters. . . . I . . . know if the porters had been able not to smile at those whom they had to carry, China would have long since been out of its present rut" (cited in Suzanne Ogden, "The Sage in the Inkpot," *Modern Asian Studies* 16.4 [1982], p. 577).

54. The rest of the paragraph, which summarizes the thrust of the entire article, is from Edward Friedman, "After Mao," *Telos*, No. 65 (Fall 1985), p. 46.

55. Reformers argue, "Although Lenin saw, in his later years, the malpractice of bureaucratism, the lack of democracy inside the Party and the growth of personal power resulting from the emphasis on centralism, and wanted to adopt measures to expand democracy inside the Party, the Russians failed to set up a complete and perfect system to expand democracy within the Party for various reasons" (Ni Yongping, "The Principles of Organization of the First International People's Congress and Lenin's Democratic Centralism," *Guangming ribao*, March 18, 1985, translated in JPRS-CPS–85–039, April 26, 1985, p. 45). Whereas the democratic reformers argue for a democratized version of Lenin, the conservatives stand with Leninist-Stalinist political institutions.

56. Paul Hockenos, "Xenophobia and Racism Unbound in the Land of the Magyars," *New Politics*, Winter 1993, pp. 69–81.

57. "Hunan Should Lead the Way and Practice Patriotic Self Government," in Asia Watch, *Anthems of Defeat* (New York: Hunan Rights Watch, 1992), pp. 200, 201.

58. James Seymour, ed., *The Fifth Modernization* (Stanfordville, NY: Human Rights Publishing Company, 1980), p. 135.

59. A debt of gratitude is owed to the intellectually brave pioneer analysts of this potential transformation whose work is cited in this chapter. Their profound insights were not appreciated by very many of their professional peers, whose paradigm of authoritarian, centralized, northern-based continuity obscured the profound achievement of that work.

Part Two

National Identity Crisis

Chapter 2

New Nationalist Identities in Post-Leninist Transformations

The complexities and contradictions of an extraordinarily diverse China full of conflicting potential do not yet define or confine China to any necessary future. This chapter explores one possible outcome linked to a theoretical model derived from general Leninist experience. What follows is not *the truth* about China but an attempt to imagine what could happen should one crucial factor change in China, as it has in other Leninist states. That factor is the delegitimation of anti-imperialist nationalism.

Leninist nationalism imagines a capitalist world as the enemy of an entire people and legitimates rule by a dictatorial Leninist system with a command economy because only such a ruling group purportedly has the insight and capacity to reject, negate, and check a murderous, predatory capitalism alleged to be the cause of a bloodthirsty imperialism that permanently threatens the nation's most precious values, and indeed threatens the very independence of the people. This core legitimation of Leninist anti-imperialism, as Professor Jerry Hough has shown, is a kind of xenophobic Khomeini-like fundamentalism that is in conflict with the reform imperative of economic openness to the world market that is necessary for growth in the era of post-steel technologies, flexible production, and instantaneous international finance. China's post-Mao rulers, who understand that economic growth at the end of the twentieth century requires tying in to a wealth-expanding world market, do not have an easy task in winning supporters from those who still give their primary loyalty to policies premised on treating that market world as an ultimate enemy. A reforming Leninist state ignites an explosive contradiction because new policies destroy the old legitima-

Originally published in 1992 in Shatin, Hong Kong, by the Chinese University of Hong Kong.

tion. To confront the delegitimation of Leninist anti-imperialism and accept the imperative of economic reform, including the loss of a hate-filled nationalism that was the emotional glue of the polity, causes a deep crisis. In addition, in a Leninist reform era the artificial "socialist" culture loses its binding force, and the command economy's place-specific, stratified mode of distribution and politically created economic disparities inevitably foster political, tax, and budget backlashes that give more power to regions, thereby reinforcing loyalties to historically regional, but newly "nationalized," primary mobilizing identities. New populist nationalisms are waiting to explode and bury the old, discredited unity previously premised on anti-imperialist nationalism. Unexpectedly for the Leninist reformers, saving the nation actually threatens the nation, at least in its Leninist guise.

The Soviet Union and Yugoslavia have broken down. Observers in the 1990s look at Ethiopia and Czechoslovakia and other reform Leninist or post-Leninist systems and wonder whether all such overly centralized, rigidified states will break apart. The consequences of reimagined communalist loyalties are earth-shaking. Do the forces undercutting the old Leninist nationalisms in ossified systems elsewhere reflect general patterns providing clues to China's future? My conclusion is that similar forces are weakening the glue of patriotic appeals of outmoded Leninists in Beijing. The evidence for such a conclusion is over-whelming.

The explosion of the new nationalisms challenges a major social science generalization of the twentieth century, that patriotic attachment to an anti-imperialist center was the strongest political binding force of the era. As the twentieth century comes to its end, this old truism is no longer so obviously true. From the end of World War II until the 1990s, only Bangladesh has succeeded as a breakaway state. But suddenly a host of new nations are joining the United Nations. All over the planet, that long-established nationalistic ideological priority seems undermined from without and from below, by both the growing weight of transnational forces, best reflected in the surging emergence of a single European economic community, and by subversion from below from state-shattering regional, ethnic, lingual, tribal, religious, and other subnational primary loyalties and identities. Penetrated and subverted, losing loyalty, effectiveness, and relevance, the old centralized nation-state identity is no longer the end-all and be-all of political loyalty. The most vulnerable of the centralized Leninist states embody command economies whose narrow and selfish rule seems to serve but one community to the exclusion of most of the people.

A denationalizing transformation has been most manifest in Leninist states, because the political logic and social dynamics of Leninist states most completely create legitimate and weighty forces capable of defeating the delegitimated and weakened anti-imperialist central governmental power. This was most obvious in the 1980s in the Soviet Union and in Yugoslavia. But similar forces have been undermining top-down centralized unity in numerous Leninist states, from Nicaragua to Angola, from Ethiopia to Czechoslovakia. The East German state has disappeared from the family of nations. North Korea was suddenly forced to seek an independent seat in the United Nations, a policy it previously damned as an imperialist plot, is likewise in trouble. The generality of this challenge to neo-Stalinist centralized state power and Leninist national centers leads to the question: What are the implications for Beijing (and Taipei and Hong Kong)? That is—can the People's Republic of China survive? Has the glue of its nationalism so desiccated that Leninists in Beijing will soon cease to be able to hold things together?

Students of Leninist China recall both those who earlier speculated that Mao's Cultural Revolution or his death might bring division or civil war and those shrewd observers who analyzed China's various field armies and found institutionalized regional forces. But these strong regional tendencies surfaced before the legitimacy of Leninist anti-imperialist nationalism had been exposed as self-serving hypocrisy. Today such regional forces might win out because the defense of the old consensus of superpatriotism, of a strong national center as required to keep out imperialists, no longer exists. In an era when citizens see the sons of the Leninist elders selling Chinese weapons abroad and pocketing the profits while China's international debt grows, the old Leninist regime can no longer attract patriotic loyalty. A real national family must be reimagined and created to oppose the selfish family of traitorous rulers.

National disintegration for China is an extraordinary question, and until recently, almost an unthinkable one. Whatever else analysts of the PRC differed on, it was beyond question that Mao's revolution was patriotic, an extreme embodiment of Chinese nationalism. Wherever a person stood on socialism or Stalinism or some other controversial ism, almost no one challenged the consensus that Mao's armed struggle unified the nation, threw out the foreigners, and built a strong and powerful centralized state that won dignity and standing for China and Chinese in the world arena. This Leninist anti-imperialist litany remained the core legitimation of neo-Stalinist ruling groups in post-Mao China. The litany now sounds like a dirge, a death knell for scoundrels and an elegy for martyrs who gave their lives in vain to a betrayed nationalism.

But do new nationalist movements elsewhere really suggest that the ground is also moving from under the feet of post-Mao power holders and that the rug can be pulled out from the seemingly stable power position of China's elders, who are backed by a conservative military and politically loyal security force? Do developments in other Leninist systems that challenge both an outmoded centralized state and anti-imperialist nationalism foreshadow forthcoming events in China? Or is China a uniquely nationalistic success?

This study finds that the logic of Leninist disintegration is already at work in China, too.

However, what one hears in Beijing, and not only from apologists for the regime, is that China is unique, almost a law unto itself. Of course, everything and everyone is unique somewhat. Still it is worth examining this portentous matter of the general weakening and discrediting of archaic Leninist nationalisms because all Leninist systems suffer the same debilitating diseases that turn fearsome tyranny into sclerotic rigidities that auger weakness, decline, and death for the anti-imperialist Leninist center.

New national explosions in Eastern Europe are, nonetheless, dismissed in China as irrelevant because those European regimes are said to reflect long-illegitimate Soviet conquests rather than indigenous, popular struggles. The great democratic revolutions of 1989 are dismissed as liberation struggles of the old anticolonial variety, merely ending foreign control by Moscow. Leninism in China, in contrast, it is claimed, results from a true national struggle, turning Chinese into death-defying loyalists of the Leninist system.

Nativistic elders in China are contemptuous of any close comparison of China to other places. China is China, a world unto itself. As for the Soviet Union, its disintegration is treated as a Gorbachev-made (and Yeltsin-made) disaster. It supposedly only represents bad leadership, a rather shallow and wholly unpersuasive explanatory argument for a profound global phenomenon. Blaming leaders is just whistling in the dark to scare away ghosts. China's elders, however, insist that what is changing the political features of East Europe, Africa, Latin America, and the Soviet Union should be treated as a mere anomaly, a triviality of no relevance to Leninist-Stalinist China. Reports of the elders seeking out the latest news from the Soviet Union belie this tale of serene Chinese rulers not at all concerned with extraordinary ruptures throughout the world of Leninist states. Surely when so many Leninist states have similar experiences, one must examine China too to learn if it also is experiencing the discrediting of Leninist nationalism.

Do Leninist developments elsewhere indeed embody mere idiosyncratic historical peculiarities such that state-centralized, anti-imperialist Chinese nationalism is uniquely deep and lasting? Or must the tendencies at work in so many and diverse Leninist states reshape the future of China, too? Is the old nationalism, the core legitimation of Beijing's anti-imperialist dictatorship, crumbling? Given the way Chinese talk about the military's role in the Cultural Revolution, in the unpopular 1979 invasion of Vietnam, and in the June 1989 massacre, that "Great Wall of Steel" is turning from a treasured protector into a rusted, outmoded relic. The wall may be crumbling. In the silence, one hears the thunder, as Lu Xun wrote. The props of the old order could fall and produce a collapse. Those within Zhongnanhai may one day be found in a rubble of traitors if a re-experienced nation and a redefined people create a new, ultimate loyalty. This chapter finds that that mind-boggling change is already underway in China.

After all, it is patently untrue that China and Eastern Europe have had fundamentally different experiences of nationalism. Yugoslavia's Leninist state was not a Soviet imposition. It embodied a powerful indigenous nationalism, one that Professor Chalmers Johnson some thirty years ago in his book on peasant nationalism and communist power correctly identified as similar to China's nationalism, a view quite publicly expressed by China's post-Mao leaders during Tito's 1977 visit to China. Eastern Europe's turn against Leninist dictators in Yugoslavia, Albania, Romania, East Germany, and Czechoslovakia is not a matter of overthrowing unpatriotic puppets of Moscow. All these regimes insisted on Leninist anti-imperialism as their core legitimation. A transvaluation of values is underway throughout the Leninist world that has redefined Leninism as the ugly enemy of the peoples.

With democratic emergences responding to Leninist delegitimation, even in Leninist regimes established by prolonged wars of liberation in Nicaragua, Albania, Mozambique, and Angola, there is little historical basis for locating the delegitimation of the old anti-imperialist nationalism or the new democratic urge only in Leninist states with a Soviet master or a European cultural heritage, either. Democracy is positively attractive, Leninism repulsive. What is happening is also transforming Mongolia and what was once the USSR. Despite the will of Leninist elders to remain a law and world unto themselves, China is inescapably part of this larger Leninist experience. The panicky search of China's elders for new legitimations, one day in Confucianism, another day in Maoism, and yet another day in traditional Han chauvinism, suggests that even the Leninist rulers know that a general process of Leninist delegitimation is occurring, that it is also at work in China and that only a new national legitimation can hold the polity together.

The old problematique of Leninist nationalism was defined by the defenders of the system in terms of a fundamentalist militarized patriotism that imagined permanent threats to the nation requiring sacrifice to obtain missiles, atomic weapons, and a large, powerful military, to require sacrifice to maintain chauvinist values and build high and great walls to keep out supposedly subversive ideas and forms. Leninism was, at its core, the war communism descended from Robespierre's French Revolution, Jacobin vigilante terror state with its state-imposed maximum price on grain. The dynamics of such a system eventually alienate a people, as Robespierre learned. Leninist developments and transcendences elsewhere reveal that corrupt privileged power and an inordinately rigid, expensive, and wasteful economic system eventually lead citizens to reimagine nationalism such that standing up in the world requires negating this old-style anti-imperialist nationalism; the system is reimagined as something that keeps the Chinese people down, an ersatz public realm and a real private realm that relegates the people to groveling, fawning, and lying to incompetent, corrupt parasites who live off the hard work of a suffering populace.

This revolutionary transformation of national political consciousness has occurred in the democratizing parts of the post-Leninist world, although sections of the old system, especially the institutions of coercive control and the regions of privileged nationalities, try to hang on to the legitimations of the old Leninist nationalism in order to maintain their privileged, arbitrary, and nonaccountable power. The poisoned potent alternative to democratization, however, does not seem to be a stagnant Leninism, but rather a reborn chauvinism of the dominant ethnic group. Not enough analytic attention has been given to Deng Xiaoping's increasing invocation of the symbols of traditional Han chauvinism.

Whatever the ultimate and unpredictable outcome of new nationalist legitimation, this transvaluation of values away from Leninism in China has already gone a far way. How many or few still believe in the one quotation from Mao that even anti-Maoists used to take as an absolute truth, that the Chinese people had stood up? The contrasting, actual popular experience that negates the ubiquitous claim of Maoist anti-imperialist nationalism was expressed by the novelist Zhang Jie in *The Ark*. She wrote:

> It has started all over again this life of pleading and begging. Whether you wanted to get a divorce, an apartment to live in or a suitable job, it always involved grovelling at the feet of others in the hopes that they would show pity and understanding. What was so extraordinary about such requests? They were not asking for more than their fair share. When would Liu Quan at last know what it felt like to stand up proud and straight? She was not yet old, but she felt as if her back had been bent for a whole long lifetime.[1]

Or, as democratic activist Chai Ling said to a Taiwan reporter in June 1989, "We must raise our heads, straighten our backs—and fight to the end. We must keep our backs straight . . . or China will not move forward." In fact, Mao's flawed and failed Leninist nationalism has kept the people down and prevented the Chinese people from standing up. That is the spreading popular perception. Chinese people know they do not stand high in the world, whether measured in Nobel Prizes, per capita spending on education, human rights, or material standards of living. They even joke about it.

> American President George Bush asks God: "When will the United States become a heaven on Earth?" "Oh, maybe twenty years or so." Bush breaks out in tears, saying, "But by then I won't be president anymore! Someone else will get all the credit!" After Bush leaves, Gorbachev shows up. "When will the standard of living in the Soviet Union equal that of the United States?" he queries. "Give it about fifty years, I guess." Gorbachev pounds his breast and weeps: "In fifty years I'll be dead! It's a day I'll never see!" The leader of mainland China then makes his appearance. "If China follows the road of socialism with Chinese characteristics, when will it surpass capitalist nations?" This time God is the one who bursts out crying: "Not even I will live to see that day!"[2]

Embarrassment, not pride, is ever more the inheritance of Leninism to China's people. Leninist anti-imperialism has been exposed as a laughingstock.

In 1958 Mao promised to overtake Britain and America. A generation later China's Communist Party leadership is seeking leadership of Asia. This failed Leninist ruling group cannot explain its policies in anti-imperialist terms. Few educated individuals read its publications anymore.

Educated people are aware that even the nation of India graduated more people from college than did Maoist China. That India, previously the fallback nation used by anti-imperialist Chinese to prove that China was doing well, that even India was known at the end of the Mao era to be doing better than China despite its extraordinary handicap of inherited ethnic and religious divisiveness reflected nationalist delegitimation in China. That Chinese more and more knew India's achievements and stated them was, I believe, a very good indicator of the delegitimation of the old Mao-era Leninist nationalism.

Hidden forces within Leninist structural dynamics inevitably undermined the supposedly unassailable walls of Stalinist power. Quietly eroding such institutionalized control in Leninist states until it produced the amazing transformation of 1989 was disillusionment, the loss of illusions. Hannah Arendt was the one and only political analyst who early on comprehended the fragility of Leninist power. She noted in the wake of Hungary's great 1956 revolution that once the spell of ideology or charisma is snapped, once the young experience their parents as forced to act immorally, surviving by complicitiousness with a hypocritical regime of selfish and cruel rulers, then these once-invincible rulers can be re-experienced as alien to the nation because they are interested only in their private successes. What presented itself as a socialist state is suddenly revealed as a private monopoly serving the personal interests of selfish rulers. In that newly illuminated world, Arendt concluded, living in truth and dignity could require linking up with historically rooted traditions and identities, presuppositional givens of a better, more decent community.[3] The world is reenvisioned. In Russia (not the Soviet Union), Lenin and the other Bolshevik founders were reconceived as non-Russian. Leninism was suddenly a betrayal of Russia.

Can one similarly imagine Chinese dismissing their Leninist state as alien? The fact is that, more and more, they already do. In the south, Chinese denigrating Deng Xiaoping note that he is a Hakka, note that Marx is non-Chinese, note that Mao was turned into a backward person by his long stay in China's most backward northern hinterland regions. This is daily gossip in China. Denationalizing Leninism is, in fact, a transformation already underway in Chinese consciousness. Leninism is re-experienced as an emanation of what is backward and foreign to any better future for the people. What is still an open question is when, where, and how the political consequences will appear.

This redefinition of the content of Chinese national and personal identity was palpable in spring 1989 in the extraordinary experience of people suddenly helping strangers. They felt a new bond of living in truth as a community. They continued after June 1989 to support each other against the discredited northern, backward, state center and, in so doing, began to give life to a new, humane society to replace Leninist tyranny. They no longer would rat on each other.

The delegitimation crisis can be delayed by war (Stalin's Great Patriotic War kept Soviet Russia legitimate) or a real threat (the United States for Fidel Castro in Cuba) or charismatic loyalty to an older generation of revolutionary nationalists, but delaying the forces of delegitimation cannot forever deny them. More and more, anti-imperialist nationalism seems a nakedly self-serving discourse of a privileged and parasitic ruling group.

Stalin defined the Leninist nation as "an historically constituted, stable community of people, formed on the basis of a common language, territory, economic life and psychological make-up manifested in a common culture." But since there was no universally spoken language in China, Leninists interpreted Lenin to mean that "those who live together learn the language spoken by the most people."[4] In practice, China's Leninist rulers took the language of the capital and a sanitized version of its culture as advanced and socialist, as something to impose on other regions and cultures, which where treated as old, backward, and traditional. Yet daily gossip reports how even Leninist leaders, from Chen Yun to Chen Yi, went to great lengths to stay tied to their very different regional cultures.

Combining Lewis Henry Morgan's racist anthropology, which privileged modern Aryans, with Marx's telos, which treats all nonproletarians as backward and bound to die out, China's Leninist state imposed all the oppressive colonialist categories of orientalism. The rulers defined groups by an anthropology of advanced and backward, with the most industrialized areas tied to the Leninist ruler's capital treated as most advanced. In other regions, communities had to make themselves over in the image of an artificial "socialist" culture or be treated as primitive and reactionary. What was demanded is deculturation. However much affectively bonded groups conform on the surface to the artificial socialist culture, inwardly and very deeply, resistance is real. Once state terror and charismatic rule evaporate, outrage against the experientially oppressive and deculturing Leninist center and ultimate loyalty to the local community of the long-suffering begin to reshape identity, community, and the polity.

Not in charge of shaping their own development, ruled by outsiders, forced to destroy their basic identities, people in diverse regions resist, finding allies in those who are truly at one with them. Natives of Hainan Island tell each other that none of their counties were run by their people until 1982–83; Shanghaiese remark that they are still controlled by non-Shanghaiese; Guangdong people comment on their 1980s good luck in their native governor. Quotidian events and daily gossip shape a new identity, an oppositional community. The shared enemy of all communities is the old anti-imperialist center. Loyalty to that murderous nation would require treason against one's own kind.

Away from the capital and exploited by the privileged regions, communities have long noted which areas and people got the least investment, paid the most taxes, suffered the worst schools. In the Leninist era, local rulers, the agents of the center, congregated in regional capitals and made themselves the major beneficiary —experienced as a monopolistic beneficiary—of the center's distribution of goods through privileged networks to the center's people. China's west not only got least, but what it got was concentrated in the provincial capitals. The Leninist war against the market locked peripheralized groups into their places, thus intensifying regional contradictions and the oppositional identities and communities. Po-litico-economic geography and cultural identity became reinforcing hierarchies. Treated crudely and condescendingly, over time the regional communities grew more conscious of the hypocrisy of the regime's socialist legitimation of fairness through administrative rationing, noting how housing—or most any other prized or scarce good—went first to the outsiders from the Leninist center and their syco-phants, noting how the notion of rationing or waiting in line as fair distribution was in fact a fraud masking intolerable injustice. To believe that Leninist socialism is just would require one to abandon one's own community bonds of belonging.

When reforms begin, a backlash inevitably occurs as these long repressed anti-Leninist valuations become potent political forces. Regionally, local people are experienced as a previously martyred community. They have come to believe that only they can care for their own. This experience is intensified by its invisi-bility to the people in previously privileged regions. There, seeing themselves and their culture also as victims of the Leninist-Stalinist system that repressed parts of their cherished culture, privileged people cannot hear, let alone respond to, the cry of distant victims that they actually experience as pampered benefici-aries of subsidized largesse. Thus, the powerful forces creating new identities and communities are allowed, even forced, to fester and keep growing. The social dynamite of revolution awaits only an igniting spark and favorable politi-cal winds.

When reforms begin, the previously excluded surge into privileged redoubts. Each region tries to maximize its gains against the center. The reformed center finds budget funds slipping through its hands. A conflict grows over budget and taxes. A war between center and regions intensifies, and barriers are erected in a struggle in which the center seems increasingly foreign even to its local suffer-ers, as it seems to stifle the reforms to which it claims to be committed. While the center loses power and legitimacy, local communities become stronger, not only politically and economically but as recipients of passionate loyalty and hope. The strongly centralized Leninist state threatens to fall apart on regional and communalist fissures. Whether the outcome is civil war, or autonomy, or federalism, or new self-determinations, or whether something else wins out, a political struggle is unleashed in which regional communities contest the legiti-macy of a Leninist center experienced as a privileged, parasitic, and incompetent plunderer. This struggle has long been underway in China.

Although the Chinese government talks about the contradiction between coastal and inland provinces, although it worries openly about nationalist tenden-cies in its central Asian region, the division that manifestly threatens to split the anti-imperialist nation is between north and south, categories with a geographi-cal core but a stronger essence in terms of national identity that boils down to a war between the nation of the old anti-imperialism and the nation of a new nationalism capable of succeeding and winning in the world market. Daily sto-ries appear in the media and in gossip about the north this or the south that. They are the defining categories of a split in national loyalty. What compels interest is the content given to north and south.

As embodied at the founding of the People's Republic in the notion of sending officials to the south (*nan xia ganbu*), Leninist nationalism embraced the idea that Chinese from the loess soil of the north, as in Mao's guerrilla headquarters in Yan'an in Shanbei, defeated the imperialists and conquered the south. Historiography treated the victory of anti-imperialist nationalism as the fulfillment of a 4,000-year history of a northern-based people. But in late-twentieth-century consciousness, Chinese talk of how, as with Taiping Tianguo, the revolution began in the south and then went north. So it did with the Northern Expedition and again with the Long March. Conscious Chinese patriots who can take the lead are now re-experienced as southerners. A transvaluation of values and spaces valorizes the south and stigmatizes the north. This profound transformation occurs with no public propaganda on its behalf. It is a reformation at the level of values that the great German philosopher Hegel noted always foreshadows a genuine revolution.

Since former Party Secretary Hu Yaobang was experienced as on the progressive side, he was decoded as a southerner. He was not seen as a Hakka, although he was Hakka, as was the much-praised former Guangdong governor. People saw friends and enemies in south–north terms. "Hu Yaobang has been staring at his head, which is characteristic of a Southern Chinese," noted a hagiographer.[5] In the south, northern official power was experienced as holding China back, and backward.

The national identity of an agrarian, northern-originating Han people that defined itself by a patriotic struggle first against the Manchus and then against foreign imperialists is a superficial cultural construction, not an emanation from society's history. The regional forces that actually helped undermine Manchu rule, the same regional forces that fostered decades of twentieth-century warlordism, have long and deep roots. In the old empire, held together by an emperor, by shared religious orientations, and by a national administration with a common written language, these regional differences did not overly conflict with the minimalist imperatives of territorial unity. But these regional cultures and communities tied to different political economies have been greatly strengthened by Leninist dynamics and by new anti-Leninist identities and regional systems. What if Subei and Jiangnan will not unite when the anti-imperialist center falls? What if the northeast or the west or minority regions emotionally close to kith and kin on the other side of a border do not wish to be at one with the new south anymore than with the old north? As with the Soviet Union, so with the People's Republic of China, pundits erred when they saw a Leninist state as a happy and full solution to a nationalities problem. The common wisdom at the height of Mao Zedong's power made it impossible even to imagine China shaped and divided by raw, powerful, inherited, primordial distinctions. One highly regarded pundit erroneously found,

All that remains of the old society collapsed under the Communist blows. . . . Now that the bulldozer of Marxism has passed over ancient China, the international type of Marxist-Leninist society is springing up. . . . The Chinese is in the course of becoming . . . a man who has placed an ocean between himself and the past.[6]

The past, however, was always there just beneath the surface, indeed perhaps growing much stronger than it had been in the recent past. The past that can reappear, then, is not uniquely a south-defined nation. Peasantries are numerous, diverse, regional communities. They may be loyal to Jiangnan, not the south, for example. All the divisions of China's multiple communities could come to the fore once the anti-imperialist Leninist state disintegrates. Fear is spreading. Parents seek to get their children out of the way of an impending disaster. Beijing woos support by claiming that its rule is all that stands between the Chinese people and chaos. All sorts of new combinations or confederations or divisions may be possible. But it is in the south that people do not fear positive association with Hong Kong or Taiwan or the rest of the dynamic world economy. Whether or not a southern-based notion of nation wins out, the Leninist elders in the north are discredited.

An outraged southerner dismisses a Deng Xiaoping he finds useless as "a dirty little Hakka," or comments on how "Deng has come to Hunan to speak that language with the other Hakka." Were Deng a favorite, the southerner might have embraced him as a southerner, as he embraces the martyred Hu Yaobang. Although officialdom categorizes Hakka as Han, southerners see Hakka as not their people. In fact, given how Hakka historically were forced to live in the high hills, the source of many of Mao's guerrilla recruits, a disproportionate number of Communist Party leaders have been Haaka. There is already an incipient tendency in the south toward dismissing China's Communist Party as not even [Han] Chinese, much as Russian patriots in the late twentieth century dismiss Bolshevik leaders as not even Russian.

The new consciousness is so deep and presuppositional as not to be upset by mere facts about the large number of dedicated democrats in the north. Despite the Beijing democracy movement, it was the south that was experienced as China's progressive part. The new national consciousness is a major force in giving meaning to what and where are China's future. The 1989 democracy movement in Beijing did not valorize the north.

To the extent that southern consciousness permeates the north, the category is not geographical. Northerners who see the south as a land of opportunity and use any means to get to Shenzhen or Canton, which are experienced as the center of China's future, have accepted the new national identity. A change in consciousness and political loyalty *need not* splinter the territorial state however much it divides people and shapes political conflicts that *could* splinter the territorial state. While this book can delineate the forces at work, only actual political combat will decide among possible outcomes.

The other side of this north–south coin is the conservative, chauvinistic north conceiving the south as alien and immoral. Southerners, in a tale recounted by Bette Bao Lord, are categorized as enemies of war communism, not on the side of the military or of anticapitalism: "Shysters, the lot of them—buying cheap down south and selling dear up north things nobody with good sense needed anyway. The bums ought to be turned up and spruced up and signed up. In no time the army would turn them into real men."[7] Southerners are not true Chinese in the eyes of antireform northerners.

An opponent of that regime in the north, Fang Lizhi, seeing the regime as reactionary predicted in July 1990 (and as reported on August 29 in *The Free China Journal*) that "The strong autonomous tendency among local authorities . . . can put an end to the oligarchy in China." Democratic forces are equated with the south. In like manner, economist Liu Guoguang predicted that if an "institutionalized, legislated track" of national democracy does not arrest the political bite in this "regionalism, total chaos and the back and forth central versus local power struggle" will deepen.[8] With a reactionary party apparatus running Beijing, with state ministries there loyal to the reactionary groups, reformers once at the center have literally abandoned the north to seek jobs in the more progressive south. Optimists are those who believe that all the efforts of the conservative north to control from the top, as through wasteful state enterprises, will eventually be subverted by local, even rural, mainly southern internationally competitive enterprises that by 1991 had earned almost 40 percent of China's foreign exchange. Reformers threw their energies into those "southern" efforts and left the outmoded northern economy to drag its region down.

One increasingly finds Chinese reimaging history so the progressive thrust comes from the south, perhaps as Huang Taopo from Hainan brought north cotton growing, spinning, and weaving. Southerner Sun Yat-sen [Zhongshan] can be seen as embodying the promise of a republic. After Sun's death, the descendants of Sun's northern adversary, Yuan Shikai, would turn the clock back, having him followed to power by the reactionary northern warlords (*Beiyang pai*) until Zhejiang's patriotic Jiang Jieshi marches north to overthrow those northern warlords. Given the transvaluation of values, Jiang is no longer a source of evil. The southern Jiang is popularly depicted as a shrewd fellow who knew how to get money from the Americans, a trick the northerners cannot perform.

The north–south split pits two Chinese national histories, an imperial and frightened northern one, and a resurgent and popularly rooted southern one against one another. But at the end of the twentieth-century, it is the past of the south as a promise for China's future that seems far more attractive to the people of China. As the twentieth-century American writer William Faulkner noted, "The past is never dead. It's not even past." Guangdong, at the outset of the 1990s, embraced its past and its promise by holding the First International Guangdong Opera Festival, bringing groups from Hong Kong, Macao, Singapore, Malaysia, Thailand, and elsewhere. Guangdong also held its first international seminar on the relationship between Guangdong and the cultures of Hong Kong, Macao, Taiwan, and over-seas Chinese. A historical museum in Canton tells the story of a southern people. The United Kingdom has recognized this growing regional southern force, with its links to numerous dynamic Chinese cultural and economic regions off the mainland of China, by sending a political officer to Hong Kong to follow these overlapping southern trends and places. The U.S.–China Business Council has held seminars to study these ties and forces of a new region and a new identity.

Chinese scholars, too, recognize the implications of the prospering south. To them, there are extreme imbalances in China in terms of local development. For example, Hainan, Guangdong, Fujian, and other coastal open cities differ consid-erably from other areas in their economy, politics, cultures, and religions. Yet, the former enjoy relatively more independence than other areas. Such an imbal-ance has a tendency to grow. The existence of such independent areas and interest groups should gradually weaken the highly centralized, vertically con-trolled political system.

The north, the Leninist regime, will demand more equality for all, meaning more subsidies from the south and coast for itself and supposedly the rest of China, but more likely subsidies will go to strategic regional allies. Or, if that is impossible, the regime will slow down reform and openness. The consequence, predicts Columbia University professor Andrew Nathan, will be that coastal "enterprises are likely to ignore the orders coming from far-away Beijing for an economic slowdown and to continue their rapid growth. If the days of reform from above are finished, the days of reform from below may be just beginning."[9] Below implies south. Above, in Chinese popular consciousness, implies north.

While the particular categories of the new nationalism reflect Chinese particu-larities, the forces at work are not uniquely Chinese. The hierarchical, status-based, frozen Leninist system of groups and categories only seems legitimate in a modern sense when a war situation and charismatic ruler can create a nation of shared sacrifice, a temporary, artificial community of ultimate meaning. But an atmosphere of permanent combat is not easy to sustain, especially if a new legitimation insists on delivery of the consumer blessings of the material world. When war fear gives way to the promise of plenty, reform becomes a moment most dangerous for the rulers. As social historian Reinhard Bendix noted, based on the insight of Tocqueville,

> "[I]n the crisis of transition, the masters retained their privileges but no longer performed their obligations. . . ." [I]n consequence, the servants considered that the traditional claims of their states had been abrogated unilaterally and/or that they were now entitled to an equality of rights with all other social ranks since in his capacity as a citizen every man was the equal of every other.[10]

Hence, normal political analysis explains why the south seeks the right to control its destiny when the north is palpably incapable of delivering the goods.

It would seem that China's old Leninist nationalism is caught on the horns of an insoluble dilemma. To dynamize the economy requires openness and labor mobility, but that undercuts the northern control of a state-run economy that provides subsidized grain to urban dwellers, the military, and the state party apparatuses. If northern conservatives energize the economy, they unleash a mobility that can undermine their Leninist system; but if northern conservatives maintain the inefficient system, then they make the economy stagnant and force Chinese to think about reappropriating their rights. Since the mid-to-late 1980s, the conservative leadership has zigged and zagged between unpalatable alternatives but has tended increasingly in the direction of a short-run political safety that could eventually unleash a demand by the alienated nation for a right to determine its own destiny.

With China's healthy forces seen as southerners, individuals such as Peng Dehuai and Zhou Enlai (imagined as informed by his Jiangnan ties) are described as southerners trying to check an irrational and backward-looking Mao Zedong (whose consciousness is seen as coming from the backward, authoritarian, traditional northern peasantry of Shanbei).[11] Mao is envisioned as in the line of closed-minded emperors who hurt China by persecuting the educated, burning the books, and shutting the country off from the common human inheritance of science, technology, and economic progress. Mao is equated with Ming emperors who eroded China's dynamic involvement with the world economy and world science.

Hated moments in PRC history, such as the Cultural Revolution in Shanghai, are imagined as know-nothing impositions by crude and ignorant northerners such as Wang Hongwen, seen as a Subei person. (Actually he was not, although his wife was Subei.) In the cinema, the cultural split pits the northern Yan'an school against the southern Shanghai school. Even the nationalism of the north is discredited as a disaster for the nation, with Mao's notion of progressive northern Boxers (*Yi He Tuan*) rejected and the nativistic, superstitious Boxers judged incapable of accomplishing any constructive, progressive purpose. Such a transvaluation of values has redefined daily discourse.

Post-Mao enterprising peasants are imagined as innovative and southern. The peasantry, as a category, is contested by south and north in order to define one's project as nationalistic, with each political tendency imagining a different peasantry. What neither side sees is that the numerous regional peasant communities and cultures may not share either northern or southern projection. As with other post-Leninist states, once the transition speeds up, it may splinter in many unexpected ways.

Reformers imagine peasants in terms of their market-oriented, politico-economic preoccupations. They support hard-working, industrious, mobile villagers. In contrast, the opponents of reform, embodied in the "roots" school of writers, embrace a virile, reactionary, chauvinist notion of a peasantry, one that excludes the successful rural entrepreneurs in factories that export and earn foreign exchange, that condemns rural consumers who buy in the city, that mocks hard-working rural construction teams that make possible speedy and cheap urban progress. Roots writers, who are virtually protofascist nativists, are contemptuous of liberal tendencies and "capitalist"-like reforms. Money, market, city, individualism, freedom, and foreignness are portrayed as alienating and dehumanizing immoralities that would subvert some romantically imagined warm village world of caring, obedient, patriarchal peasants who suffer much and ask little so a tough, pure, simple, militarized nation survives. A good woman, as a traditional peasant, sacrifices for the patriarchal nation. A roots writer can find the essence of the essentialized peasantry in the tale of a woman who sold "herself for a bit of grain to feed her starving husband. She stripped off her cotton tunic in exchange for two sesame seed rolls and stuffed them into his hands as she left. It was then that I began to really know our suffering motherland and our people."[12]

The struggle over national identity in China, over who is the martyred people, stretches from high culture to popular gossip. It is a pervasive reality. A key question is whether the policies and strategies of the rulers in the capital city in the north, abandoning Leninism and trying to make maximum use of extreme chauvinist appeals, will backfire and make the rulers instead seem like traitors to the nation.

The north is ruled by people who rely on Japan, a nation that can be seen by nationalists as the enemy of China's people, since Japan perpetrated the Nanjing massacre (and at times denies it), since Japanese cheated China at the Baogang Steel Plant in Shanghai, and since Japan refused throughout the 1980s to make modern technology available or to invest large sums in high-tech industries in China. Although southerner Hu Yaobang was scapegoated by the northern elders for closeness to the Japanese, the northern Li Peng government seems forced to rely on Japan, because Japan is silent about human rights abuses and is generous with cash aid to rulers in Beijing as long as rich business deals ensue. Dalien almost seemed a Japanese semicolony by 1991. In the 1990s, will the northeast come to seem an old-fashioned Japanese sphere of influence? Will dependence on Japanese loans and goodwill make it seem as if the purportedly patriotic rulers in the north are actually traitors to the original anti-imperialist revolution? Will even northern people turn on them, redefining them as enemies to the Chinese nation?

Based on an analysis by the Li Peng government, Japan modernized in the nineteenth-century Meiji era through state socialism. Hence in emulating Japan, China supposedly can stick to its socialist principles of protecting the people from a cruel polarization that Chinese supposedly would suffer if market forces were allowed to dictate China's economic development. In contrast to this imagined Japanese state socialism, market-oriented and democratic America, Europe, and Eastern Europe, dwell on human rights and therefore would intervene in Chinese domestic politics, supposedly wounding China's sovereign dignity. The new, enlightened patriots note, however, that China is a signatory of the United Nations' Universal Declaration of Human Rights. They see the northern regime that arbitrarily disregarded human rights, wounding the dignity of the Chinese people, and lowering China's standing in the world community. They see the northern Leninists as isolating China from the world, leaving the Chinese people only with friends like Myanmar and North Korea. The northern regime seems ridiculous.

The out-of-touch old guard in the north mocks Taiwan as a weak economy requiring the succor of the socialist state; in contrast, in the south, where investment money comes from Chinese from Hong Kong, Macao, Taiwan, Singapore, and Thailand, people know they can benefit from openness to the world economy that actually expands ties among Chinese. The south, with Chinese help from elsewhere, grows at an extraordinary rate because it knows how to do business in the world economy. The north is slow, stagnant, and scared. The north, dominated by money-losing, resource-inefficient, noncompetitive state industries is forced to plunder the south, to beg and borrow from Japan and other nonnational resources, and to turn the printing presses to churn out more money for wasteful subsidies that threaten to create an explosive and destructive inflation. Given the hidden forces transforming popular consciousness, the failure of the northern regime raises the prospect of a politico-economic crisis being explained by Chinese in terms of the spreading transvaluation of values or as a legitimating cause of a very different national identity that privileges the experience of the anti-Leninist southern patriots. For any hopeful future for Chinese, the northern rulers are, at best, an irrelevancy.

This does not mean that China must split north from south around the Yangtze; it means that this reconceptualized nation is a challenge to the old and outmoded anti-imperialist nationalism that previously legitimated chauvinist rulers in Beijing who appealed to Leninist anti-imperialism. That Leninist system is no longer seen as protecting the nation. The Leninist order is a self-wounding economic system that brings decreased productivity while increasing heavy industrial output that serves no human purpose, with much of it left to rot, rust, and run to ruin in heavily guarded warehouses lest the scarce goods be stolen or sold on the market and put to productive use by nonstate entrepreneurs. Those ever-present warehouses, more impregnable than high-security prisons, are symbols of a national potential now locked away to die. Chinese know where those warehouses are. They symbolize the wasted opportunity that rule by the north has come to mean. To save China, its people seek a new nationalism. They find it by identifying with the dynamism of the south.

All over China, in the interstices of the outmoded center's ever more inefficient command economy, local, small industry grows to meet public demand and satisfy needs. The optimists in China are those who believe that in the not too distant future the old guard will die off, the political orientation will change, and this economically dynamic force outside of the control of the north, an economic force that is especially strong in the south, will then be channeled successfully as part of a renewed and rapidly developing Chinese nation.

The Li Peng government, trying to hold power in the 1990s by promoting Confucianism, opposing the heterodox, and fearing the south's successful opening to the world economy, is deepening a historical fissure that has split China for a millennium, creating a stark division between north and south in which the rule of the obscurantist north can only widen the gap that leaves the Chinese ever farther behind the rapidly developing world.

Archeological discoveries are sensitizing Chinese to the fact that the Han people are not Mao's monolithic descendants of the yellow soil of the loess regions of north China and that civilization in China has multiple sources originating in diverse parts of a multicultural land. The northern peasant, the base of Mao's anti-imperialist revolution, is no longer privileged as China's true patriot and savior in preconscious nationalist categorization.

Imperial China can be conceived as a multinational empire of military conquest. As European settlers in the Americas or Australia experienced themselves as on virgin territory, in like manner, imperial court-centered Chinese notions treated peasant land or the land of the next region as virgin territory. Historically tillers and outsiders are lower than people (*min*). They are seen, as Mao pictured them, as simple and natural, a blank sheet of paper. Hence the rich cultures that in fact distinguish, say, a *minnan* peasant culture from a *huabei* peasant culture have long been virtually invisible in a twentieth-century imagining of Chinese historical development as a unity. In the nineteenth century, these rich cultural differences began to be seen by the educated Chinese elite as a hodgepodge of local ties, unscientific religions, and useless superstitions that had to be destroyed if China were to modernize. A Han nation was invented. Imagining all Chinese as united in overthrowing the foreign Manchu monarchy, would-be patriots ignored the power and diversity of regional cultural communities. In Hebei, where I have done research, the revolution's restoration of order permitted the local community to invest in Hebei opera, which Mao's Cultural Revolution subsequently treated as a feudal fossil that should be destroyed. The Leninist order was the enemy of passionately experienced community bonds and regional cultures.

Superficially, the old Khomeini-like anti-imperialist chauvinism seems a potent source of popular support for the post-Mao rulers. This manipulated passion resembles East Germany's pride in its nation building a wall that seemed unassailable until the day the wall fell. Then the new national legitimation of raising consumer standards of living revealed the old Leninist ideology as almost without adherents, except for a small strata of intellectuals and a part of the old statist hierarchy. Because the imperatives of survival in a Leninist order force people to be complicitious, and because people try to maintain a good conscience, they embrace the most popular part of Leninist ideology—in China, patriotism. Therefore, even honest informants are unaware of how rapidly and completely they can change when that artificial and corrupting Leninist system disintegrates. As soon as complicity is no longer required, most people simply stop bowing to the fraudulent gods of Leninist chauvinism.

To be sure, the regime endlessly reproduces ritual proof of its eternal nature to impress the complicitious, and foreign observers. To doubt this reality while the regime continues its rituals of manufacturing support may invite ridicule. But the history of post-Leninism globally is a warning against the danger of overestimating the staying power of what is manifest but superficial.

Yet that does not mean that the alternative to post-Mao chauvinism must win. Consider the czarist autocracy of the mid-nineteenth century. It was a useless anachronism. There was no positive reason for it to survive. And yet its life was prolonged into the second decade of the twentieth century. When it finally disappeared virtually without a trace in the blink of an eye during World War I, a sixty-year-old analysis of the emptiness of the czarist body politic was proved right. And yet it had lived for at least sixty years too long. It would not self-destruct. Something had to deliver the final, fatal blow.

So it is with post-Mao chauvinistic Leninism and the northern regime. It too just might survive on inertia, complicity, fear of worse, chauvinism, the provision of guaranteed minimums, and the like. It need not disappear tomorrow. Politics will be decisive. One cannot predict the varying forces of what shapes politics: leadership, alliances, timing, strategy, coalition building, appeals, etc., or how they will combine. Still why would one wager on no final blow burying the northern corpse, that is, the Mao-era anti-imperialist nationalism? Either one believes that the same forces that undercut Leninist states elsewhere are at work in China, or one embraces China as a peculiar entity. This chapter has offered reasons for betting on the global tendencies delegitimating the old northern, Leninist nationalism.

To quote the theologian and historian Paul Tillich, "The present is a consequence of the past but not at all *an* anticipation of the future." In China, the Leninist past virtually guarantees that the regime in the north will fail. But the fate and future of the nation continues to be contested. Even who and what the nation are is contested. But such struggles reflect similar explosive or implosive potentialities in post-Leninist states elsewhere that should lead one to anticipate some Chinese future premised on a new nationalism, or nationalisms.

Notes

1. Zhang, *The Ark*, in *Love Must Not Be Forgotten* (Beijing: Panda Books, 1986), p. 159.

2. Cited in *Inside China Mainland*, September 1991, translated from *Fandou Monthly* (Hong Kong), July 1991, p. 62.

3. Arendt's essay on the 1956 Hungarian revolution as a paradigm for the democratization of Leninist tyrannies appears as a concluding appendix to her classic study, *The Origins of Totalitarianism*. Her theory's implications for democratization in China are spelled out in Edward Friedman, "Was Mao Zedong a Revolutionary?" *Issues and Studies* 26.8 (August 1990), pp. 38–42.

4. Chen Zhangtai and Chen Jianmin, "Sociolinguistic Research Based on Chinese Reality," *International Journal of the Sociology of Language* 81 (1990), p. 31.

5. Pang Pang [pseud.], *The Death of Hu Yaobang* (Honolulu: University of Hawaii Center for Chinese Studies, 1989), p. 45.

6. Robert Guillarn, *600 Million Chinese* (New York: Criterion Books, 1957), p. 264.

7. Lord, *Legacies* (New York: Knopf, 1990), p. 190.

8. "Zai zhili zhendun jichu shang jin yibu shenhua gaige de sikao" [Thoughts on further deepening reform on the basis of retrenchment], *Caimao Jingji* [Finance and Trade Economics], No. 99 (March 11, 1990), pp. 3–10.

9. Andrew Nathan, *China's Crisis* (New York: Columbia University Press, 1990), p. 120.

10. Bendix, "The Lower Classes and the 'Democratic Revolution,'" *Industrial Relations* 1 (October 1961), pp. 91–116.

11. For example, 1980s military histories of the late 1940s civil war written by Li Ruqing praised Jiang Jieshi's strategy but criticized Mao's strategy as "feudal" (June Teufel Dreyer, "The Role of the PLA in the Post-Tiananmen Period," *Asian Outlook* 26.5 [July–August 1991], p. 14).

12. Helen Siu, ed., *Furrows* (Stanford: Stanford University Press, 1990), p. 307.

Chapter 3

Ethnic Identity and the Denationalization and Democratization of Leninist States

Ethnic and regional resurgence in China is a particular manifestation of a process threatening the disintegration of Leninist and post-Leninist states in general. The Bolshevik conquest of communities previously locked in the Russian czar's "prisonhouse of nationalities" (Shapiro 1984) was followed by "nativization" (locking the community on a territory) and forced Russification through police terror, resulting in "resistance [that] took the form of retreat into the national culture, refusal to learn or speak Russian, and determined efforts to increase ties with the West" (Suny 1990).[1] Outsiders know of similar resistance in China from the prideful assertions by Tibetans in a historic homeland. However, Leninist rulers in China, seeing themselves as members of a 90-plus percent dominant ethnic group dubbed Han, have suppressed Tibetans in the name of Chinese national unity.[2] But many people in China do not embrace this Han identity as primary. It seems the artificial construction of a discredited rulership. Instead, in keeping with the instrumental needs of some more regional group, peoples have been imagining themselves in more important terms.

The almost thirty million Muslims who live all over China began, in the post-Mao era, rebuilding and returning to their mosques in an expression of communalist identity as explosive as the Tibetans' (Gladney 1991). The subversive essence of this

Originally published in M. Crawford Young, ed., *The Rising Tide of Cultural Pluralism* (Madison: University of Wisconsin Press, 1993). Reprinted with permission of the University of Wisconsin Press.

asserted identity was obvious inside mosques where, within tame Chinese characters, ink-brush Arabic strokes conveyed Islamic declarations of faith.

This bold embrace of ethnic identity, a challenge to the Han and their values,
is also powerfully revealed in the doubling of registered Manchus between
China's 1982 census and its 1990 census, while Han population grew by but 8
percent. The Manchus, the rulers of China's last multicentury dynasty, had been
vilified by Leninists as reactionaries. Much of the growth in ethnic population
was not a result of high birthrates—although that is how the Han tended to see
it—but the result instead of a conscious choice of a revalued community. In the
Mao era, politically stigmatized Manchus tried to hide their identity and sought
to pass as Han, persuading observers that, as modern myth had it, the Han had
absorbed nomadic invaders from the north beyond the Great Wall, forgetting that
the 1911 revolution that overthrew the Manchus was legitimated by their resistance to absorption. By 1990, the northern-steppe Manchus stood up, confidently
and publicly asserting an ultimate moral claim higher than that of the dominant
Han ruling group, whose center was Beijing.

So it was with Mongols, too. In Inner Mongolia, where Mongols had been
overwhelmed in the Mao era by a massive influx of Han migrants, Mongol
informants, according to anthropologist Dru Gladney, reported joy on hearing of
the Beijing massacre of June 4, 1989. Finally Han were killing Han instead of
the minorities. The Turkish peoples in China's far west suffered a similar Han
inundation and persecution. Among Tibetans, Muslims, Manchus, Mongols, and
others, a discredited Han ethnic Leninist despotism was challenged. A Harvard
researcher in southwest China, seeking to interview a minority, found himself
directed to a group he had previously studied as Han; the entire group had since
abandoned the Han identity. Inadvertently, Leninism brought denationalization.
The survival and identity of China itself was at issue.

Similar communalist movements exploded against Russians at the end of the
1980s among ethnic groups in the Leninist Soviet Union, in Leninist Yugoslavia
against Serbs, and in Leninist Ethiopia against the Amharic. The structured
dynamics of Leninist systems inadvertently yet inexorably strengthened ethnic
challengers to the nationalistic essence of the previous Leninist despotism, identified, in China's case, as the Han. What cries out for explanation is how the
Leninist political system fosters this ethnic assertion against a state-centered
group, re-experienced by victims as so oppressive as to be virtually genocidal.
To be sure, this ethnic reassertion is well-nigh universal. But Leninist politics, as
this essay will show, leaves an extraordinarily deep imprint on identity politics
that makes more likely strong, antiregime forms of consciousness ready to be
mobilized.

An inevitable consequence of the unintentionally subversive dynamics of Leninism was the recognition that a far higher priority must be placed on resolving
the national question. Strong ethnic reassertions imposed that new political
agenda. A Hong Kong reporter finds of China that, as with the former Soviet

Union, there can be no "doubt that . . . parts of the country, held together now only by brute force and coercion will want to break off. . . . Ethnic-religious nationalism . . . will spring back to life, once the lid is off" (Pan 1990, 46). The political emergence and ascendance of ethnic communal identities requires a general explanation in terms of shared Leninist dynamics, an explanation that fits China and similar Leninist polities.

Leninism and Its Mark on Ethnic Identity

Leninism, both as institutional structure and policy practice, is driven by a perverse logic that creates the obverse of its proclaimed purposes. The Yugoslav writer Mihajlo Mihajlov explained how the actual dynamics of Leninism are more like racist fascism than progressive egalitarianism, since "recruitment for the republican police [is] based on ethnic criteria, the bans on the sale of property [are] based on the same principle, etc. Regrettably, very often nationalist savagery is not recognized from a distance. The red star on the helmet of a tank crew totally misinforms" (CADDY 1991, 2).

Leninists of the dominant group do not see themselves as racist fascists. Rather, Leninists define themselves as anti-imperialists saving a people from parasitic plunder by a deathbed capitalism supposedly temporarily resuscitated only by blood money sucked from the poor nations of the third world. In reality, Leninist rulers therefore opt for economic autonomy. The communities defending against injurious Leninist autarky imposed by the ethnic group at the capital usually seek the blessings offered by open and deep involvement with the world's advanced technology, knowledge, and products. To communities opposing the disastrous economic policies of the center, Leninist anti-imperialism seems a force keeping other communities locked into backwardness and poverty.

Leninist rulers imagine themselves commanding the physical resources of the economy and redistributing them to achieve justice and equity. This is offered in contrast to a hypostatized capitalism that is alleged to operate by a logic of polarization and immiseration in which the rich get richer and the poor get poorer. In practice, the Leninist state distributes a physically confiscated surplus by institution and locale. Groups that are not part of the dominant ethnic bloc at the state center find that distribution by institution means privileging the ruling Leninist party, its governmental ministries, and the military hierarchies, all benefiting the dominant group.

In fact, the Leninist system creates fantastic inequality. W. Brus recounts, "I never saw more inequality than in the Stalinist, pre-reform epoch when distribution was centralized and a large part of remuneration was made in kind. The injustices were in both the relative and in the absolute sense" (Brus 1981, 34). Watching the transformation from Leninist inequalities toward a market-oriented, post-Leninist society, Eric Foner (1990, 800) noted,

Even those in a position to benefit from this [Leninist] system find it unfair and humiliating. To a large extent, whom you know now determines your standard of living. There is something positively egalitarian about the way money in a market society can erase other social distinctions, about a world in which anybody with the cash can walk into a store and purchase whatever goods he or she pleases, without incurring personal obligations.

Only reform that permits market and mobility and advancement on merit can counter alienating Leninist dynamics. When the Leninist Han center hesitates on reform, it reconfirms the experience of other groups of the dominant group as selfish exploiters. But the ruling group believes it is acting in good faith, taking from its central urban areas to redistribute to the regions dominated by minority language, ethnic, and religious groups. While the minorities find themselves getting last and least, the dominant group feels itself sacrificing to lift up benighted groups. That each and every community feels itself the loser can facilitate a rapid crumbling of that Leninism when it is finally confronted by a serious challenge. The numbers, beyond elites and organs of coercion, who ultimately experience themselves as beneficiaries with a stake in the traditional Leninist system turns out to be quite minute. Leninism stands on fragile legs of dessicated legitimacy and shriveled support.

Who actually benefits from redistribution from the ethnic center to the minority regions? In fact, such regions mainly receive state-imposed, below-market prices for their agricultural products and raw materials. They are forced to self-exploit to fund local education and medicine from remnants left behind by the center's metropolitan-biased pricing system that leaves the minority regions the poorest areas with the least medicine, the worst education, the lowest income, and the highest malnutrition. Hence what the dominant Han group experiences as the privileging of the inept minorities, such as providing expensive beef at lower pork prices for Muslims and less strict controls on childbearing, the minorities, in contrast, experience as small change to buy off victims who have been peripheralized and immiserated by the systems of pricing and distribution.

Partial reform produces the worst of all worlds for the center. China's communities in the northwest and southwest find themselves paid below-market prices by an exploitative center, thereby intensifying reasons for alienation from the old center.

Still, it is true that funds from the state center do go to the capitals of the minority regions. But the beneficiaries are mainly the power holders, usually members of the dominant group. Local turncoats, the equivalents of Indian Indian agents, as one Mongol described them to me, are seen as doing the dirty work of the dominant group. The monies sent from the center tend to stay in the regional capital, whose population increasingly becomes the dominant group; in China's case, Han officials, traders, and an occupying army. The minority experiences benefits as going only to the dominant group.

Yet so perverse is the Leninist system that Han beneficiaries experience themselves as poor because so much goes to purportedly lazy, unproductive minorities. People living in Leninist systems learn that reward is related to personalistic politics and not to merit or productivity. The dominant group, in fact, has kept the minorities down. But the dominant group, conscious of its own pain and focused on how the undeserving—including minorities—benefit, is oblivious to the actual sufferings of minorities. Hence in the spring of 1989, when the Twenty-seventh Army marched from Inner Mongolia to Beijing to crush the movement for democracy, the rumor in Beijing was that an army of minorities was coming to crush the Han. Actually, what arrived was a Han army that had been repressing the Mongol minority.

It is systematic peripheralization of minorities that characterizes Leninist dynamics. Local people are locked into regional poverty by Leninist controls that keep them from fleeing state-imposed, place-specific collectives, a system that also uses internal passports, region-specific food coupons, and police registration in hotels to prevent minorities from even temporarily enjoying the greater resources monopolized elsewhere by the dominant group. The system fosters a divisive process, privileging the dominant group, peripheralizing the minorities. Because a nation-state is a shared space, this absolute geographical split fostered by Leninist structures threatens to split the nation itself. The logic of Leninism is denationalization.

Thus the Leninist system creates a situation where the dominant group monopolizes all the best in jobs, education, and residence, while the plundered minority is left with the dregs. A member of the local minority, whether Latvian or Tibetan, waits endlessly on lines and on lists, hoping for key items monopolized and politically rationed to favorites—say, a new apartment—only to discover that the new and best are given to officials of the alien group from the state center. Consequently, the distribution system commanded by the Leninist apparatus appears as an embodiment of racist injustice. For a minority to be prosocialist would be to play the fool or to be a traitor, the enemy of one's own community.

In addition, Han officials in the minority area tend to be disgruntled, upset because they failed to obtain postings in Han regions with better services, schools, and housing. They take their disappointment and anger out on the local people they rule. The minority community experiences occupation by an army that hates and ridicules the local community it dominates. Consequences include quotidian degrading treatment of the minorities, resentment, and tension The rulers find themselves sitting on a powder keg that at times explodes, intensifying the opposing identities and angers.

In a Muslim region of China, "three times government troops came to suppress their revolts against cadres who ruled so callously that their subjects lopped off their hands in frustration and revenge" (Lord 1990, 174). In another Muslim village, in response to protests by the faithful against the closing of a mosque, tanks sent to the village killed "all those living within it. The village itself was reduced to rubble" (Gladney 1990, 64).

Given the polarized identities fostered by the Leninist system, once terror ends and reform begins, local leaders who had been long stigmatized by the ruling group as reactionary agents of imperialism return from exile or prison to be greeted as heroes (Madsen 1989). Long-suppressed identities congeal and implode. The occupying army then intensifies communal strife by repressing local cultural reassertion.

> In April 1989 . . . 4,000 policemen armed with electric batons descended upon a Catholic [Chinese] village of 1,700 people; more than 200 were injured, 100 very seriously, including octogenarians and children. Local hospitals were forbidden to treat them. The . . . savagery surpassed even that of the bulldozing of Crossroads and other black townships in South Africa. And the villagers' only offense had been to insist on erecting a tent as a makeshift church. (Chan 1990, 7)

The grounding of this oppositional relationship lies in the Leninist project. The impact has fallen both on Koreans in China and in the Soviet Union, and on Lamaists both in China and Mongolia. Koreans under Stalin, about 200,000 of whom had fled Japanese occupation, were forcibly deported in 1937 to barren land in Kazakhstan, where "the dead were taken away in carts every morning for the first six months" (*Far Eastern Economic Review*, 1991, 18). Two thousand or so were deported to slave-labor camps and death, intellectuals were exterminated, teaching in the Korean language was outlawed, and assimilation was imposed (ibid.). Likewise, among Chinese of Korean descent, "Several tens of thousands were imprisoned, isolated or investigated," while "about 4,000 persons died due to persecution" (Lee 1986, 89). The official story was that "the use of ethnic language meant cultural degeneration and political retreat. . . . [P]rograms to train minority teaching personnel and to produce minority language textbooks were thoroughly destroyed" (ibid., 91).

In China, the slaughter of some 30,000 Mongols has been admitted. Almost every permanent structure in Inner Mongolia in the late 1960s turned a room into a torture chamber to make Mongols confess that they were foreign agents. In like manner, Stalin's declaration of war on religion devastated Buddhist Lamaism in Soviet-dependent Mongolia, where outside of Tibet live the only other people who are Lamaists. More than seven hundred monasteries were destroyed, religious books were burned, and thousands of Lama Buddhist religious leaders were murdered. It is a general and cruelly oppressive phenomenon of Leninism that requires explanation, not a supposed Han Chinese chauvinism.

V. Zotov, a Soviet analyst, finds: "The key sociological feature of the Stalinist model of socialism to which China had belonged is . . . crowd mentality. . . . [A]ntagonisms under socialism will be found above all in the ethnic and denominational spheres" (Zotov 1990, 2). Leninism in minority areas brings military occupation by a force felt to be foreign, whose daily conduct intensifies alienation and the primacy of ethnic identity and communalist politics. Consider, for example, this account by a Tibetan refugee:

> When Tibetans arrive at a check-post and speak Tibetan, the [Han] soldiers will react by telling them they [the soldiers] don't understand and they [the Tibetans] must speak Chinese. They [the soldiers] check all luggage and confiscate knives, keeping them instead of giving them to their officers. The soldiers are also patrolling and when they don't like somebody, they will take this person to the police headquarters, interrogate him and beat him. In the daytime, they beat people in the street with their sticks without any reason, and, at night, this regularly happens. One evening, through my window, I saw five Tibetan pilgrims prostrating on the Barkhor [Lhasa's central market]. Then eight Chinese soldiers came to harass them, treated them badly and took a watch and money that one of them had in his money belt. Another time, in the evening, around the Barkhor, a girl on a bicycle passed Chinese soldiers; Tibetans passing Chinese soldiers have to dismount and bow to show respect to them. She did not, and the soldiers were annoyed; so they started to beat her very badly, even on her breasts. A Tibetan who witnessed the scene and only asked the soldiers not to beat her was also beaten very badly for intervening. (Tibetnet 1990)

Daily experience reinforces a dichotomy of polarized communalist identities. In China's case, the dominant Han and all others are dichotomized into evil oppressor and innocent victims. In Tibet's case, these cruelties have been extreme, including a famine that forced starving Tibetans to seek survival on the droppings of Han army horses. That is, the dumb beasts of the oppressor were better off than the minority people.

> Parents fed dying children their own blood mixed with hot water and tsampa [barley]. Other children were forced to leave home to beg . . . and old people went off to die alone in the hills, [as] thousands of Tibetans took to eating the refuse thrown by the Chinese soldiers to the pigs each Han [military] compound kept, while those around PLA outposts daily pieced apart manure from the soldier's horses looking for undigested grain. (Avedon 1984, 237)

The Han have taken over the non-Han areas and grabbed power, land, and all the best state-run opportunities. In addition, the Han blame the non-Han for the minority community's poverty, claiming, "The one fundamental reason for poverty is the lower quality of the people" (Ellingson 1991). The system fosters condescension that gives good conscience to those high in the system, making the losers seem naturally inferior. Leninism operates as a racist form of settler colonialism.

While each Leninist state has its particular way of treating minorities, there is a shared content to the system that, over time, delegitimates the national center of the dominant group that has predefined the minorities as enemies of the nation and socialism. Leninist rulers believe that only they can save the entire nation from foreign exploitation. Minorities, often on the frontiers and frequently involved with foreigners in a prior era of chaos or openness before the Leninist state was established, seem to Leninists not only incapable of defending the nation against imperialism but often, as with the trade-oriented bourgeoisie and urban workers in port regions, also appear to be allies of imperialism and enemies of "the people." The ultimate expression of this general tendency that defines the urban and cosmopolitan as traitorous was the Khmer Rouge Pol Pot war of annihilation against cities and city dwellers.

In building anti-imperialist nationalism, Leninists define a pre-existing *volk* as glorious because of a struggle to hold the land. The actual early story of the Han seizing the territory of other communities and slaughtering minority peoples who once occupied that land is eliminated from the imagined national history. So are the glories of the minority people and their civilization. Seen as dwelling in empty space, the non-Han, a veritable fourth world, find their lands the target of nuclear tests and dominant ethnic-group settlers.

Protoracist Leninist nationalism is similar to the German nationalistic response to French Enlightenment nationalism, an anxious chauvinist response that treats the project of freedom as an excuse for expansion. This anxious nationalism is a response to an equivalent of a Napoleon marching into Germany and carrying the promise of republican governance premised on a generalizable legal code. In anti-Enlightenment nationalism, the project of law, freedom, and careers open to talents is experienced as an apologia for foreign domination. The threatened people respond with pride in a particular culture, finding their new nationalism in a rejection of an open, liberal project. Hence, national military defense and ideological fundamentalism to preserve the purity of some threatened people become the essence of Leninist anti-imperialist nationalism, an explicit rejection of European expansion, and an implicit protofascist project proclaiming itself socialist and progressive because it is antiliberal, anti-Enlightenment.

Ironically, Leninism thereby negates the haughty Eurocentric Hegelian-Marxist tradition that saw Europe as the maturity of the human race and perceived Africa and Asia to be its transcended childhood, understanding history as progress in reason and freedom. Instead, as this expanding and chauvinistic Europe defined the non-European other as immature, so the anti-European Leninist response defines its valued essence as the rejection of European categories, commerce, and culture. Survival as a people seems so all-encompassing that stories of progress are treated as sources of the death of the nation. The oppositional identity rejects the vital baby in throwing out the dirty bathwater. Imperialism versus anti-imperialism is a conflict of arrogant irrationalities, a pitting of one haughty chauvinism against another, leaving little space for humane purposes.

Leninist Nationalism in China

In China, Mao Zedong's Leninist movement defined itself as the rejection of the Europe of the Opium War, a Europe represented by Bible-carrying soul stealers and foreign gunboats serving narcotics traffickers. If Hegel and Marx chauvinistically defined China's fate to be submission to European commercial civilization because the latter was superior to alleged Asian fatalism and barbaric customs, in contrast Chinese Leninists would re-create the endangered nation as a defender threatened with obliteration by murderous Europeans who would devitalize the Chinese people. Constitutional representation or mutually beneficial economic interaction has no part in this nationalist epic of survival through the sacrifice of lives to save the race-people. A militaristic mobilization insists on absolute self-sacrifice as the price of sacred national survival. The technically and scientifically advanced is redefined as a morally bankrupt criminal, enriched only by theft.

Rather than understand how industrially advanced groups applied science and technology to expand wealth at a pace the world had never before witnessed, Leninists explained the accumulation of capital as the plunder of poor laborers. "Under the spur of the vilest and most shameless greed, the bourgeoisie . . . used cruel and remorselessly barbarous devices to suck the blood of millions of laboring people" (Crozier 1990).

But by the end of the twentieth century, Chinese leaders have acknowledged that the problem they confronted was not a dying, parasitic capitalism but a new stage in a continuous scientific revolution. Leninist policy has been revealed as a disaster. At first, however, it appeared as an ethical imperative. In the Leninist project, a vulnerable, pure nation needs protection from penetration by the evil and strong foreigner. In China, in response to the Opium War, the conservative cultural advice was to keep the rapacious foreigner out:

> [T]o defend the open ocean is not as good as to defend the seaports, and to defend the seaports is not as good as to defend the inland rivers.
>
> The phrase "enticing the enemy to enter the inland rivers" means that soldiers . . . are sown on land and in the water as if making a pit to wait for tigers. . . .
>
> The strength of the British barbarian is on the ocean. . . . On the shore, they will lose their strength.
>
> Except for your ships being solid, your gunfire fierce, and your rockets powerful, what other abilities have you?
>
> If we do not exterminate you English barbarians, we will not be human beings. (Wei 1842, 30–31, 36)

In this view, anyone who reached out to welcome the values of the Europeans was seen to be on the side of the immoral enemy of the people. Progress in Europe was invisible or tainted. Consequently, a deeply conservative traditionalism infused purportedly modern anti-imperialist Leninist nationalism. The Chinese rejected the European calendar and cosmology and killed Chinese astronomers who found modern science superior. The project of anti-imperialist nationalism was to militarily occupy the threatened borders, the regions of the minorities, and to treat all who trafficked with the foreigners as traitors. This made every minority, from the Muslim traders from the Silk Road to Tibetans dealing with British or Indians, seem similar to compradores working for (meaning selling out to) foreign firms. Nationalists were those who defended the sacred soil from those immoral groups.

The Leninist nation, organizing in self-defense against imperialism, did theoretically include minorities. Yet such communities, which previously found foreign allies to keep the territorially expanding central group, the Han, at bay, were also redefined as subverters of unity, friends of the new nation's enemies. The Leninist-Stalinist project insisted that it brought modern power by resisting the threat from a parasitic foreign commerce and polluting foreign culture. Stalinism was an autarkic fundamentalism claiming to guarantee military strength and national independence.

The national project was presented by the Han as controlling a national space. Since minorities, in fact, controlled much of that space, either the space was redefined as empty or the minorities as so backward that they had to obey the vanguard ethnic group that could more productively and patriotically employ the space. This vision demanded the suppression of indigenous peoples, redefined as invisible, anachronistic, or traitorous obstacles. Those farthest from the foreign impact, hinterland Han peasants, were valorized as patriots who suffered to keep outsiders out. By stigmatizing what the outside had to offer, Leninists tended toward autarky, import substitution, and the mobilization of mass manual labor. The wealth-expanding worlds of trade, capital, technology, and knowledge transfer were excluded.

When hinterland Han people turned out to be religious and family-oriented communities whose standard of living required temporary urban jobs, peddling, hauling, and other "bourgeois" economic practices made them targets of Leninist fundamentalists out to purify the nation of superstitious, private, parochial, money-oriented pollution. Chinese editions of Marx's work mistranslate his description of religion as an "opium of the people," meaning, according to Marx, "the heart of a heartless world," so that religion is defined by Leninists as a "poison," something that the body politic must be rid of at any cost. The rulers who lead a war on the poison of religion, ethnicity, and family see themselves as saving lives and purifying an authentic nation. In reality, they are the enemies even of their own community and its culture.

The only morally pure group becomes the party–state leadership of the dominant group engaged in a cultural war against the sacred bonds of all. After all, even the dominant group has a particular culture. Thus Russians in the 1990s who are trying to reclaim a heritage that had been shattered by Leninist tyranny denationalize even Lenin, imagined as anti-Russian, and see him as Mongol, not Russian; and Han Chinese who reject the Leninist system that warred against the sacred rituals of lineage can denationalize Deng Xiaoping and see him as Hakka, not Han. Hakka are a community with their own language and culture who fled south and were forced many centuries ago into southern hills, an area from which Mao's earliest guerrillas were disproportionately recruited. Although the Beijing government defines Hakka as Han, antiregime Chinese, especially in the south or east or on coasts, often find the regime as backward hinterland, northern conservative—or Hakka—and therefore not truly Chinese. Even the dominant group must redefine its communalist nationalism, so morally discredited and isolated does Leninism become.

It is striking how little emotional hold persists in Leninist nationalism beyond antiforeign chauvinism. The culture of the Han anti-imperialist state is artificial and readily discarded once power and fear are no longer obstacles. Leninist national identity was never integrated into daily life. Its "national holidays, for example, have little cultural meaning and elicit no special behavior whatsoever except for that arranged by local cadres. The contrast with the lunar New Year and other traditional festivals could not be greater" (Cohen 1991, 128). Austere, group marriages were imposed on regime-defined holidays. This alienating artificiality is not a peculiarity of Chinese Leninism. Jacek Koron of Poland's Solidarity finds that Leninism "is a system artificially created and artificially designed, and such a system destroys all life around it" (1990, 24). Leninism creates a hunger and a need for a genuine community. It leads people to search for truer and deeper identities. Inadvertently but inevitably, it denationalizes and recommunalizes.

Morgan, Lenin, and Stalin: The Roots of Leninist Minority Policy

National minority policy in Leninist states combines the ideas of anthropologist Lewis Henry Morgan, as adopted by Friedrich Engels, with the practices and theories imposed by Lenin and Stalin. The newly dominant group defines its rule as one of civilization replacing barbarism. What is sacred to an ethnic community is thus redefined as ready either for the dustbin of history or for a museum.

With ethnic communities seen as outmoded, mere living fossils, the politics of anthropology in Leninist-Stalinist societies finds little progressive value in the cultures of minority peoples. They are mere economic moments whose time has passed. To be rid of them is like removing the dead but unburied, virtually an apologia permitting genocide. Mao Zedong called for the destruction of the old to make way for the new; his supporters took that as a call to destroy the cultures of those who were not steel-factory proletarians.

In smashing the bonds of other communities, the central power group experiences itself as merely speeding the pace of history in removing an outmoded economic group that would die anyway. In reducing communities to mere economic moments, a destructive project is proclaimed an advance in the mode of production. Han leaders show no concern that in Buddhist Tibet during the Mao era, over six thousand "monasteries . . . were blown up. . . . They burned the scriptures. All the statues were taken away. . . . They drove the monks away." Nor did they wonder "what the world's reaction would have been if the German occupation of France had left the cathedrals at Chartres, Reims and Rouen in charred ruins. That, and worse, is what had happened in Tibet" (Gargan 1990, 193–94).

This Leninist project of ethnocide is overdetermined. Engels took his anthropology from Lewis Henry Morgan's expression of the chauvinistic and racist myths of his time and European place. Sympathetic to the plight of Amerindians, Morgan saw family societies as the earliest division of labor and Amerindians as tied to a hunting mode of production that could not rise and to a prior golden age, which Engels could dub primitive communism. While stressing historical contingency rather than biological essence, racist culture and superior technology were nonetheless linked in Morgan's apologia for his people and time. "The Aryan family represents the central stream of human progress, because it produced the highest type of mankind, and because it has proved its intrinsic superiority by gradually assuming control of the earth" (Jenkins 1984, 19). For Tibetan, Ukrainian, Albanian, and Tigrean, who each and all lost their piece of the earth to the Han, Russian, Serb, or Amhara, Leninist rulers act the Aryan role, presenting a threat of genocide.

In 1912 in *Marxism and the National and Colonial Question*, Stalin defined the Leninist nation as "an historically constituted, stable community of people, formed on the basis of a common language, territory, economic life and psychological make-up manifested in a common culture." For China's Leninists, this meant that "those who live together learn the language spoken by the most people" (Chen and Chen 1990, 31). In practice, Leninist Chinese rulers take the language of the capital—a language unintelligible to minorities, southerners, or even most northern peasants—and a sanitized version of its culture as advanced and socialist and impose it on other regions and cultures, which are treated as old and backward. The rulers define the people of other regions by an anthropology of advanced and backward, with the most industrialized areas tied to the capital treated as the most advanced. In other regions, people have to make themselves over in the image of an artificial "socialist" culture or be treated as primitive and reactionary. What is demanded is deculturation. However much people conform on the surface, inwardly and very deeply, resistance is real. Ever more, people value their martyred and moral community. Once state terror and the charismatic rule of the first anti-imperialist generation evaporate, little is left other than desires for autonomy, revenge, and renewal. A Leninist nationalism that once seemed all powerful suddenly appears as a rejected evil, the target of all communities, even the dominant one.

Not responsible for shaping their modernization, ruled by outsiders, and forced to destroy their basic identities, in diverse regions, communities resist, finding allies in those who act, speak, dress, or worship truly like them. The enemy is the anti-imperialist center, the old Leninist nationalism. The Leninist war against the market locked people into their places, thus intensifying communal contradictions and the oppositional identities. In market societies, mobility and individuation weaken community identities. In a Leninist order, over time, in contrast, the regional and religious communities grow more conscious of the hypocrisy of the regime's legitimation. To live in truth and justice means to oppose the Leninist center.

When reforms begin, local people experience their group as a previously martyred community. They believe that only they can care for their own, an experience intensified by its invisibility to the people in previously privileged regions. Seeing themselves and their culture also as victims of the Stalinist system, which repressed parts of its cherished culture, the people of privileged regions do not readily hear the cry of distant victims, whom they have learned under Leninism to experience as pampered and undeserving beneficiaries of subsidized largesse. Thus the divisive forces of Leninism that had strengthened ethnic identities and communities allow, or even force, these communities to assert independent claims.

To see just how divisive Leninist nationalism is one should look at what was hidden by invoking the concept of the Han peasant to cover most rural dwellers in China. While Mao praised suffering, sacrificing, ascetic, hinterland Han peasants as the patriots who liberated China, in fact, even before 1949 the Leninists were trying to destroy rural customs and religion, treating diverse community bonds as reactionary obstacles to material progress. Villagers were dismissed as a remnant of a dying mode of production, to be allied with, used, and transformed. Chinese Leninists in the 1920s and 1930s portrayed villagers as victims, exploited and oppressed both by Confucian landlords and Japanese invaders. Mao conceived of the fate of China's peasantry in objectified alternatives defined by Stalinist Russian ideological distortions, kulak oppressors, or state-imposed collectives. He simultaneously imagined the obstacle to China's prosperity to be contemptible peasant practices, from family particularism to nonproductive dowries and festive drinking. Rural resisters could be cruelly treated and branded as kulaks who purportedly would return China to polarization and famine. The writer Liu Binyan has noted that the impositions of Mao's nonaccountable group of imperious lords actually brought more rape and rapine to the peasantry than did even the pre-Stalinist lords of the land. If peasants of the dominant community are properly understood as regional historic communities with rich, diverse cultures, then it is not surprising that their fate is the same as that of the ethnic communities. All particularistic, primary passions that limit commitment to the antiforeign cause are experienced by Leninist rulers as traitorous convictions to be extirpated.

When reforms begin, members of these previously excluded communities surge into privileged redoubts. But Han identity that was legitimated by a war against the foreign, including national, minorities loses meaning as minorities and communities are valorized and the foreign is no longer stigmatized. Each revalorized region tries to maximize its gains against the discredited center. The previously supercentralized Leninist state threatens to fall apart on regional fissures, especially where the fault line coincides with a communalist and group identity. Where there is a joining of cultural, economic, and lingual grievances on "sharply regional lines," political scientist Dankwort Rustow noted in 1970 about political regimes in general, there "secession . . . is likely to result" (Rustow 1970). Because the central regime in Leninist anti-imperialist China has been located in the north and legitimated in terms of a historical narrative that privileges hinterland northern creative dynamism and peripheralizes southern coastal links to world commerce as treason, the regional fault lines tend to pit the south against the north, with the south constructing a new historical discourse that links it to China's future.[3] Whether the outcome is instead a new, cruel central control, or civil war, or federalism, or new self-determinations, a political struggle is unleashed by post-Leninist politics in which regional communities ever more self-confidently contest the legitimacy of a previously dominant center.

That center finds itself threatened and surrounded by atavistic, surging rural dwellers. The fate of the peasantry is struggled over in order to define one's project as properly nationalistic, with different political tendencies imagining different peasantries, but with the center ignoring the powerful identities inherent in regional, lingual, and cultural assertions. An almost genocidal wish infuses this imperial nationalism at the center, as urbanites tend to agree that China has too many people, meaning that the number of peasants must be reduced, that it would be better if city people had two children and peasants were restricted to one so peasant numbers would decline. Rural mobility into cities, followed by urbanization, is almost universally opposed by the urban, who fear dangerous ex-villagers flooding into cities as criminals who destroy and create disorder.

But peasants do not unite. A notion of a broad national peasant class attracts only a few villagers in diverse regional communities, boundaries of identity being defined by opposition to the next "peasant" culture. Han and Hakka may or may not be antagonistically different. Around the Yangtze River, Subei and Jiangnan peasant communities are antagonistic worlds. South, coastal Minnan and northern, plains Huabei peoples differ more from each other than many foreign countries do. The political assertions of these revalorized communities could reject a Han racial nationality, which in fact is a modern invention, not a genetic essence. In the early years of the twentieth century, while some called for the "race originating in the Yellow River Valley to become the largest unique stock of human beings on earth," according to John Fei and Charlotte Furth, actually "the myth of ethnicity proved less durable than the myth of culture" (Wakeman 1991, 25). That is, the Chinese were not a race, and after progressives delegitimated inherited culture as an obstacle to national regeneration, the anti-imperialist state could not be premised on a common culture, either. The notion of a Han people who arose thousands of years ago in conquering the Yellow River and who in 1949 brought Leninists to power to keep out rapacious foreigners is a potted history with a short life span. It can be dispensed with in the communal reassertions of the post-Leninist world.

China in a Post-Leninist World

China in the post-Mao era is no longer envisioned as the longest continuous national civilization, with a unique history from a founding Han people in the loess soil of the north China plain, running without stop from more than four thousand years ago to the present. Instead, Chinese history is reconceived to imagine very different national projects, as Zhang Yufa described it in *The Interactions of Divided State(s)* (1989). According to Maria Hsia Chang in an unpublished paper from 1991, China actually was only unified for 40 percent of the time in its more than four-thousand-year history. For an equally long time it was a federation. The rest of the time, China was not even united. The future suddenly is as open as the past. Political history and national identity are both contested.

The struggle over national identity reaches from high culture to popular gossip. While cultural identities are truly valued, the struggle over culture is preeminently political. The outcome will be decided in political combat and not merely by continuing cultural consciousness. It is a matter of politics whether the newly politicized ethnic identities lead in a fundamentalist or a federalist direction. The contrast is stark between those valuing community and those seeing no possible good in community. Asking "What Comes After Marxist Regimes?" the Marxist Ralph Miliband (Miliband and Panitch 1991, 324) responds: "A nationalism that readily slides into an exclusive, aggressive, xenophobic chauvinism . . . drawing on the most backward and reactionary interpretations of religion." In contrast, the anti-Marxist Alasdair MacIntyre (1981, 262–63) answers the same question, finding "the constitution of local forms of community within which civility and the intellectual and moral life can be sustained." Denationalization of identity in a post-Leninist system opens a struggle over the nature of all communities in the territory, with possibilities ranging from racist despotism to federalist pluralism.

The overly centralized national state was too rigid to respond flexibly to the economic challenges of a penetrating world market with instantaneous finance in an era of poststeel microtechnological lead sectors (Friedman 1991). Whether one looked to the formation of the European Community or the rise of Pacific Rim economies, the defensive, closed premises of Leninist anti-imperialism, import substitution, and dependency theory were revealed as suicidal prescriptions. In addition, that unitary, centralized defensive nationalism was also subverted from within, as diverse communities and regional groups insisted on their moral and political priority. Penetrated and subverted, ineffective and illegitimate, the old Leninist anti-imperialist nationalism seems to rattle as in its death throes.

Leninist states, such as China, threatened by these international and subnational forces, reveal generalizable dynamic forces building new political forms.

These overly politically centralized, economically rigid, and culturally artificial Leninist states seek, in a post-Leninist era, to benefit from the expansion of the world economy and seek to craft more federal structures. But these are complex tasks. Valorized ethnic communities approach them with the fear of learned experience from the prior era of a cruel Leninism that alienated them, outraged them, and energized them. Communalist demands, often irreconcilable, can explode in bloody and hate-filled fights, or, perhaps, lead to truly democratic and communitarian federalist republics.

These new and powerful potentials challenge Leninist China. While reforms permit some decentralization and international economic openness, the Leninist dictators fear the calls for democracy or autonomy, and crush the claimants. It is not obvious, however, that the anti-imperialist Leninist center can hold. It increasingly seems ossified, archaic, and profoundly hypocritical. The regime represses and silences, and yet new communities, new identities, and new political projects keep erupting. It is difficult to see, given the international economics of wealth expansion at the end of the twentieth century, how Han China can prevent the ascension of a reimagined Chinese nation. This newly imagined China is being invented in terms of a south tied to an Asian-Pacific economic dynamism that brings in most of China's foreign exchange earnings and foreign investment.

With finance breaking free of national constraints, there is a virtual guarantee that in addition to imposing growth-efficiency criteria, international finance will also act in a predatory way that undermines families and threatens communities and thereby unleashes a powerful backlash against money's mobility. Since social life is impossible without value-based bonds, communalist attractions may win out over economic openness and democracy (Sampson 1990, 233). Even a democratic breakthrough can be reversed, as rulers manipulate primordial identities and hates to win backing for communalist tyrannies. That the future is open does not mean it will be better.

Conservatives in China's Communist Party, a political group that began with an attempt to destroy Confucianism and the reactionary interests that the inherited authoritarian culture defended and preserved, were by 1990 describing authoritarian Confucianism as "the historical guiding principle for the Chinese people's political structure ... different from any western model" (Zhang Xinhau 1990, 103–6). Confucianism, Leninist traditionalists found, contained "the essence of humanism and democracy" and was a culture "which aided in the establishment of benevolent and moral government." These "positive ingredients usable by socialism" also were the source of success in the "launching of the East Asian economies." Therefore it made no sense "blindly mouthing empty slogans about democracy and freedom ... to promote an Enlightenment in China. ... Compared to the West, China's cultural thinking ... just might be ahead" (ibid.).

The Leninist fundamentalists in power in Beijing have tried to revive the previously vilified culture, especially its most authoritarian features, and ally

with fundamentalists among the minorities against secularist democrats and political reformers whose cultural creations, such as sex education and uncensored
depictions of the body, are damned as foreign cultural pollutions. When the old
Han center of Leninist power pridefully and superpatriotically claims to be preserving sacred cultural verities, it in fact opposes federalist, democratic, pluralist,
and multicultural possibilities. The racist protofascism of Leninists—in Serbia,
Russia, or China—can readily re-emerge in a pure racist, fascist nationalism.

But progressive possibilities also persist. Victims of the Leninist regime, communities of ultimate meaning—family, ethnicity, religion—have bound together
to survive and give moral meaning to life against a culturally vacuous Leninism
that leaves a profound moral crisis and a widespread popular desire to live in
truth. These ethnic communities can build democracies or share in a federal
republic. They are not inherently and inevitably reactionary. Envisioning ethnic
communities as mere backward irrationality was the Leninist-Stalinist policy
misunderstanding that created the ethnic backlash in the first place, leaving "a
yawning void to be filled" (Starr 1990, A6).

The most intriguing of these protocommunities reaches out from southern and
coastal China to embrace the Chinese diaspora. If E. J. Hobsbawm is right that
"the area of national studies in which thinking and research are most urgently
needed today" is how "national identification . . . can change and shift in time"
(Hobsbawm 1990, 11), then this research suggests that changes in military technologies and wealth-expanding imperatives for shaping political communities
that can deliver protection and prosperity with participation in the postmodern
world are definers of new national communities that can value openness, self-
rule, and pluralism. That is, in the new world of easy physical mobility and
immediate long-distance communication, where place-specific bonds of meaning
are threatened, the link between national identity and living on a particular piece
of land may weaken (ibid., 174). The Chinese nation could come to include what
previously had been a diaspora. Market capacity rather than military power could
become more central to national identity. Hobsbawm suggests that the rise to
international centrality of ministates such as Singapore and Hong Kong reflects a
transcendence of the nineteenth-century vision of "national economies" that supposedly were decisive for Bismarck and Stalin, the paradigmatic leaders of modern centralized despotism. To the large extent that Leninist anti-imperialist
nationalism presumed Bismarckian presuppositions of steel and grain autarky as
the essence of a supercentralized nation-state, it is not peculiar that a state system
premised on nineteenth-century notions of nation should be dying as humanity
enters the twenty-first century.

What this essay suggests, in addition, is that to the extent that symbolic
communities permit humans to deal with the joys and pain of life itself, and to
the extent that ever more rapid, incomprehensible, unsettling changes impinge on
poststeel or postmodern life, the ultimate value of transnational "national" communities may intensify: perhaps that helps explain the rise of religious national-

ism from Sinhalese Buddhists through Amerindians, from Shi'ite fundamentalists to Hindi patriots. As with the Chinese diaspora, territorial exclusivity may in the postmodern world be less decisive for experiences of communalist ties. In an age of satellite electronic communication, bonds among people are neither fixed nor bounded by walls at frontiers. If this analysis is accurate, then the old state center can hold only by greatly loosening its grip in an open, democratic, and decentralist direction.

Communities of ultimate identity could be central to a new democratic Chinese identity with roots spread to include diverse, ethnic, and diaspora communities. These communities of recharged ethnic identity that were bloodied and vilified in the Leninist era are in the reform and post-Leninist era both actors trying to shape their own destiny and a potential new nation in which Leninist denationalization could be the premise of democratization. Still, a future of ethnic warfare beckons if chauvinistic, centralizing Han rulers are incapable of meeting the self-governance demands of regional and ethnic communities. The old center has the power to welcome democratic federation or to practice bloody repression, a delegitimated repression that can even lead to the breakup of the old nation-state.

Notes

1. Since Leninist states incited outrage and vengeful passions in ethnic communities, E. J. Hobsbawm (1990, 173) errs in claiming, "It was the great achievement of the communist regimes in multinational countries to limit the disastrous effects of nationalism within them."
2. A good one-volume compilation of the suffering imposed upon Tibetans compiled by the German Greens is Kelly et al. (1991).
3. The emergent construction of a south China regional identity is a momentous new development.

References

Avedon, John. 1984. *In Exile From the Land of Snows* (New York: Random House), p. 237.
Brus, W. 1981. "Is Market-Socialism Possible or Necessary?" *Critique*, No. 14, p. 34.
Chan, Anita. 1990. "China's Long Winter." *Monthly Review* 41.8 (January), p. 7.
Chen Zhangtai, and Chen Jianmin. 1990. "Sociolinguistics Research Based on Chinese Reality." *International Journal of the Sociology of Language*, Vol. 81, p. 31.
Cohen, Myron L. 1991. "Being Chinese." *Daedalus* 120.2 (Spring), p. 128.
Committee to Aid Democratic Dissidents in Yugoslavia (CADDY). 1991. Translation of Mihaljo Mhajlov in Borba. CADDY Bulletin, No. 65, p. 2.
Crozier, Ralph. 1990. "World History in the People's Republic of China." *Journal of World History* 1.2 (Fall), pp. 151–69.
Ellingson, Peter. 1991. "Where Poverty Begins at Home or Stays with Scant Relief." *Financial Times* (March 12).
Far Eastern Economic Review. 1991. (July 11), p. 18.

Foner, Eric. 1990. "The Romance of the Market." *The Nation* 251, 22 (December 24), p. 800.

Friedman, Edward. 1991. "Permanent Technological Revolution and China's Tortuous Path to Democratizing Leninism." In Richard Baum, ed., *Reform and Reaction in Post-Mao China* (New York: Routledge, Kegan Paul).

Gargan, Edward. 1990. *China's Fate* (New York: Doubleday), pp. 193–94.

Gladney, Dru. 1990. "The Peoples of the People's Republic." *The Fletcher Forum of World Affairs* 14.1 (Winter 1990), p. 64.

————. 1991. *Muslim Chinese* (Cambridge, MA: Harvard University Press).

Hobsbawm, E. J. 1990. *Nations and Nationalism Since 1870* (Cambridge: Cambridge University Press).

Jenkins, Francis. 1984. *The Ambiguous Iroquois Empire* (New York: Norton), p. 19.

Kelly, Petra, et al. 1991. *The Anguish of Tibet* (Berkeley: Parallex Press).

Koron, Jacek. 1990. "The Overcoming of Totalitarianism." *The Journal of Democracy* 1.1 (Winter), p. 74.

Lee Chae-jin. 1986. *China's Korean Minority* (Boulder, CO: Westview Press), pp. 89, 91, 90.

Lord, Bette Bao. 1990. *Legacies* (New York: Knopf), p. 174.

Macintyre, Alisdair. 1981. *After Virtue* (South Bend, IN: University of Notre Dame Press), pp. 262–63.

Madsen, Richard. 1989. "The Catholic Church in China." In *Unofficial China*, edited by Perry Link et al. (Boulder, CO: Westview Press), pp. 103–20.

Miliband, Ralph, and Leo Panitch. 1991. *Communist Regimes: The Aftermath* (London: St. Martin's Press), p. 324.

Pan, Lynn. "Make or Break." *Far Eastern Economic Review* (November 29), p. 46.

Rustow, Dankwurt. 1970. *Comparative Politics* (April), pp. 337–63.

Sampson, Anthony. 1990. *The Midas Touch* (New York: Penguin), p. 233.

Shapiro, Leonard. 1984. *The Russian Revolution of 1917* (New York: Basic Books).

Starr, Frederick. 1990. "The Disintegration of the Soviet State." *The Wall Street Journal* (February 6), p. A16.

Suny, Ronald. 1990. "Nationalities and Nationalism." In *Chronicle of a Revolution*, edited by Abraham Brumberg (New York: Pantheon), pp. 108–28.

Tibetnet. 1990. Interview of a Tibetan refugee by a Swiss Tibetan support group (June 13).

Wakeman, Frederic, Jr. 1991. *In Search of National Character* (Berkeley: Center for Chinese Studies), pp. 25, 3.

Wei Yuan. 1842. In Ssu-yu Teng and John King Fairbank, eds., *China's Response to the West* (Cambridge, MA: Harvard University Press, 1954), pp. 30, 31, 36.

Zhang Xinhua. 1990. "On Using Traditional Culture as a Wellspring to Build a Socialist New Culture." *Shehui Kexue*, No. 3 (March 15); translated in JPRS-CAR–90–049 (July 11), pp. 103–6.

Zhang Yufa. 1989. *The Interactions of Divided States* (in Chinese) (Taipei: Institute for International Relations).

Zotov, V. 1990. "Political Crisis in China." *Far Eastern Affairs* (Moscow), No. 2, p. 72.

Chapter 4

A Failed Chinese Modernity

As with all former Leninist dictatorships, rulers in Beijing also confront a crisis of legitimation.[1] Surface tranquility in China hides moving tectonic forces that are reshaping China's national project. The most politically conscious Chinese already have dismissed the Leninist system, with its claim to embody the interests of all Chinese in an anti-imperialist nationalism, as a betrayal of the nation. The millions of democracy demonstrators in spring 1989 dubbed their movement "patriotic," in contrast to a regime that they found had wasted the people's hard-earned wealth on luxury: imported Mercedes-Benzes for a parasitic ruling caste.[2] Increasingly in the post-Mao era, reformers in the government are abandoning the capital of Beijing in the north to work in the dynamic south, in coastal regions, or at local levels with entrepreneurs who have brought China some of the world's most rapid economic growth, a high level of both foreign confidence and investment, and an extraordinary record of export success.[3]

Slighting this delegitimation crisis, ruling groups hope that mass money-making will absorb the energies of China's people. Their hopes for political stability seem to have been realized, but only on the surface. This political quiet is premised on a merely momentary consensus in which party conservatives, lacking economic alternatives, accept economic reform, and in which reformers, lacking political alternatives and believing the reform project irreversible, accept a temporary bracketing of political change to avoid the chaos and decline of post-Leninist Europe and to escape the vengeful wrath of China's ruthless senior troglodytes.

Meanwhile, those shifting tectonic plates are remaking China. Strong shoots of a new nationalism are breaking up out of the old discredited

This chapter is reprinted by permission of *Daedalus*, Journal of the American Academy of Arts and Sciences, from the issue entitled "China in Transformation," Spring 1993, vol. 122, no. 2.

debris, producing a new identity holding the promise of a better future for all Chinese, though not inevitably a democratic future. The anti-imperialist nationalism embodied in Maoism that once won Chinese hearts has been discarded.

Nationalism at one time seemed to be the essence of the legitimation of Mao Zedong's popular, anti-imperialist revolution. It seemed so presuppositional to the identity of proud Chinese responding to the Communist Party's proclaimed mission of helping the people "stand up" to foreign exploiters, domestic traitors, and imperialism in any form. Almost no one realized that this patriotism was actually a very recent and fragile construction and not the essence of some imagined, eternal China. What appeared as permanent national truth was merely passing national mythos. Increasingly, educated Chinese are aware that the once presuppositional Leninist notion of a Chinese nation uniting behind and sacrificing for a Communist-led movement of paradigmatic, poor, hinterland peasants who suffer and even die to keep out foreign invaders, especially the Japanese, in order to maintain Chinese independence was merely a creation of the mythologized Yan'an era[4] (1936–47), when Mao's guerrilla headquarters were situated among the poorest of north China's peasants.

This extraordinary myth, in which the Yan'an-era north China peasants sacrifice to save China, is a story that trivializes the tremendous regional variety in China, where many Chinese, including peasants, actually opposed Mao's movement as anti-Chinese. In the pre–Yan'an era, for example, remnant Communist armed forces in south China, fleeing for their lives, tended to ally with Hakka people in hill regions. And they were opposed by indigenous southerners, tenants, and owner-tillers as well as landlords. Mao embraced a minority to survive.[5] The partiality and particularity of the Communists are coming to consciousness again in the post-Mao era. The myth of an intrinsic and indivisible nation of the poor supporting the Communists is increasingly challenged by a very different nationalist identity for China.

Bubbling up from beneath a merely superficially tranquil political surface, new nationalisms have arisen, much as they already have surfaced and spread in other Leninist and formerly Leninist nations where anti-imperialist patriotisms have disappeared in an instant, leaving the Soviet Union, Yugoslavia, Czechoslovakia, and Ethiopia split and others teetering on the brink of instability.[6] It is worth exploring similar forces in China. It is remarkable how swiftly an artificial Leninist nationalism can disappear.[7]

Knowledge of China illuminates central features of conflicting notions of national identity that discredit the previous Maoist anti-imperialist patriotism. Some researchers point to the growth of the idea that a progressive China has historically always been tied to areas other than the isolated and insulated northern Chinese mountainous hinterland, and that China's dynamism is tied rather to the south, or the coasts and oceans, or to the west for international trade along the ancient Silk Road toward the Middle East and the Mediterranean.[8] These

revisions of national identity transform northern hinterland peasants from paradigmatic patriots, Mao's Yan'an-era hope of an armed, struggling Chinese people pushing foreigners out, into xenophobes who bound the nation captive to a
backward concept of isolationist patriotism that kept China painfully apart
from the dynamic and progressive scientific, technological, and commercial
forces of the world. Increasingly, Yan'an-era anti-imperialism seems as self-
defeating as fifteenth-century Ming Dynasty nativism that burned ship blue-
prints and executed astronomers. Maoist nationalists are re-experienced as
know-nothings keeping China backward.[9]

One set of works, revealing the unjust politics behind the purported Leninist embrace of the rural backward as China's pure patriots, investigates the
historic conflict in China's major metropolis of Shanghai between Subei people and Jiangnan people, a conflict involving invaders from the poorest countryside who failed to subsist on the soil and brought stagnation and decline
into the People's Republic after seizing power in Shanghai from longtime,
dynamic, educated, market-oriented dwellers from the riverine plains of both
Jiangsu and Zhejiang provinces.[10] In promoting Subei over Jiangnan, Mao's
anti-imperialism is felt to have privileged the incompetent. Politicized nationalism is totally devoid of legitimacy in a world seeking the economically competent.

Another illuminating approach to the rapid deconstruction of this Maoist–
Great Han nationalism, that turned into traitors all not at one with suffering
subsistence farmers, studies the recent renaissance of numerous primary identifi-
cations in China that are cultural, regional, linguistic, and/or religious—for ex-
ample, the Muslim, Buddhist, Taoist, Christian, or neo-Confucian; the
Cantonese, Fukienese, or Wu speaking; the Yueh, Chu, or Ba ancestry in
Jiangsu, Hunan, and Sichuan; the Manchu, Mongol, Turkic, Tibetan, and Hakka.
The prior chauvinism that celebrated a Han people is re-experienced as a fraud.
No Chinese asserts intrinsically, "I am a Han." None![11] So who is a Chinese?
What, in the post-Mao era, makes for a legitimate patriotism?

It is important to focus on alternative sources of identity because when the
Maoist, anti-imperialist notion of Leninism implodes, a conflict over a new
nation or nations is likely to emerge from these other, still somewhat subterra-
nean, forces. Not all of what is now sprouting, however, is open or tolerant, let
alone liberal or democratic.[12]

The conflictful potentials in the new national identities are revealed in the
popularity of the heavy metal band, Tang Dynasty.[13] On the one hand, it borrows
Western music as well as Chinese minority music and lionizes the Tang-era
capital as an open, global cosmopolis. On the other hand, it celebrates a great
Chinese empire and imagines a glorious Chinese future including a war to destroy Japan. Aspects of the new nationalism often include bitter chauvinism.[14]
My own 1992 experience found an expansive, militarist identity within the
delegitimated old nationalism, as is portrayed in the following dialogue:

Beijing worker: We Chinese are not patriotic or powerful like you Americans. We're tremendously impressed by what you did in 1991 to Saddam Hussein's force in Kuwait.

Friedman: America's power is in relative decline. It is most important for America to revive the forces of long-term economic growth.

Beijing worker: Our nation should be able to do what you did. We should be able to sell weapons and make money so we can buy modern weapons and get strong. But mainly we need a government that is at one with the people, as yours was in the Los Angeles riots.

Friedman: The Los Angeles riots?

Beijing worker: Your government stood with the people against the forces of crime and disorder. Here, [African] blacks gang rape a Chinese woman and the government does nothing. We too need a strong government on the people's side.

As elsewhere in the post-Leninist world, the experience of ruling Communists as hypocritical, corrupt criminals and greedy parasites produces an openness to politics redefined by purist, tough notions that could, as elsewhere, respond positively and strongly to virtually fascist, militarist appeals of demagoguery. In China, as in other post-Leninist systems, reactionary leaders appeal to patriarchal notions in which women are kept in their place and evils such as prostitution, AIDS, drugs, divorce, and juvenile delinquency are blamed on outsiders who would corrupt a pure people.[15]

In noting that national identity is contested in China, one is not claiming that good replace bad, but that a failed anti-imperialist, nativist project has opened up a Pandora's box of possibilities in which democracy is not necessarily the most popular alternative, a situation where nativistic chauvinisms grow in strength, feeding on the hateful, poisoned seeds sown in the anti-imperialist era.

Two ideas have almost become presuppositional in Leninist China, as in other transforming Leninist and post-Leninist states, in discrediting anti-imperialist, nationalist identity. First, people speak as if no progress had occurred under Leninism, as if time has been wasted.[16] In China, this means rethinking history so that Leninist rule, instead of being a rupture away from a benighted past, is identified as one of a number of similar failures, such as the crushers of the 1898 reform to modernize the monarchy, or the defeaters of the 1911 revolution to establish a republic, or the rejectors of the May Fourth Movement's message to build a popular, democratic, and scientific culture. There is a popular feeling in China of lost time, of having "returned to square one," as Wang Gungwu has characterized it. In fact, by attacking *feng, yang,* and *xiu* (feudalism, the nonnative, and revisionism), the Leninists are understood to have attacked or annihilated, as Ying-shih Yü says, the proven good of the Chinese essence. Hence, there is a popular desire to return to what is authentically Chinese, which often is patriarchal, nativistic, and authoritarian. Democracy, in this historical re-emergence, is discredited, as is Leninism, as just another foreign imposition. Reborn jingoists oppose both Leninist despotism and liberal democracy for imposing on China unsuitable foreign ideas, models, and projects picked up in Japan, Bolshevik Russia, and the West. People instead embrace Wang Shuo's stories in the local argot and flock to the traditionally restorative breathing regimens such as Qi Gong,[17] in which masters save disciples. Exclusive, authoritarian localism is ever more potent as a source of identity.

The second popular view that Chinese share with others elsewhere who likewise discarded a Leninist national identity is the conclusion that violent political revolution, the essence of Leninism, only brings evil. What is desired is a peaceful transformation based on presumed real national essences instead of hateful, splintering political struggles premised on violence. In this popular understanding, revolution can achieve no unifying national good, for it merely turns Chinese against Chinese. The apologists for the June 4, 1989, Beijing massacre unconsciously appealed to these presuppositions that actually delegitimate Mao's violent Leninist revolution that pit group against group, portraying innocent prodemocracy victims as violent hooligans instigated from Hong Kong or Taiwan. A violent project is an antinational project.

But with peaceful and open political challenges illegal, the new, hopeful national agenda must come from inherited social identities. An equation of reform progress with a peaceful continuity leads people to identify true Chineseness with one or another ongoing communalism, an emotional imperative strengthening and enhancing many ultimate communities that elsewhere have splintered post-Leninist nations to disintegration, chaos, or civil war. This ideational process receives tremendous impetus from the logic of economic reforms that necessarily transfer economic initiative away from the center of the stagnant command economy to the rapidly advancing regions. In a hidden struggle, each region tries to build locally and to keep its funds from going to the center. A powerful process with divisive tendencies is underway.

To free ourselves from seeing the future of China wrongly as an endless, large unity built on now discredited, yet previously quintessentially Chinese, Maoist nationalism, it is worth remembering just how recent is the construction of Maoist-myth history. This narrative creates an identity of a Han people arising millennia ago in the inland Yellow River Valley, defending against steppe barbarians, and spreading out to unify all of China by transforming all people in the territory, such as the Manchu, into the superior civilization of the Han. In fact, opponents of that last dynasty of the foreign Manchus found them to be a group that did not become Han, that, in fact, would not assimilate. At the outset of the twentieth century, Chinese patriots often identified the hated, conquering Manchus with an alien north and a backward czarist Russia, while identifying patriotic Chinese (not Han) with the south and modernizing Japan. As Helen Siu points out, the south cheered for Japan in the 1904–5 Russo-Japanese War. The Southern Study Society appealed "for physical education to create a new martial *chün-tzu* robustly modeled on the Japanese samurai."[18]

Southern patriots embraced southern languages, or even Esperanto, as superior to the north's Mandarin Chinese, the tongue of the traitorous, foreign court. The patriotic heroes of the last dynasty, such as Tan Sitong or Sun Yat-sen, tended to come from the south, identifying with the nativistic Ming Dynasty and experiencing the north as a traitor that had allied with British imperialism to survive against the people's popular patriotism. These northern traitors were seen as heirs of other northern groups over the millennia who had been made over by aliens.[19]

Southerners in the late Qing opposed British imperialism's plundering of China from the colony of Hong Kong and the foreign concession areas of Canton (Guangzhou) and Shanghai. In the racist nationalism of the late nineteenth century, the patriots identified with Japanese success, interpreted in the hegemonic discourse of the then-dominant racism such that China and Japan were joined in a struggle of yellow races to throw out white or European races from Asia.[20] Chinese went into Japan for exile, inspiration, and aid, hoping to achieve what Meiji Japan had achieved—national vigor sufficient to defeat the white race from European Russia as Japan did in the 1904–5 war, a victory that thrilled and attracted even west Asians in Persia.

Few Chinese at this time imagined China's future in terms of hinterland north China peasant courage. At the end of the nineteenth century, the influential nationalist popularizer, Zhang Binglin, synthesized China's plight,[21] using globally hegemonic categories, to conclude that

> yellow people who achieved a higher level of social integration and organization . . . fared better than the black, the brown, and the red; and . . . were being trampled under by white people, who were better organized.[22]

By the first decade of the twentieth century, Zhang championed a violent and vengeful liberation struggle of all peoples against expansionists. He imagined a Han people who rose in an area to the west of what was now China and who, based on cultural heroes such as the Yellow Emperor and Minister of Agriculture (Shen-nung), were being oppressed by a Manchu government.[23] Zhang imagined Han Chinese, in contrast to Japanese, as especially egalitarian and nonfeudal. He sought to comprehend China's unique cultural essence. He privileged idealistic Mahayana Buddhist analogues such as Wang Yangming's spiritual teachings, which "played an important part in the success of the Meiji Revolution in Japan."[24] Whether as a yellow race or a Han nation, Chinese and Japanese shared a moral cause of national liberation, according to Zhang, who was born in Zhejiang in south China.

In a similar manner, another leading patriotic publicist, Liu Shipei, from

Yangzhou prefecture in Jiangsu Province in south China, identified anti-Manchu Chinese independence with a long history of struggle against barbarian invaders.[25] For Liu, the formalistic particularism of Confucianism blocked this national project. It served the ruling Manchu family at the expense of the Chinese people.[26] He "found Rousseau's notion of democracy congenial . . . , a moral quest . . . for a good society . . . expressing the goodness inherent in human nature,"[27] as an ethic superior to the paternalism, authoritarianism, and hierarchical quality of Confucianism.[28] Therefore, Chinese should sacrifice self and narrow utilitarianism to serve the national, liberating cause of true equality, held to be superior to mere parliamentary democracy or a system premised on private property. There was in the Chinese heritage a this-worldly temper "expressed as an urge to dissolve the self into a large whole," a vision most attractive to neotraditionalists who privileged "immersion into a selfless whole."[29] Such themes of organic monism helped undermine parliamentary democracy and market-oriented economics, understood as legitimatizing selfishness, narrow interest, and endless conflict. This national selflessness did not yet define the nature of the nation being liberated; or rather, that notion was still contested and changing.

By 1915, when Japan imposed the Twenty-One Demands on China's independence (the final demand being the right to proselytize Japanese religion in China as Europeans did with Christianity), Chinese national sentiment began to be traumatized in an anti-Japanese direction. China, which previously imagined itself a superior culture that was borrowed by the Japanese more than a millennia earlier in the Tang Dynasty, seemed in need of a new culture that could stand up to the Japanese who were using the Great War in Europe to take over German concessions in China. As Chinese fought among themselves, both as selfish parliamentary politicians and greedy, regional warlords, it increasingly seemed that what China needed to be free and independent was a mobilization of all China's people in a unified effort to push Japan out of China and back across the Yalu River that separated China's northeast from Korea. The invading Japanese military crossed the Yalu River and turned the northeast into a Japanese puppet state called Manchuguo (Manchukuo). They then invaded deep into the China heartland, massacring, raping, and pillaging as they came. The pro-Japanese, anti-British, yellow-race nationalism of the pre–World War I south needed to be discredited if everyone (even Europeans) was to be mobilized to save the Chinese nation.

After 1935, Mao Zedong's guerrilla force in the northern hinterland of Yan'an became a national salvation movement of liberation that met the imperatives of the new circumstances. Modern China was reimagined as a victim of imperialist invaders since the Opium War of 1839–42. The lesson from that war was that

> to defend the open ocean is not as good as to defend the seaports, and to defend the seaports is not as good as to defend the inland rivers. . . . The phrase "enticing the enemy to enter the inland rivers" means that soldiers, guns and mines are sown . . . as if making a pit to wait for tigers.[30]

This guerrilla strategy, a narrative of national defense, was read large in the lessons of the Ming Dynasty, which threw out the foreign Mongols and built the Great Wall while smashing seaborne commerce.[31] This heroic Chinese tale of defense against invaders was identified with human liberation in general by linking it to the national resistance of the motherland of socialism, which defeated fascist invaders on Socialist soil after Stalin's Red Army fell back to the Ural Mountains. This militaristic nationalism harmonized with a purportedly universal Leninist-Jacobin tradition of human liberation through Spartan virtue in which citizen-soldiers sacrificed everything to save the nation. The poor, young, courageous boys from China's villages who joined Mao's revolutionary army faced every hardship and sacrificed life itself to defend the nation and save the people from Japan's imperialistic invasion became model personalities, idealized and worthy of emulation. Chinese history was reimagined in terms of a Han race from the northern plains whose virtue had, time and again, unified and defended China against savage invaders, as represented in the sacrifice to build the Great Wall of China. The People's Army in Yan'an, under Mao, came singularly to embody this new narrative project, a historical Chinese nationalist essence, a unified and indivisible force that alone knew how to save China's people from imperialist domination. In 1949, Mao proclaimed that the Chinese people had stood up and asserted themselves. It seemed obvious that it was a new chapter in a continuous history of Chinese struggle and sacrifice that won the Chinese people yet again their independence in the People's Republic of China.

By the 1990s, however, this nationalistic narrative is discredited. Maoism, in the post-Mao era, is seen as having kept China poor and backward, as having even made the military weak, as proved by its costly 1979 venture into northern Vietnam. Southern China, peripheralized in the Maoist mythos, has been reprivileged, once again made the central focus of imagination and yearning for a better Chinese future. In the view of Mao's Yan'an-era nativistic nationalism, the south was the home of weak gentry and foreign-facing merchants who made China vulnerable to foreign invasion and foreign subversion. Former guerrilla soldiers sent down from the conquering north after the establishment of Mao's People's Republic had been ruling the south in state-imposed collectives of virtual serf (or slave) labor since 1949. The south's liberation has recently been locally reimagined as some date, usually in the 1980s, when these northern outsiders passed on and local people, at last, rose. Whereas the northerners were scandalized by southern mourning rituals, preferred a different diet (e.g., black tea, not green; flour, not rice), and spoke differently, in the post-Mao era, empathetic, capable local people are taking over. China is returning again to win glory as in ancient times. The great economic gains of the post-Mao era are credited to southerners, whose inventiveness skirted around northern bureaucrats envisioned as useless, corrupt parasites. Contrary to popular newspaper reports, southerners do not credit China's recent extraordinary growth to the policies of rulers in the north.[32]

In the south, the anti-imperialist capital of Beijing is ridiculed as a backward town of mere talkers who live off the people's wealth and contribute nothing to wealth expansion. Northerners are mocked as people who would not even recognize money lying in a street. The new doers and shakers ridicule northerners who spout propaganda, saying, "in Beijing, people say anything, while in Canton people do anything." In Canton, China's fastest-rising metropolis, southerners sarcastically repeat the northern canard that "northerners love the country (*ai guo*) [are patriots] while southerners sell the country (*mai guo*) [are traitors]," knowing that people interpret the phrase to mean that while northerners talked, southerners did the business that earned China the foreign exchange that raised the people's standard of living. To survive, the regime in Beijing needs a stronger nationalism to compete with the open-market orientation of the south.

Northern proponents of fascist chauvinism are the natural heirs to Leninist-fascist socialism[33] in Beijing, as well as in Serbia, or anti-Semitic Pamyat in Russia. Yet changed consciousness puts northern chauvinists on the defensive. Beijing residents nervously joke about a new encirclement of China's cities. Mao's revolution had been presented as the pure, rural, patriotic soldiers liberating weak, corrupt, urban centers, whose passive people welcomed capitalism and then were polluted by foreign imperialist germs. But by the 1990s, Beijing was full of economic actors from the outside who were not allowed to reside legally in Beijing. These moneymakers established residence by illegally buying household registration permits in the villages that surrounded Beijing and other similar cities. The problem for northern tyrants in Beijing is that even Beijing residents welcome the southern project, which promises to raise both China's standing in the world and the standard of living of the Chinese people.

Inside Beijing, people paid a premium price for Cantonese food. New restaurants in Beijing featuring various regional cuisines highlighted regional virtues. Beijing and northern hinterland soldiers were no longer considered central to the Chinese future. Even in Beijing, people understood that the future was coming into China from the commercial south and the trading coasts. Cantonese language and culture spread. Northerners are popularly adapting to a new consciousness that imagines China's future as in the economically open south; they flood the south seeking jobs. Even though the north controls the media and the secret police, northern chauvinists feel encircled and endangered.

In China's capital, Beijing, there is an elite response to the attraction of a new national identity equated with southern virtues, insisting that the south has nothing to offer. In this northern perspective, the south is at best a cultural desert with nothing of value to offer. In fact, the south, as in Mao's nationalist defense against an imperialist culture of Christian missionaries and commercial markets, is seen by supporters of the old anti-imperialism as the opening through which AIDS, drugs, venereal diseases, prostitution, juvenile delinquency, disrespect for elders, consumerism, and other supposed foreign capitalist inhumanities flow. In contrast, Beijing is imagined and presented by such anti-imperialists as virtue incarnate, the capital of a Confucianism that has supposedly provided the economic basis and the moral glue for the miraculous development of Pacific Asia, of which Confucian[34] China is to be an ever more crucial element, a joining of a coercive hierarchical authoritarianism with a state-managed economy, a fascist socialism.

Northerners who identify with this worldview of wanting to join the successful world of Japan and South Korea, among others, will declare themselves to have felt more at home in Tokyo than in Canton. The ancient north is reimagined as China's Confucian essence, the core of the rise of Pacific Asia. China's southern national project is consequently stigmatized by such people in a discourse of romantic nostalgia as the antithesis of a warm, caring community. China's good Confucian heartland is felt to be home to an ethical people opposed to money-making, materialist, selfish greed. A communitarian north, presented as the antithesis of alienating individualism, favors cultural mutualities bonding people across gender and generation in a purportedly caring patriarchy. The south, in contrast, stigmatizes these northern claims as old-fashioned and sellouts to exploitative Japan, while southerners appear as both individually free and communally rooted with humane openness to all the world and at one with individualistic Taoism.[35] This southern project could, but need not, be compatible with democracy and liberalism. It certainly is stigmatized by old-fashioned anti-imperialists as liberal.

To the extent that any northern nationalist vision is disbelieved and discredited as a mere self-serving rationale of parasitic tyrants to block needed reform toward democracy or human rights, then even the apolitical are predisposed to reinterpret the regime's frantic recent appeals in ways that actually subvert the regime. The regime's propaganda line defending its dictatorship and opposing peaceful evolution into democracy is taken to mean only that one should not hurry toward democracy and inadvertently fall into chaos, as in the former Soviet Union; evolution toward democracy is good.

The northern message of opposition to peaceful evolution is in fact popularly interpreted as a rationale for peaceful evolution, for patience now, for gradual change that, as throughout Confucian East Asia, will in a not-too-distant future win a better world of democracy peacefully for all Chinese. When the northern regime points out that it took four decades before the perpetrators of the February 28, 1947, massacre in Taiwan were openly recognized and the victims rehabilitated, Chinese interpret that to mean that China too will democratize. Given the prior deconstruction of the northern national narrative, even northern chauvinist propaganda is interpreted to legitimate the inevitability and the desirability of the southern national project, a vision not of a separate south, but of a new Chinese nation enlivened by the southern ethos.

Having lost any robust promise for a happy future, northern anti-imperialist nationalists are left appealing unconvincingly to worst-case anxieties, hates, and fears. China's media play up all violence in the former Soviet empire and play down all the gains from democracy, human rights, and initiatives from society. Rulers in Beijing fear losing control. Yet they have already lost command of the categories and narratives that give meaning to a desirable future. The legitimate discourse has been reconstructed.

At the level of cultural magnetism, for the new generation of young northerners, the conservative Confucian appeal for patience is wholly unpersuasive. They want a better life now. They already buy goods with southern brand names, prefer beauty parlors promising Cantonese style, and identify the open and rapidly prospering south with better-paying job opportunities and a happier future for China.

There seems no way for the anti-imperialist old guard to relegitimate their nationalistic project. In the post-Mao era, they have tried to modernize the military to make China respected (feared?) in Asia and influential in the world through arms buildups and arms sales. But rather than feel pridefully uplifted, what ordinary Chinese see are corrupt rulers allowing their children to enrich themselves illegally in arms sales and caring not about China's suffering people.

The old-guard rulers do not even win credit for post-Mao economic successes that have swiftly raised standards of living. Instead, people see success in terms of getting around a system imposed from the north in which villagers are ordered to be patriots and grow grain, but then are not paid a living wage for the grain. In the countryside, villagers condemn a corrupt rulership imposing arbitrary taxes that Communist Party party bosses are believed to pocket.

This delegitimation of anti-imperialist nationalism does not mean that tomorrow China will change its political direction and choose between the now rising nationalist projects, a racist chauvinism of the old guard, and a democratic constitutionalism of the new forces. Other possibilities could explode. As with the re-Balkanization of the Balkans and the experience of finding 1917–89 in the former Soviet Union an era when time was wasted, Leninism's inheritance is a poisoning of communalist forces. In Europe, all the World War I–era divisions and problems have re-emerged in a more poisoned form. So it could be with China. One must remember what China was before the temporary domination of Mao's artificial anti-imperialist nationalism.

China, at the end of the nineteenth century, experienced power flowing to regions. By the early twentieth century, cruel regional warlords ruled. And Leninist economic reforms, all analysts agree, strengthen local tendencies, intensify alienation from the old state center, and worsen intraregional (language, ethnicity, culture, religion, etc.) divisions, as groups struggle over taxes, prices, and monopoly shares while raising economic barriers, with each blaming all others. One should not underestimate the potency of the divisive forces that China's Leninist rulers correctly assert are spreading just beneath the surface.

The longer the old guard delays political reforms, the stronger these angry and divisive political forces grow. Chinese outside of China, in touch with China's diverse explosive angers, aware that there is no longer a binding anti-imperialist Han chauvinism as an easy, unifying glue, suggest the creation of a federation with great autonomous local power that could preserve order and progress and also hold the allegiance of Tibetans, Muslim Turkestanis, Cantonese, and Taiwanese. (There was a federalist movement in China in the earlier part of the twentieth century that even appealed to Mao Zedong.) Although there is much wisdom in that wise and humane confederated vision, an analysis of the comparative experience of other post-Leninist transitions suggests that achieving that happy outcome will require great political wisdom and also, perhaps, a bit of good luck.

Meanwhile the old guard clings tenaciously to power and rejects needed political reform. This political stagnation permits nasty communal identities to grow in frustrated outrages, leaving less room and less hope for new democratic shoots to flower and flourish.

Mao's anti-imperialist nationalism has long since died, but its corpse cannot be buried. A cadaver sits on the Leninist throne of national power. It is not possible to predict when this still-fearsome corpse will be permitted a burial. One cannot predict which straw is a last straw.

Notes

1. Edward Friedman, *New Nationalist Identities in Post-Leninist Transformations: The Implications for China* (Hong Kong: Chinese University of Hong Kong, 1992).

2. Edward Friedman, "Permanent Technological Revolution and China's Tortuous Path to Democratizing Leninism," in Richard Baum, ed., *Reform and Reaction in Post-Mao China* (New York: Routledge, 1991).

3. "Guangdong has become a haven for refugees from the former Government of Prime Minister Zhao Ziyang. His loyalists have set themselves up as independent economic consultants in Guangzhou, and in the special economic zones. Some are researching reforms like the legalization of bankruptcy, a quick way of getting state enterprises off the dole. Others advise local governments on such matters as real estate investment and how to tax wage earners rather than making employers carry the whole burden" (Jay Gao, "Is Guangdong Asia's Fifth Tiger?" *New Zealand Herald*, January 28, 1992).

4. See David Apter and Tony Saich, *Revolutionary Discourse in Mao's China* (Cambridge, MA: Harvard University Press, 1994).

5. See I. Yuan, *Mao Zedong and the South China Peasantry* (Ph.D. thesis, University of Wisconsin, Department of Political Science, 1993). He finds the Chinese-language *World Herald* of February 26, 1993, reporting that Mao's family was itself originally Hakka.

6. Edward Friedman, "Ethnic Identity and the Denationalization and Democratization of Leninist States," in M. Crawford Young, ed., *The Rising Tide of Cultural Pluralism: The Nation-State at Bay?* (Madison: University of Wisconsin Press, 1993).

7. Lowell Dittmer and Samuel Kim, eds., *China's Quest for National Identity* (Ithaca: Cornell University Press, 1993).

8. This theme of a China that includes its diaspora versus a China whose core is in the hinterland far from the coast is highlighted in *Daedalus* 120.2 (Spring 1991).

9. Edward Friedman, "The Eclipse of Anti-Imperialist Nationalism in China and the Rise of a Southern National Project" (forthcoming). Similarly, in Vietnam people say, "Hanoi has no seaport; it was the capital of the peasantry" (Murray Hiebert, "Vietnam's Dichotomy: North Dominates Politics, But South Drives Economy," *Far Eastern Economic Review*, October 15, 1992, p. 47).

10. Historian Emily Honig has been publishing on this topic.

11. See Dru Gladney, *Muslim Chinese: Ethnic Nationalism in the People's Republic* (Cambridge, MA: Harvard University Press, 1991).

12. Tony Judt, "The Past Is Another Country," *Daedalus* 121.4 (Fall 1992), pp. 83–118.

13. Andrew Jones, "Beijing Bastards," *Spin*, October 1992, pp. 1–8.

14. See Michael Sullivan, "The 1988–1989 Nanjing Anti-African Protests," *China Quarterly*, No. 132 (Summer 1994).

15. Edward Friedman, "Consolidating Democratic Breakthroughs in Leninist States," in M. L. Nugent, ed., *From Leninism to Freedom* (Boulder, CO: Westview Press, 1992).

16. See Zhang Xianliang, *Getting Used to Dying* (New York: HarperCollins, 1991).

17. For an introduction to the reception of Wang Shuo and Qi Gong, see Geremie Barmé and Linda Jaivin, eds., *New Ghosts, Old Dreams* (New York: Times Books, 1992).

18. Frederic Wakeman, Jr., "The Price of Autonomy: Intellectuals in Ming and Ch'ing Politics," *Daedalus* 101.2 (Spring 1972), p. 60.

19. William Stevenson reminds readers, "The desire for an independent Yunnan state was always known to exist among leaders who regarded the Chinese as intruders. . . . The Mongols . . . drove the Burmese Shans out of this territory and turned it into a part of China. As recently as World War II, the feeling of separation from China was strong. The Governor of Yunnan had even suggested a distinctive Yunnan assistance program to U.S. officials" (*The Yellow Wind* [Boston: Houghton Mifflin, 1959] pp. 93–94).

20. See Frank Dikötter, *The Discourse of Race in Modern China* (Stanford: Stanford University Press, 1992).

21. See Kauko Laitinen, *Chinese Nationalism in the Late Qing Dynasty: Zhang Binglin as an Anti-Manchu Propagandist* (London: Curzon Press, 1990), and Martin Bernal, "Liu Shih-pei and National Essence," in Charlotte Furth, ed., *The Limits of Change* (Cambridge, MA: Harvard University Press, 1976), pp. 90–112.

22. Chang Hao, *Chinese Intellectuals in Crisis* (Berkeley: University of California Press, 1987), p. 110.

23. Ibid., pp. 112–16.

24. Ibid., p. 144.

25. Ibid., pp. 146–147.

26. Ibid., p. 163.

27. Ibid., p. 165.

28. Ibid., p. 167.

29. Ibid., p. 191.

30. Wei Yuan in 1842 in Sss-yu Teng and John K. Fairbank, *China's Response to the West* (Cambridge, MA: Harvard University Press, 1954), pp. 30, 31.

31. Arthur Waldron, *The Great Wall of China: From History to Myth* (Cambridge: Cambridge University Press, 1990).

32. Guangdong leaders responded to claims that Beijing is responsible for the south's post-Mao growth, "What have they invested here?" "We pay for our railroads, our highways, our power plants." "They have no right to tell us what to do" (Jay Gao, "Is

Guangdong Asia's Fifth Tiger?" *New Zealand Herald*, January 28, 1992).

33. For an introduction to the Chinese democratic analysis of Leninism as a fascist socialism, see Edward Friedman, "The Social Obstacle to China's Socialist Transition," in Victor Nee and David Mozingo, eds., *State and Society in Contemporary China* (Ithaca: Cornell University Press, 1983), pp. 148–71.

34. Confucius was a northerner.

35. For some in the south, the southern cultural renaissance is a re-emergence of the vibrant, open culture of the ancient southern state of Chu that northern Confucians had tried to repress and suppress. The ecstatic poems "came to be 'superseded, discouraged, persecuted and mocked' (though fragments of its mythology survived, particularly in popular Taoism). When . . . Chu was destroyed . . . , Confucian-minded scholars . . . seldom deigned to mention them. . . . The world of erotic imagery and . . . beliefs from which . . . shamistic hymns sprang only filled them with repugnance, and they allowed it to pass out of existence or to subsist in corrupted form among the illiterate masses" (Burton Watson, *Early Chinese Literature* [New York: Columbia University Press, 1962], pp. 242–43).

Chapter 5

China's North–South Split and the Forces of Disintegration

In the 1970s, when the Soviet Union considered Communist China both a major adversary and a dangerous competitor, Victor Louis, understood to be a Soviet intelligence operative, published *The Coming Decline of the Chinese Empire*, a tract prophesying the disintegration of China as a result of "the national aspirations of the Manchu, Mongols, Uighurs, Tibetans, and other non-Chinese peoples." Today, China's media portray anyone who raises the topic of a possible breakup of China as an enemy and saboteur—like Victor Louis, an agent of black propaganda.

On the surface, it does seem that the non-Chinese peoples inside the People's Republic have been reduced to insignificant minorities by waves of Chinese immigrants in what had once been huge non-Chinese regions—Tibet, East Turkestan, Mongolia, and Manchuria. (Tibetans protest this population invasion as cultural genocide.)

In the twentieth century, nationalistic Chinese have tended to take the fate of the Manchus, who conquered all of China in the seventeenth century, as a preview of the destiny of the non-Chinese. To maintain their communal identity, the Manchu kept their northeastern homeland free of female Chinese settlers and maintained Manchu as a national language. Yet nearly 300 years later, the population of what was once Manchuria—known in China merely as the northeastern provinces—is less than 10 percent Manchu, and only a small minority of these can speak Manchu. That Chinese civilization conquers all is the usual conclusion drawn from the sinicization of the Manchu.

The Chinese view is that in what were once non-Chinese regions, tens of millions of Chinese settlers went to live in once-inhospitable terrain to block

Originally published in *Current History*, September 1993. Reprinted with permission.

expansionist neighbors: the Russians, Central Asian Muslims, Indians, and Japanese. These settlers are seen as having suffered to make once-barren regions productive, and also as having brought with them a superior civilization that sincized the indigenous peoples, making China one homogeneous people. If this is the case, why even raise the issue of breakup?

One reason is that China cannot escape the global tendencies of the information revolution and the rise of soft technologies. In China, as in Lombardy in Italy, Quebec in Canada, the Breton region of France, the Punjab region in India, or the southern states of Brazil, there is an extraordinary resurgence of communalist, or shared, identities. There is a desire for a new nation-state, as people imagine that they would be better off without a useless, corrupt, tax-taking, distant, central government bureaucracy. That is precisely how the rulers in Beijing are popularly characterized in China. They know it and they fear the consequence: a breakup of China.

The new international economy based on technologies that can instantaneously penetrate borders welcomes an international culture that subverts Confucianism–Leninism throughout China. Pocket-size shortwave radios pick up BBC and Voice of America Chinese-language broadcasts, and television satellite dishes are turned toward Taiwan and Hong Kong. The Mao-era national center founded on a monopoly of information and economic autarky is dead, although China's rulers still engage in a fruitless struggle to keep out so-called cultural pollutants from abroad.[1]

Because China's leaders are worried that the country could split apart, they have mounted a propaganda campaign against it. Almost no day goes by without lead stories in the media calling attention to the chaos, killings, and decline that accompany ethnic and nationalist strife around the globe, from the former Yugoslavia and Soviet Union to Northern Ireland, Germany, Czechoslovakia, India, and Africa.

Regional communal identities in China have grown so strong so rapidly that most Chinese are genuinely worried that the toppling of the Leninist dictatorship in Beijing would lead to the disintegration of China, a disintegration in which they would suffer all the privations, pains, and terrors associated with hate-filled civil strife. Anxiety, not affection, holds China together at the end of the twentieth century. The Chinese do not want to end up like the Lebanese or Somalians or Yugoslavs. But can fear long serve as a national glue?

The Two Chinas?

The central government in Beijing contends that China's post-Mao economic success, understood as an integral part of East Asia's phenomenal growth, is a consequence of the spread of north China's ancient and eternally valid Confucian values throughout East Asia. As the home of these virtues of hierarchical authority, thrift, education, family, hard work, respect for seniors, and submersion of self for the larger good, China, its rulers believe, will surpass the other East Asian countries and become the largest economy in the world by the early twenty-first century. In this vision of the future, the Chinese people will take great pride in a respected, militarily powerful, and politically active nation that will keep Asia free from Japanese or extraregional domination. China will be the new global center. Such is the new nationalism promoted by rulers in Beijing.

This authoritarian, militarist, Confucian nationalist project of the north is challenged by a vision emanating from the dynamic metropolises of south China. The south's alternative to the north's military authoritarianism imagines an open, confident Greater China. (The World Bank has recognized the reality of this project by adding a new statistical category for its collection of economic data, the Chinese Economic Area.) The media inform Chinese that the total investment capital available in mainland China, Taiwan, Hong Kong, Macao, and Chinese communities in Southeast Asia is greater than the foreign exchange reserves available to the Japanese. The south's Greater China, a China that crosses borders, is successfully and fearlessly open to the world. It is a China that celebrates a multiplicity of religious sects and worldviews, one not constrained by the anachronisms of northern Confucianism, with its denigration of the young, the female, and the commercial—and one not manipulated and glorified by self-serving, parasitic northern bureaucrats. The southern project is not afraid of multiple communities of identity.

Central to the south's vision of a new Chinese national identity is the conviction that the Leninist regime, rather than being admirably responsible for successful post-Mao economic growth, is increasingly an obstacle to China's continuing development. The rural economy was freed not by a decree from Beijing that wisely decollectivized agriculture—as the foreign press has portrayed it—but by local people taking advantage of a small opening and a weakened state apparatus resulting from traumatic Mao-era campaigns. Together these allowed Chinese far from the reach of the center to get around the system. Innovative and entrepreneurial Chinese did so well, despite the rulers in Beijing, that the old-fashioned time-servers in the capital finally had to legalize much of what had succeeded so brilliantly in diverse localities.

Reform, however, still has far to go. The old system lingers, a potentially malignant cancer. The frightened old men who rule from Beijing have not legalized private property, and the corrupt Leninist apparatus enjoys the fruits of not permitting peasant households to rent, buy, or sell land. Instead, when a family member dies, moves out, marries in, is born, or finds work elsewhere, permission must be sought from the all-powerful, arbitrary, local village party boss for changes in land allocation, as well as in the imposed state quotas for farm products to be delivered to the state at ridiculously low prices. Consequently, villagers hate the exploitative power holders. Their belief that an oppressive system remains in place and that a new world is not in the offing is the view of most Chinese. This perspective, delegitimating the claims of Beijing, is captured in the poetry of Bei Dao:

> The Ice Age is over now.
> Why is there still ice everywhere?

Peeking Into the Abyss

Though the government in Beijing and its reactionary authoritarian project are ever more illegitimate, and a southern-based, open image of a Greater China ever more legitimate, no one in China calls for the country's breakup. If the nation disintegrates, it will be because the southern project fails to encompass the communalisms of language, region, religion, and ethnicity that are exploding everywhere.

In fact, one attractive feature of the more open southern worldview is that it seems capable of attracting yet more Chinese so that China is not limited to *Zhongguo*, a Chinese state on the mainland, but is open to *Zhonghua*, all who identify with a Chinese nation, including overseas Chinese. If the south's project is a supranationalism that is appealing because it is in part a supernationalism, why then raise the question of a breakup of China?

Part of the answer lies in the global technological forces undermining the center's control. In addition, in reforming Leninist systems, or in post-Leninist regions, centrifugal tendencies rooted in past and present history are also tremendously reinforced by the economics that accompany reform of the system. Enterprises and regions are thereby empowered, and the economically irrational statist command economy is consequently undermined. Each region then tries to collect its own taxes for local investment and competes against every other region. Unless a new nationalism can reintegrate all China's diverse communities, then disintegration threatens.

Communalist identities and conflicts are heightened by the experience of the Leninist system's inhumanity. In China as elsewhere, communities tied to the capital benefited by keeping down other communities. Local community members therefore view themselves as having been martyrs and as having survived because they helped each other out in the face of the alien Leninist system, seen as a foreign, Russian, or Western imposition. The rulers are "them"; the local community is "us." These numerous local communities could become protonationalisms as people seek revenge against rulers or release from domination.

China is also experiencing an explosion of communalist identities down to temple sects, secret societies, and lineage associations. Violence and the potential for violence among such groups seem pervasive. An unintended consequence of perverse Leninist irrationalities is that all groups believe themselves to be victims and find all the rest to be unfairly privileged. Even Tibetans will not be seen as sufferers. Instead, they and other victims of the regime will be imagined as wastrels who have been given subsidies that keep the rest needlessly poor.[2] The irritation among localities has led to the widespread fear that hate-filled, bloody chaos could engulf the country. It is this fear that Beijing relies on for China's continued stability.

The conservative ideologues who rule China are very conscious of and concerned about these disintegrative forces. They are well aware that the idea that China is one homogeneous people with a shared culture is nonsense. In fact, what they see everywhere are the differences. Communities mourn differently. They prefer different teas. Cuisines are regional. Most importantly, it is not even obvious now that Chinese share a culture since they view each other as speaking different languages. Northerners who travel to the south increasingly are confronted by Cantonese who speak Cantonese and Shanghaiese who speak Shanghaiese. Outside the Beijing region, the Mandarin language (the administrative language of the old empire) is treated like an alien tongue.

Reactionaries contend that only by stepping up Confucian socialization and increasing propaganda for Marxist-Leninist socialism can China overcome its ever more powerful diversities and remain unified. These hard-liners clearly do not believe that fear of chaos will prove to be the glue that holds China together. But can they woo outraged communities to ancient verities and a discredited ideology?

The Seductive South

The conventional wisdom has it that the conservative north will win out against the dynamic south because the southern coastal regions have zoomed ahead so fast that the rest of China, resenting the south's wealth, will join together against the region. In this view, most Chinese will respond to the Confucian language of reciprocity and the socialist appeal of economic equality, and therefore unite with the dictatorship in Beijing as it taxes the south, redistributes the region's wealth, and keeps military power out of southern hands. The south would become a milk cow for a united nation, not a harbinger of a new nation or nationalism.

But there is much evidence that most of China identifies more with the south's project than with the north's. In the hinterlands, museums have been redone that reimagine these regions to be in conflict with Beijing's idea of Chineseness; local people are not part of a Chinese nation working to resist the penetration of foreign ideas, as the ideologically purist, Confucianist-Leninist north would have it. They instead see the local community, and all of China, developing because of open international exchange from the ancient Silk Road to the glorious civilizations of the Mediterranean, the Nile, the Tigris, and the Euphrates, and because of a welcoming of Buddhist religion and sculpture. (The south coastal city of Changzhou claims to be the most Chinese city because it has had the longest continuous history of trading overseas.)

In addition, people living in the hinterlands are all too aware that they suffer when they are forced to accept Beijing's state-imposed low prices for their raw materials instead of the south's significantly higher world-market-oriented prices. One should not underestimate the large extent to which those in the hinterlands also identify their future and all of China's with the southern project.

In reality, the economically dynamic south has become the source from which China is increasingly being reintegrated as an entity. Thirty percent of Hong Kong's currency already circulates inside China. The Cantonese language and southern styles, songs, and customs are spreading north, as is southern investment. Workers come for jobs in the south, send money home from the south, and eventually return with a southern nest egg and a southern tongue. The rise of the south is experienced as benefiting all local communities. It, in contrast to the north, is imagined as friendly to the new communalism.

Before the Cultural Revolution ravaged its economy, Shanghai was seen by Chinese as the best place in the country in which to live. In the late Mao era, with everything decided by narrow political interests, Beijing was viewed as the place that had the greatest opportunities for a good life. But now, in the post-Mao reform era, Chinese pollsters find that people want to live in their own community, with that community enriched by cultural and economic ties to China's future: the Greater China of the southern project. The old center, it would seem, cannot hold.

A Revised History

China's rulers and many foreign analysts contend that the Leninist state is still embraced as the beloved savior of the motherland from Japanese invaders during World War II. The People's Republic is Chinese patriotism incarnate. Profound experiences such as China's war of resistance are seen as having established a difficult-to-change nationalist identity that benefits the government in Beijing, the heir of the liberation struggle. This deep nationalism is said to make for continuity and stability in China in contrast to Eastern Europe, where Leninism was supposedly merely imposed by the Red Army, and thus lacked a nationalist bond to hold the loyalty of the people.

But this concept of Chinese exceptionalism ignores the powerful forces that delegitimate even a nationalistic Leninist system, as in Albania, Mozambique, or Russia itself. The failures of Leninism foster an experience of lost time. A growing number of Chinese see the Mao era as one when time stood still, continuous with the outmoded empire. The People's Republic was not, and is not, believed to have succeeded as a modern nation.

Massachusetts Institute of Technology political scientist Lucian Pye has been virtually isolated in his insistence that

China is really a civilization pretending to be a nation-state. . . . China today is what Europe would have been if the unity of the Roman Empire had lasted until now and there had not been the separate emergence of the separate entities of England, France, Germany and the like.[3]

Pye's view is similar to the long-mocked but ultimately accurate voices in the field of what used to be Soviet studies that found the Soviet Union to be the Russian Empire refurbished—in other words, a prison house of nations, a political entity that could not hold up against the strong and unyielding urge for independence by diverse communities. Is Pye not right then that China—like Russia, Ethiopia, and Yugoslavia—is an empire that cannot survive growing regionalist communal identities?

Manifest evidence of this coming Chinese identity transformation can be found in the vicissitudes of anti-Japanese nationalism. By the 1990s, Chinese in the northeast saw their rewoven ties to the Japanese economy as a happy return to pre-Leninist growth that had been unfortunately interrupted by economic stagnation and the cultural disruption of Beijing's Leninism. The ruling groups in post-Mao China claim credit for having won beneficial economic ties with Japan, including large aid packages and generous loan terms. Those outside these groups see instead a government selling out to Japan for its own narrow, selfish interests, such as corrupt deals that enrich the children of the elite but do not benefit Chinese people.

Indeed, Chinese increasingly imagine themselves as a long-suffering people who have been continuously betrayed by leaders who did not insist on a large indemnity for Chinese victims of the Japanese massacre in Nanjing or for Japan's Nazi-like medical experiments on Chinese in the northeast, or for the millions of other Chinese victims of Japanese rape, pillage, and slaughter. The anti-Japan slogans that have accompanied virtually every democratic movement in post-Mao China should be understood as antiregime manifestations, a way of expressing the sentiment that today's rulers of the Chinese state are in fact traitors to the Chinese nation. *Zhongguo* is suspect today; *Zhonghua* is the real and future China. A new notion of nationalism, or of nationalisms, has already largely replaced the bond that once held Mao-era China together. The old anti-Japanese nationalism has been reimagined so as to discredit the regime in Beijing.

This delegitimation of anti-Japanese Leninist Confucianism appears in another form when people note that the Soviet troops that invaded northeast China in 1945 at the end of World War II also raped and pillaged. China's Communist dictators covered up the crimes, ignored the suffering of the Chinese people, and allied with the enemies of the Chinese people, again for the benefit only of the party's elite. The new thinking holds that Beijing welcomed Russian rapists and forgave Japanese rapists. Such a regime must be illegitimate; it cannot represent the best interests of the Chinese nation.

This re-evaluation, which no longer credits China's rulers for saving the nation in an anti-Japanese war of liberation from imperialism, has gone so far that Chinese scholars can now ask even of Wang Jingwei, previously conceived as China's Pétain and considered the ultimate traitor for having gone over to the Japanese during the war, what alternative did he have? Moreover, the victory of Mao's side is no longer understood as a deep expression of Chinese nationalism. Leninist rule instead seems a mere contingent event, made possible only by external forces such as America's defeat of Japan. Mao thus was lucky; Wang was not wrong.

In another similar and fundamental transvaluation of nationalistic identity, it once was obvious that China's Communists were the carriers of the patriotism of the Ming Dynasty, which had overthrown a foreign Mongol imperialism, only to be defeated by the tragic, foreign Manchu conquest. The modern drive to free Chinese from Manchu rule was often sloganized as restoring the Ming. Patriotism was the Ming, treason the Qing.

Yet by the 1990s, Chinese scholars were defending Ming collaborators with the Qing Dynasty Manchus.[4] It turns out that the Ming rulers, predecessors and surrogates for the Communist dictatorship, were disasters for the Chinese people. In such a situation, patriots can and must reach out to ally with any groups, even beyond China, to save the Chinese people from parasites parading as patriots.

The Chinese writer Xiao Qian likens the nation to an organism that is murderously sick; its body is full of deadly poisons and suffers from constipation. Only diarrhea can get the poisons out; even though this would leave the body weak, it is a price worth paying to escape the continuing tragedy of entrapment in one's own poisons. In short, the militarized, anti-imperialist appeal to a nationalism based on sacrificing everything for military power—as with the Opium War, the Boxer Rebellion, and the anti-Japanese war—is rejected.[5]

In like manner, Zhou Bo, in the February 1991 edition of the Shanghai newspaper *Wen Hui Bao*, rejects maintaining Mao's militarized anti-imperialism to ward off evils such as those the British brought in during the Opium War. Instead, rulers who isolated China are blamed for making China vulnerable and backward. Only "open dynasties such as the Tang and Yuan" brought real "national strength and dignity." Pride in a Chinese Ming defeat of foreign Mongols of the Yuan is an error. Parochial arrogance makes for an empty patriotism that kept Chinese impoverished.

Instead of stubbornly clinging to Mao's worldview, one should note that Chinese who risked their lives to flee to Hong Kong from coastal Guangdong province in the Mao era, now, in an era of maximum openness in south coastal Guangdong, are trying to return home. It was the Guangdong patriot Sun Yat-sen who, in the nineteenth century, likewise understood how to revive the nation. The choice for patriots, then, is isolation versus openness, the nativism of the Ming, the Qing, and Mao, or the openness of the Mongols, the Yuan, and Sun

Yat-sen. A Chinese patriotism that promotes the Mongol Yuan Dynasty and has nothing good to say for the fighters of the Opium War expresses an extraordinary transvaluation of values. It regards the proud Confucian-Leninist authoritarianism of the late-twentieth-century north as heir and purveyor of empty slogans and real poisons that have kept China poor for centuries and still block a full, albeit painful, opening to what can again make all Chinese prosperous—and again make China a great civilization.

To the extent that the notion of a Greater China as an alliance of *Zhonghua*— a coming together of Chinese who escaped the shackles of Leninism by going to Hong Kong, Taiwan, Macao, or Southeast Asia—allows successful economic competition with Japan, the southern project seems most attractive to patriotic Chinese who are still working out their identity in opposition to a successful Japan but who no longer see China's Leninist dictators as real or successful opponents of the Japanese threat. The increasingly legitimate counter to Japan is the economic power of a southern-based Greater China.

Yet however much southern consciousness spreads, it need not win. If the lessons of other post-Leninist states have significance for China, they suggest that it will not be easy to knit together a new, democratic confederation of peoples identified with diverse communalist concepts of language, region, and culture legitimated in the wake of Leninist decline. If those lessons from elsewhere hold, Leninism has so poisoned communalist identities that demagogues who can find a popular response to appeals to hates of other communities will likely emerge. That was already the reality of the late-nineteenth-century Qing Dynasty and the early-twentieth-century republic when the center could not hold and warlords, gangs, and regional satraps violently ruled and ravaged China. It is a frightening alternative to the discredited regime in Beijing. But it may well be what is simmering just below the surface in the boiling cauldron of angry communalist identities:

> During the Qing, inter-ethnic conflicts . . . became common between Han and Muslims, Hakka (a minority group of southeast China) and Hoklo (Hokkien-speaking Chinese), and Hakka and Punti (native Cantonese). Ethnic feuds strove to "clear the boundaries" by ejecting exogenous groups from their respective territories. Such ethnic clashes could be extremely violent: a major conflict between the Hakka and Punti in 1856–67 took a toll of 100,000 victims.[6]

Other outcomes, of course, are possible. The southern project could integrate a more open polity. Still, tough northern chauvinists could win out in vicious combat. It is also possible to imagine a succession crisis temporarily resolved by the choice of a regional leader as head of state who is committed to the southern project but who is not from the south coastal area. That could legitimate regional representation and serve as a step toward eventual democratization. Such a course is imagined in China as a gradual but inevitable process, akin to the one that has supposedly already transpired in Taiwan and South Korea. It is taken as the happily shared project of Greater East Asia.

The future is unknown, open, and uncertain. Whatever it proves to be, it will require grappling with the forces that could precipitate a breakup of China.

Notes

1. Edward Friedman, "A Failed Chinese Modernity," *Daedalus* 122.2 (Spring 1993), pp. 1–17.

2. Edward Friedman, "Ethnic Identity and the Denationalization and Democratization of Leninist States," in M. Crawford Young, ed., *The Rising Tide of Cultural Pluralism: The Nation-State at Bay?* (Madison: University of Wisconsin Press, 1993).

3. Lucien Pye, "How China's Nationalism Was Shanghaied," *The Australian Journal of Chinese Affairs*, January 1993, p. 130.

4. Wang Hongzhi, *Hong Chenchou zhuan* [Biography of Hong Chenchou] (Beijing: Red Flag Publishing House, 1991).

5. Yi Yueh, "On Diarrhea, Constipation, and Reform—Xiao Qian's Three Political Allegories," *Dangdai* [Contemporary], No. 23 (February 15, 1993), translated in JPRS-CAR–93–029 (May 6, 1993), pp. 61–62.

6. Frank Dikötter, *The Discourse of Race in Modern China* (Stanford: Stanford University Press, 1992), p. 70.

Chapter 6

Reconstructing China's National Identity

By the 1990s, it was a commonplace that Mao-era anti-imperialist nationalism in China was dead. The anti-imperialist perspective had pitted an exploitative foreign imperialism against a courageous Chinese people (Hu 1955). This nationalist understanding of Chinese history was encapsulated in the Great Leap Forward–era film on the Opium War, *Lin Zexu*, which drew a contrast between patriotic Sanliyuan villagers and traitorous ruling groups in the capital city. If the brave peasants would join with all patriotic Chinese and not fear to die, then under correct leadership the foreign capitalists who got rich in making Chinese poor by forcing opium into China would be thrown out. But ruling reactionaries, afraid of popular mobilization, preferred to sell out to the imperialists. As with patriots who had led exploited peasants throughout Chinese history, Mao's Communists would save the nation by providing the correct leadership that would mobilize patriotic Chinese, push imperialists out of China, and thus permit an independent China to prosper with dignity.

By treating the capitalism that China had supposedly experienced starting with the Opium War in 1839 as pure imperialism, a total evil made up singularly of "aggression, plunder, national humiliation, etc.," Maoist anti-imperialism was imagined in the post-Mao era as having kept Chinese from embracing the other side of a two-edged sword, that is, "the modernizing role of foreign capital" required for "a catching-up type of economy." In short, even former Marxist-Leninists found that anti-imperialist nationalism that built a wall around China to keep out foreign influence was a disaster that had kept China locked in poverty and backwardness (Glunin and Grigorev 1991). The Qing Dynasty's error was no longer a failure to mobilize peasants to wall out foreign influence, but instead

Originally published in *The Journal of Asian Studies*, February 1994. Reprinted with permission.

the very attempt to wall out the world. "China ... had gradually fallen into decline because of the feudal and isolationist policies adopted by the Qing government. The muddleheaded rulers forbade contact with other countries. ... At the same time, the economies of the western capitalist countries were undergoing rapid development" (Zhang Tianxin 1993).

Anti-imperialist nationalism had previously seemed to express the true story of China. The 1978 National College Entrance Examination at the end of the Mao era limned this soon-to-be discredited narrative of a Han people rising in the ancient north, spreading by civilizing other peoples, surviving by keeping out barbarians, facing new threats from imperialism, and surviving yet again by mobilizing China's popular forces under Communist leadership. The student was to fill in the blanks that completed this long, single-strand, militaristic, nationalist narrative (pp. 72, 73):

> 1. During the Shang Dynasty, the laboring people of our country used an alloy of copper and tin to cast tools and weapons called _____ implements. It signalled a new level in the development of the forces of production.

> 2. During the reign of T'ai Tsung in the T'ang Dynasty, the Tibetan leader _____ married _____, thus promoting economic and cultural interchange between the Han and the Tibetan peoples and effecting a close relationship between the Han and Tibetan peoples.

> 3. During the peasants' righteous rebellion in the final days of the Yuan Dynasty, Chu Sheng proposed to _____ that "the walls be built high, grain be widely stored, and the assumption of the title of prince be postponed."

> 4. Toward the end of the Ming Dynasty, the peasant revolt led by Li Tzu-ch'eng raised the revolutionary slogan of _____.

> 5. During the Opium War, people in the northern suburb _____ of Canton stoutly resisted the invading English army, displaying the Chinese people's heroic spirit of being unafraid of the strong and the cruel, and daring to engage the enemy in battle.

> 6. During half a century beginning in the 1850s, Tsarist Russian imperialism forcibly occupied _____ square kilometers of our country's territory.

Questions 7, 8, and 9 were on the rise of China's Communist Party.

> 10. In May 1938, Chairman Mao published "_____," clearly pointing out the objective laws for development of the War of Resistance Against Japan and the path to victory, and criticizing the _____ theory and the _____ theory, thereby greatly inspiring and strengthening the belief of the people throughout the country that they would be victorious in the war.[1]

The Maoist mythos left out how Chinese civilization also grew from an intermixing of cultures from diverse spots in China, how China's rise was facilitated by international exchange across both the Silk Road and the South China Sea, how the large territory that Chinese nationalists claimed for themselves was conquered by Mongol and Manchu, how the foreign project that Mao imported from Soviet Russia carried with it cruel and arbitrary repression and self-wounding exclusion. That the anti-imperialist nationalistic project misidentified the causes of China's backwardness in focusing on a need to keep out foreigners, British, Russians, and Japanese was popular wisdom by the 1980s.

Even paramount leader Deng Xiaoping blamed closed-door policies for China's backwardness, a view reflected in the political education manuals subsequently used by college political instructors. Deng pointed out on October 22, 1984,

> Isolation would prevent any country's development. We suffered from this and so did our forefathers. However, it was probably a case of an open door policy ... when Zheng He was sent on voyages in the western oceans by the Ming Emperor Zhu Di.... The Ming Dynasty entered a decline with the death of Emperor Zhu Di and China was subjected to foreign aggression.... As a result, China fell into poverty and ignorance.... Later, we closed our doors and economic development slowed down. (Deng 1985, 61)

Chinese now tend to find the source of the nation's backwardness not in external imperialism beginning with the Opium War, as Mao had declared, but in a lack of openness to the world. Because

> the rulers of the Ming and Qing stubbornly adhered to the old ways, disdained science and technology, and suppressed or even throttled the development of an industrial and commercial economy, they closed off the country to the outside world. Thus they lost the opportunity for a transformation to an industrial society and impeded social progress. (Lu 1991, 53)

As bad as imperialism was, it was not, in fact, the unique source of what made China backward. Key causes of underdevelopment long preceded the Opium War.

> When Britain was moving ahead with capitalism in the early seventeenth century, China was just then in the final years of a Ming dynasty characterized by factional fighting, chaos caused by war, and a ban on maritime trade and intercourse with foreign countries. Being a step behind others, China was forced into a passive position and became vulnerable to attack. The result ... was that China became more and more backward. (Zhu and Cao 1987, 7)

A 1980s article in the official newspaper of the Central Committee of China's ruling Communist Party asked why China, which had been a world leader in science and technology through the fifteenth century, was so backward at the end of the Mao era. It answered that a Chinese people, injured and humiliated by imperialist attack and plunder, unintentionally intensified its wounds by trying to save itself by isolating China from the capitalist world market. To fend off evil, the anti-imperialist nation inadvertently committed slow suicide by entombing its living people in an airless enclosure in which the fresh winds of world progress were blocked out (Qiao 1987, 5).

As anti-imperialist policies were self-wounding, so anti-imperialist ideology was alienating. It suffocated society and imposed an unwelcome statist artifice. "During the Maoist era . . . Marxism-Leninism was taught . . . to integrate the new modern society. . . . This attempt to replace culture with ideology largely failed" (Duke 1989, 31). Chinese in the post-Mao era are in the process of creating policies and a mythos to replace the failed anti-imperialist praxis of the Mao era. The new national narrative must supplant its predecessor by offering a compelling vision of a happy future that is, as its predecessor, rooted in a celebration of a glorious past. This chapter sketches an increasingly popular version of reconceived national history—one that is contesting for Chinese hearts and minds at the end of the twentieth century—of a historically dynamic southern core that holds the promise of a great national future for all Chinese.

The Eclipse of Anti-Imperialist Nationalism

The People's Republic of China in the Mao era presented itself as the heir of a Han people who had come together millennia earlier in the north China plain of the Yellow River Valley, built a great civilization, fought to preserve it, and expanded over the centuries by civilizing barbarian invaders. Mao's anti-imperialist revolution was the culmination of this Chinese national history. The National Museum of History in Beijing displayed this nationalist history as an ascent from Peking man through an expansionist, amalgamating, and unifying Han culture to the founding of the People's Republic.

An anthropologist explained:

> The ascendancy of the Communist Party and creation of New China are both understood as the inevitable outcome of China's historical process. . . . [T]he antiquity and continuity of Chinese culture . . . give China a respectable status. . . . Creating a sense of national cultural identity requires persuading all of the non-Han peoples that they have a stake in the fate of the Han majority. If ethnic groups always place their "Chinese" citizenship behind their own ethnicity, the state will fragment. (Thorp 1992, 18, 19)

By the 1990s, however, Chinese teachers forced to repeat this story of a singular north China origin to Chinese civilization, which was recapitulated and advanced in Mao's north China peasant movement, described it as a lie.

[A]n essentially unilinear evolutionary model . . . no longer enjoys universal acceptance in China. . . . [T]he old, hypersimplistic notion that increasing social complexity during the north China Neolithic period is best explained as an inevitable evolutionary process by which a highly localized early Neolithic Yangshao culture spawned a late Neolithic Longshan culture forming the foundation for the genesis of Chinese Bronze Age civilization is no longer tenable. Most Chinese archaeologists now agree that the late Neolithic and Bronze Age of China were a rich amalgam of influences from many areas, including those outside the middle Yellow River valley itself. (Olsen 1992, 4)

As soon as reforms began in the post-Mao era, archeological and anthropological associations, journals, and conferences, aware since the mid-1960s of data for "a new conception of the Chinese past," swiftly undermined the northern, Maoist mythos of national genesis, insisting that scientific findings made impossible "the viewpoint of linear development . . . of cultural development . . . from one central point . . . radiated out. . . . Late Paleolithic cultures in the southern part of our country . . . represented . . . a continuation of their own type of development." Measurements today revealed "proportionate differences between the residents of the North and the South. . . . This type of regional differentiation can be traced back to the human fossils of the late Paleolithic."[2]

In the "Neolithic Revolution," while the Yellow River basin of the north centered on "dry farming and millet," in contrast, "culture in the Yangzi River basin as far back as seven thousand years ago was already proficient in rice crop agriculture." In sum, "The Yellow River basin . . . , taken to be the cradle of the most ancient civilization in China, . . . would not be in conformity with the reality discovered through archeological excavations. . . . [T]he genesis of China's civilization came not from one source, but from many . . . that were scattered throughout the different regions . . . through their mutual influence and blending." In short, "[T]he Yangzi River valley . . . was just as much a cradle of Chinese civilization as was the Yellow." Furthermore, one had to look at the "importance of foreign contacts in the development of Chinese civilization and culture and the relative impact of non-Han peoples on Han" (Guldin 1990, 16, 135, 134–135, 124, 81, 77, 75, 80, 22).

"Many Chinese archaeologists became converted to the multilinear view during the mid-1970s, when a decentralized archaeological apparatus brought about major discoveries outside the Zhongyuan cradle, and when the new carbon–14 dates showed that some of the 'marginal' cultures were as early as the Zhongyuan center" (Chang 1992).

Swiftly, all over the country, from Xian on the Silk Road to Changzhou on the south China coast, museums were reorganized or new ones were built to tell stories that contravened the notion of a northern origin.[3] More and more, Chinese by the 1990s were envisioning the south as integral to the future of China, reimagining their history such that the promise of China was no longer premised on a northern-based purist history. Democrats organized in Hunan Province in

June 1989 described the virtue of "the people of Hunan" as a result of their "being the offspring of centuries of intermarriage between northerners and southerners" (*Anthems* 1992, 201). The anti-imperialist regime's legitimating national myth of a pure ethnos was subverted.

Imagining a Nation

Analysts see nationalism less as the fruit of an evolutionary budding and more as a consequence of a historical contestation in which some interest or agency successfully imagines or seems to embody a history that persuades people of shared primordial origins (Young 1976; 1993). The late imperial debate in China did not privilege an anti-imperialist north. That worldview became pervasive and persuasive starting only in the 1930s. By the 1930s, Jiang's Nationalists and Mao's Communists, both dedicated anti-imperialists, put together the old idea of the centrality of the northern plain (*Zhongyuan*) with recent archeological discoveries in the north, so that these political adversaries shared much at the cultural-political level.

When Chinese at the end of the nineteenth and the beginning of the twentieth centuries asked why they lacked nationalist consciousness, however, answers included a history of "denigration of the individual and the seclusion of the country from the rest of the world," a lack of " 'the ocean faring' commercial soul" and the freedom-loving and anti-despotic "democratic soul." With identities defined by parochial social bonds such as lineage, village, and language, regional division precluded national unity. It was believed that Chinese were "prone to separation."

> The northern Chinese were martial in spirit but lacked "political ability." The customs of Fujian and Guangdong were most different from the rest of the country . . . , [with] Jiangsu natives . . . most effeminate and disappointing.

Chinese lacked national spirit because "each province had its own character and sentiment, customs, and language." One analyst traced the flaw back to ancient Yellow River origins.

> Chinese despotism . . . emerged early because the flatness of the Yellow River basin enabled a geographical unification of peoples with "contrary feelings". . . . [by] compulsion, which not only sapped the people's political ability but "lowered their intelligence, enfeebled their spirit, and silenced their voices." In such a nation . . . people . . . do not know the existence of a nation, and each individual pursues his selfish ends. (Young Lung-chang 1988)

It was not until the late Qing, when racist ideas spread from Europe, that a story was put together of a Han race descended from the Yellow Emperor defending a northern sacred plain, the Middle Kingdom, against barbarians (Sun

1992). Prior Qing discourse on " 'sincization'. . . *hanhua*, 'to become Han'. . . culturally, . . . is silent on the self-identification that is so fundamental to a sense of ethnicity in China or anywhere else" (Crossley 1990, conclusion). While the Han is in fact the river crossroads that connected the upper reaches of the Yangtze River and Yellow River plain (Sage 1992), the twentieth-century racial mythos of a pure ethnos obscured this reality of an ecumene of exchange. The Maoist national narrative was indeed a mythos.[4]

The mythos was that a people from the northern plain had assimilated all would-be conquerors. As Zhou Enlai put it in 1957, "The Han are so numerous simply because they have assimilated other nationalities" (Conner 1984, 428).

> In Chinese history, many powerful nations, which had swept through the length and breadth of the country for several centuries disappeared one after another, such as the Huns, the Eastern Hus, the Turks, the Sienpis and so forth. . . . China of the present is the continuation and development of China of the past. If we love our country, we certainly love the cradle of the Chinese nation, which has an outstanding cultural tradition of more than 2,000 years. (Chen 1992, 4, 5)

Unity was actually forged in the early twentieth century on an agenda of all Chinese uniting to expel the Manchu rulers of the Qing Dynasty, with the ruling Manchus understood as conquerors who "refused to be assimilated but, instead, attempted to destroy Chinese culture and obliterate Chinese history." A consequent vengeful war on Manchus did not make them into assimilated Han patriots. "The Taiping armies expressly targeted Manchu communities for extinction. . . . [I]n . . . the 1911/12 Revolution, Manchus . . . were slaughtered . . . hunted . . . and executed for spite after the fighting had subsided." In response, the "Manchu community . . . [was] susceptible to the overtures of the Japanese . . . who . . . established the Manchukuo state" (Crossley 1990, 227, 228). In fact, Chinese before the 1930s did not see themselves as a nation happily born in the north who peacefully, through a superior culture, amalgamated the Manchus and succeeded as a people because they were protected by a Great Wall. That was a twentieth-century construction, a particular reading of history in the service of anti-imperialist nationalism.

That jerry-built construction has crumbled. During the 1978–79 Democracy Wall Movement, people began to reject explicitly the narrative of Han assimilation with the north's Great Wall as a protector of a superior people–civilization. Instead, Chinese increasingly looked outside of China for the source of scientific progress, echoing the views of Lu Xun, who imagined China's walls as confining the energies of the people. When, at the end of 1978, the Democracy Wall Movement exploded, no one invoked the image of a glorious Great Wall that could still protect China. Instead, people cried out for openness, travel, an end to isolation, and access to the fresh winds of all the world. The publication of the Human Rights Alliance declared that "we should never again take such a narrow view of 9,000 years of cultural heritage, but start to use a broader perspective to survey the surrounding horizons" (Goodman 1981, 10). A poet sang of the end of the Mao era as the end of China's long nightmare. "Three thousand years of darkness gone, never to return" (ibid., 45). The manifesto of the Thaw Society found that "China, isolated from the world for thousands of years is facing an unprecedented . . . great thaw" (Lin n.d., 19). The Great Wall imagery was mocked by another poet: "A weak master depends on solid gates" (Goodman 1981, 24). Two poets pined, "Why did people say there is no warmth under the collective system? Why did they say countless walls separate us?" (Lin n.d., xii). The Enlightenment Society in Guiyang declared that "the spiritual Great Wall erected by Qin Shi Huang's progeny to maintain their tyranny . . . is the theoretical structure of feudal despotism, and we must not fail to shatter it" (Seymour 1980, 109). The journal *Enlightenment* asked,

> We stand behind the Great Wall. . . . We see the blue ocean and a mast that brings peace and friendship. Now it sails with culture and science toward the ancient civilization of the Orient. . . . Should we bravely break out of the Great Wall and welcome change, or should we remain dead in our tracks just looking around? (ibid., 126)

Li Jiahua commented that Huang Xiang's poem, "The God of Fire," appeared in "a kind voice with southern accent familiar to the 800 million people" (ibid., 279). Huang wrote of creativity:

> You have broken down the well-guarded gate
> That locked people behind walls of ignorance and prejudice.
> You have removed the pathological veil
> From those who resist freedom more than tyranny. (ibid., 275)

A historical narrative of nationalist anti-imperialism, understood as keeping foreigners out beyond the Wall, had lost its attractive power in less than fifty years.

No National Language of Shared Myths

As in most Leninist systems, the Communist Party's discourse failed to bind the people.[5] Ruling groups were aware of the problem. Mao noted about China's most popular writer, "Ba Jin says it is difficult to write essays." Mao reported that he also heard "that some literary writers do not at all like this thing called Marxism. They say . . . it is not easy to write a novel anymore. . . . Some people say that they do not dare to write even when they have things to say, for fear that they might . . . be criticized." Nonetheless, Mao insisted that "in the area of literature . . . there is only the worker-peasant-soldier orientation" (Leung and Kau 1992, 519, 368, 385, 468). Official literature did not offer heroes, villains, and plots that resonated with lived experience. As C. T. Hsia and numerous other students of Mao-era Chinese literature have shown, unattractive and didactic patriotic posturing presented in "psychologically simplistic, socially formulaic, thematically tendentious, and artistically pedestrian literary documents" appealed to so few Chinese that "Maoist discourse" was "almost universally recognized as the conservative and self-serving utterances of a rapidly aging ruling caste" (Duke 1993, 46, 61).

Ted Huters finds that early-twentieth-century Chinese writers struggled to combine popular accessibility with the preservation of the national essence, until Mao, between 1938 and 1942, silenced them by using "the new exigencies of the war against Japan" to "abuse" writers who wrote other than in class terms that served the power interests of the Communist Party. The result was post-1949 publications in which "nothing much was done that deserved the name of literature." Writers who "blamed . . . party dogmatism" in the 1957 Hundred Flower Movement were crushed. The Party despots after 1957 intensified their insistence on the production of "bright encomia to the new society." When writers failed to produce these, "the role of professional writers" was diminished. But the literature of propagandistic amateurs proved so "shrill" in tone and "narrow" in plot and character as to move very few people. Because of Mao's Leninist practices, the great power of the novel to foster the bonds of national identity was squandered (Huters 1989).

Students of nationalism have found that the modern novel and the modern nation are mutually reinforcing forces. Therefore it may be decisive that the People's Republic could not produce a great literature. By the 1980s, defenders of the regime blamed the Nobel Prize committee's racism for China's lack of a winner. Chinese chauvinists dismissed out of hand this supposed racist imperialist prize, because "China, like any third-world nation, can never win" (Larson and Kraus 1989, 160).[6] Most writers, however, blamed a suffocating atmosphere. These writers were conscious that the official story, China as a pure civilization guarding against barbarian polluters for millennia, was a mythos to prop up a discredited system. An ideology of class struggle anti-imperialism had, in fact, from the outset precluded a bonding among the nation's people with the artificial, inhuman, and alienating discourse of official Leninism.

In 1935 Tian Jun's patriotic novel, *Village in August*, offered contemporaries a compelling propagandistic vision of the nation's wartime plight. But Leninist censors opposed "the outspoken and unashamed sexuality of the relations between the soldiers and their women" (Herdan 1992, 46). Novels were purged of authentic passions and novelists were compelled to use a language that did not resonate with popular pains and aspirations. Tian Jun was expelled from the Party in 1958, when rulers decided to no longer tolerate any language other than that of militarized class struggle against the bourgeoisie, a language that split, numbed, and paralyzed nationalist emotions. Consequently,

> [m]any of the best revolutionary writers from the late May Fourth period stopped writing creative works before or during the Civil War between the

CCP and Guomindang of 1948–49. Several others continued to write up until the Anti-Rightist campaign of 1957, and then stopped. Virtually none of them have published anything since the Cultural Revolution. (Berninghausen and Huters 1976, 12)

In 1992 a writer further noted that "no outstanding full-length novel has emerged" since the June 4, 1989, Beijing massacre (*CD*, April 28, 1992, 5).

As soon as the People's Republic was established, China's great patriotic comic writer, Lao She, was criticized for flippancy toward the proletariat in his novel *Camel Xiangzi* (Rickshaw Boy). He edited out supposed coarse language and apologized for his lack of faith in the working class before a new edition of the book was published. He was barbarously tortured and driven to death at the outset of the Cultural Revolution. He noted just before his death that there was no place in China for a bourgeois. As Innes Herdan explained, those "out of step" "had to go" (Herdan 1992, 59, 95, 122). Those out of step turned out to be most Chinese writers and readers.

In Mao's China, no powerful national literature or national culture emerged after 1949 to bind a new anti-imperialist consciousness. Instead, censorship that preimposed a myth about class struggle to build a socialist nation excluded ever more Chinese from the category of "the people" and kept China's best writers from writing. When they wrote in terms of a shared nationalism, as in the 1950s movie script *The Lin Family Shop*, which made all the people victims of imperialism, they were denounced for prettifying the bourgeoisie.

But the problem of *The Lin Family Shop*—the problem of excluding the petty bourgeoisie from the nation and from the nation's culture—was already obvious to the writer Mao Dun in the 1930s. He complained then:

> [I]f you are describing the hard lot of the petty bourgeoisie, then you will automatically incur the charge of being counterrevolutionary.... Do petty bourgeois people nowadays suffer? ... Then why should the revolutionary writers look upon them as outcasts from civilization, not worthy of soiling their sacred brush-tip? (Herdan 1992, 37)

Mao Dun never wrote an "original literary work" after the Leninist state was established (Herdan 1992, 43). The great Sheng Congwen's pen stopped writing. The Leninist project had no way to integrate most Chinese into the nation. They were not part of the nation. Hence it is a consequence of Leninism itself that its momentary anti-imperialist appeal can rapidly disappear in China as in so many other places.

The Party insisted on literature for "the people," but "the people" were defined by a discourse that treated all toilers as socialist utopianism would have them. Such descriptions would not portray recognizable people, the diversity and difficulties of people as they were, because they were treated as they absolutely were not; that is, as masters of the state. A compelling language that could touch the shared real plight of the powerless who were victims of the new state, when they had already been imagined by Leninism as the nation's masters, was impossible. Instead, "the people" were invited to hate, and then to hate yet again, both their own inclinations and the supposed continuing impact of defeated adversaries, alleged vengeful oppressors from the pre-Leninist era.

Life was a lie, complicitousness in self-enslavement, an Orwellian reality where slavery was proclaimed to be freedom. Writer Zhang Xianliang's sarcastic paean to socialist labor exposes the ideology's inherent unattractiveness. In the post-Mao era, Zhang wrote in mock praise of life in a slave labor camp:

> Work creates man, bringing out an instinct long ago submerged in advanced [i.e., bourgeois] culture. It takes man back to the primitive state [i.e., communism] when he gloried in the process of creation. . . . Go to a labor camp and try it for yourself. (Zhang Xianliang 1986, 8)

Zhang's fine 1985 novel, *Half of Man Is Woman*, is in part a story of how a person from the north and one from the south must divorce. It describes northern peasants who serve in Mao's army and in the Communist Party as simple and traditional, incapable of the continuous creativity demanded by the modern world.

China is not linguistically united. Even in the north, peasants are presented as not speaking the language of Beijing. In fact, the Red Army used translators for peasants less than 200 miles from Beijing. Most important for the purposes of this chapter, Zhang describes how no shared literary language or common life-enhancing purpose developed in the Leninist era to bind a people in love of their land.

In Mao-era China, peasants were locked in to their village in ignorance. Even rural teachers were illiterate. "[A]lthough she had never finished primary school and it was doubtful if she could write her own name properly, she was still the teacher in the village school." Party policy transformed intellectuals and literate people into stupid people. "What would I be doing reading a book? The few characters I ever knew I've almost forgotten." The " 'works of Marx and Engels,' these were the only books that could be shown to the world." Cultural life was moving backward toward the Dark Ages, where signs, superstition, and gossip had a higher payoff than reading newspapers. Books? "What use are they?" The system "would use words and writing" only for "violently declaring war against its own people." It "destroyed a sense of trust among men." "A movement that really belongs to the people? That would immediately be branded a 'counter-revolutionary incident.' " "[T]rampled on and ravaged, . . . [m]y land" no longer existed. The "only thing to do is protect your own little life" (Zhang Xianliang, 55, 63, 94, 100, 74, 93, 108, 74, 116, 225, 222, 220, 227, 83). In sum, common literacy and popular plots in novels and the press in the Mao era held little positive significance for national bonding in Leninist China. Without a universal tongue or popular literacy or attractive narratives toward a shared and better future, there was little likelihood of creating a united Chinese nation from diverse regions, villages, lineages, religions, languages, and cultural identities.

When writers in 1957, during a liberalizing moment known as the Double-Hundreds Campaign, complained about how imposed categories precluded compelling creativity, they were condemned as antipeople. An antirightist movement followed. High school teachers were attacked as alien, meaning to local speakers, Mandarin-speaking. Good people, the formerly exploited, were taken to be the less educated who spoke the local language (Friedman, Pickowicz, and Selden 1991, 210–11). An inability to read became an indicator of revolutionary virtue (Qian 1986, 253). Consequently, throughout the Mao era, no powerful national literature or culture was produced. Local people spoke the local language and built on local ties. Hence the divisive tendencies of nineteenth-century regionalism and twentieth-century warlordism were intensified by the failed project of modern Leninist anti-imperialist nationalism.

In the early-twentieth-century debates over language reform to serve the goals of popular literacy and national unity, it became clear that if one were to agree to write in the vernacular to facilitate mass literacy and to reach a mass audience, then one had to acknowledge that most Chinese did not speak the Beijing dialect. If one did not wish most Chinese first to have to learn a new language of the north as a precondition of literacy, then one would have to allow regional alphabetizations. By 1937, however, with the political imperative of uniting all Chinese to resist Japanese invaders, superpatriots denounced "the 'dialect romanization' movement . . . because it denied that China was a single nation . . . and by dividing the country into a large number of separate linguistic units was opening the way to imperialist division of the country" (DeFrancis 1984, 247). "Nationalistic feelings" led to an abandonment of a policy of bilingual transitional alphabetization for merely pursuing instead some character simplification. The topic of alphabetization became a taboo. According to John DeFrancis, Mao Zedong supposedly declared clandestinely in 1956, "If the Latin alphabet had been invented by Chinese, probably there would not be any problem. . . . If we make use of it [the Latin alphabet], will we then be strongly suspected of selling out our country? I think it is not necessarily a betrayal [laughter]." But Great Leap–era policy stressed the superiority of Chinese characters over foreign alphabets as part of "euphoric expectations of progress by uniquely Chinese means." Mao Dun's urging in 1962 of focusing on children acquiring *pinyin* [alphabetic spelling] capabilities "fell on deaf ears." Some additional simplification of characters was promoted in the superchauvinist Cultural Revolution, which denounced *minnan* promoters of alphabetic writing as "foreign lackeys," while "xenophobic Red Guards . . . tore down street signs written in Pinyin as evidence of subservience to foreigners." Despite the ongoing power of "a belief in the unifying force of the [historic] script in the face of disparities in speech," DeFrancis concludes that it is the continued propagation of ancient characters and the northern dialect that impedes mass literacy and modernization and consequently pushes most modernization-minded Chinese against the northern dictatorship, making more likely the "political breakup of China" (DeFrancis 1984, 258, 263, 275, 268, 270, 285, 287).

Mao's regime had tried to integrate all peoples inside China through a territory-wide print culture in harmony with common speech, which meant Beijing speech. But so few speakers of Mandarin, the tongue of Beijing-area people, existed in most of the country in 1949 that primary school teachers were allowed to teach all courses but Chinese language in the local language. In ordinary life, people spoke diverse, regional languages. Because of the regionalization of the previous century, the oral cultures of radio, stage shows, opera, pop singers, and the like were the oral voices of the diverse regions in the first half of the twentieth century. It was not to the tones of the north's Beijing dialect that they appealed when reformers in the Southern Society proposed "to use our southern accent to keep alive the memory of our ancestors," who had for centuries fought and died defending against northern invaders such as the Manchus (Schneider 1976).

Mao's northern capital in 1949 confronted regions whose early modernization and nationalism were not necessarily linked to or admiring of the Mandarin-speaking northern center.[7] Cultural pluralism was eventually deemed incompatible with Leninist monolithism. The subsequent failure to create a compelling national literature reflective of a single spoken language consequently left in place, and indeed strengthened, prior regional identities and tongues, not only in China but in all Leninist systems.

Hence, as in other Leninist states, regional cultures and languages re-emerged and were revalorized. In China, this tendency was strengthened by Mao-era policies that undercut national administration and reinforced local autarkies. The "cellularity and localism of the Mao era ran directly counter to integrative trends" (Perry 1989, 590). Peasants of one region did not share a common spoken language with peasants of another. In addition, Mao launched a war on both minority cultures and various Chinese regional peasant cultures. These attacks were alienating. Mao's project precluded the building of an emotionally or economically binding nationalism. It kept China frozen at the moment of what Ernest Gellner, a leading historian of nationalism, calls agrarian empire.

Gellner finds that a modern national consciousness results from universal education in a common spoken language of previously parochial peasants who, through urbanization and physical mobility (for jobs, schooling, army service, trade, etc.), become part of a territorially interdependent division of labor furthered by a national center that invests in the infrastructure of national integration (e.g., railroads, mass communications). But the Mao regime weakened such integration, locked people into their regions, blocked physical mobility, treated economic interdependence as an enemy, demeaned the literate, and demolished the literature that could have furthered a shared national culture. Phrases such as cellular economy were invented by scholars trying to comprehend Mao's failed nationalism.

People survived by living a two-faced life, combining superficial public loyalty to the self-defeating anti-imperialist project with profound ties to local networks of protection and advancement. The public proclamations of loyalty to a failed, official nationalist story and project throughout the world of Leninist states would turn out to be a poor predictor of actual loyalties at moments of national crises. Reforms further weakened the center and strengthened the regions. Just beneath the surface, the devalued was being revalued.

The Rise of a Southern-Oriented National Identity

Although Leninist anti-imperialism is a self-negating discourse that must implode, what will rise to replace it is not predictable. The winning narrative must emerge from a political contest that includes the cultural construction of a more compelling national project. In the 1990s, one such project involves a reimagination of the role of the south in China's history.

In the Mao era, speech in the language of the north had been rewarded. Cantonese were urged to speak Mandarin. The language of the capital region in the north was the language of status, power, and career prosperity. "[Y]ou have to learn Mandarin to have a good career in China" (Frolic 1980, 104). In the early years of Mao's rule, Beijing residents openly ridiculed the purported ugliness of southern speech. By the end of the 1980s, in contrast, a writer would comment, "His soft, kindly voice was clear and pleasant; he had a southern accent" (Barmé and Jaivin 1992, 377). Mandarin-speaking northerners visiting the south now felt themselves as foreigners. One said to me that he might as well be in Hanoi as in Canton. Merchants in Canton pretended not to comprehend Mandarin, humiliating northern visitors, turning them into peripheralized outsiders. Meanwhile, southerners declared, "We've no need to speak Mandarin. . . . We have our own language. China's like Europe, and we want to speak our own language just as in France people speak French" (*NYT* 1992). Southern tongues again resonated with the beauty of a better national future. In place of Mao-era anti-imperialist nationalism that privileged poor, hinterland, Yellow River, north China peasants as the source of nation building—a people whose culture fostered frugality and bravery and permitted sacrifice and martyrdom for the national cause of independence from imperialist exploitation—national success by the 1980s was identified with the market-oriented activities of southerners who joined with Chinese capital from diaspora Hong Kong, Macao, or Southeast Asia to produce world-competitive products that earned foreign exchange that could be invested in building a prosperous China.[8] In the new narrative, northern peasants were recategorized as backward, ignorant, superstitious, insular, and static. And as for able northern intellectuals, southerners announced that "sixty percent of Beijing intellectuals come from the south" (*Geographical Knowledge* 1992).

The discredited myth of a salvationist north did not prefigure China's real and better future. Young Chinese began to abandon the artifacts of the ancient north and instead took honeymoon trips to the south to see the future, buy clothes, and learn about contemporary household interiors. Whereas in the Mao era, southerners "eagerly sought out those who came from the north with more reliable information," in the post-Mao era, in contrast, a "fashionable magazine" of the south, *"Nanfeng Chuang"* (The window to the south wind), introduced "an alluring world of style, freedom, comfort, capital, technology and experience." (Vogel 1989, 19, 63)

From the chitchat of ordinary folk to highest-level intellectual production such as archeology, with all linked by a new cultural discourse that challenged and subverted the Maoist discourse, Chinese experienced a transvaluation of values. The anti-imperialist mythos disintegrated and a new national project that privileges the dynamism of the south was constructed. This is a future- oriented political project, not an accurate scholarly explication of new discoveries in archaeology.

The pervasive presupposition that shaped popular gossip and elite analysis was that, in China, what was good originated in the south. When China's paramount leader went south at the outset of 1992 to reinvigorate policies of openness and reform, the line that spread from his talks was, "I had to go south to speak because in the north many people won't listen to me." It became presuppositional that successful change originated in the south.

> Ever since the Opium Wars, the southern and northern parts of China have evolved in different directions; in the south, Western influence has been strong and politics relatively liberal, while in the north, Western influence has been kept to a minimum and politics remained rather conservative. At his wits end after the 1911 Revolution, Sun Yat-sen went down south to organize a revolutionary government, and . . . opened a new chapter in modern Chinese history. And before he outmaneuvered Liu Shaoqi and Lin Biao, Mao Zedong . . . headed down south. Given such precedents, it is believed that Deng Xiaoping's recent trip to the south of China is a signal of an imminent showdown with Chen Yun. (*Baixing* 1992, 17)

A cultural reconstruction transformed political discourse throughout China. I heard southerners describe their liberation not as occurring in 1949 with the establishment of Mao's rule, but as a moment, usually in the 1980s, when "northern sent-down officials" who had (mis)ruled since 1949 or so and made southerners the dominated objects of an imposed northern project, were finally replaced by local people, southerners, us (1949 was them).

People literally heard the language of Great Wall closed-door despotism as the hated dialect of outmoded conservatives in Beijing. Perry Link reports that "in Cantonese . . . Mandarin is known colloquially as . . . 'big brother speech,' meaning the language of the big brothers who descended from the north after the

Communist revolution." Given this popular reinterpretation of crucial rhetorical polarities, antireform leader Chen Yun declared that he would play the Chinese card and ally with speakers of Beijing dialect to defeat reform, stating "I speak the Beijing dialect. [Reform leader] Hu Yaobang speaks a local dialect," it was obvious that "in Chen Yun's view, 'Beijing dialect' conflicts with 'local dialect,' and, of course, 'Chinese card' is in conflict with 'openness card' " (Ruan 1992, 5). The Mandarin language of Beijing and its self-serving chauvinism had been particularized and revealed as the narrow interest of a backward-facing group situated in the northern capital. The promise of a reformed China open to the world and prospering lay elsewhere.

Chu Shall Rise Again

When the past is reimagined to preview a more hopeful future, a new national project can be legitimated. Students of nationalism find that a nation must be popularly imagined before it can be politically established (Horowitz 1985). Studies of the history and archeology of the south have become a growth industry of enormous proportions. The civilizing force in Chinese historical imagination has migrated to the south. Scientific findings validate the project of the south. Nationhood has been reimagined to include the southern state of Chu before the ancient era of Confucius.

An inexpensive 1988 volume, *A History of Chu Culture*, with magnificent color pictures of ancient items from the state of Chu, argues in rich detail that the ancient southern state of Chu was essential to Chinese culture; the Chu contribution made Chinese culture "higher" and permitted it therefore to spread "more broadly" (Zhang Zhengming 1987, 520). Chu culture had "exerted a lasting influence on . . . Chinese civilization." The old view that Chu culture "had been imported" from the north was denied.[9] Instead, Chu culture was seen as largely indigenous. Ancient Zhou influence was found to be particularly weak in Chu because Shang remnants held out longest in a buffer between the two. The great 1923 Henan archaeological finds were no longer judged distinctive products of the north, but instead were found to have a "style [that] was formed in the state of Chu and then spread northward." By the sixth century B.C., distinctive Chu culture, "among the most advanced of the bronze cultures," spread north, south, and west and "united the southern half of China," "exerting important influences on its neighboring states" (Lawton 1991, xi, 6, 9, 10, 12, 21, 22). During the Warring States period, because of the advance of a Chu army into present-day Yunnan, "Advanced culture and superior productive methods of the Chu kingdom were introduced, greatly promoting . . . economic and cultural development" (*CD*, August 30, 1992).

By 1992 a "hot tide of studying Chu culture" was celebrated in national exhibitions (*PD*, April 20, 1992). Museums sprouted up along the south coast with exhibitions on the ancient trading culture of the south. International conferences were held. Celebrations of Chu civilization became a matter of national moment. In fact, "monographs about virtually every possible aspect of Chu culture appear[ed] regularly" (Lawton 1991, x). Non-Chinese archaeologists at a 1990 international symposium on Chu found that culture powerful and original in ways "unmatched by anything comparable in Western Zhou." The weight of shamanism and unique burial practices clearly distinguished Chu from Zhou (Lawton 1991, 186, 165, 147, 159, 156, 166).

In general, the south, including the Wu people of the Yangzi region, were portrayed as cultural and commercial innovators going back many millennia (*Wu Yue Wenhua* 1991).[10] Some people understood the new national narrative as Chinese culture moving from an ancient northern hinterland origin to a modern southern littoral future. Others note that

> most archaeologists believe that China's culture did not derive from a single root or source and then slowly radiate outward ... ; rather, even before the neolithic period, China's culture was already pluralistic. . . . In the early period of its development, Chinese culture took shape under the mutual influence and impetus of agricultural and pastoral civilizations. (Tu 1991b, 302–3)

Whether focusing on a progressive move to the south, a southern creative origin, or a continuous and dynamic synthetic ecumene, the new identity had no place for a pure northern origin, with continuous northern inspiration legitimating war mobilization to keep impure forces outside of heavily guarded gates.

What was not bought was what the regime sold in school.

> In kindergarten, I learned that Beijing was the capital of the People's Republic of China, the place where Chairman Mao lived. In primary school, I learned that it was an ancient city with a long cultural history, the cradle of China's 5,000-year-old civilization. (Luo 1990, 313)

In the Mao era, which privileged the north, an anti-imperialist discourse had stigmatized the south as the enemy of the nation. On May 18, 1966, Lin Biao legitimated his rise to power in a report to the Politburo of the Chinese Communist Party's Central Committee by claiming that his military would prevent a coup, as the regimes of Nkrumah, Ben Bella, and Sukarno had not. The first major Chinese coup that served as a negative lesson involved the southern state of Chu. In Lin Biao's only reference to the south,

> Rebellions broke out soon after the establishment of the Zhou dynasty.... Within a single state, men killed one another. Shang Zhen, son of Emperor Zhen of the state of Chu, encircled the palace ... to compel Emperor Zhen to commit suicide. . . . Emperor Zhen was forced to kill himself at once. (Kau 1975, 329–30)

Invoking the south as the enemy of a strong, united state is virtually inconceivable in the new national narrative that privileges the south as China's future.

Political consciousness has experienced a transvaluation of values. The force of societal imagination has resisted and reversed statist propaganda, now seen as propaganda.

By 1989, even the democratic movement actually centered in Beijing was often not credited to the north. Instead, Chinese observers noted, even in the far northern city of Shenyang during the 1989 Democracy Movement, "The leader, Ji Futang . . . had originally come . . . from [the southern city of] Wuhan and the south China component was said to be strong. One student at the Northeast Engineering Institute claimed that there was no student from the Northeast on the students' steering committee or think tanks. Some student leaders dismissed people from the Northeast as being 'asleep' " (Gunn 1990, 244–45). In May 1989, Beijing democracy activists found hope in the rumor "that the Shanghai branch of the Communist Party had declared itself separate . . . and that the southern provinces were thinking of breaking with the central government" (Shen 1990, 308). Student broadcasters at Beijing University falsely announced, "The Mayor of Shanghai has joined the pro-democracy demonstrations." "Liang Xiang, the provincial governor of Hainan Island, has proclaimed his disassociation from the government" (Duke 1990, 16). Movement leaders hoped the garrison in Canton would side with them.

In response to the new view that Mao's anti-imperialism was unnecessary or counterproductive, a still-fervent supporter of the now-discredited anti-imperialist view noted, "I heard that some students in Jilin Province said that if we still had the Japanese in Changchun, construction work would definitely be better than now." He angrily retorted, "If we still had the Japanese occupation . . . the population of Changchun would be only 20 percent Chinese because by 1945 60 percent . . . were Japanese" (Yu 1991, 1).[11] Amazingly, a new national narrative that the old guard portrayed as national suicide won over ever more Chinese.[12]

Responding to the eclipse of northern anti-imperialism to keep out aggressors and the rise in its stead of a southern openness to international exchange as hopeful nationalism, the reactionary octogenarian General Wang Zhen acidly commented, "If the Japanese were to invade, these assistant professors would all be on the welcoming committee. . . . [T]he Party and the State will be finished" (Bodman and Wan 1991, 20). General Wang Zhen's denunciation of the promulgators of the new southern project ("You are unpatriotic; you curse your ancestors" [Tu 1991b, 308]) was hopefully understood as a last gasp of reaction on its deathbed. In fact, the anti-Japan rhetoric of the old guard was dismissed as a fraud to obscure the fact that the delegitimated rulers actually abandoned China's anti-Japan nationalism by not obtaining an indemnity for the losses suffered during Japan's brutal war against China so that these actually anti-nationalist Chinese rulers could personally have their family members benefit from private deals with the Japanese at the expense of the suffering Chinese nation. Given the new presuppositions that privilege the historical role of the south, the northern-imagined anti-imperialist nationalism was discredited as hypocritical when it claimed to be anti-Japanese. Representative of this delegitimating discourse is Zhang Jie's 1986 short story "What's Wrong With Him?" in which an enterprising Chinese importer of clothing from Hong Kong is bankrupted by the selfish collusion of corrupt and unpatriotic Chinese officials with sharp Japanese merchants. The northern narrative of having saved the Chinese from Japanese imperialists is now seen as pure fiction.

Already in the Cultural Revolution, when travel revealed that the south was relatively prosperous in comparison to a miserably poor north, it was a conscious matter to punish by dispatching people to the northern hinterlands. Increasingly, southerners presumed that nothing healthy could grow in that hinterland, while the south had long been enriched by absorbing the good of the world. The 1974 Li Yizhe big-character poster in Canton defended the south's introduction of democracy and legal rights in this language: "Exactly like someone from the well-watered south visiting the desert and realizing for the first time the preciousness of water, the broad masses during the Cultural Revolution only realized the preciousness of democratic rights when they were robbed of them."

Powerful hidden forces of change have even altered the consciousness of the ruling elite. Reporter Harrison Salisbury's narrative tying together the memoir impressions of China's ruling elite families and colleagues who spoke with him contrasts Mao and anti-Mao as the ancient northern mythos against the revolutionary south. Mao, a "modern Emperor Qin . . . had unified China and devastated its people." In contrast, Marshall Ye, the leader of the effort to end the Maoist project, "was a native of Canton. . . . Since before the time of Sun Yatsen, Canton had led its own political life, often independent of Beijing. It was the traditional base for insurrection" (Salisbury 1992, 349, 348). Even elites in Beijing shared a discourse in which "the south shall rise again."

A Southern National Narrative

In the northern anti-imperialist mythos, China's choice was dictatorship or disintegration, because only a despotic center could make China strong so foreign forces could not invade and plunder the nation. Regime apologist He Xin (*GMRB* 1990) still sings the old tune. He worries that democratization could undermine "national cohesiveness" and "destroy" prospects for development, threatening both a "splitting and [a] civil war" "whereby politicians and warlords set up their separatist regimes and fight with one another" causing a loss of "Xinjiang and Tibet," whose "rich underground and mineral resources" supposedly make speedy economic growth possible. He Xin finds that China could again "fall into great chaos and disintegration" because the nationalism of Leninist anti-imperialism has failed to forge a common Chinese identity, such that "a Beijinger and a resident from the hinterland provinces . . . can probably be as far apart as heaven and earth." In sum, even to an apologist for the discredited regime, China remains bedeviled by the unresolved and divisive political challenges of the late nineteenth and early twentieth centuries.

The same persistent divisive tendencies are also described by a critic of China's Leninist dictatorship, economist Liu Guoguang (*Caimao Jingji* 1990, 96). The "visible phenomena" he finds in China's dynamic is "regionalism, total chaos, and the back and forth central versus local power struggle." Canton scholar He Bochuan notes the prospect of "chaos and division of the nation," finding that China's "unification is only superficial" and that "in the age of regional economies which lies ahead ... it will be difficult to avoid conflict between the regions and the central government" (He 1991, 155).[13] Hence a foreign scholar who does "not see regionalism in China," who concludes that "separatism in the core areas is not likely to become a problem" (Womack 1992, 181), is at odds with the shared perception of the widest spectrum of Chinese. A democratic opponent of China's Leninist dictatorship can even see the strength of centrifugal forces as a hopeful opportunity.

> As soon as Deng Xiaoping dies, central control will weaken and local forces will rise, Guangdong, Fujian and Shanghai will ask for more democracy.... The strong autonomous tendency among local authorities is not entirely a bad thing. Maybe it can put an end to the oligarchy in China. (Fang 1990, 5)

In China, according to Harvard professor Wei-ming Tu, "the center no longer has the ability, insight, or legitimate authority to dictate the agenda for cultural China." "Either the center will bifurcate or, as is more likely, the [coastal] periphery will come to set the economic and cultural agenda for the center, thereby undermining its political effectiveness" (Tu 1991a, 27, 28, 12). Ever more Chinese imagine a more open future as the heir to a more open past.

The Chinese scholar Chen Kun in 1981 denounced the tyrannical impositions of the Qin Dynasty of 221 B.C. that unified a large state, slaughtered intellectuals, and built the Great Wall to keep others out. "Qin people did not have time to grieve for themselves. Their descendants did. The descendants grieved but did not learn. Later generations were made to grieve for the descendants again." For Chen, an autocratic China is not a strong nation. Rather, it is an inhuman one. Chen equates "autocracy and atrocity" (Schwarcz 1986–87, 594, 601). Mao's identification with a continuous tradition of a strong exclusionary state is thus exploded.

In the new national narrative, as described by the Chinese scholar Tang Yijie, China is not the nation of the Qin dictators, with supposed strength found by hiding behind a Great Wall. Instead "Chinese ... vitality" lies in an "open attitude toward foreign cultural influence," as exemplified by the hybrid vigor inherent in China's millennia-long absorption of Indian Buddhism. "Therefore, all purist talk of 'native culture' or 'national essence' cannot but harm the development of national culture and reflects the withering of the vitality of a nation's culture" (ibid., 603). Hence a project of military defense to wall out alien influences actually weakens the Chinese nation.

Anthropology, archaeology, and history have been revolutionized so that Chinese are no longer imagined as a people descended from an isolated, northern-plain culture but instead are seen as the consequence of the southern Chu and other cultures, each involved outside of China, all merging with the others. There is no center in the north that can spread. The focus now is on the normality of decentralization, the power in local creativity, a need for confederation premised on federal divisions of power rather than military concentrations of power.

In the new cultural consciousness, the identity of Mao with the *ancien régime* that hid behind walls reveals both as reactionary and antipopular, the antithesis of what a vital, future-oriented national community requires. Mao's anti-imperialist roots are ridiculed:

> [T]he cultural conservative Gou Hongming ... wore a long pigtail down his back ... and mocked May Fourth activists by calling the proponents of democracy "demo-crazy." That is what Mao thought about intellectuals as well—crazy and dispensable. (Schwarcz 1992, 7)

Mao and his project are redefined as at one with the most reactionary, outlandish, narrow nativists, from superstitious Boxer rebels to Qing Dynasty diehards.

In contrast, a new national project seems a palpable reality in a mobile south China that reaches out through the Chinese diaspora to the world. What Chinese are increasingly conscious of is not a single northern Han people who filled an empty space, but a land long peopled by plural groups with "extreme linguistic heterogeneity ... mainly characteristic of the southeastern coastal provinces in an area extending roughly from Shanghai, through Guangdong, and somewhat into Guangxi" (Cohen 1991, 115). Chinese are reimagining themselves as diverse, not homogeneous, not a nation that is supposedly 95 percent Han. "The regionally defined groups ... Cantonese, Shanghaiese, and Taiwanese, including those living overseas—have obvious ethnic differences in speech, dress, customs, religious beliefs, and so on.... [T]he difference between two Han groups can ... be more pronounced than that between a Han and a so-called minority nationality group" (Wu 1991, 167). The Chinese press comments about how different regions prefer different teas or celebrate holidays differently. It is difference that catches popular attention. It is how people talk and see.

Given this Chinese reconstruction of national identity, the southern narrative could become a self-fulfilling prophecy. Chinese find that this more open south embodies "littoral vitality" and that "the coastal cities on the lower Yangtze River and ... the provinces of Fujian and Guangdong" will "become increasingly internationalized," a "transnational and cosmopolitan" part of the Pacific Rim (Lee 1991, 224).

So much is it a presupposition that the southern people, understood as the heirs of the state of Chu, are revitalizing China that even the official press describes the dynamism of southern people as "a history of leading change in China." "As early as in the spring and autumn period (770–476 B.C.), the Chu Kingdom already offered fertile soil for the 'Chu culture' whose salient features have doubtlessly influenced people in today's Hunan Province, the intellectuals in particular." (Historians accept Hunan intellectuals as quintessential true patriots.) The purported "industrious" and "pioneering" nature of such people was said to have been reinforced by "massive migration" that brought vigor to the area and by "the development of waterways for transportation," turning the area "into a traffic hub" (CD, March 26, 1991). The presupposition is that nonmobile, rooted northerners, toiling away on ancestral land, are obstacles to progress. A renewed Chinese nation must build on a national vision imagined in southern terms of openness, mobility, and decentralization.

Contrasting north/south experiences are interpreted as causes of two national projects, anti-imperialist centralized dictatorship and open decentralist confederation. In the twentieth century, desperate north China peasants fled to northern and western frontiers. Fixated on the misery of leaving home to dwell in poor, minority, and climatically harsh regions, northern oral culture and folk songs celebrated the virtues of staying home with the family, thus embracing Mao's conquest of state power as ending their painful dilemmas where "a poor house is hard to abandon, one's land is hard to leave."

In contrast, poor southerners were imagined as having fled overseas. Their family members who stayed home in south China experienced economic benefits from overseas remittances and openness to the world. The northerners pushed minorities off land and gave themselves good conscience for their racist chauvinism in terms of ethnonationalist superiority. Southerners, in contrast, defined patriotism to harmonize with continuous ties to a non-Chinese world. The southerner was open to a world of market, money, mobility, and other people. The conflict between north and south is imagined as a conflict between closed and open, intolerant and tolerant, the failed project of a self-wounding Leninist anti-imperialism and the rising project of a successful nation (Cheng 1988). The northern project is seen as a dead-end error.

The experience now is one of taking off blinders. Ever more Chinese see reality as do southerners. Traditionally, north China cities were built around an enclosed governmental or aristocratic center. The emperor's back was literally turned to the merchants' quarter. By the Tang Dynasty, the cities of the south, in contrast, were bustling, irregular commercial centers with numerous foreign visitors. The north–south split seems historical, profound, and obvious.

A happier future is imagined as the fruit of the southern project.[14] With its facilitating of a dynamic commodity economy of material progress, "Guangzhou could be the cradle of China's new culture," proclaimed a Cantonese analyst in 1986. The city's glory, wrote Cantonese historian Ye Chansheng, came from its distance over the centuries from northern "feudal influences." The south was popular, not elitist; democratic, not aristocratic.

By the 1990s, people in Canton were the biggest newspaper-reading audience in China. Chinese elsewhere sought out Canton newspapers. Cantonese intellectuals projected a new national culture, premised on Canton's open, plural, entrepreneurial, amalgamated, mass culture. The south has a common print culture giving voice to a shared narrative of a hopeful future, a new national consciousness in embryo.

Inside families, southern children are being taught to hate cruel northerners. The south, southerners now say, has always been more advanced than the north. In fact, southerners find the north has lived off the earnings of the south. The grain of the south even fed the north. The south has always been open to trade and other peoples. China has been held back by northerners who are indigent, insular, and ignorant.

In Song times, southerners note, reform was needed. The southern reformist Wang Anshi opposed the northern reactionary Sima Guang. Unfortunately, the Song court was dominated by northerners who sided with the reactionary Sima Guang. The south lost. Reform was blocked. All China consequently suffered. China was conquered in the north by the Liao, Jin, and Xisha, and then by the Mongols. Blood, language, and culture were intermixed in the north. Teachers of Cantonese tell students that Cantonese is closer to the original Chinese language, while the tongue spoken up north is more of a foreign imposition.

When the Mongols momentarily conquered the south, they graded their subjects into four tiers. First came the Bannermen, the Mongols themselves. Next came the colored-eye (*Simu*), people of the west seen as coming from places where eyes were not black. Third were the mixed groups of the north previously conquered by the Liao, Jin, and Xisha. These were labeled Han. The actual survivors of the ancient Han era, now in the south, often the descendents of Chu, were called southerners. They were the true Chinese, an advanced people, the hope of a revitalized China.

The resurgent Chinese Ming Dynasty, based in the south, envisioning the north as an area for many centuries corrupted by non-Chinese rule, decreed that all Chinese return to the dress of the Tang Dynasty and that Mongol costumes and surnames be discontinued. When the Ming capital was moved to Beijing to help sinicize alien northern territory, the north became economically dependent, culturally conservative, and politically bureaucratic; while the south monetized its economy, expanded its trade, and increased its urban component. South China benefited greatly from silver carried there through international trade. The rulers in the north never figured out how to reform to compete in that world economy and instead increased the tax burden on productive people. The Manchu conquest and the subsequent Mao era are imagined as the consequence and continuation of a politically bureaucratic, culturally conservative, economically unreformed northern rule.

Thus it seems natural that modern ideas and practices were first established in China's south; the north's conservatism led the northern people to reject modern ways. The southern reformer Tan Sitong, a hero of the young who identify reactionary post-Mao elders with the Empress Dowager, used an eclectic cosmopolitan ethos to attack Confucian hierarchy. Reactionaries in the government, trying to hold power in the 1990s by promoting Confucianism, opposing heterodoxy, and fearing the south's successful opening to the world economy, seem caught in a time warp that would leave the Chinese people ever farther behind in the rapidly developing world.

Defensive, anxious, Mao-style anti-imperialist nationalism is now revealed as a false path to suit a particular and parochial political project. The recent transvaluation of values reveals some of the repressed political alternatives that the anti-imperialist myth made invisible or treasonous.

The growing presuppositional popularity of the new national history does not mean that China will democratize, or that a southern-based consciousness will establish a new national polity, or that the nation will split, or even that the anti-imperialist reactionaries legitimated by the old northern narrative will be deposed. Political culture in itself is not decisive. But a new cultural consciousness popularly legitimates political projects that are more diverse than imagined by observers still mesmerized by the old northern narrative. These possibilities include confederated democracy or an open, southern-based state. While politics will decide among numerous contending projects, the southern narrative that privileges Chu and peripheralizes Qin is ever more potent.

Scholars of national identity tend to find that people engaged in a political struggle are likely to identify with one national history or another, to choose between perceived poles in an oppositional binary. Democracy Movement representative Chen Ziming wrote in early 1991 while in prison, "I cast aside . . . serving the state of Qin in the morning and Chu in the evening" (*AW* 1992, 16). The data assembled for this chapter suggest that choosing Chu over Qin is not an individual idiosyncrasy but a broadly shared identity transformation that may be full of significance for China's national future.

Notes

1. I think the correct answers are: (1) Qing tong qi, (2) Song-tsen Gompa and Chengwen, (3) Zhu Yuanzhang (Ming Taizu), (4) Suspension of taxes on grain, (5) Sanliyuan, (6) Almost 1.5 million, (10) On Protracted War, Quick Victory, National Defeat.

2. There are even claims of a genetic boundary around the Yangzi River (*Proceedings*, n.d.).

3. For the importance of museums to national identity formation, see Anderson 1991.

4. A forthcoming book from Harvard University Press by David Apter and Tony Saich offers an explanation of how, in the Yanan era, the Maoist mythos came to seem truth incarnate.

5. For a sketch of this process in Russia, see Remnick 1992.

6. Actually, there have been winners from Africa, the Caribbean, and South America.

7. Southerner Mao Zedong complained of his earlier mistreatment by northern speakers. "They had no time to listen to an assistant librarian speaking southern dialect" (Snow 1984, 55).

8. This north–south peasant opposition is captured in Siu 1990.

9. In contrast, Kang Yuwei saw Chu people as having become Han Chinese in ancient times as Manchu supposedly had in modern times (Duara 1992, 25).

10. This book, *Wu Yue Culture*, depicts the independent power of Wu people in the Yangzi Valley going back to 1100 B.C., including a major influence from exchanges with non-Chinese peoples. In contrast to this narrative of the dynamic, open, and commercial south of Chu and Wu Yue, Han Dynasty historian Sima Qian characterized the region as "large territory sparsely populated where people eat rice and drink fish soup . . . where people enjoy self-sufficiency without commerce. The place is fertile and suffers neither famine nor hunger. Hence the people are lazy and poor and do not bother to accumulate wealth" (Lung-chang Young 1988, 42).

11. "A provincial official of a Northeastern province informed the author that during previous student demonstrations some student leaders had openly said that Manchuria would have developed faster if it had remained under Japanese rule" (Ch'i 1991, 320).

12. Likewise, Taiwanese national identity includes the notion, rejected by Jiang's anti-imperialist heirs, that Taiwan has done so well in part because of the Japanese and would have done better yet had the Japanese stayed and anti-imperialist Chinese never come.

13. In general, "newly acquired financial power has caused them [regional leaders] to identify themselves more and more with local interests." In particular, the regional military has had to cooperate with these interests to make military enterprises profitable. "Another reason why the military has sought to improve its ties with local administrations is that demobilized servicemen have to rely on local governments to obtain employment" (Fu 1992, 81, 78).

14. The next two paragraphs draw on White and Cheng 1993.

References

Anderson, Benedict. 1991 [1989]. *Imagined Communities* (London: Verso).
Anthems of Defeat: Crackdown in Hunan Province, 1989–92 1992 (New York: Asia Watch).
Asia Watch (AW). 4.18, June 10, 1992.
Baixing (Hong Kong) 1992 (March 1). Translated in *Inside China Mainland* 14.5, May 1992.
Barmé, Geremie, and Linda, Jaivin, eds. 1992. *New Ghosts, Old Dreams* (New York: Random House).
Berninghausen, John, and Ted Huters. 1976. "Introductory Essay" to "The Development of Revolutionary Literature in China." *Bulletin of Concerned Asian Scholars* (January–March 1976).
Bodman, Richard, and Pin P. Wan, eds. 1991. *Deathsong* (Ithaca: Cornell University East Asia Program).
Caimao Jingji. 1990 (March 11). Translated in JPRS-CAR–90–049, July 11, 1990.
Chang, K. C. 1992. Letter to Edward Friedman (July 31).
Chen Kuiyuan. 1991. "Study Marxist Nationality Theory and Correctly Understand National Issues in the New Period." *Shijian* (October 1). Translated in JPRS-CAR- 92–021, April 16, 1992.
Cheng Tiejun, Ph.D. dissertation, SUNY-Binghamton, citation of "Xibu zai Yimin" [There is a migration to the West] *Xinhua Wenzhai*, No. 10 (1988), pp. 98–119.

Ch'i Hsi-sheng. 1991. *Politics of Disillusionment* (Armonk, NY: M. E. Sharpe).

China Daily (CD). March 26, 1991.

China Daily (CD). April 28, 1992.

China Daily (CD) (Supplement). August 30, 1992.

Cohen, Myron. 1991. "Being Chinese: The Peripheralization of Traditional Identity." *Daedalus* 120.2 (Spring).

Conner, Walker. 1984. *The National Question in Marxist-Leninist Theory and Strategy* (Princeton: Princeton University Press).

Crossley, Pamela Kyle. 1990. *Orphan Warriors* (Princeton: Princeton University Press).

DeFrancis, John. 1984. *The Chinese Language* (Honolulu: University of Hawaii Press).

Deng Xiaoping. 1985. *Build Socialism with Chinese Characteristics* (Beijing: Foreign Languages Press).

Dikötter, Frank. 1992. *The Discourse of Race in Modern China* (Stanford: Stanford University Press).

Duara, Prasenjit. 1992. *Rescuing History from the Nation-State* (Chicago: Center for Psychosocial Studies).

Duke, Michael. 1989. "Reinventing China." *Issues and Studies* 25.8 (August), pp. 29–153.

———. 1990. *The Iron House* (Clayton, UT: Peregrine Smith Books).

———. 1993. "Thoughts on Politics and Critical Paradigms in Modern Chinese Literature Studies." *Modern China* 19.1 (January), pp. 41–70.

Fang Lizhi. 1990. *Free China Journal* (August 2).

Friedman, Edward, Paul Pickowicz, and Mark Selden. 1991. *Chinese Village, Socialist State* (New Haven: Yale University Press).

Frolic, Michael. 1980. *Mao's People* (Cambridge: Harvard University Press).

Fu Feng-cheng. 1992. "The Decentralization of Peking's Economic Management and Its Impact on Foreign Investment." *Issues and Studies* (February).

Gellner, Ernest. 1983. *Nations and Nationalism* (Ithaca: Cornell University Press).

Geographical Knowledge, No. 1. 1992. Republished in *People's Daily* (Overseas Edition), February 6, 1992.

Glunin, Vladimir, and Alexander Grigorev. 1993. "A Conception of China's Recent History." *Far Eastern Affairs* (Moscow), No. 3.

Goodman, David. 1981. *Beijing Street Voices: The Poetry and Politics of China's Democratic Movement* (London: Marion Boyars).

Guangming ribao (GMRB). 1990 (June 12), p. 4. Translated in JPRS-CAR–90–049, July 11, 1990, pp. 13–19.

Guldin, Gregory, ed. 1990. *Anthropology in China* (Armonk, NY: M. E. Sharpe).

Gunn, Anne. 1990. "Tell the World About Us." *The Australian Journal of Chinese Studies*, No. 24 (July).

He Bochuan. 1991. *China on the Edge* (San Francisco: China Books and Periodicals).

Herdan, Innes. 1992. *The Pen and the Sword: Literature and Revolution in Modern China* (London: Zed Books).

Horowitz, David. 1985. *Ethnic Groups in Conflict* (Berkeley: University of California Press).

Hu Sheng. 1955 [1948]. *Imperialism and Chinese Politics* (Peking: Foreign Languages Press).

Huters, Ted. 1989. "Between Praxis and Essence." In Arif Dirlik and Maurice Meisner, eds., *Marxism and the Chinese Experience* (Armonk, NY: M. E. Sharpe), pp. 316–37.

Kau, Michael Y. M., ed. 1975. *The Lin Biao Affair* (Armonk, NY: M. E. Sharpe).

Larson, Wendy, and Richard Kraus. 1989. "China's Writers, The Nobel Prize, and The International Politics of Literature." *The Australian Journal of Chinese Affairs*, No. 21 (January), pp. 143–60.

Lawton, Thomas, ed. 1991. *New Perspectives on Chu Culture During the Eastern Zhou Period* (Princeton: Princeton University Press).

Lee, Leo Ou-fan. 1991. "On the Margins of the Chinese Discourse." *Daedalus* 120.2 (Spring).

Leung, John K., and Michael Y. M. Kau, eds. 1992. *The Writings of Mao Zedong 1949–1976*, Vol. II. (Armonk, NY: M. E. Sharpe).

Lin Yih-tang, comp. n.d. *What They Say: A Collection of Current Chinese Underground Publications* (Taipei: Institute of Current Chinese Studies).

Lu Xueyi. 1991. "Several Problems in the Study of Current Rural Social Strata." *Gaige*, No. 6 (November 20), pp. 157–63. Translated in JPRS-CAR–92–093, April 24, 1992.

Luo, Zi-ping. 1990. *A Generation Lost* (New York: Avon).

New York Times (*NYT*). 1992. (April 23).

1978 National College Entrance Examination of the People's Republic of China. 1979 (Washington: U.S. Department of Health, Education and Welfare's Office of Education).

People's Daily (*PD*). 1992. (overseas edition, April 20).

Perry, Elizabeth. 1989. "State and Society in Contemporary China." *World Politics* 41.4 (July).

Proceedings of the National Academy of Science (USA). 85, pp. 6002–6.

Olsen, John. 1992. "Archeology in China Today." *China Exchange News* 20.2 (Summer), pp. 3–6.

Qian Jiaoju. 1986. *Qishi Niande Jingji* [The Experience of 70 Years] (Hong Kong: Post Cultural Enterprises).

Qiao Huantian. 1987. "What Were the Effects on Modern Chinese Society of the Invasion of the Western Powers?" *Renmin ribao* (June 26).

Remnick, David. 1992. "Defending the Faith." *The New York Review* (May 14), pp. 44–51.

Ruan Ming. 1992. "The Political and Economic Situation in China after the June 4th Massacre of 1989," *A Changing China* 2.3 (Summer).

Sage, Steven. 1992. *Ancient Sichuan and the Unification of China* (Albany: State University of New York Press).

Salisbury, Harrison. 1992. *The New Emperors* (Boston: Little Brown).

Schneider, Laurence. 1976. "National Essence and the New Intelligentsia." In Charlotte Furth, ed., *The Limits of Change* (Cambridge: Harvard University Press), pp. 57–89.

Schwarcz, Vera. 1986–87. "Behind a Partially Open Door." *Pacific Affairs* (Winter).

———. 1992. "Memory and Commemoration." In Jeffrey Wasserstrom and Elizabeth Perry, eds., *Popular Protest and Political Culture in Modern China* (Boulder: Westview Press).

Seymour, James, ed. 1980. *The Fifth Modernization: China's Human Rights Movement, 1978–1979* (Stanfordville, NY: Human Rights Publishing Company).

Shen, Tong. 1990. *Almost A Revolution* (Boston: Houghton Mifflin).

Siu, Helen, ed. 1990. *Furrows* (Stanford: Stanford University Press).

Snow, Edgar. 1984. *Red Star Over China* (New York: Vintage).

Sun Lung-kee. 1992. "Social Psychology in the Late Qing Period." *Modern China* 15.3 (July), pp. 235–62.

Thorp, Robert. 1992. " 'Let the Past Serve the Present': The Ideological Claims of Cultural Relics Work." *China Exchange News* 20.2 (Summer), pp. 16–19.

Tu Wei-ming. 1991a. "Cultural China: The Periphery as the Center." *Daedalus* 120.2 (Spring).

———. 1991b. *"Heshang*: Whither Chinese Culture?" In Richard Bodman and Pin P. Wan, eds., *Deathsong of the River* (Ithaca: Cornell University East Asia Program).

Vogel, Ezra. 1989. *One Step Ahead in China* (Cambridge: Harvard University Press).

White, Lynn, and Li Cheng. 1993. "China Coastal Identities." In Lowell Dittmer and Samuel Kim, eds., *China's Quest for National Identity* (Ithaca: Cornell University Press), pp. 154–93.

Womack, Brantley. 1992. *The Australian Journal of Chinese Affairs*, No. 28 (July).

Wu, David Yen-ho. 1991. "The Construction of Chinese and Non-Chinese Identities." *Daedalus* 120.2 (Spring).

Wu Yue Wenhua. 1991. (Shenyang: Liaoning Education Publishing House).

Young, Crawford. 1976. *The Politics of Cultural Pluralism* (Madison: University of Wisconsin Press).

———, ed. 1993. *The Rising Tide of Cultural Pluralism* (Madison: University of Wisconsin Press).

Young Lung-chang. 1988. "Regional Stereotypes in China." *Chinese Studies in History* 2.3 (Summer).

Yu Xinyan. 1991. *Xuexi yu Yanjiu* (May 9). Translated in JPRS-CAR–91–052, September 23, 1991.

Zhang Jie. 1987. "What's Wrong With Him?" *Renditions* 27–28 (Spring-Autumn).

Zhang Tianxin. 1993. Review of Yang Gongsu, *Diplomatic History of the Late Qing Dynasty* (in Chinese) (Beijing: Beijing University Press, 1993). In *China Daily*, September 20.

Zhang Xianliang. 1986. *Half of Man Is Woman*. Translated by Martha Avery. (New York: Ballantine).

Zhang Zhengming, ed. 1987. *Chu Wen-hua shih* (Shanghai: Shanghai People's Publishing House).

Zhu Huaxin and Cao Huanrong. 1987. "The Historical Position of China's Reform," *Renmin ribao* (October 6 and 7). Translated in JPRS-CAR–87–056, November 9.

Part Three

After Socialist
Anti-Imperialism

Chapter 7

Anti-Imperialism in Chinese Foreign Policy

Nationalism

The Communist Party led by Mao Zedong that conquered state power in China in 1949 seemed the embodiment of heroic anti-imperialist nationalism. A portrait of the Red Army as China's patriotic force contrasts its brave and bold response to imperialist invaders with northeastern (Manchurian) warlords' surrender to Japan in 1931 and the failure of Chiang Kai-shek (Jiang Jieshi) and his Nationalist Party government to block the barbarous rape of Nanking (Nanjing) by the Japanese military. From this viewpoint, the only fighting patriots in China, the Communists, waged a courageous guerrilla war to protect China's people from the Japanese. This nationalist tale of modern Chinese resistance to foreign marauders is imagined as at one with the struggle of China's people throughout history to defend their land from foreign invaders. It links time, place, and people in a unifying grand narrative that begins with the building of the Great Wall of stone in ancient times to defend against wave after wave of barbarian plunderers, goes on to describe the successful fourteenth-century resistance of what became the Ming Dynasty to its Mongol conquerors (the Yuan Dynasty), and ends with the unifying liberation of China by a people's army—China's modern Great Wall of Iron.[1] This grand narrative of patriotic history is given its modern origin in 1839, with a failed popular defense against Britain's barbaric attempt to force civilized Chinese to buy British opium. This losing Chinese effort carried the historic lesson that Chinese should not try to imitate the seafaring pirate-merchants; Britain could not be defeated with ships on the sea, but on

Reprinted from Samuel Kim, ed., *China and the World* (Boulder, CO: Westview Press, 1994), by permission of Westview Press.

the nation's sacred soil invaders could be submerged and drowned in a sea of popular resistance.[2] A force that could mobilize Chinese villagers could defend China's independence. In this narrative of Chinese Communist national legitimation, the imperialist armies of Japan are finally defeated in 1945, when the Red Army of the Soviet Union comes to the aid of China's Communists, the people's guerrilla resisters, and helps to liberate Manchuria from the Japanese. The victory of Mao's anti-imperialist forces was the victory of an international socialist mission that alone was capable of unleashing the might of the Chinese people in pursuit of its independence. As Mao put it in 1949, at long last the Chinese people stood up.

Any historian can easily poke large holes in this pretended seamless fabric. In fact, ancient China rose through trade and cultural exchange with surrounding peoples. About half the students in the National Academy in the Tang Dynasty capital (today Xian) were foreign. The Great Wall was completed by the Ming Dynasty and reflects a self-inflicted injury to Chinese development—a nativistic and isolationist turn that cost the Chinese people the potential benefits of openness to the early industrial revolution and thereby made them vulnerable to foreign attack. Modern astronomers were executed so that the emperor alone could comprehend and command the heavens. The Communist Soviet Union helped detach Mongolia from the Chinese empire in the 1920s and thereafter fought to hold onto special (imperialist?) privileges in Manchuria. It was the United States that defeated Japan in World War II, in alliance with Chiang's Nationalists, who fought brilliantly in Burma. Many non-Communist forces in China courageously resisted the Japanese military occupiers. By the 1990s, as Chinese nationalism was being redefined, even Deng Xiaoping blamed Ming Dynasty isolationism for China's modern weakness.[3] The controlled and censored film industry of China could, in the 1990s, present movies of non-Communist anti-Japanese resistance. Mao-style anti-imperialism has lost its credibility. An overview of Chinese foreign policy as an attempt to respond to imperialist challenges shows that Mao's policy perspective injured the Chinese people and is being discarded.

Understanding the degree to which the notion of communism as the national essence pursuing independence from imperialism is a temporally constructed and temporarily legitimating narrative makes it clear that the anti-imperialist national project depended on maintaining the popular credibility of this empowering mythos, celebrating and miming the nativistic and isolationist aspects of the Ming Dynasty. Mao identified with the founder of the Ming.[4] This narrative of total mobilization for a war of defense is increasingly less capable of winning the allegiance of patriotic Chinese. In an era in which world-market competitiveness seems to define national success, Maoist anti-imperialism engenders a crisis of post-Mao legitimation. In the post-Mao era, a new national project is emerging from the renewed efforts of China's people, to benefit from the common wealth of the entire human race, even to the point of purchasing potentially profitable businesses as far away from China as in Peru and the United States. How can one legitimate anti-imperialism when China has become the top investor in the century-old British colony of Hong Kong?

Independence

"The Chinese people have stood up" is Mao's best-remembered phrase. With the establishment of the People's Republic of China on October 1, 1949, rulers and ruled looked forward to freedom from the incursions of imperialist powers. The new foreign policy makers saw themselves as engaged in a continuing struggle to free China from and defend China against imperialism in all its aspects— economic exploiters, military invaders, and cultural polluters. To counter imperialist challenges, a Communist Party dictatorship would strive to make China completely independent; that is, economically self-reliant, militarily strong, and in matters of values and beliefs, pure. Freedom was sought not for individuals but for the new nation-state. In political practice, this meant all power to the dictatorial rulers of the Leninist state.[5]

State leaders had to transform their anti-imperialist project into workable policies. In the post–World War II, bipolar, Cold War world, Mao concluded that China needed to ally with the Soviet Union to defend against the imperialist United States, allied with revanchist Japan, and with counter-revolutionary armies loyal to the defeated side in China's civil war.

Compromising with the Soviet Union

Mao Zedong and the other rulers of Communist China believed that state power had been redefined by the U.S. use of atomic weapons in war. Even before establishing themselves in the restored national capital of Beijing, Mao's followers sent agents to an anti-American peace conference in Paris, the declared purpose of which was to ban the use of nuclear weapons. Ironically, the agents' mission was purchasing material so that China could one day build its own nuclear weapons. At the same time, Chinese agents approached Chinese scientists and engineers abroad, mainly in the United States, to persuade them to return home to work as patriots on a Chinese atomic bomb project. Mao's ruling group found that to be a great power in the age of nuclear weapons required possessing nuclear weaponry. Only the most advanced weapons would free the Chinese people from fear of invaders or blackmailing threats.[6] The Soviet Union was open to an alliance with China because World War II ended with the United States occupying Japan and turning its military might in Japan toward Russia.

In addition to placing a high priority on restoring China's dignity and greatness through military might (a project that soon involved Chinese in learning from the Communist Party dictatorship in the Soviet Union, which exploded its first nuclear weapon in 1949), the new Chinese ruling group believed that it had to act immediately to stave off direct foreign threats of aggression on behalf of counter-revolution. Its concern was that the United States might try to overthrow the Leninist socialists and restore to power the defeated Nationalist Party led by Jiang Jieshi.[7] Mao Zedong's belief in the need to resist imperialists supporting counter-revolutionary forces reflected his understanding of both global revolutionary history and Chinese anti-imperialist goals. For Mao, all of the modern revolutions—the 1789 French Revolution, the 1871 Paris Commune, the 1917 Bolshevik Revolution, the Spanish republic (crushed by international fascism in the 1930s), and the Greek partisans of the 1940s—had been attacked by foreign-sponsored armies allied with domestic counter-revolutionaries. In addition, China had since its origin been engaged in a continuous struggle to defend itself against invaders. Division at home made China vulnerable to foreign threats. Only the Leninist one-party dictatorship could resist imperialism by mobilizing Chinese resources against it. Consequently, anti-imperialist China's top priority was to smash all opposition to Mao's correct line and to prepare to defend China's revolution against expected imperialist invaders. This in 1949 meant the United States, which was seen as establishing itself next door to China in Japan.

Mao worried about imperialist America aggressively joining with a revanchist militarist Japan and Jiang Jieshi's counter-revolutionaries. Consequently, on Valentine's Day 1950 China signed a pact with the Soviet Union that committed the latter to come to China's aid should it be attacked by Japan or any nation allied with Japan. This was a formula that appealed to popular anti-Japanese sentiment in China while actually targeting the United States, understood as not merely capitalist but a re-embodiment of the barbarian invaders who had threatened China from time immemorial. The new regime's legitimation was based on its ability to defend against foreign enemies to China's national independence.[8]

The Korean War

War in Korea between June 1950 and July 1953 tested the alliance of Beijing and Moscow against Washington. The Communist forces in northern Korea were beholden to the occupying army from the Soviet Union for their very existence. The Korean Communists[9] sought Moscow's support for a war to liberate the south from military occupation by U.S. imperialism and its client regime, headed by the patriotic tyrant Syngman Rhee. According to the 1980s memoirs of Russians and Koreans involved in the 1945–50 events initiating the war, agents from Moscow planned the war, including a withdrawal of Russian advisers just prior to the initial attack to conceal their involvement, but Stalin checked with Mao before giving North Korea's dictator, Kim Il Sung, the go-ahead.[10] The Chinese allowed Korean troops then fighting with China's Communist armies to join the armies that invaded South Korea on June 25, 1950. A mock attack was staged to look like a thrust from the south so that the north could camouflage its offensive with a pretext, as the Nazis did in 1939 against Poland. The United States nonetheless won United Nations approval for military action to defend South Korea against aggression, and General Douglas MacArthur headed the UN force.

In August 1950, when U.S. forces finally held against the North Korean Communist armies at a beachhead in southeast Korea, Mao began to worry that the north was overextended and a U.S. counterattack was possible. Concerned that the United States would move on to threaten China's revolutionary independence, he began sounding out colleagues about how China should respond.[11] Most Chinese leaders felt that the nation should build itself up before taking on the United States—that the Chinese people were exhausted from a century of war, plunder, and turmoil and needed tranquility. But Mao believed in getting the inevitable war with the United States over with as soon as possible. After MacArthur's maneuvers in September had isolated the North Korean forces from the rear, the general in October ordered a march north toward the Chinese border. Chinese signals aimed at deterring this advance went unheeded.[12] Because Stalin did not want to provoke America, Mao was largely on his own when he committed China to send troops into Korea to fight the largely U.S. troops. The United States responded by persuading the UN to declare China an aggressor, backing Jiang Jieshi's regime on Taiwan, and intensifying its embargo against China. As Communists in China saw it, the imperialist United States had intervened in China's civil war on the side of reaction in an attempt to reverse the verdict of history.

The logic of events seemed to lend credibility to Mao's political project of anti-imperialist war communism. Industry on the coast, being bombed and blockaded by Jiang's forces, was moved north and inland. A campaign to ferret out counter-revolutionaries who might aid imperialist invaders targeted southern elites. Cultural pollution in the form of foreign missionary education was brutally uprooted. Schools were reorganized away from U.S. forms (treated as subversively capitalist) in the direction of a Soviet model, called socialist. All of China was to be mobilized to secure China's independence from imperialist enemies.

A long, bloody stalemate and war of attrition ensued in which almost half a million Chinese gave their lives. The U.S. president, Harry Truman, tried to restrict the fighting to Korea. In 1951 he fired General MacArthur, who had insisted on expanding the war into China, using Jiang Jieshi's troops from Taiwan, treating the war as global, and rejecting limitations on weaponry and targets ("refusing to fight with one hand tied behind one's back"). Had MacArthur's policies prevailed, Mao's worst fears would have been realized. Although specialists still debate how close MacArthur came to succeeding, it was close enough to strengthen the hold of Maoist presuppositions on Chinese patriots.

Even after the war was stalemated in mid-1951, an end to the fighting still took another two years to negotiate. Mao insisted that China's dignity required that all Chinese prisoners be repatriated to the motherland—that they never be surrendered to imperialism. Truman insisted that prisoners on both sides be free to choose not to return to totalitarian control. Finally, in late 1952, Mao decided that the draining war in Korea was increasing China's dependence on the Soviet Union and delaying China's emergence as a great power, and therefore he conceded that the war in Korea could end with stalemate and free choice by prisoners on repatriation. But Truman could not meet China halfway. Only a Republican president might have the anti-Communist credibility to compromise with Communists in China.

In November 1952, Dwight Eisenhower was elected to replace Truman as president, and immediately after taking office he offered an exchange of wounded prisoners. Mao readily agreed, and disengagement began. The final obstacle to peace was the opposition of the South Korean government, which wanted the United States to fight on at all costs. The United States allowed Mao's China to pound the South Korean anti-armistice forces into submission— an early signal that on a pure realpolitik basis, with neither Beijing nor Washington benefiting from war in Asia with each other, the interests of the two countries overlapped. This overlap was obscured by China's belief that only an all-out defense, including a willingness to risk nuclear attack, had saved China and the U.S. assumption that it was the threat of nuclear attack that had forced China to compromise in Korea.[13]

The Bandung Era

True to Communist anti-imperialist nationalism, Mao began to yield to pressures from the Chinese military for military action to liberate the southern offshore islands held by the counter-revolutionary forces of Jiang Jieshi.[14] The ultimate goal of the Leninists in Beijing was reunifying China, including Taiwan, and eliminating any remaining reactionary pretenders to Chinese state power that denied the People's Republic its rightful place as a great power. They also increasingly identified with a global anti-imperialist mission given meaning by third world independence, seeking to participate in the first conference of independent states of Africa and Asia held in Bandung, Indonesia, in 1955. Moreover, to obtain the material goods required to construct an independent, strong, and prosperous China—one that would have the wherewithal to contribute to a global struggle against imperialism—the government in Beijing welcomed trade with any partner. This set of policies is often characterized as united front, peaceful coexistence, or détente. It included overtures to and talks with the United States in Geneva and Warsaw—participating in the 1954 Geneva conference to settle the wars against French imperialism in Indochina, in which China had armed Ho Chi Minh's forces and urged similar compromises in a split Vietnam as in a split Korea. China's independence could be obtained by policies other than war mobilization.

These Bandung-era policies were still completely congruent with China's great-power, anti-imperialist ambitions. Mao's government cooperated with the

Soviet Union to obtain nuclear weaponry and stepped up efforts to allow China to work on its own for nuclear bombs. It tried to keep imperialist forces away from China's borders in Korea, in formerly French Indochina, in the Fujian-Taiwan Straits region, in Burma, and in the Tibet/India border. In short, China was creating space and time in which to turn itself into a great power, a nation that could be truly independent of imperialist dangers and help other global forces that were similarly inclined.

Agrarian Socialism

By mid-1955, Mao had concluded that Chinese independence and great-power goals would not be served by following the Soviet path or intensifying economic or military dependence on the Moscow regime. After all, Soviet agriculture was a disaster. Rejecting the Soviet notion that collectivization required prior mechanization, China collectivized agriculture with no machinery inputs from modern industry—a project known by Communist critics in China as agrarian socialism. The tough, disciplined, heroic Chinese villagers who had fought the imperialist invaders could, in Mao's view, build agrarian socialism without tractors and diesel fuel from the Soviet Union. With such a devoted people, an agricultural surplus could be produced to fund the speedy military buildup that would allow an independent China to ward off any threat.

Pushing aside other leaders who criticized independent agrarian socialism as adventurism, in 1957 Mao launched a series of initiatives designed to make China independent, prosperous, strong, and great. Seeing the Soviet dictator Nikita Khrushchev as unworthy, Mao urged the crushing of the great October 1956 Hungarian revolution and insisted on reading Tito's Yugoslavia (which believed in détente, decollectivization, and other reforms) out of the Communist movement. Disappointed that Moscow had done so little for Nasser's Egypt after the 1956 Suez Crisis, China tentatively challenged U.S. military commitments to Jiang Jieshi over the islands of Jinmen (Quemoy) and Mazu (Matsu), across from Taiwan, islands occupied by almost one-third of Jiang's military. This war posture seemed in Washington and Moscow to threaten a struggle of Mao's side against Jiang's that could drag America and the Soviet Union into a war that neither wanted. Mao meant to contribute with China's military to a global anti-imperialist effort; his shooting policy backfired.

Khrushchev saw Mao's initiatives as threatening to undermine the Soviet priority of détente with the United States to block a U.S.-backed militarization of West Germany. A Moscow–Washington agreement to avoid war required opposition to Taiwan-area globalizing policies premised on the power projects of Mao and Jiang. Suddenly Mao was faced with two possible outcomes that could weaken his nationalist cause: that Taiwan might be permanently split from China and that China might be left isolated against both the Soviet Union and the United States. Consequently, he dropped his explusion policy toward Jiang's troops on Fujian's offshore islands, instead pointing to their presence as evidence that the Chinese Revolutionary Civil War was unfinished and that only foreign interference had kept the People's Republic of China from incorporating Taiwan Province. He also intensified efforts to resume talks with the United States on problems such as Taiwan.

To enhance their ability to defend China against potential invaders, all regions, down to the gargantuan, multivillage collectives whose misnomer was "commune," were to become self-reliant. The intention here was to reduce the need for markets and money (the world's most deadly famine followed, leaving over twenty million Chinese dead) and to enhance the ability to survive as a socialist entity against any potential invasion. In the countryside, virtually everyone was ordered to become a soldier. Elements of culture that did not serve the purposes of the militarized anti-imperialist regime came under attack. Textbooks were rewritten to read that dying in defense of China against invaders was the ultimate glory. Rituals such as lineage burial mounds and prolonged familial celebrations of the New Year were attacked for detracting from the primary purpose of mobilizing everything to win the anti-imperialist struggle.

Mao's insistence on his own, better way to build a great power alienated both other leaders of China's anti-imperialist cause and the rulers of the Soviet Union. In 1959 Moscow broke its commitment to help China build atomic bombs, and in 1960 it recalled all Soviet scientists working on that project and others in China. Mao responded by ordering full commitment to the most rapid development of the nuclear project, even if it meant—as it did—more starvation for ordinary Chinese.

In 1961, according to Hu Hua, a keeper of the Party archives, Mao prodded his new Minister of National Defense, Lin Biao, to suggest to the leadership that with both Moscow and Washington as adversaries and tensions along China's Tibet border with India it was necessary for China to mobilize in self-defense. China, he argued, should devote all its efforts to preparing to survive as the world's only true anti-imperialist socialist society, building locally self-reliant economies without market relations that could survive a blockade and support a war effort. Other leaders insisted, however, that recovery from the murderous 1959–61 famine had to be priority number one, and Mao temporarily yielded to this consensus. The Soviet Union was blamed for Mao's famine and the other miseries caused by the disastrous policies of the Great Leap.[15] The deep presuppositional nature of a Chinese nationalism defended by martial anti-imperialism virtually guaranteed Mao the capacity to win massive support from Chinese patriots for subsequent initiatives in harmony with the grand anti-imperialist narrative.

The Third Front

By 1963 world events permitted Mao to persuade many fellow leaders that China was confronted by an imperialist United States in collusion with a revisionist

Soviet Union and could become dangerously vulnerable if it did not act swiftly and fully in its own defense. Now China alone was the world's hope for anti-imperialist socialism. In 1962 Chinese rulers found themselves responding to an advance of Indian troops, armed and supported by both Washington and Moscow, into Tibet. After China had forced the Indian troops back across the original border, both the United States and the Soviet Union had increased their military support for expansionist India, seen in China as a subimperialist power. In addition, the United States and the Soviet Union had signed treaties against atmospheric nuclear testing and for a halt to nuclear proliferation. In the capital of the PRC, it seemed obvious that their goal was not peace but dominion. Their shared purpose was to keep China from succeeding in its costly pursuit of nuclear military might that would supposedly permit it to act independently on behalf of anti-imperialism worldwide. U.S. President John Kennedy was even considering scenarios for destroying China's bomb-building installations before China could explode its first nuclear device. Chinese participants in a Pugwash Conference* in the Soviet Union in 1963 found Americans and Russians wanting to discuss how to keep China from going nuclear. China increasingly seemed the target of military collusion by the superpowers.

Local events reinforced the overall threat. After a 1962 clash in China's far western province of Xinjiang, an exodus of Turkic Muslims from China to Soviet Russia was welcomed by Moscow. The Soviet view was that irrational Maoist economics would bring more famine in China and hungry people would be seeking land with food in Soviet territory. In 1963 the Soviet Red Army was therefore redeployed in greater numbers into China's border region, including Mongolia.[16] Already in 1962 Mongolia had been taken into the Soviet-run economic bloc, thus squeezing China out of Mongolia and making China's northern border a Soviet monopoly. At this time of danger, China's air force was weaker than Egypt's. If war came, it would be fought on China's soil.

Although the Soviet Union increasingly seemed the most active threat to China, it was not alone. Jiang Jieshi's forces on Taiwan maneuvered militarily in May to spark a rebellion in China in 1962. Mao ordered a pullback of government institutions from the Taiwan Straits coast of Fujian and mobilization as far inland as Nanjing. President Kennedy halted Jiang's thrust. A consensus was developing among China's leaders that China had to defend itself against potential aggression from numerous directions.

Even south of China proper, in Indochina, the United States and Soviet Union were increasingly involved against Chinese interests. A crisis in Laos permitted the Soviets to use their airlift capacity to supply the Communist Lao forces from the territory of North Vietnam in 1961–62 and threaten to squeeze China out. The United States was backing a losing group in Laos and arming the Saigon regime in South Vietnam, far from China's borders, and therefore Chinese lead-

---

*A Soviet-American dialogue on how to avoid nuclear war.

ers did not envision a U.S. invasion from Indochina. As Soviet forces, arrayed in a half moon to the north, west, and south, pressed hard against Chinese territory and broadcast into China on behalf of a military coup against Mao, the United States seemed to complete the encirclement of China from the U.S. bases in Japan, the Ryukyus, Taiwan, and the Philippines. Mao's policy initiative of 1961—Lin Biao's failed trial balloon—would seem wise to many Chinese leaders in 1964–65.

With leaders in Washington and Moscow discussing how to destroy a purported Chinese threat to world peace, Mao won support in late 1964 for an all-out attempt to save China from a coming war imposed on China that might be immediate, nuclear, and widespread. Facing an ultimate imperialist aggression, China reached out to any friend it could find. It armed liberation struggles at no charge against white racist Rhodesia and Portuguese colonial Mozambique. It reached out to anti-imperialist organizations in Southeast Asia, such as Sihanouk's in Cambodia and Sukarno's in Indonesia. It approached dissidents within the U.S. and Soviet camps, hoping to split each from within. Within the U.S. camp, France recognized China, and Beijing hoped that Japan would follow. Within the former socialist camp dominated by the Soviet Union, China became the sole support of super-Stalinist Albania, pressing rulers in Tirana to persuade other Eastern European regimes to break with Moscow.[17] China's October 1964 explosion of an atomic weapon earned it more stature in the third world and more animus from Moscow and Washington. In both capitals more people in power were looking for ways to destroy China's growing military power.

Many anti-imperialist initiatives failed. Sukarno was overthrown in Indonesia. The Afro-Asian movement changed after Ben Bella was overthrown in Algeria, adopting a more pro-Soviet orientation based on the prestige of Nehru in India and Tito in Yugoslavia. In response, China frantically offered arms aid free to all anti-imperialists. These Chinese efforts did, however, persuade Washington that U.S. intervention in Vietnam was needed to stop a Chinese policy of global subversion by proxy. More important, the post-Khrushchev rulers in Moscow from 1965 on saw nuclear-armed, economically irrational, antirevisionist (i.e., anti-Soviet) China as their major enemy, with Beijing wooing anti-imperialists in Africa, trying to subvert Moscow's hegemony in Eastern Europe, and working to cause Communists internationally to see Moscow as their major enemy and Beijing as their only friend. When Moscow responded to Mao's taunts about U.S.-Soviet détente by mocking China's accommodation with colonial Hong Kong, Mao snapped back, calling attention to czarist Russia's land grabs from China. The Brezhnev regime subsequently intensified military preparations targeting Mao's government in China.

By 1965 China was moving military industry into its hinterland, away from both the Soviet border and the coast. First-line defenses were built on China's west, north, and east, on China's long, exposed border with the Soviet Union and

Soviet-occupied Mongolia and facing the U.S. military bases in a Pacific island chain. Second lines of defense were prepared in defensible mountain regions behind the first. A third front, the secure militarized hinterland, was prepared in China's southwest, not far from Indochina. Mao believed that if America invaded it would do so from the Pacific island chain off of China's east coast, not from the jungles of the south. More powerfully than ever, the premise of all-out war mobilization of the entire people defined China's policy project.

With everyone mobilized for war communism, China's economy was grievously wounded. Moscow, rapidly building its forces on China's borders in aggressive array was enemy number one. The Soviet Union's purportedly phony communism, called revisionism, was taken as the major enemy in China. Revisionists in China—opponents of Mao's mobilizational priority—were portrayed as traitors and potential allies of anti-imperialist China's major foe. Mao launched a series of movements, the Cultural Revolution being the best known, to root out so-called revisionists and to institutionalize anti-imperialist economic policies so that each region of China could be self-reliant and survive war and invasion.

Mao's China became isolated from all but the most militant anti-imperialists. From countries all over the world these zealous Communists, dissatisfied with Moscow's détente with Washington and with the Soviet Union's grey stagnation, flocked to China for political lessons and military support for real revolution, total revolution, continuous revolution. The choice for them was between Maoism, whatever its unfortunate excesses, or global Armageddon. Revolutionary tourists came from annihilationist groups all around the world, from Pol Pot and his genocidal Khmer Rouge in Cambodia, from the Naxalites in India, from dissident Communists in Peru following Alberto Guzman, who would form the monstrously murderous Sendero Luminoso. Tied to the International Liaison Office of the Party's Central Committee, led by the 110 percent Maoist Kang Sheng, a Maoist anti-imperialist international was in the making.

After the Soviet Union crushed a Czechoslovak effort to build "socialism with a human face" in 1968 and announced its right to do the same to any nation undermining what Leonid Brezhnev called the socialist commonwealth, and after Moscow had responded to a Chinese incursion in March 1969 with an overwhelming pummeling of the Chinese border area, Mao grew open to a tactical entente with the United States against it. Rulers in Moscow from 1968–69 on debated whether to attack China.

Cooperation with Washington that would check the threat to Beijing from Moscow could also permit a Chinese opening to the U.S.-dominated world economy and, consequently, a reinvigoration for the Chinese economy, which had stagnated and declined because of third-front policies that imposed sacrifice on China's people. A political struggle in Beijing pitted Mao, who believed the Chinese people needed a respite from all-out struggle, against Defense Minister Lin Biao, who continued to promote mobilization against both the United States and the Soviet Union.

By 1970 what anti-imperialism meant to Mao was defeating the Soviet Union, perceived as the greatest danger to China because of the prestige it retained from its earlier era of true anti-imperialism. The key partner for this effort was the United States. President Richard Nixon's arrival in Beijing, after three years of secret negotiations, in February 1972 won Mao and China's people relief from third-front war-mobilization pressures. Lin Biao, still committed to the third-front policies against both the United States and the Soviet Union, had fallen in the autumn of 1971. In the tremendous succession struggle that followed, Mao's continuing commitment to the war communism model precluded Maoist legitimation for the forces whose titular leader was the premier, Zhou Enlai, and who were committed to policies of reform, openness, and international maneuvering aimed at making China a militarily strong, economically prosperous, socialist country. Under this leadership China normalized relations with Japan and imported means for promoting economic growth from capitalist imperialist countries, such as fertilizer plants from the United States. Anti-imperialism meant anti-Sovietism.

The Soviet Union grew ever angrier at this American-Chinese détente, but after 1974 it increasingly blamed Washington rather than Beijing. Not until after Mao's death in September 1976, with the ascension of Premier Zhou's protégé Deng Xiaoping in 1977–78, were the policies of the third front legitimated by Mao's anti-imperialist worldview finally reversed. But anti-imperialism remained the premise of the nationalism that still legitimated China's post-Mao Leninist system rulers. China was to try to make itself the anti-imperialist center of the world not through mobilization of an armed, self-reliant people but through economic growth, providing the wealth to build a modernized, militarily powerful China that could not be bullied by anyone.

The grand narrative of Chinese history as popular mobilization against potential foreign invaders clashed, however, with increasing economic involvement with imperialist economies. If Great Walls and opposition to foreign commerce were no longer the building blocks of a modernizing and militarizing China, then how could the rulers of Leninist China legitimate their new policy direction?

Modernization and Legitimation

China's post-Mao leaders agreed that autarkic policies intended to make it strong and respected by maximizing distance from the world market had in fact left it poor and weak. Although the state had mobilized resources to manufacture nuclear weapons and rockets, the basic equipment of the military copied 1950s deliveries from the Soviet Union that even at the time had not been the most advanced weapons available. When in 1979 Deng Xiaoping dispatched China's army into northern Vietnam after Hanoi's Soviet-backed armies had toppled Pol Pot's Chinese-backed forces in Cambodia, Chinese soldiers paid a terrible toll for China's military backwardness. It was clear to the leaders in Beijing that

China's military required a modernization that could only be based on access to the world's most recent science and technology. This required opening commercial and cultural exchange relations with the advanced industrial democracies to win access to their markets.

In general, the post-Mao leadership grew ever more aware that China under Mao had stagnated economically while the rest of East Asia had raced ahead. Mao's anti-imperialist policies of self-reliance had isolated China from the dynamic forces of economic progress. In a world in which the United States was still the leading economic, military, and political power, the Deng government could win access to the sources of growth by normalizing relations with Washington, especially to win cheap loans from the international financial institutions in which China now participated. The Leninist anti-imperialist notion that dealing with capitalist international finance was surrender to a blood-sucking monster consequently lost credibility.

In mid-December 1978 Deng agreed to allow the United States to continue arms sales to Taiwan as the price for obtaining the key goal of a normalization of relations. The Beijing rulers were caught on the horns of a dilemma. Their basic legitimation had been nationalistic. To modernize, to create a dynamic economy, and to begin to satisfy the pent-up demands of Chinese people for the material benefits of modernity (washing machines, baby strollers, toilet paper, sanitary napkins; quality and style in everything) required changes that undermined the prior anti-imperialist nationalist appeals. Since 1949, incorporating Taiwan into the People's Republic had become central to this legitimation. Yet if Taiwan kept obtaining weapons from the United States, why should it surrender to an amalgamation with the People's Republic? And if China's growth required foreign capital, foreign technology, and foreign trade, what did it mean to be a socialist anti-imperialist state? Success in modernization clashed with legitimation by anti-imperialism.

The political struggle in China seemed to foster no stable compromise. On the one hand, by not disbanding unprofitable state enterprises or allowing the private ownership and sale of farm land, the state preserved jobs for those loyal to the money-wasting party–state machine. On the other hand, it welcomed, at local levels, the emergence of entrepreneurial efforts tied to foreign investment, especially by Chinese from Hong Kong and Taiwan, overseas Chinese from Southeast Asia and the United States, and others from the European Community and Japan. As money poured in, mainly via Hong Kong,[18] two very different Chinas seemed to develop—a flourishing, dynamic south tied to Chinese the world over and a conservative Confucian north ever more involved with Japanese loans, trade, and investment. To the large extent that anti-Japanese sentiment had been the heartbeat of Maoist anti-imperialism, the north was at risk of losing legitimacy to the south.

In addition, with economic growth through openness to the world economy an overall policy priority, Beijing normalized relations with Moscow, eliminated the last remnants of the third-front policy, and instructed the military to earn funds through commercial transactions at home (e.g., selling motorcycles from Sichuan) and abroad (e.g., Silkworm missile sales to Iran, nuclear technology to Pakistan and Algeria, rockets to Saudi Arabia and Iraq). There no longer seemed to be an imperialist threat to China against which to mobilize support, except for a popular experience of exploitation by Japan.[19] The Deng government adopted the Japanese model of aggressive exporting to earn the foreign exchange to buy what it needed to modernize.[20] It abandoned its embrace of stagnant, miserable Stalinist North Korea to normalize relations with capital-rich South Korea, seen as selling Japanese-quality products at third world prices. Likewise, to win friendly economic ties with the rapidly rising economies of Southeast Asia, Beijing stopped backing the Khmer Rouge and reduced military pressure on Vietnam.

And yet a tough nationalism still characterized the legitimating patriotism of China's ruling group. In negotiating with Britain for the return of Hong Kong to China in mid-1997, Beijing would tolerate no democratization or shared British rule. Although Beijing capital was heavily invested in a profitable Hong Kong, China would not guarantee Hong Kong the autonomy that its residents wanted and even threatened to send in its troops to keep Hong Kong in line. Increasingly, the hope of Hong Kong people was the rise of a Canton-based southern force that would not be a tool of Beijing's despotic northern chauvinists. This growing regional identity was enhanced by the economic reforms, which strengthened regional forces against the old capital. Consequently, even the remnants of the old anti-imperialism as applied against Hong Kong were delegitimating for China's Leninist rulers because they seemed the antithesis of what was needed to permit Chinese to prosper.

The Leninist dictatorship's old guard still believed that its power rested on tough military chauvinism. It abandoned the conciliating initiatives of early post-Mao reformers toward the Tibetans and used harsh military means to crush them while an endless stream of trucks carried out of Tibet its precious timber and other resources. Similar force was used against a democracy movement in June 1989. The question remained whether economic modernization could combine with military chauvinism to buttress the old order. The consequences of this contradiction were manifest in Beijing's policy dilemmas with Taiwan.

By 1990 investment from Taiwan had surged, but if Beijing dealt normally with Taiwan, then so could others. The United States, France, and Germany stepped up arms sales to Taiwan. Japan welcomed Taiwan's foreign minister as an "unofficial" guest. Taiwan politics became Taiwanized. Beijing condemned each and every one of these changes, but also fostered the environment facilitating these actions by strengthening normal economic ties with Taiwan.

By the late 1980s, the political conservatives in Beijing committed themselves to the project of restoring China to great-power status. Hoping to free itself of unwanted human rights pressures from the United States or the European Economic Community,[21] China would try to buttress shaky Leninist dictatorships elsewhere; for example, in Pyongyang, Hanoi, and Havana. It would seek to maximize beneficial economic relations with all nations (e.g., Russia was no longer a military superpower to be feared) and continue its open economic policy. It would make maximum use of economic ties with South Korea, Japan, Taiwan, Hong Kong, and Southeast Asia to modernize rapidly. The future seemed to lie in Asia.

By 1991 Japan was the world's number-one aid giver and the largest repository of capital in the world. The United States seemed in economic decline as Japan continued to rise. Beijing's rulers redefined China as the origin and center of East Asian Confucianism, the core dynamic that supposedly facilitated Asian economic growth and political stability. Their assumption was that no Asian nation wanted to deal with an economically mighty Japan that would also be a military superpower; China would act as a military-political counterweight to Japan. Economically, China would ally itself with Japan. Politically and militarily, however, it would ally with all others in Asia to check Japan. This combination of policies was expected to take China into the twenty-first century as the leading power of Asia, itself the leading region of the world. The humiliation and weakness caused by imperialism's oppression would become a matter only for history; China would finally have defeated imperialism.

Maneuvering between two military superpowers was a thing of the past, with the United States in economic decline and the former Soviet Union having disintegrated. China in the 1990s was responding to very different international forces. Realization of its vision of a great China leading a great Asia in the Asian twenty-first century was, however, far from guaranteed. Regional forces[22] were pulling the economic center of China south and into a Chinese diaspora, and memories of a long, cruel war made many Chinese doubtful about Beijing's intimate adversary friendship with Japan. In a world where the logic of modernization had discredited the discourse of Leninist anti-imperialism, it was uncertain whether Beijing's failed Mao-era legitimations could inspire the loyalty of the Chinese people into the twenty-first century.

Notes

1. Arthur Waldron, *The Great Wall of China: From History to Myth* (Cambridge: Cambridge University Press, 1990).
2. This view was popularized by Wei Yuan, the most influential writer of the times on foreign policy.
3. Chinese historians in the 1990s do credit the contributions of non-Communist resistors in the anti-Japanese struggle.
4. A grandson of Mao is said to be writing a biography of the Ming founder to highlight Mao's understanding of the identities of the two state leaders.
5. A Leninist state is an overlapping of four institutional networks legitimated by anti-imperialism: (1) a militarized, secret Party based on a hierarchy of cells, (2) a perva-

sive police covering residence, work, travel, and all other aspects of life, (3) a command economy in which the central government imposes prices, runs industrial production, and distributes inputs and outputs, and (4) a nomenklatura—a list of names of the politically loyal who can be appointed or promoted to official positions by various levels of the state–party hierarchy rather than being chosen on the basis of merit, exam, election, or seniority.

6. John Wilson Lewis and Xue Litai, *China Builds the Bomb* (Stanford: Stanford University Press, 1988), contend instead that China's atomic bomb project was a response to the 1954–55 Taiwan Straits crisis threat of American nuclear blackmail. Mark Ryan, *Chinese Attitudes Toward Nuclear Weapons* (Armonk, NY: M. E. Sharpe, 1989), details how China's rulers presumed nuclear war as inevitable from the outset. See also Chongpin Lin, *China's Nuclear Weapons Strategy* (Lexington, MA: D. C. Heath, 1988).

7. For an overview of the foreign policy of the Nationalist Party on Taiwan, see Hung-mao Tien, *The Great Transition* (Stanford: Hoover Institution Press, 1989).

8. Book-length studies of Chinese foreign policy capturing this essence include Peter Van Ness, *Revolution and Chinese Foreign Policy* (Berkeley: University of California Press, 1970) and Gerald Clark, *In Fear of China* (Melbourne: Lansdowne Press, 1966).

9. The writings of Bruce Cumings are the best sympathetic guide to the calculations of North Korea's rulers.

10. These memoirs of the pro-Moscow faction of North Korea's Communist Party have been regularly reported on in *Moscow News*. These individuals were given asylum in the Soviet Union at the end of the 1950s to escape a murderous purge of faction members by the North Korean tyrant Kim Il Sung. South Korea has been systematically mining the now-open Russian archives, the best new, rich source on Chinese foreign policy.

11. In the post-Mao era, military memoirs by now-retired Chinese army commanders have been full of details on Mao's strategic thinking.

12. Compare Allen Whiting, *China Crosses the Yalu* (New York: Macmillan, 1960) and Edward Friedman, "Problems in Dealing with an Irrational Power," in Edward Friedman and Mark Selden, eds., *America's Asia* (New York: Pantheon, 1969), pp. 207–52. The best overall study of Chinese security calculations is Harvey Nelsen, *Power and Insecurity: Beijing, Moscow and Washington, 1949–1988* (Boulder, CO: Lynne Rienner, 1989).

13. On peacemaking in Korea, see John Lewis Gaddis, *The Long Peace* (New York: Oxford University Press, 1987) and Edward Friedman, "Nuclear Blackmail and the End of the Korean War," *Modern China* 1.1 (January 1975).

14. Scholars in China with access to the military agree on this.

15. There is a large and diverse literature on the causes of the Moscow–Beijing split, with analysts varying on when the rift became unhealable, ranging from 1955, when Mao began to criticize the Soviet Union in internal Chinese statements, to 1963, when Moscow began dispatching troops to the Chinese border. The first solid book on the topic was Donald Zagoria, *The Sino-Soviet Conflict, 1956–1961* (Princeton: Princeton University Press, 1962). A more recent study is Gordon Chang, *Friends and Enemies: The United States, China and the Soviet Union, 1948–1972* (Stanford: Stanford University Press, 1990).

16. Good introductions to Soviet views are Roy Medvedev, *China and the Superpowers* (New York: Basil Blackwell, 1986) and Arkady Shevchenko, *Breaking with Moscow* (New York: Knopf, 1985). For a more propagandistic presentation of Moscow's views, see G. Apalin and U. Mityayev, *Militarism in Peking's Policies* (Moscow: Progress Publishers, 1980).

17. The supposed memoirs of Enver Hoxha, *Reflections on China*, 2 vols. (Tirana: 8 Nentori, 1979), are a good introduction to China's attempt to split the Soviet-led bloc.

18. Ezra Vogel, *One Step Ahead in China* (Cambridge, MA: Harvard University Press, 1990); Yung-wing Sung, *The China–Hong Kong Connection: The Key to China's Open Door Policy* (Cambridge: Cambridge University Press, 1991); Wang Gungwu, *China and the Overseas Chinese* (Singapore: Times Academic Press, 1991).

19. See Allen Whiting, *China Eyes Japan* (Berkeley: University of California Press, 1989) and "China and Japan," *Annals of the American Academy of Political and Social Science* 519 (January 1992), pp. 39–51.

20. Paul Kennedy, *The Rise and Fall of the Great Powers* (New York: Random House, 1987), pp. 447–58, concluded that China was succeeding and would become a superpower. Kennedy's book was quickly translated and published in China.

21. See Peter Van Ness, *Analyzing the Impact of International Sanctions on China* (Australian National University, Department of International Relations, Working Paper 1989/4), and "Human Rights and International Relations in East Asia," *Ethics and International Politics*, July 1992, pp. 43–52.

22. See *Daedalus* 120.2 (Spring 1991).

Chapter 8

Democracy and Peace Versus Dictatorship and War

Introduction

Looking toward the twenty-first century, Japan's role in Chinese politics can be clarified by illuminating three large changes in China's nationalist identity since the late nineteenth century. Chinese in the post-Mao era are experiencing a great failure caused by Mao-era anti-imperialist (basically anti-Japanese) nationalism. Consequently, Chinese often look beyond the second era, the period of Maoist nationalism that began in the 1930s when Japan's military invasion threatened the entire Chinese nation. Instead, Chinese in the post-Mao era reimagine their ongoing crisis of national identity and state legitimacy in terms of missed opportunities in the initial era of national-identity formation, an era that began in the late nineteenth century. Indicatively, in 1981, when the leading spokesperson for democracy in south China, Wang Xizhe, was warned that he was about to be made a political prisoner for his nonviolent dissemination of democratic ideas, Wang

> instead of fleeing expressed a preference to follow in the footsteps of late Qing reformer Tan Sitong and sacrifice himself for China's democratic reforms. Wang . . . stated from jail, "Tan Sitong said that 'Too few people are willing to shed blood for reform, so if someone must do so let it begin with me.' China hasn't enough people like that—I'm willing to be one of them."[1]

Chinese democrats in the post-Mao era feel there have not been enough Tan Sitongs. They ask why Chinese have been unwilling to make the ultimate sacri-

---

This chapter was previously published in *Asia-Prashant: The Journal of the Indian Congress of Asian and Pacific Studies* 1.2 (October 1994).

fice to build a free China. In discussing the slaughter of 200,000 or more Chinese in Nanjing in 1937, the so-called "rape of Nanjing" or "Nanjing massacre," the writer Bai Hua asked why Chinese, who far outnumbered Japanese troops, lacked the courage to fight and die and perhaps win, and instead surrendered.[2] Thus even when Chinese in the post-Mao era, the third period of Chinese national-identity formation, imagine their dilemmas and options by looking back to the pre-Mao era, they are not merely repeating a path once taken. Rather, they now see China's destiny and Japan's place in it with lenses sharpened by a century of painful disappointments and defeats.

Harvard University history professor Akira Iriye concludes *China and Japan in the Global Setting*, which investigates the China–Japan problematique in terms of a similar three periods, finding that

> global developments . . . cut across national boundaries and can be solved only through transnational cooperation. Chinese–Japanese cooperation . . . will be a good test of whether humanity is . . . ready.[3]

Professor Iriye's excellent work contemplates the China–Japan relation in terms of larger global concerns and central human issues. He finds that in the first period of Chinese nationalism, a late-nineteenth-century opportunity for China and Japan to go forward cooperatively was lost because of military expansion by the government of Showa-era Japan on the soil of China. But he notes that a similar opportunity has been re-created in the post-Mao era, where Japan is a major shaper of Asia's future. How Japanese policies shape China–Japan relations will help decide whether Asia's future will realize or frustrate larger humane purposes. Much now depends on Japanese initiatives.

Professor Iriye argues that if Japan envisions only "some sort of counterpart to the European Economic Community," if its aim is only "an Asian-Pacific economic community," if cooperation is not built on "a common concern for human rights, the rights of all people to live with dignity and freedom," then the outcome will be as great a disaster for Chinese and Japanese and the world as was the prior failed attempt to build unity on a common cultural understanding.[4] However, as Chinese democrats know, Leninist China opposes human rights activism in Asia. Chinese nationalism in the present era, the third period, is contested. The value orientation of rulers in Beijing does not support the humane values promoted by Professor Iriye.

The rulers of post-Mao China promote emulation of Japan, but of a very specially constructed notion of Japan, one that ignores Japan's democracy. These Chinese leaders are attempting to build a strong state, as militarist Japan did in the Meiji era; to build a powerful economy through state-leveraged export aggressiveness, as Japan supposedly did after World War II; and to build a forceful, authoritarian, hierarchical system, as has long undergirded the dynamic success of Japan and all the rest of purportedly Confucian East Asia, at least as that achievement is imagined by China's authoritarian, post-Mao government.

If these post-Mao militaristic, authoritarian tendencies obstruct open, cooperative, international efforts suitable to the new era of globalization, what then should Japan do? Policy in Japan is confronted by a difficult situation, by authoritarian Asian nationalisms, a major part of whose legitimacy derives from indigenous anti-Japanese passions rooted in Showa-era suffering from Japanese aggression. Antidemocratic forces in China and elsewhere in Asia do not make it easy for democratically oriented Japanese to build a future of freedom, peace, and cooperation. Nasty forces may portend far less happy outcomes. Can Japan act so that it is obvious that a truly open and international, deeply democratic, human rights–oriented Japan is not a friend or model for militaristic, chauvinist authoritarians?

The Era Prior to the Legitimation of Mao's Anti-Imperialist Nationalism

Professor Iriye notes that in 1895, during the first era of Chinese nationalism, the Japanese literary figure Kunikida Doppa found "Chinese as totally devoid of national consciousness."[5] Chinese patriots were in fact constructing a national identity to replace loyalty to the old empire. This national identity was at first racist and anti-imperialist; the yellow race would remove the white race from Asia. Given shared opposition to European domination, Iriye notes a quest by Chinese and Japanese for deep cooperation premised on a common identity. In 1895,

> [a]t the Shimonoseki peace conference, . . . Foreign Minister Mutsu Munemitsu was able to read and comprehend what the Chinese delegate Li Hongzhang wrote in Chinese. . . . Li proclaimed that the two countries shared a common language.[6]

Actually, the claim of those promoting yellow-race nationalism was that China and Japan shared both a common language and a common race.

Sun Yat-sen became the most important Chinese nationalist leader promoting this racial-cultural Chinese-Japanese unity.[7] Sun Yat-sen's Japanese was better than his Mandarin.[8] After all, Sun, a Cantonese raised in Hawaii, had lived in Britain and Japan but not in Mandarin-speaking areas of north China.[9] The Japanese language was so useful to Chinese in dealing with new challenges that needed new words—freedom, nationalism, socialism, imperialism—for grappling with new issues that these terms were taken over from the Japanese. Chinese patriots in the south identified with Japan's struggle. They rooted for Japan against Russia in the Russo-Japanese War, identifying Japan with their struggle against the Manchu emperor's rule over Chinese. These Chinese hoped that all yellow people would grow strong enough to throw out foreign or European or white invaders.

Perhaps because of Manchu recalcitrance, China was the last of the East Asian nations to try to institutionalize and popularize a national vernacular written language. Patriotic opposition to the old state system of the Manchus included opposition to its administrative language (*guan hua*), centered in the northern capital, Beijing. The first Chinese alphabetic writing system was modeled "on Japanese katakana." The Manchus banned it in 1901.[10] Nonetheless, China continued to borrow, translate, and use Japanese textbooks.[11]

China's south experienced itself as the region that had historically opposed and suffered from savagery by northern invaders and that had recently led the struggle against British imperialism, which was based in the southern ports of Hong Kong and Shanghai, as occurred in the Opium War. The south was the heart of China, the source of rice, silk, landscape painting, and neo-Confucianism. The Southern Society was the center of new nationalist thinking, as China's south was the center of opposition to the Manchu Dynasty of the north. Revolution, Don Price's scholarship on Song Jiaoren shows, was imagined as a loyalist act of filial piety (*xiao*), revenging alien northern wrongs done to southern ancestors.

At a 1913 national language conference, the Mandarin language of the north was attacked as unsuited to state strengthening.[12] The leader of the pro-Mandarin group tried to win by changing the voting rules. Passions flared. A fight broke out. The southern leaders walked out. A "suggestion to change the voting procedure was adopted, and ... the Mandarin faction had its way."[13] Nonetheless, "The first standard for pronunciation decided on in 1913 by the Society for Unification of the National Language was a ... compromise, containing features of both Northern and Southern Chinese."[14]

Still, most nationalists focused on resistance to Britain from south China. The May Thirtieth incident of 1925, the slaughter in a southern port of Chinese by British-led troops, intensified this southern, anti-British notion of Chinese nationalism. Anti-imperialists did not inevitably imagine a Chinese modern vulgate as rooted in the conservative and warlord-dominated north. Radicals and Communists in China, after Russia's Bolshevik Revolution, did not look to reactionary mandarins but instead began to look to modern Latinization experiments with the Chinese language in Russia.

Only with the 1930s Japanese military expansion in north China did Chinese national consciousness and language politics change to opposition to Japan. The south then suddenly seemed too soft on Japan. A new era began that required a nationalism that embraced the martyrs of the north who resisted Japan. That project made invisible the prior, more hopeful era of Chinese relations with Japan.

Akira Iriye details the subsequently hidden Taisho-era prospect that China and Japan could both have democratized and cooperated in opposition to the West's racist and imperialist practices.[15] Into the 1930s Japanese trade and investment with China surpassed Britain, and Japan endorsed a policy toward China of "coexistence and coprosperity." Iriye recounts a project of democratic cooperation, the vision and friendship of May Fourth–era Chinese and Taisho-era Japanese.[16] He asks if Chinese and Japanese in the post-Mao era can build a better future on this unfulfilled potential.

Of course, one should not forget or diminish the cruelties of aggressive Japanese militarism in China or Korea or elsewhere in Asia. But Iriye reminds us that Japan's dealings with China were not exhausted by atrocities. Even in the era of alliance with Germany, Japan never accepted Nazi racism. Japanese in northeast China imagined a harmony of "five races—Han Chinese, Mongols, Manchus, Koreans and Japanese."[17] In fact, despite the alliance with Hitler, some Japanese helped save thousands of Jews from annihilation by the Nazis. One of these humane Japanese officials, Chiune Sugihara, is celebrated as a hero in Israel.[18]

Maoist Anti-Imperialist Nationalism

Only in the 1930s did Chinese patriots almost universally comprehend nationalism as defense against Japan's military invaders. That posture required subsuming all other struggles into the one against Japan. Only then did Japan's 1894–95 victory in Korea become a defeat for China rather than for the Manchu Empire.[19] Only then did the Twenty-One Demands of 1915 become a central moment in the failure of non-Communists to defend China against Japan rather than a betrayal by the reactionary northern warlord Yuan Shikai, who had served the northern Manchus and tried to restore czarist-like monarchy.

In contrast to the 1930s anti-Japanese narrative, when Mao Zedong's guerrillas at the end of the 1920s established a base in southern mountains, they declared themselves an independent polity, a stance that a decade later would have been almost inconceivable since it would have been taken by Chinese patriots as a betrayal of the national cause, the need for all Chinese to unite to defeat Japan.[20]

Professor Iriye notes that the first period of Chinese nationalism was infused with the goal of state power. By the 1930s, it seemed to Chinese patriots that China's rulers had failed in that quest and that Japan's state power success was immoral. Hence Chinese nationalism had to be built on an identity that opposed both failed Chinese elites and inhuman Japanese militarists. Mao Zedong identified China's anti-imperialist nation with a project and group that could oppose Chinese elites and Japanese militarists, the resistance of poor, pure, northern hinterland Chinese peasants.[21]

The southern writer Chen Xuezhao caught how these northern wretched of the earth had become modal personalities of Chinese patriotism. She wrote of that peasantry:

> They believed in their country, revered the party leadership. . . . They had endured the Japanese invasion . . . without surrendering. When the Japanese were robbing and arresting innocent people and raping the women, the peasants hid in the mountains for days without food.[22]

A northern writer, Mo Yan, in *Red Sorghum*, captured the same peasant patriotic essence.

> [T]hey defended their country in a valiant, stirring ballet that makes us unfilial descendants who now occupy the land pale by comparison.[23]

In the nationalism of this second epoch, the Communist-led peasant war against Japanese invaders was imagined as a continuation and culmination of millennia of Chinese history. It built on 1920s archeological discoveries of ancient humanity in the north and redefined the Opium War–struggle against British imperialism as resistance to foreign penetration. This nationalistic history legitimated Mao's ascendancy and his power project of Spartan, autarkic war communism. Japan was presented as the most recent avatar of the enemy of the Chinese people, the villain in a long nationalist narrative.

Contemporary Chinese were taken as direct descendants of a great civilization that had arisen in the Wei River bend of the Yellow River millennia ago. These north China peasants survived by sacrificing in defensive struggles to keep out armed invaders and spread by settling and civilizing the landmass of China.[24] The victory of Mao's Red armies achieved what Chinese had failed to win in the Opium War, the establishment of a strong and independent state that could fend off foreign threats. Mao was pictured as having derived the strategies that won an opportunity for China to be independent and to again create a great civilization; this time, true communism.

The 1950 treaty with the Soviet Union that cemented these policies was aimed against "Japan or any nation allied with Japan." The 1958 Great Leap Forward was Mao's first thorough attempt to institutionalize Communist purposes. It followed a break in trade talks with Tokyo when the government of Prime Minister Nobusuke Kishi—Kishi had been arrested after Japan surrendered in August 1945 as a war criminal—allowed a Chinese flag to be desecrated in Nagasaki. Mao, China, and communism, in this second moment of Chinese nationalism, would prosper through a self-reliant Leninist command economy, and against export-oriented Japan, without profit-oriented Japan, and in contradistinction to world-market-oriented Japan, with Japan portrayed as a permanently poor and exploited dependency of a voracious American imperialism. Instead, Japan surged ahead and China stagnated.

In the post-Mao era, it would be obvious to Chinese patriots that the project inherent in the Maoist anti-Japanese nationalist narrative was self-destructive, miring Chinese in socioeconomic wretchedness, even as Japan and all others in East Asia zoomed forward. Hence post-Mao Chinese patriots see the Mao era as a disaster for the people.

Post-Mao Chinese Nationalism

Professor Iriye identifies economics as the central feature of the third era of Chinese nationalism. Mao's 1969–72 overtures to the Nixon administration had a major economic component. Living standards in China were stagnant. Beijing sought new economic policies. Messrs. Nixon and Kissinger, however, focused on Cold War strategic issues (the Soviet Union and war in Vietnam). But Japan swiftly normalized relations with Beijing and signed generous commercial contracts. Tokyo allowed Beijing to boast that it still did not take economic aid from anyone by calling aid-like loan arrangements with Japan "commercial" terms. Iriye contends that Japan owed China such aid because, before the all-out invasion of China,

> much of Japan's economic gain had come about because China offered it reparations, territory rich in resources, and easily accessible markets for trade and investment. Without the reparations of 1895, without the cessation of Taiwan and the lease of the Liaotung Peninsula, and without the unequal treaties . . . which kept import duties low and protected foreign merchants and industrialists from Chinese jurisdiction, Japanese industrialization would have been much slower.[25]

In addition,

> Japan owed its positive economic development to a war in which it was not a direct participant but in which China had to divert scarce resources to fight American forces equipped with Japanese material. Japan benefitted even as China suffered from the Korean war.[26]

Post-Mao Leninist dictators in China insist that one reason they have done better than Mao is because of their good ties with Japan, the leading aid donor to China. Yet Japan's friendliness to the ruling despots in Beijing during the post-Mao era is actually held against Japan because Mao-era nationalism and China's Leninist polity are no longer legitimate to most Chinese. According to Nicholas Kristof, the *New York Times* correspondent in China, in early 1993,

> [m]any ordinary Chinese protest that the Communist authorities are being too friendly to Japan, and are trying to prevent anti-Japanese organizations in China from speaking out. The [Chinese Communist] party rose to power partly because it gained nationalist credentials by fighting Japan; today it is losing some of its dwindling legitimacy because it is widely seen as too chummy with those still known in Chinese as the wokou, the "Japanese bandits" [dwarf pirates—EF]—a term often pronounced with real hatred.

In August 1990, when Japan's Prime Minister Kaifu visited China to symbolize the renormalization of relations following the June 4, 1989, Beijing massacre, the Chinese government staged and televised for Chinese people to see a "super reception" (*chaoji jiedai*).

Chinese people believe, however, that "Japanese firms . . . refuse to transfer high technology" because "Japan intends to prevent China from developing quickly."[27] Dismissing the Japanese contention that China cannot absorb high technology, Chinese ask themselves why their rulers praise a Japan that exploits China.

East Asian specialist Robert Scalapino notes that China has "exempted Japan from the charge of interfering in China's internal affairs" because the government in Tokyo is quiet about Chinese human rights violations against the Chinese people.[28] In response to Tokyo's supposed support for and collusion with unpopular Chinese dictators in sweetheart contracts, all of China's popular democratic movements in the 1980s targeted Japan. In fall 1986, when student demonstrators protested against a second Japanese invasion, this time economic instead of military, a poster at Beijing University featured a Japanese soldier of the first invasion boasting of the second, which had just produced the Hainan Island scandal, during which the semi-smuggling of vehicles and electronics to the mainland through the island resulted in an outflow to Japan of over $1 billion. The Japanese solider boasted, "Forty years ago I chopped fifty Chinese heads off with my sword, but now my firm sells you color televisions in hundreds of thousands."[29] In sum, a historically unremorseful and contemporaneously greedy Japan discredits Chinese rulers who embrace Japan.

The Japanese description of East Asian economic progress as a pattern of flying geese in which Japan is always the leader is experienced in China as relegating Chinese to a state of permanent dependency on Japan. But "there is nothing in the long history of Sino-Japanese relations to suggest that the Chinese would willingly accept the position of a junior partner in a relationship defined by Japanese priorities."[30] Not only because China is the world's most populous nation, but because it is a nuclear power, and because it is a state with veto power as one of the five permanent members of the United Nations Security Council, and also because the prior greatness of Chinese civilization fosters expectations of future greatness, a Japanese discourse that permanently reduces China to second-rank dependency cannot help but produce anti-Japanese resentment in China.

Anti-Japanese gossip spread like wildfire after a tragic train accident in central China took the lives of touring Japanese high school graduates. The Chinese government apologized only to have the Japanese bring up the issue of reparations. That Japanese demand was felt as such an injustice by ordinary Chinese, given no reparations for the Japanese Showa-era invasion of China, that Chinese characterized Japanese to each other as pure exploiters. Such attitudes are popular, spontaneous, and rooted in history. Consequently, Chinese are susceptible to demagogic appeals that turn the piece of the truth on Japanese gains at Chinese expense, sketched above in quotes from Professor Iriye, into outrage that focuses on Japan because Japanese supposedly are rich because Chinese have unfairly suffered.

Hence the issue of no Japanese indemnity for what Japan did to Chinese in World War II, while Japanese-Americans were indemnified for mistreatment by the American government during World War II, intensifies a Chinese experience of Japanese as uniquely selfish and unjust. The emotion is so strong that the government in Beijing could not repress all pro-indemnity activities during the Japanese emperor's 1992 visit to China. It could not even crush an unofficial pro-indemnity group. A Beijing poster read, "Never Forget the Criminal Activities of Japanese Aggression to China."[31] A list of demands included: (1) a U.S. $10 billion interest-free loan to help China complete its eighth five-year plan, (2) a study commission on what Japan should pay China for destruction during the Japanese invasion, with China to seize Japanese property in China if the commission outcome were unsatisfactory, (3) Japanese return to China of the Ryukyus and Diaoyutai islands and the promise of respect of China's territorial integrity, (4) no sending of Japanese military overseas, (5) an apology by the emperor at the Beijing airport for Japan's aggression and crimes. If Japan did not agree, China should initiate a second war to resist Japan.[32] "More than 150 prominent intellectuals jointly petitioned the National People's Congress. . . . They suggested that if Japan refuses to compensate the war victims, China should stop payments on its debts."[33]

Hence there is chauvinistic receptivity in China to Beijing's attack on all Japanese leadership initiatives—e.g., conditioning economic aid on environmental responsibility or calling for meetings to address the regional arms race—as revealing a return of big-power dreams. An essay of analysis concluded that Japan's crimes left it unsuited for an international position of leadership. Besides, China cannot tolerate a Japanese leadership role in Asia when Japan has not abandoned a policy of trying to keep China weak.[34] A list of problems in China–Japan relations in another essay included: (1) the error of both Jiang Jieshi and Mao Zedong in sacrificing the Chinese people to foreign policy by not demanding an indemnity from Japan, (2) Japan's occupation of China's sacred territory of Diaoyutai and Deng Xiaoping's willingness to put off dealing with this continuing aggression, (3) Japan's rapid resumption of loans to the Beijing government after the June 4, 1989, Beijing massacre.[35]

North China superpatriots could not tolerate a Japan that was contemptuous of China occupying the Asian vacuum of power created by the departure of the American military.[36] What made this anti-Japanese sentiment so potent and potentially explosive was a prior discrediting of the Communist Party dictatorship's patriotic credentials and a consequent feeling that a Chinese government was needed now that would truly stand up for China, a passion that could be filled with popular anti-Japanese appeals. An end had to be put to the alleged practice of Chinese rulers preferring deals with foreign governments over aiding the victimized and long-suffering Chinese people.[37] Mao, as Jiang, had put his power-aggrandizement purposes above alleviating the poverty of the Chinese people, a perverse priority that continued after the establishment of the People's Republic when Japan was permitted not to indemnify the Chinese people so that Beijing rulers could get what they wanted from Japan. At its inception, the Chinese Communist government likewise shut its eyes to the orgy of rape by the

Soviet Army when it invaded northeast China in 1945.[38] Chinese now want instead a government that will stand up to immoral behavior such as Japan's claimed mistreatment of China.

Thus a Chinese policy of military buildup in Asia to fend off Japan's rise to great-power status is popular in China. Despite the post-Mao regime's economic search for a maximum of economic benefit from Japan and Beijing's political attempt to use lack of Japanese concern for human rights violations in China to help quell a popular Chinese movement for democracy, the regime's broader Asian strategy is premised on taking Japan as its enemy. "In Chinese eyes, the danger of a resurgence of Japanese militarism combined with Japanese economic hegemony looms on the horizon." China appeals to other Asian nations on an anti-Japanese basis for support for China's military buildup because, like China, these countries also feel a need to "maintain a degree of vigilance against Japan." As seen in China, the real obstacle to this needed growth of Chinese military power in cooperation with all of Asia against a dangerous Japan is Japan, for "Japan is afraid of China's becoming strong enough to pose a threat to Japanese domination of Asia."[39]

The Beijing government's policy is to have China rise to become the dominant power in East Asia by playing to the fears that other Asian nations already have about a return to Japanese domination, as with Showa-era military expansionism. In East and Southeast Asia, there is indeed "fear [of] a new Japanese hegemony."[40] Foreign policy elites in China and North Korea and a number of other Asian places tend to believe that "it takes [little] for Japan's *past* militarism to resurface in *today's* world."[41]

China increasingly has a capacity to project military power. Kyorin University professor Shigeo Hiramatsu, an expert on the Chinese navy and previously a researcher at the International Institute for Strategic Studies, has noted that since the 1973 global oil crisis, China has been expanding its navy and its offshore territorial claims with an eye on oil. It first moved against Vietnamese islands in 1974. "China intends to convert the South China Sea into the 'All China Sea,' seeking hegemony in the region and filling the vacuum forming in the wake of the Cold War."[42] China's "200,000-member navy" includes "the world's third largest submarine force of 181 vessels, five nuclear-equipped."[43]

Michael Swaine, RAND Corporation specialist on the Chinese military, found China becoming more than just a threat to offshore, oil-rich territories of Asia that are disputed hot spots, potential trigger points for war.

> China's ongoing attempt to enhance its power-projection capabilities through the acquisition of Russian long-range transport and advanced fighter aircraft, aerial refueling technology and more advanced blue-water warships—combined with indications of a more assertive political and diplomatic posture towards Asia—is producing growing concerns over the emergence of a Chinese "threat" to the region.[44]

The challenge from China to Japan is consequently multifaceted and difficult. Can Tokyo imagine and implement economic policies that do not relegate Asian nations to a permanent status of dependent follower? Can Japan resolve the issue of war reparations? Can Japan join with other Asian nations both to resolve outstanding territorial disputes from the Spratleys to Diaoyutai (Senkaku) and to agree on arms-control measures that will defuse the dangerous arms race? Can Japan distance itself from unpopular despots in Beijing without igniting a chauvinistic Chinese backlash against Japan? Can Japan advance ecology, human rights, and democracy without seeming a threatening hegemon?

The alternative to such large and creative policies by Japan may be Chinese bullying or Chinese military action in Asia that could threaten Asia's fledgling democracies and ignite a constitutional crisis in Japan on the issue of troops overseas.

Japan has already shown diplomatic creativity in finessing seemingly insoluble conundrums. In 1972, in recognizing Beijing, it was Tokyo that pioneered nonofficial relations with Taiwan as part of its normalization agreement with Beijing, an innovation that has mightily contributed to peace and prosperity in East Asia and been copied by the United States and numerous other nations. Japan thereby has proven its capacity to lead in peace-directed diplomacy. Indeed, given the increased emphasis on using the United Nations in global peacekeeping since the end of the 1980s, one could even conclude that the best part of Japan's postwar foreign policy public consensus has received a global stamp of approval. Also, Japan in 1992–93 got the World Bank to consider Japan's approach to development instead of discredited neoliberal policies of privatization and liberalization. This raises the prospect that poorer countries will gain from steering credits to firms and sectors that serve national objectives and will not be penalized for protecting strategic economic sectors. Criticism of Tokyo too often ignores key arenas, such as the three just noted, that show that Japan can succeed as an enlightened global leader.

The International Crisis of Changing National Identity

The underlying problem in both China and Japan has to do with the need to legitimate a new national identity and new national purposes for our new era. What became Mao's regime in Beijing, only in 1944 committed itself to imposing the northern Mandarin dialect on all the nation.[45] Southerners in the People's Republic after 1949 found it necessary to learn the northern language in order to succeed in life. Over time, as the Leninist dictatorship based in north China was discredited, southerners increasingly resented having to speak the northern tongue. With the rise of China's economically dynamic south in the 1980s, the Cantonese language has spread, as has pride in regional identities, in contrast to the north's old imperial language and singularly political identity. What the south represents is not southern separatism, but a national economic and cultural revival for all the diverse peoples that reside in China.[46] The Mao-era notion of one nation with one culture coming from the north is disappearing from Chinese consciousness.

When Japan's Prime Minister Ohira Masayoshi visited China and appealed to a "shared two-thousand year history of cultural exchanges,"[47] he probably was unaware that in the rapidly prospering Jiangnan area around the Yangtze River Valley, local Chinese saw Japan's borrowings in the Tang Dynasty as proof of the vitality of their region. The Yangtze region's *Wu yueh* culture was centered on dynamic southern cosmopolitan cities such as Hangzhou and Yangzhou, which connected to international exchange over land by the Silk Road and over sea through the South China Sea and the Indian Ocean to West Asia, East Africa, and the Mediterranean.[48] In other words, in the post-Mao era of world market intensification, a new epoch in which the Maoist anti-imperialism of war communism's economic autarky makes no sense, the nationalist mantle in China is contested and is ever more defined by an open ecumene of international exchange, as supposedly manifested in the long history of the south. The old guard in power in Beijing, however, still identifies with military chauvinism, as sketched above, as well as with a revived authoritarian Confucianism that has no need for democracy or human rights universalism. The notion that China *is* Confucian and that Confucius *is* a northerner and that Confucianism *is* the secret of East Asian economic success is the line of northern authoritarian chauvinists with militarized, great-power ambitions.

In contrast, in contestation with this north-based chauvinism, there is a south-based openness that can imagine itself as including Chinese capital in Hong Kong, Taiwan, and Southeast Asia, a group with more foreign exchange than Japan. This self-confident greater-Chinese identity, which is neither afraid of Japan nor vengeful toward Japan, became in 1993 an official statistical category for the World Bank, listed as CEA, the Chinese Economic Area.[49] This south could identify China with a future of global openness and democratization. This Greater China challenge to the heirs of Mao's militarized anti-imperialism, which I will call postmodern nationalism to reflect its opposition to a notion of modernity as a top-down, centralized, closed identity, is spreading throughout China.

No one, however, opts for a division of China into smaller states. All Chinese patriots imagine a united Chinese future. The question is whether that purpose is best identified with the north's closed-door chauvinism or with post-Mao openness that could include sufficient democratic federation to appeal even to residents of Hong Kong and Taiwan.

For Japan looking to China, the question is whether Japanese national identity can adapt to this new era of intensified international exchange and cross-national cooperation in a democratic way, as promised by China's southern-based national project, or will Tokyo instead identify with the Confucian authoritarian and militaristic expansionism of China's north, while at the same time treating China as Japan's adversary in Asia, to be matched militarily by Japan or by a Japan tied to American military might in Asia? What will it mean to be a proud Japanese in the twenty-first century?

This crisis of national identity is global, one that faces all people. Australia is reimagining itself as part of Asia rather than as an heir of British culture. The

United States is re-envisioning itself as truly multicultural rather than as singularly a direct descendant of European culture. From Mexico to India, once proud and relatively closed anti-imperialist nations are struggling to reimagine themselves as open to and benefiting from the intensified world market.

There are those who say that Japan's national identity is so deep as to be unchangeable, that there is a unique and prolonged historical essence to a Yamato people that allows Japanese to borrow Confucianism or Buddhism or European-style modernization, indigenize them, and yet remain uniquely, ethnically Japanese (*minzokushugi*). In contrast, there are those who insist that as Japan absorbs workers from Asia, as it emerges as the leader of Asia, as it represents itself to itself as a global leader for the new and complex postmodern age, Japanese cannot help but reimagine their history and identity. Perhaps Japanese will remember and re-emphasize that Japanese are a combination of language and peoples from North Asia, Southeast Asia, and elsewhere; that in early medieval times at least one-third of Japan's aristocratic families traced their lineages to China or Korea; that Japanese wealth long expanded with overseas international exchanges via the ancient Silk Road and the historical link to India, the Middle East, and the Mediterranean via the South China Sea and the Indian Ocean. Pacific wind patterns allowed easy trade with the Spice Islands.

> Like the Europeans and Bugis, the Japanese could shift back and forth between plunder and trade. They could trade with or attack the Chinese mainland as the opportunity presented itself. Japanese merchants also went out to Southeast Asia in large numbers, establishing Japanese trade-diaspora communities in the Philippines, Makassar, and especially in Siam. Between 1604 and 1635, 355 ships sailed from Japan for destinations in Southeast Asia. . . . Siamese trade with Japan was more valuable than all other [Siamese] foreign trade combined.[50]

Japan has always benefited from being part of the ecumene. Okakura Tenshin imagined Japan as "part of a thalassocracy of Yamato, Korea, and southeastern Chinese."[51]

The challenges for China and Japan in the new age include not relying on authoritarian adversary identities and instead embracing open identities premised on cooperation and mutual benefit. The problem confronting China and Japan also challenges the entire human species in the new international era. How China and Japan relate is of global significance. Akira Iriye concluded his volume on China and Japan arguing just this point, that the key conception of cross-national cooperation and open engagement that can foster peace and democracy requires "a new conception of culture" by and between both nations,[52] indeed all humanity. It is a most difficult challenge. But the alternative—not changing—makes more likely an ultimate disaster.

Notes

1. Austin R. Hsu, "Wang Xizhe—A Forerunner of the Chinese Democracy Movement," *Inside China Mainland* 15.4 (April 1993), p. 76.

2

2. Bai Hua's critique of Chinese "thankful for being able to survive for one more hour" was denounced by Chinese chauvinists as an apology for Japan's mass murders.

3. Iriye, *China and Japan in the Global Setting* (Cambridge, MA: Harvard University Press, 1992), p. 133.

4. Ibid., pp. 134, 141, 142.

5. Ibid., p. 32.

6. Ibid., p. 30.

7. Maurius Jansen, *The Japanese and Sun Yat-sen* (Cambridge, MA: Harvard University Press, 1954). The hegemonic force of European racial justifications for imperialism fostered a counterhegemonic language of anti-European racism virtually everywhere, not just in the embrace of yellow race nationalism in China. For Africa, see Kwame Anthony Appiah, *In My Father's House: Africa in the Philosophy of Culture* (New York: Oxford University Press, 1992).

8. Sun's ally, He Xiangning, recalls of their time in Japan, "I could not speak Mandarin. . . . I was unable to communicate (except with my Cantonese friends), because our speech was mutually unintelligible. Even when we would have liked to have a long talk, it was impossible . . . since we could not understand each others dialects . . . , we said little to each other." (Li Yu-ning, ed., *Chinese Women Through Chinese Eyes* [Armonk, NY: M. E. Sharpe, 1992], p. 142.)

9. The centrality of Sun Yat-sen to Chinese nationalism is argued in Dru Gladney, *Muslim Chinese: Ethnic Nationalism in the People's Republic* (Cambridge, MA: Harvard University Press, 1991).

10. Jerry Norman, *Chinese* (Cambridge: Cambridge University Press, 1988), pp. 257–58.

11. Iriye, *China and Japan*, p. 33.

12. S. Robert Ramsey, *The Languages of China* (Princeton: Princeton University Press, 1987), p. 7.

13. Ibid., p. 8.

14. Norman, *Chinese*, p. 176.

15. Iriye, *China and Japan*, pp. 45 ff.

16. Ibid., p. 65.

17. Iriye, *China and Japan*, p. 74.

18. *Points East* 8.1 (February 1993), a publication of the Sino-Judaic Institute, offers great detail on this history.

19. See Iriye (*China and Japan*, p. 29) for pro-Japanese sentiment in China even after Japan's victory in the 1894–95 war.

20. I, of course, am indebted to Professor Iriye for my three periods. However, in contrast to Iriye (*China and Japan*, p. 8), my first period does not end with World War I, but with the Japanese invasion of China; and my third period begins with the post-Mao era (or Mao's opening to economic rationality after 1969) and not with the end of World War II. Perhaps Iriye's periods reflect Japanese perceptions, while I am trying to comprehend changes in terms of Chinese national consciousness.

21. Thus the long march, in which the Red Army fled from the south to the north, was experienced in terms of the northern base and not the southern exodus, which imagined an invincible army as Shi Dakai the Second, the renaissance of a southern Taiping peasant rebellion of the mid-nineteenth century. (See Harrison Salisbury, *The Long March* [New York: McGraw-Hill, 1987], ch. 21.)

22. Chen, *Surviving the Storm* (Armonk, NY: M. E. Sharpe, 1990), p. 33.

23. See Mo, *Red Sorghum* (New York: Viking, 1993).

24. Iriye takes as truth this Maoist nationalistic narrative. "Most military conflicts took the form of protecting the Middle Kingdom against the nomads, barbarians of the steppes. Within the Great Wall, which separated the two kinds of societies, military force was of much less

significance than culture as a symbol of authority and greatness" (*China and Japan*, p. 9).

25. Iriye, *China and Japan*, pp. 24–25.
26. Ibid., p. 105.
27. *US–Japan Policy Dialogue on China* (New York: Asia Society, 1992), pp. 8, 9.
28. In Chong-sik Lee, ed., *In Search of a New Order in East Asia* (Berkeley: University of California Institute of East Asian Studies, 1991), p. 18.
29. Laura Newby, *Sino-Japanese Relations* (London: Routledge, 1988), p. 14.
30. Robert Scalapino, "A Regional Review," in Chong-sik Lee, ed., *New Order*, p. 18.
31. *Tansuo* [Quest], No. 105 (September 1992), p. 6.
32. Ibid., pp. 6–7. Seeing the Ryukyus as an 1870s imperial conquest by Japan fosters a feeling that Japan's claim to Diaoyutai (the Senkakus) is endlessly expansionist at China's expense. The intrinsic value of Diaoyutai is not at issue.
33. *China Focus* 1.2 (March 30, 1993), p. 7.
34. *Dangdai* [Contemporary], No. 19 (October 15, 1992), p. 23.
35. *Dangdai* [Contemporary], No. 16 (July 15, 1992), p. 87.
36. *Dangdai* [Contemporary], No. 24 (March 15, 1993), pp. 82–83.
37. Foreign aid in the Mao era went to nations (e.g., Indonesia, Vietnam, and Albania) that then turned against China. Arms were delivered free to rebels. Billions went into nuclear weapons and missiles. All that can seem like waste and theft to Chinese in the post-Mao era, who feel humiliated by their economic standing vis-à-vis Japan and who want to catch up economically.
38. *Tansuo* [Quest], No. 107 (November 1992), pp. 46–47.
39. Wu Chan, "A Chinese View," in Lee, *New Order*, pp. 62, 56, 62. Consequently, despite the proclaimed policy of friendship with Japan, rulers in Beijing attacked Japan for robbing China in the Baoshan Steel complex and accused Party Secretary Hu Yaobang of too much genuine friendship toward Japan. On the day before the third anniversary of the Beijing massacre of Chinese democracy activists, "In the early afternoon, a cameraman of the Tokyo Broadcasting System named Atsushi Yamigawi was brutally attacked by at least a dozen plain clothes agents in Tiananmen Square and then detained, together with an unidentified Asian man with whom he had been talking for several hours. The Japanese journalist later required numerous stitches to his face and mouth, having been denied medical attention in police custody" (*Asia Watch*, March 21, 1993, p. 10).
40. Edward Mortimer, "Asia as a Region," *The Financial Times*, March 10, 1993.
41. Donald Klein, "Japanese Perceptions," in Ilpyong J. Kim, ed., *The Strategic Triangle* (New York: Paragon, 1987), p. 110. Cf. William Nester, *Japan's Growing Power Over East Asia and the World Economy* (London: Macmillan, 1990).
42. *Japan Economic News*, December 12, 1992.
43. Beijing, UPI, January 27, 1993, citing data from London's Institute of Strategic Studies.
44. Swaine, "The PLA and China's Future," *The Financial Times*, March 4, 1993.
45. Norman, *Chinese*, pp. 260–61.
46. As democratic leader Wang Dan put it in spring 1993, "The south is the future hope of China."
47. Iriye, *China and Japan*, p. 130.
48. *Wu yue wenhua* [Wu yue culture], (Shenyang: Liaoning Education Publishers, 1991).
49. *Investor* (August 1991), pp. 29–43; David Lampton et al., *The Emergence of "Greater China"* (New York: National Committee on U.S.–China Relations, 1992).
50. Philip Curtin, *Cross-Cultural Trade in World History* (New York: Cambridge University Press, 1984), pp. 167, 168.
51. Steven Tanaka, "Imagining History: Inscribing Belief in the Nation," *The Journal of Asian Studies*, vol. 53, no. 1 (February 1994).
52. Iriye, *China and Japan*, p. 142.

Chapter 9

Confucian Leninism and Patriarchal Authoritarianism

Introduction

In the post-Mao era, China's Leninist rulers found they lacked legitimacy. They tried, starting in 1978–79, to prove themselves by economic performance, that is, by delivering ever higher standards of living to the Chinese people. That effort at relegitimation failed because most people did not credit their material gains to the ruling system and because the socialist structure of power skewed the gains in ways that seemed profoundly unfair.

Another effort to legitimate Leninism began in 1984. The regime tried to identify with the values and potentials of conservative Confucianism. Given the popularity of various tough, authoritarian, patriarchal, communalist appeals in other postsocialist societies, one might have expected great success for this shrewd tactic of identifying the regime with the nation's sacred culture, which had been ravaged in the Mao era.

That culture subordinated women to a private sphere. Treating women as Furies to discredit a more democratic politics is a ubiquitous authoritarian ploy. Madame La Farge knitting while heads roll to the guillotine of the French terror encapsulates this symbolization. Prostitutes burning down Paris likewise repre- sents the Paris Commune to many antidemocrats. A similar antiwoman tendency seemed hegemonic in the early reform era in China. With Jiang Qing taken as evil personified, cultural creations made women in politics into evil geniuses, as in Xie Jin's direction of the movie *Hibiscus Town*. Outside observers found that China was heading toward more patriarchy.

149

Post-Mao China prevented the emergence of a self-representing women's movement. Consequently, no group opposed layoffs predominantly of women from state enterprises, no one opposed continuing college entrance exam scoring biased against women, and no one opposed a persistent denial of better jobs to qualified women. Margery Wolf therefore could conclude in 1985 that the reform project in China would "do little to improve women's lot." Its goals, she found, precluded "autonomy and a heightened sense of personhood." Worse yet, "Men are again likely to become structural as well as ideological patriarchs" (Wolf 1985, 267, 270).

Ruling groups then propagandized the discourse of Confucian authoritarian patriarchy. But unexpectedly, the consequence tended to discredit both patriarchy and the Leninist system. Ironically, the conservative Confucian appeal not only backfired, but it even inadvertently increased support for independent young women, the usual victims of authoritarian patriarchy. The cause of freedom for the young and female actually became experienced by many as the cause of freedom for all Chinese. This chapter probes the dynamics and potential consequences of this most remarkable development.

In contrast to societies where democracy facilitated the organization of women for women, the Chinese discourse occurred more at a symbolic level, one in which women served mainly as markers deployed, often by men, at times in sexist and stereotyped ways, although self-consciously prowoman. The southern artist Ni Haifeng explained how all China is in the position of the young female victim of state socialist rape.

> When culture invades private life on a large scale, the individual cannot escape being raped. From this viewpoint my zero-level writing can be taken as a protest against the act of rape. I also want to warn people of the dangers inherent in cultural rape. (Andrew Solomon 1993, 51)

In elite cultural enclaves, creators identified with victimized women, imagining the party–state as manned by political prostitutes parading as paternalists claiming to protect, but actually oppressing and violating, women. Because post-Mao rulers presented themselves as promoters of Confucianism, those who would challenge the dictators logically had to oppose the patriarchy of Confucianism. This meant revealing the unhappy outcome of violent patriarchy, the cruel repression of women, especially young women. The cause of freedom for sexually active young women increasingly seemed identical to the cause of freedom for all people opposed to the despotic Confucian patriarchs.

The protest against patriarchy was a quotidian experience, as when the unmarried daughter returned home late. Stylishly dressed, she sat down and started smoking in front of her father, a bodily presentation whose explicit message was that she could reject the repressive patriarchy of both her father and the Party, which presented itself as national *paterfamilias*. The consequent legitimating discourse of autonomy for young women may be contributing to the democratic project, because Chinese thinkers find it "extremely difficult to have the principle of human equality accepted, and to acknowledge human equality, and to acknowledge human nature as freedom and the value of the individual subject" (Tang 1993, 407).

The attempt to legitimate the regime via authoritarian patriarchy, however much it has for the moment rebounded and instead enhanced the language and logic of autonomy and pluralism, is not the end of the political struggle. At another time, anti-Leninist traditionalist authoritarianism could win. Legitimate identification with the victims of patriarchal injustices has perhaps only temporarily strengthened democratic possibilities. Because political success is a matter of timing, if the moment is missed, subsequent opportunities could instead favor authoritarians.

The Campaign for Confucianism

A pro-Confucius campaign began in 1984 with the formation of a Confucian society and state investment in restoring Confucian relics. China's rulers tried to create public opinion respectful of authoritarian patriarchy in both private and public realms. Beginning in 1984, these conservatives promoted a media campaign to celebrate women who manifested patriarchal Confucian virtues and did not give up home and family for life in the public realm. They argued that women should stay home to educate their (male?) children so the children did not turn into juvenile delinquents and instead became productive assets in a national effort of economic catch-up.

Women seeking individual fulfillment are still denounced as selfish and unpatriotic. Indeed, they are presented by the old guard as alien ingrates who do not understand that socialism already has granted them moral equality—the ability to play their "natural" role in the family and the larger society. Starting in the mid-1980s the Party praised "wives' sacrifices." Xie Lihua, who then edited the Marriage and Family column in *China Women's News*, reports that

> [w]eeks before March 8 [Women's Day], stories would pour in about wives sacrificing for their husbands' careers—all ... written by men. ... She particularly remembered one "model family" story. The wife was praised for staying with her paraplegic husband instead of divorcing him. She had lived in self-denial for eight years when local officials "discovered" her "shining merits." (Wang Rong 1993, 6)

> In 1986, six women were extolled ... who had ... sacrificed their sexual desire, or career or time ... taking care of their sick in-laws or maintaining their loyalty to their impotent, or sick, or criminal, or soldier husbands. Among them was a widow ... eulogized for maintaining widowhood and taking care of her deceased husband's parents for 23 years. (Bao 1980, p. 15)

In November 1989, the Party General Secretary Jiang Zemin proudly declared that "the Chinese women's ability to bear hardship [is] well known through the world" (Rosen, 1990).

The regime promotes beauty contests and fashion shows as evidence of "Oriental" (*Dongfang*) female virtue. At the ice festival in Harbin in 1994, the flimsily clad young women who paraded in subzero temperatures in bathing suits were praised for displaying the heroic virtues of "northern modern girls." Fashion awards are celebrated as proof of the "beauty of Oriental women." Feminine graces are described as "eternally beautiful" and called the "essence of the Orient." In serving the nation through female beauty, these northern, Oriental women supposedly negate the notion of learning from China's south or a global West. Women should not transgress prescribed female roles; they should be northern Oriental women and thereby serve the nation.

Patriotism, self-denying patriarchy, and prosperity are joined as the antithesis of an imaginary West, meaning an anarchic civil society of individuals free to satisfy their needs and desires. China's post-Mao rulers insist that a secret to Japan's success was the strength of the Confucian family in which women were not liberated as in the West. Instead, women stayed home and helped educate the children for success in the competitive world economy. For a woman to accept patriarchy therefore is to be a patriot. A feminist would be a traitor. In this mode, *China Youth Daily* argued in its initial 1992 issue, as translated by David Kelly, for the essentialness and superiority of antiliberal Confucianism.

> China . . . is an Oriental country, with unmistakably distinctive forms of civilization and value concepts. The Confucian tradition and its moral ethic of collectivism and altruism, its secular attitude of "not truckling to authority or might, shunning licentiousness whether rich or poor," is a source of values indispensable in the process of socialist modernization, especially in a backward country trying to catch up. Asian economic growth has in recent decades proven the great contribution of Confucian culture.

The place that symbolizes success in the campaign to re-establish Confucian morality is Singapore. China's Deng Xiaoping noted on his early 1992 tour of the south to reinvigorate reform, that

> Singapore boasts good public order under a strict administration. We should learn from their experience and surpass them in this regard. Since China opened its door to the outside world, decadent things have come in . . . drug-taking, prostitution and economic crimes. (Deng 1992)

By self-repression, women will be kept from vices such as prostitution.

But China's elite cultural creators instead stood with women, even prostitutes, as morally superior to ruling Confucian Leninists. It was subsequently noted that "Most contemporary Chinese literature attacks the evils and limitations of traditional Chinese clan families and describes the wail and woe of young people who try to break away from the old family shackles." By 1993 the regime responded. It explicitly promoted novels that offered a conservative response to the notion in pre-1993 novels that China would be better if not shackled by its Confucian past. The conservatives celebrated the north China "Loess Plateau, which both nurtured China's forefathers and 're-incarnated' the Chinese nation during the modern revolution." The traditional value system, uniquely Chinese, that emerged supposedly made it possible for a united Chinese culture to last "more than 2,000 years." This celebration of Confucian north China culture was advertized as having "great popularity in Hong Kong, Taiwan and Southeast Asia, where neo-Confucianism is widespread." Hence national unity and prosperity were tied to the old ways.

Mao-era propaganda and May Fourth–era intellectual work had long argued the opposite. Chinese had long been taught by Communists that the nineteenth-century Confucian Zeng Guofan was "a man who suppressed the peasants' uprising and their Heavenly Peace Dynasty (1851–64) and who supported the Qing Dynasty's (1844–1911) yielding of China's sovereignty to foreign imperialism." The regime suddenly reversed itself and argued that old-fashioned Confucianism was not the enemy of Chinese independence and progress. They were not sure "whether this trend for traditional culture . . . will satisfy the public. . . ." (Zong 1994). This chapter explains why official propagandists had good reason to doubt their ability to make Confucianism popular and define it as at one with Leninism.

In the late-Leninist period, people were aware that socialism actually did badly by women and the family. The late-Leninist popular consensus was that women should be liberated from a triple burden of onerous household responsibilities, heavy work outside the home, and special difficulties caused by command-economy scarcities and production priorities that led to endless waiting in lines, sitting at meetings, engaging in "voluntary" extra, unpaid labor, and not having access to such consumer goods as sanitary napkins, washing machines, dishwashers, refrigerators, or fast food. Freedom based on this experience meant freedom from even superficially well-meaning statist initiatives. Day care for one's children is experienced as just another pseudopublic realm where the immoral state intrudes with its poisonous propaganda against the sacred family.[1]

In post-Mao China, the Party dictators knew that people saw Mao-era policies, premised on a vacuous egalitarianism, as hurting the family. The regime therefore tried to relegitimate itself by focusing on any attempt to achieve equality as unnatural. The post-Mao rulers would instead offer supposedly weaker women the protection of conservative Confucian authoritarian patriarchy, identifying gender equality as the evil cause both of Mao's project and of post-Mao political reform toward democratization. Both are presented as anti-Confucian, as disrespectful of the distinct value of hierarchical Chinese culture. The regime offers itself as the vehicle of conservative communalism.

Securing Women

There has been an explosion of individually liberated women whose behavior seems immoral to conservatives in nations where Leninism has been delegitimated. Prostitution at times has seemed the fastest-growing profession. The government of post-socialist Hungary decriminalized prostitution as a human right. In Russia, a poll of fifteen-year-old females found three-quarters insisting that prostitution should be a free choice. Andrei Codrescu reports that he heard an Italian cameraman ask two Romanian girls:

> "Are you two lesbians?"
> "We don't have that in Romania yet," one of them answered earnestly.
> "Maybe when democracy comes," the other said, just as sincerely.
> (Codrescu 1991, 93)

In China by 1992, especially in the south, there were a spate of sex-change operations, sought as a way to realize one's authentic self, a true avant-garde of individual freedom. A new market-driven need to win readers produced stories stressing the scandalous. Writing on sexually explicit themes proliferated. With consumerism in the era of post-Mao reform providing short-sleeved blouses made of light fabrics, and with China joining an international world of sports, bathing suits, and physical fitness, it could seem from a conservative authoritarian perspective that visually immorality was threateningly pervasive. Besides, what did Chinese women have to complain about, patriarchal opinion had it, given the gains since the death of Mao Zedong? "Indeed, Chinese women have been 'liberated' ever since the first package of sanitary napkins was made in the Beijing No. 11 Paper Mill in 1982" (Cai 1990).

This new morality of assertive young females claiming control of their bodies could seem immoral to many. The young and liberated embraced what the elderly and conservative abhorred. "To write about love-making, to celebrate sexual desire . . . [i]n China . . . is a revolutionary way of writing . . . because it produces 'fresh desires' " (Wang 1993, 379). Pornography proliferated. Freedoms for women, in patriarchal consciousness, appeared as sexual immorality, the degradation of women parading as a sexual revolution. Many Chinese could conclude that they did not need another revolution, at least not a sexual revolution.

Market-oriented reforms in China have included the removal of subsidies from most cultural productions, although the dictatorship has kept subsidizing its own few chosen house organs. But liberal cultural outlets often find that to win readers, purchasers, or viewers, nudity and some salaciousness are a great help. To monopolize the media, the authoritarian patriarchs launched a war on pornography, obscenity, and immorality in the name of protecting young women and preserving sacred values. Democracy and liberty were damned as enemies of sacred and protective patriarchal norms.

A spate of divorce in the reform era is a hot topic of gossip. The family, the moral bedrock of the culture, can seem threatened by the liberation of women, by a turn away from stable patriarchy. In conservative national consciousness, feminism is synonymous with alien values.[2] A feminist is a foreigner. Chinese "women writers refuse to have their names associated with feminism" (Liu 1993, 197; Wang Zheng 1993, 164, 165, 188, 193, 195, 205). Feminism is predominantly experienced as a foreign disease, indistinguishable from AIDS, syphilis, or gonorrhea.

Reactionary patriarchal authoritarians find independent or assertive women permissive and licentious, neither women nor Chinese. From the patriarchy there is a backlash of violent rage against women—rape and beatings—blamed (not only in China, indeed not only in nations reforming out of Leninism) on the female victim. These violent actions are seen as the consequence of

> Western intrusiveness, "democracy" and the liberalization of sexual mores. It is worth remembering that the men who attempted a coup [in Russia] in August 1991 declared, "Never before has the propaganda of sexual violence assumed such a scale, threatening the health and lives of future generations." (Vanden Heuvel 1993, 872)

Subordinating Women

While the authoritarian appeal is reasonable to conservative villagers, who believe "that nothing is wrong with buying a woman or selling one to a man" (Sun 1992, 18), in reality, Leninist Confucianism does not protect women. Hence a Chinese woman sold into a marriage or even a brothel is assumed to have been properly obtained. *China Daily* reported on December 22, 1993, on one abduction ring.

> A 69-member ring engaged in abducting and trading women . . . based at the Jiulongyang Labor Market in Chengdeu, Sichuan Province, had abducted more than 200 women aged 15–41 in Yunnan, Shanxi, Sichuan and Shaanxi provinces and Inner Mongolia under the guise of offering them business and job opportunities. The women were sold to rural and pastoral areas of Inner Mongolia.

The hidden problem is that some people still imagine violence, prostitution, and rape such that patriarchy gives a husband the right to sell his wife and a man the right to buy a woman (see Gilmartin 1990; Hershatter 1991; Tanner 1994). Such values do not actually advance the cause of women.

Although my own interviewing suggests a great frequency to these horrors, the arrest of one enslaved woman for the murder of a man claiming to be her husband received media attention. After this young woman from Hunan province failed the college entrance exam, her parents negotiated a price for an arranged marriage with a much older man. The girl fled to escape the forced marriage. On the road, she hitched a ride in a truck whose driver sped to a remote village and sold her as a bride. The police and the official Women's Federation were no help. The girl, a victim of kidnapping, enslavement, and rape, however, fled as soon as possible. Other villagers captured her and returned her to the man who had bought her. Drunk and angry, he beat her brutally with the flat side of an axe. Exhausted, he fell asleep. The battered victim took the axe and killed the rapist, the torturer, the enslaver. She then was arrested.

More typically, forced prostitution begins as a way out of misery. Buyers visit a poor rural area. To families locked into unprofitable grain production by state fiat, they offer cash plus a good salary for a daughter, perhaps U.S. $1,500 a year in an area where per capita income is not even a tenth of that amount. Once the girls are alone in a distant city, they are forced to work as prostitutes. Any resistance is met with extreme physical brutality, including gang rape. By 1993 there were more than two million prostitutes in China, perhaps one-quarter, according to Chinese analysts, of the illegally coerced variety.

Kidnapping and sale are protected by corrupt tough males in China's various police forces. The Chinese press reported an instance where a Ms. Wu was sold against her will to a farmer named Gong, who raped her.

> Considered ugly and bad-mannered, Mr. Gong nonetheless enjoyed the sympathy of villagers for his failure to find a local woman who would marry him. Friends and relatives joined in a forced marriage ceremony a few days after Ms. Wu's capture. Mr. Gong's friends, including officers in the local public security bureau, later kept an eye out to make sure that Ms. Wu would not flee or phone for help.
>
> When she did once attempt to escape, Mr. Gong stripped off her clothes, tied her to a roof beam in his home and scorched her thighs with a lit cigarette until she promised not to try again. (*Dallas* 1993)

The conservative discourse on learning of women being "bound and gagged, gang raped by their captors, shipped along illicit trade routes and paraded in flatbed trucks before eager buyers in rural villages" concludes that "For girls, it is safer never to leave home." Hence young women are to devote themselves to cultivating dependable dependence. Women would be better off subordinating themselves, a reality reflected in literature that presents love and marriage in virile Confucian terms in which authoritarian men are presented as morally upright and women are properly submissive (Louie 1989, 55). This patriarchal perspective has cultural resonance. "Recent studies and surveys reflect the prevalent view among Chinese men and women that women are physically weaker and inferior to men, display negative personality traits (e.g., gossip, pettiness, disrespect for authority), and inherently do not possess the same abilities to learn and study" (Hom 1992, 183). Indeed, a good son or husband would see himself, and be seen as, a strong male who protected both wife and mother. Conservatives insist that only tough Confucian patriarchy can save China.

Patriarchy as Salvation

Reforming a wasteful command economy where women's labor had been seen as "expensive labor" allowed state enterprises now aiming at profitability to cut costs by laying off women (Moghadam 1992, 6). Firing women first is, of course, a patriarchal priority in all sorts of economies. In the prereform era, women seemed to patriarchal males to be redundant or low-value producers earning too much and receiving benefits that appeared undeserved in an economy of redundant employment. Women could retire earlier, could receive maternity leaves, and be assigned lighter tasks. Yet women were palpably inferior by proletarian standards of heavy manual labor. Socialist values reinforced Confucian values. The undeserving seemed unjustly favored. It seemed right that women should return to a household realm.

The fraud in Mao-era gender equality also seemed manifest in the political realm where token females aped the party line. In addition, the overemployment of women as neighborhood spies led to a depiction of women in public life as "the fanatic utterly intransigent woman apparatchik" (Bollobas 1993, 203), a generalized image reinforced in China by widespread hate for Jiang Qing, the leading Mao-era fanatic fundamentalist.[3]

With women consequently seen to have no good role to play in the public sphere, a cult of domesticity is actually embraced by "many women [who] seem to want to retreat to the domestic sphere" (Moghadam 1992, 21). It is a tranquil refuge from the impossible triple burdens that judged women at work by heavy labor standards and denied women modern conveniences so that household burdens intensified, while new onerous obligations from socialist dynamics brutally piled up on already weighted-down shoulders.[4]

Many women enter the reform era believing they are weaker or so different that they should stay out of the public sphere. Chinese customarily believe both that lost blood cannot be restored and that women's blood is inferior, weaker, watery. Political scientist Kate Xiao Zhou reports in an unpublished paper that soldiers, who predominate among blood donors, reinforce their image and self-image as uniquely brave and altruistic by giving their rich, strong, precious blood. Their sacrifice of blood makes the life of the nation possible. In contrast, women are thought not to have a real contribution to make and so are not pressured to give blood. The nation would suffer if wounded soldiers received women's supposedly thin blood that does not support martial courage.[5] Many women agree that the immoral socialist system promoted a false egalitarian ideology and an unfairly burdensome inequality by treating women as other then women. They consequently "breathe a sigh of relief at the possibility of relegation to the domestic sphere" (Einhorn 1992, 66).

Since much in socialism was a "natural catastrophe," buffeting women with "exhausting housework, abortion or birth control, lower salaries, lack of prestige" (Bollobas 1993, 206), many women imagine a return to their different and "natural" role as better. There is a "desire to maintain the family as a non-politicized sphere" in opposition to the previously "ubiquitous state presence" (Einhorn 1992, 61). Prior socialism is blamed for forcing women to abandon a proper place in a supposedly natural hierarchical order, a removal of a prop that threatened society's very stability.[6]

In the reform era in postsocialist societies, many "women . . . accept unemployment . . . looking forward to the opportunity to be able to spend more time with their children or attending domestic responsibilities." Staying at home is becoming "fashionable, as women seek greater involvement in raising their children" (Fong and Paull 1992, 48). The early 1990s model village of Daqiuzhuang was praised because all women could stay home. Since opposition to the immorally intrusive state valorizes the private sphere, less money spent on items such as day care can therefore seem an end to the subsidization of immorality.[7]

The writer Dai Qing believes that "China faces the question of whether women should return to the home rather than the question of how to leave the home" (Wang Zheng 1993, 193). She finds that employing women and then paying an underemployed labor force low wages because many people actually share one job (as was the case in the Mao era) hurts productivity and is blamed on women. China, she argues, also is still too poor "to pay for women's maternity leaves" (ibid., 202).

Women had experienced "Communist policy . . . as forced masculization" (Katzarova 1993, 149). "[S]ocialists failed . . . to recognize any essential *positive* contributions of engaging in unpaid reproductive labor. . . . [W]omen's 'difference' . . . [was] defined as deficiency" (Ferrel 1993, 110). In China, women who engaged in the heaviest manual labor were singled out for praise as "Iron Women." Because all were to share the monolithic interest of the ruling party, the proletarian rulers, on gender, as on religion, race, ethnicity, etc., denied any validity to the notion of societal interests that should be able to diversely represent themselves. The top-down dictatorship claimed a monopoly on a monist truth. It ended "up denying difference to women" (Liu 1993, 196).

In the first post-Mao elections at Beijing University, however, a woman ran on a prowoman ticket of being allowed to dress and adorn oneself femininely. Bicycles, previously only built with a bar from seat to handlebar, making skirt wearing inconvenient or seemingly immodest, were now manufactured so as to permit skirt wearing. The bikes sold like hotcakes. In like manner, watches now were also made with narrow wristbands. There was a virtual riot the first time they appeared at the stores. In general, "The emphasis on woman's need to realize her 'feminine essence' as the major women's issue" seems "a progressive demand" (Heitlinger 1993, 97). It negates prior unjust impositions.[8] Young women ought to be home bearing and rearing children and nurturing broader family harmony. (That is even what marrying women swore to work for in Cultural Revolution–era marriage ceremonies.)

Writer Wang Anyi finds, "In China women are only now beginning to have the right, the luxury to talk about differences between men and women, to enjoy something that distinguishes women from men" (Wang Zheng 1993, 165). Another woman writer, Dai Qing, whose politics are far more reformist than Wang Anyi, nonetheless agrees.

> God made females' biological structure different from males; women give birth to babies and breast-feed them, so their brain structure must be different, too. Women have to bear more important responsibilities in life. . . . Nature has made human beings this way for millions of years. . . . [H]uman biology is not irrational. . . . Men and women . . . are born different and cannot be equal. (Ibid., 201)

Wang Anyi cries out, "Female factory workers do the same physical labor as male workers. Now many women have difficult labors and few have milk. Women are tremendously fatigued" (ibid., 166). "[W]omen's health is deteriorating. Women are so tired. So, when they come home they are foul-tempered and mistreat the children; children don't get an adequate education. . . . [W]e are very, very tired. . . . [O]ur energy has been totally exhausted" (ibid., 167). The poet Shu Ting acknowledges that a mother is supposed to sacrifice to rescue mankind, but as a poet she cries out in pain "Oh motherland," because women are "worn out, exhausted, wilted, dilapidated" (Kubin 1992, 143, 144).

Thus there is appeal in the notion that women should be protected. Confucian Leninists claim that their strong arm will keep Chinese women from ending up as sexual playthings of foreigners who have come with money to trade and invest. Fifth-generation movies made with funding from Hong Kong or Taiwan or Japan, which depict women as suffocated to death by the feudal-like patriarchy, can be attacked by northern conservatives and even women, who now seek the safety of their "natural" role in an authoritarian hierarchy, as "Western" attempts that expose Chinese women in a pornographic way to the gaze of foreigners and besmirch the moral core of China's great culture. Openness to the world market, and not only in movies, is presented by chauvinistic authoritarians as a danger through which pour the dirty pollutants of foreign cultures.[9] A binary opposition pits the moral family values of one's own sacred culture against the immoral ways of the alien, understood in China as an amorality that has, in the United States, destroyed the family; created unmarried teen-age mothers;[10] abandoned elders; and caused juvenile delinquency, street violence, and the spread of drugs.

Authoritarian opposition to democracy tries to build on antifemale patriarchy.[11] Preform maltreatment of women under the hypocritical banner of equality can produce a demand for an end to the hypocrisy, understood as a movement against false equality. Young women freeing themselves from hated Leninist patriarchy may well choose to embrace an indigenous patriarchy.

In reforming Leninist systems, there is support for policies to free women from involuntary emancipation and return them to the family, where they fill the role of mother, keeper of the hearth, and bulwark of the nation. This patriarchal authoritarianism is legitimized by the perception that alien influences export prostitution and pornography to the wounded nation of fragile families. Women who stood with family and nation against alien freedom gained fame in the former Soviet Union. As American conservatism and fundamentalism see women made licentious by portrayals of sex in the media, by the availability of antipregnancy pills, by legalized abortion, and by the so-called sexual revolution's war against the double standard, so in China, many experience a sharp response to similar, indeed, far more sudden and revolutionary changes.[12] The mystery therefore is why, with so many Chinese accepting a conservative definition of how to protect women from immorality, has Confucian Leninism nonetheless still done so poorly. The logic of a counterhegemonic discourse links subversion of the palpably illegitimate authoritarian rulers with subversion of their rationale of Confucian patriarchy.

Subverting Authoritarian Patriarchy

Even though there was a popular base for conservative patriarchal authoritarianism, at first almost anything emanating from the discredited leadership was dismissed. Consequently, the post-Mao efforts of Leninists to appear as Confucians seemed just another hypocritical fraud. People knew that socialism hurt women. Socialism, in the Mao era, divided the family physically, insisted on loyalty to the supreme leader over one's parents, and increasingly left unmet the needs of family members. People in the reform era, when Party members seem out to enrich themselves and to be purely parasitic, experience more blows against a prospect that paternalism could happily unite rulers and ruled in a Leninist state. Consequently, the campaign to relegitimate Communist dictators as Confucian patriarchs instead helps to delegitimate both the socialist polity and Confucianism, tarring both with the same brush. Hence democratic freedom and the struggle of the female for autonomy are united in the post-Mao era by their common adversary. To oppose political tyranny involves opposing patriarchy. For many among the great majority fed up with the hypocritical regime, freedom for women is freedom for China.

A new logic of legitimation deploys the fate of women to subvert patriarchy in both spheres. This delegitimation of authoritarianism is occurring without a women's movement for human rights in general or for the righting of particular wrongs; it is happening without even an equivalent of the silent oppositional presence of the mothers in the Plaza de Mayo in Buenos Aires. This politics is largely a symbolic discourse (see Jelin 1990).

A new historical narrative redefines Leninists as betrayers of women. In the last years of the revolutionary civil war, much Communist propaganda focused on how women in capitalist-imperialist Shanghai could survive only through immoral prostitution and how schoolgirls in Beijing were raped by American soldiers. There was a hope that socialism would save women. As writer Liu Binyan experienced it:

> When the People's Liberation Army marched into Beijing, the first thing it did was to close all brothels. This move alone conquered the people's hearts (Liu Binyan 1990, 1)

Maoist practice, however, cruelly betrayed this promise.

> When you had to beg the party branch secretary every year for "relief grain" or "resold grain," or when you had to present your wife or daughter to him in exchange for his favor, would you still have personal dignity? (Liu Binyan 1990, 3)

The 1993 volume *Dreams of Educated Chinese Youth* by the young Sichuan writer Deng Xian chronicles the unnatural death of 153 educated young women in one construction corps in Yunnan, as well as a plague of rape. Society is rife with similar accounts that discredit pretended Leninist Confucians. In 1992, the Inner Mongolia Cultural Press published a report by Jiang Hao titled *Bloody Black River* that told of how in early 1976 twenty-four female university students from Beijing returned from the countryside just as the city erupted in mass demonstrations on behalf of the recently deceased premier Zhou Enlai. The women were then sentenced to prison along with five others accused of having sexual relations with Germans and charged with "illicit relations with a foreign country." In prison, the women were overworked, underfed, and continually raped and gang-raped. Eventually they escaped. They ran into an army unit that tried to protect them. Instead the leaders of the army unit were tortured and executed.

The investigation that led up to the book was blocked and the circulation of the book was banned because the truth would "affect the image of public security personnel" (Mo 1993), socialist officials reportedly in on the big business of sexual enslavement through forced prostitution. The socialist state had not stopped rape. Writer Liu Binyan found that there was more rape under communism than under either the Japanese or the Nationalists. Statistics may not exist, but the belief does.

The message that the regime has continued the rape it promised to end comes from many sources. Born in a northern village, fiction writer Mo Yan, author of *Red Sorghum*, depicted China's countryside as "a nightmarish world of ignorance, poverty and cruelty, full of suffering, sadness and misery" When the landlord rapist and the bandit rapist are defeated by forces that bring to power the hired hand, then this rural proletariat, the new Party official, also rapes. The

Party dictatorship, far from being a rupture and a new start, continues and intensifies viciousness (Duke 1991). This seems obvious to many today. It is the message of the movie *Farewell My Concubine*. In this view, Confucian Leninism is shameless hypocrisy.

Some youth believe that the hypocritical moves of parasitic, raping, prostituting political elders kept the people so repressed that the Cultural Revolution, in which constraints were lifted from the oppressed and repressed young, naturally exploded in the orgy of libertinism and sexual sadism that characterized Cultural Revolution–era cruelties. Liberating women now is a way to negate the social-psychological force that made the sadism of the Cultural Revolution possible.

An unusually large number of suicides during the Cultural Revolution, Chinese historian Jane Wu reported, were committed by previously respected women who were humiliated when their private diaries were read publicly, their heads were shaved, their blouses ripped open, and their faces smeared. In cities, divorced, alone, and publicly degraded, women often committed suicide because they could not bear life in the brutal patriarchal order. Feeling isolated and betrayed, with no hope for a life of dignity, they often ended their lives.

In China during the Cultural Revolution, urban families with a son and daughter were ordered to send one child to the countryside. The parents had to choose between losing the son, the support of their old age, or sending a young daughter into a world where survival could well require trading sex for favors, a world where there was no recourse against sexual abusers in power. With everything riding on dependent ties to all-powerful males, women lived in a casting-couch society. Trading sex for survival was ubiquitous. The regime so institutionalized rape and prostitution that it lacks moral force in blaming post-Mao reforms for a spread of prostitution. Instead, the rulers and their system are blamed.

In guaranteeing that women belonged to men, the new order killed women. "In the village, say, if a young man is recruited into military service, they feel they must get a match for him. . . . If she wants to marry someone else, then she committed a crime, violating military marriage. Lots of young women have committed suicide because of marriage problems" (Wang Zheng 1993, 189).

People find proof that the self-proclaimed moral paternalists are dangerous frauds. When Wu Ningkun returned to China from his graduate education in the United States at the outset of the People's Republic, he felt "national pride" on seeing what was no longer there: "Gone were the opium dens and whorehouses that had been the curse of my generation" (Wu 1993, 10).

But then Wu discovers that the new order in fact degrades women. They "body-search my pregnant wife and aged mother" (ibid., 54). Wu is sent away from his wife so she has "to cope by herself" (ibid., 71). Violent crimes against women, such as beating and rape, and patriarchal attitudes such as the wife as the property of the husband and the murder of infant girls persisted (ibid., 99, 268, 104, 318). In fact, the system left women vulnerable to and without recourse against repeated rape by absolute power holders (ibid., 289). In the countryside, the "raping" of urban "teenage girls" by army officers and others supposedly responsible for the "sent down" girls' protection was so ubiquitous that it soon was "no longer news" (ibid., 327).

Anti-imperialists, during the pre-1949 revolutionary struggle for liberation, in envisioning port cities as bastions of imperialism and prostitution, came to contrast the immorality of imperialism versus the purity of the native soil as an opposition of the city against the countryside in which the city was full of demeaning lures that could seduce, sully, and destroy innocents from the countryside. The binary of foreign colonizer versus native colonized treats the outside as decadent, artificial, and contaminated and the native as healthy, authentic, and pure. The prostitute was pitted against the virgin; the greedy and corrupt against the ascetic and altruistic. This binary was limned in the mass culture of Chinese cinema of the 1930s and 1940s (Pickowicz, 1991). Women should be protected.

But they were not. Worse yet, they were not even allowed to be women. What caught people's attention eventually was that women were measured by male heavy-labor work norms and had to look like men, wearing shapeless clothing and "wearing the same dark colors as men, keeping their hair short, and using no makeup" (Liu 1993, 196). Would men instead be invited to rouge their faces and wear long hair? The regime came to seem unnatural in not allowing women to be women. Consequently, in opposing this antiwoman dictatorship, Chinese experience themselves as truly on the side of women. The unpopular regime's contrary propaganda seems a lie.

The anti-Confucian promise of May Fourth, the liberation of women from patriarchal inhumanities, seems so betrayed by the socialist system that when the post-Mao regime promotes Confucianism many see it as traitorous. Regime opponents, in embracing the unfulfilled May Fourth agenda, align with the cause of young women against post-Mao self-styled Confucian despots who denounce the anti-Confucianism of May Fourth. The rulers had betrayed their promises to the people. In opposition, democracy and the rights of young women have become mutually supporting.

A Prostituting State

Given nativistic patriarchal attitudes, one might expect that prostitution for foreigners in post-Mao China would ignite male rage over proprietorship and support Confucian Leninism. That it has not may be partially related to Chinese economic success, experienced as attracting white Russian females back to China as prostitutes for Chinese men. Still, as is generally the case when industrialization takes off, most prostitutes do sex work for indigenous laborers.[13]

Chinese know well that prostitution is not an alien import. They can, on the one hand, treat sex for sale in a matter-of-fact way as a ubiquitous side effect of rapid growth and, on the other, historically celebrate women (such as the ancient heroine Wang Zhaojun)—including prostitutes—whose bodies were given to foreigners as the price of saving the nation. They learn early about the beautiful prostitute Cai Jinhua, who dissuaded German forces from bombarding Beijing.[14]

Prostitution, however, also includes young freelancers who have a daytime job but want to earn more money, or wives seeking investment funds for a family business,[15] or show-business starlets who take high pay for serving the newly rich. Chinese students of the subject find that prostitutes in the last category are never arrested. In any case, workers in the sex trade seem more like workers, while the rulers seem the real prostitutes.

Immoral prostitutes are experienced not as the young women forced into perhaps humiliating behavior to earn a better living, but as the older men who sell out China to Japan. Prettifying such political prostitutes would be a lie. The political system is the real prostitution. Perhaps the 1928 comment of Party leader Zhou Enlai will keep growing in popularity, "For the sake of the revolution, we must even become like prostitutes."

The popular writer Wang Shuo contrasted himself with the prostitutes in power. "I can't just go out and lie to people, can I? . . . Although writing isn't entirely the same as prostitution [i.e., politics], you can get away with it as long as you're shameless enough." Strikingly, opponents of the parasitical state actually identify the quest for truth and dignity with the cause of real prostitutes, the victims of the political prostitutes. Gao Shijian found in 1993:

> In a conversation in his semi-autobiographical book, *I am Wang Shuo*, Wang writes, "I'm just like a whore." Jia Ping'ao [author of *Fei Du* (Defunct Capital), which captures life after the failure of the 1898 Reform Movement—meaning the crushing of the spring 1989 Democracy Movement]—makes a similar first person confession in *Defunct Capital*. In fact, many Chinese authors today seem to embrace the worldview of the prostitute. In terms of form and structure, the novels of Wang Shuo and Jia Ping's can be called "Whorehouse Social Criticism." (Gao 1993, 71)

Although she is militantly antifeminist and has proconservative values, the writer Wang Anyi nonetheless, praises prostitutes.

> Don't feel contempt for them. Most have ideals in life and a dream of something higher than the sky. Last month, I went to a female prisoner's reformatory farm. Most . . . are imprisoned for prostitution. Lots . . . did it to secure a happy life. . . .
> They simply do not want to fall into the fate of common female factory workers, crushed every day on the bus, with a tiny little pay pocket every month and then to make everything worse, getting saddled with a baby . . . and that they think is very normal. Many of them are the most ambitious among us. (Wang Zheng 1993, 161)

As a symbol, woman is both the victim of brutal state enslavement in prostitution and an individual who should freely be allowed to fulfill her personal goals, even through the sexual use of her body for pleasure or profit. The really evil are the Confucian Leninists in power who hypocritically preach the virtues of paternalism but act instead on an amoral ethos that crushes young women.

What comes through to most Chinese is that a corrupt, nepotistic, and narrow system of cruelty can ruin Chinese young women. They are the martyred. Their cause, the cause of legal protection and secure independence, is the progressive cause of all Chinese. Truth, self-realization, and justice require that one identify even with women who choose prostitution, since they are morally superior to ruling parasitic hypocrites who profit from the brutal enslavement of women.

Against Patriarchy

In the above perspective, it seems right that young women be empowered. Soon after post-Mao reforms began, social anthropologist Fei Xiaotong found that nuclear families, instead of enlarged families, had become most prevalent. Even in joint families, daughters-in-law increasingly cooked their own meals. That is, they were making a claim on autonomy from elder in-laws. While inadequate child care and a housing shortage artificially depressed the number of nuclear families, the rising status of wage-earning daughters-in-law won more respect for women. Patriarchal purse strings were being snapped by young women who insisted on their right to assert themselves as women.

> In recent years permanent waves have become popular—something that costs [a villager] about two yuan in a neighboring town. For a young woman to get this sum from her father is difficult—he is all too likely to detest this newfangled style. So young factory workers have taken to deducting the cost of a permanent before they turn their wages over to the family head. He may fume a bit, but cannot really prevent it. . . . [R]ural Chinese women have not achieved complete economic independence, but gradually they are gaining increased autonomy. (Fei 1989, 132)

Actually, beauty parlors have long been places where women can renegotiate their identity, making self-interested decisions about where to place themselves in—or how to face themselves toward—a more cosmopolitan and open world (Thompson n.d.). In fact, in the white terror of the late 1920s, short hair on young women was often taken by reactionaries as proof of radicalism. To reactionaries, this was a bodily confession of betrayal of the nation meriting execution. With politics inscribed on the body, regular visits to the beauty parlor in the reform era can be a vigorous assertion of female self and autonomy and a rejection of repressive patriarchy.

The old Confucian values no longer predominate. Two social surveyors report,:

> The idea that a wife could ask for a divorce was something unheard of among most Chinese half a century ago. Only the husband had the right to "dismiss"

his wife if and when he should choose to do so. Now the majority of our respondents supported the idea of divorce if the couple could not get along. (Chu and Ju 1993, 285)

"Mothers-in-law have lost a lot of power. . . . Daughters-in-law have a new respect" (Wolf 1985, 237). Kinship structure is moving toward an egalitarian nuclear family. Daughters-in-law will quarrel openly with unfair mothers-in-law (Chu and Ju 1993, 288) and discuss the difficulties of caring for elderly in-laws in a socialist China that has never had a national pension or rural free health-care system. Increasingly, independence is legitimate such that more and more young parents feel "the correct way to bring up children is to let them develop freely" (ibid., 301).

In like manner, anthropologist Margery Wolf noted in 1980–81 the reversal of Maoist northern "monotonous uniformity in both thought and appearance." "Certainly life in the communes without the annual cycle of religious festivals is colorless. Efforts to keep weddings and funerals simple have further diminished the once frequent breaks in village monotony." But in the post-Mao era, the communes have been disbanded and colorful ritual and religion have returned. Immediately southern women "liked to wear colorful blouses . . . curl their hair, and even wear a bit of makeup" (Wolf 1985, 48, 54). Southern color spread even into the northern countryside. It was, Jing Wang reports, "a visual spectacle, witnessed daily in Chinese women's fashions in the streets," a proclamation of the legitimacy of self "that reached deeply into every socio-economic sector of post-Mao China" (Wang Jing 1993, 349). Southern styling is spreading nationally, propagandizing on behalf of independence for young women.

By the 1980s, women writers who asserted a right to sexual fulfillment were published. Noticing that Confucian convention and Leninist alliance politics both produce loveless marriages, a voice on behalf of allowing women to marry when in love seemed right and natural to most people, even if seemingly immorally selfish to Confucians and orthodox Communists. Women and men both supported sex education in the schools, an end to the Confucian taboo.

Within the old mores, the insistence on liberty, self, and rights for women remains immoral. The choice appears as the old order or democracy with liberty for women. The old guard, in trying to co-opt patriarchal authoritarianism, embraces a Confucianism that was attacked as reactionary in the May Fourth Movement at the outset of the twentieth century. In now reversing themselves and attacking May Fourth, the Communist Party dictators appear reactionary and far behind the times, trying to return China to a premodern ethos. As if time has stood still, Sylvia Chan points out, Chinese women are again fighting the issues of the late Qing Dynasty, attacking the cult of chastity, seeking to protect single or divorced women from defamation as loose women (Chan 1989). For women, patriarchal communism is experienced as a disaster.

The historian of Chinese thought, Julia Ching, depicts dehumanized patriarchy as the core of China's Leninist despotism. "[A] nominally patriarchal style distinguishes Chinese leadership ... inherited from the imperial days, when the supreme lord ... had the power of life or death over all his subjects. ... [T]he Communist usage ... has stripped the patriarchy of any sentiment of paternalism" (Ching 1990, 193). Increasingly, the arbitrary despotism is seen as offering no protection of the weak by the strong. A feudal-like Confucian-Leninist dictatorship is imagined by the 1990s as a vicious old man; democracy is envisioned as young and female. The much-jailed human rights activist Ren Wanding prophesizes that "the infant girl democracy may be killed in its cradle, but she will definitely be born again" (ibid., 206). The novelist Ya Ding agrees on the inevitability of death for the old one and life for the new youth. "An old man is dying but a child is born" (ibid., 226–27). The Beijing massacre of June 4, 1989, only reinforced what was already obvious, that the promise that socialism could save China's young had been massively betrayed.

Anti-Confucian Cultural Creations

Cultural creators played a major role in furthering this new narrative of promoting self, especially the personal happiness of young females, as part of a self-conscious subversion of Confucian Leninism and authoritarian patriarchy. A Chinese movie star titled her memoirs, *My Way*. The Party elite was scandalized since the one right way was supposed to be the Party's way. But the subjective and the personal, as indicated by the extraordinary popularity of the philosopher of aesthetics, Li Zehou, were now legitimate and young women were the vehicle of freedom.

Women movie directors were celebrated in 1986 for a decade of work that reflected a new women's consciousness. In these movies, body and color were celebrated, but in ways that related gender to national identity, such as Zhang Zhen reported at the 1994 meeting of the Association for Asian Studies, when the northern Chinese woman Li Chun chose to replace her drab clothes with the colorful garments worn by Dai women in the south. In place of the monotonous military-style clothing prescribed by Mao that desexualized women, women now insisted on a gender-specific voice and softer-looking colors and clothing. "Iron Women" are reimagined as not made of flesh and blood. Those who had been obedient daughters of Mao's militarized, proletarian state are portrayed as having lost time, love, and life.

Young male creators, the so-called fifth generation of moviemakers, also identify with the plight of young women, although as mentioned earlier, their way of making prowoman statements often ends up unintentionally alienating many Chinese women. These fifth-generation films represent freedom for all people, as embodied in the struggle for freedom of young women. Virtually all their films feature the struggles of assertive women, usually younger and often sexually independent. Writing of the independent young woman featured in the movie *Red Sorghum*, Yuejin Wang notes, "The establishment of autonomous female ecstasy . . . is highly subversive politically" (Wang Yuejin 1988, 47). Likewise, the movie *Farewell My Concubine*, featuring a prostitute as heroine, is seen as a cautionary tale about the dangers of repressing one's true self.

Progressive and humanistic Chinese literature and film by the 1980s no longer treated the Communist Party as the people's savior from Japanese rapists. While Chen Kaige's film, *Farewell My Concubine*, won "The top Palme d' Or award at the Cannes Film Festival . . . the party's propaganda chief Ding Guangen was said to have been enraged by the film's suggestion that there was little difference between the persecution Chinese people suffered at the hands of Japanese occupation forces, corrupt Kuomintang officials, and Communist party cadres" (*Far Eastern Economic Review* 1993). Actually, the film depicts the Communists as the most repressive. Literary critic Wang Ruowang had made the same equation about torture in his *Hunger Trilogy*. The message was that socialism had continued and intensified the evils plaguing the people. That increasingly presuppositional view, which dismissed the socialist era as a disaster, turned the attempted co-optation of Confucianism by Leninists into a discrediting of both.[16]

Zhang Yimou's film *Red Sorghum*, in contrast to Lu Xun's plaint about Chinese looking on passively as Japanese soldiers executed Chinese people, makes it impossible not to be outraged, in part, by making women vitally active agents capable of ecstasy, not just passive victims of imperialism or patriarchy. The Party, in the new narrative, however, does not save the people from rape and torture. The people have to save themselves. Likewise, in the movie *Yellow Earth*, neither the Party nor the Red Army can save the young woman.

The state that had promised to protect the endangered nation, a vulnerability symbolized by foreigners raping young women or turning Chinese girls into prostitutes, is found by cultural creators at the end of the twentieth century to have failed and left women more vulnerable, while promoting repressive sexuality. In opposition to the hypocritical patriarchal ethos, China's most popular writer of the early 1990s, Wang Shuo, speaking for an antipolitical generation, celebrates individuality through the experience of cynics, hoodlums, and petty traders. In opposition to the notion of an attractive, authoritarian Confucian ethic as a glorious cultural inheritance, Wang Shuo comments,

> Chinese are without cultural background. Chinese do not have a soul. Essentially they have the mentality of degenerate bastards. It is said that we have several thousand years of culture, but actually our background is more bleak and desolate than a desert. (Liu Xiaobo 1993, 3)

Those Chinese creators in the post-Mao era see what Lu Xun saw in the Confucian language of salvation. They see it as saving the ruling groups, the old guard. The creative artists increasingly insist on saving the people. One could no longer legitimate sacrificing individuals to save this ruling group. National liberation could only have meaning if it were premised on individual liberation, virtually all Chinese intellectuals now agree.[17]

Because Leninist hypocrisy discredits politics as such, because the purportedly public sphere is actually a private monopoly of illegitimate dictators, the discourse of freedom and fulfillment tends to focus on society and the private sphere. Freedom is the particularistically authentic, even an alternative culture of religion or community or jazz musicians or rock bands or pop singers that could embody a demand for personal meaning. This cultural delegitimation of Communist Party dictatorships was not peculiar to China. Self, individuality, and local community were valorized, while the dictatorial center was delegitimated.

National Identity and Gender Theory

The linkage of patriotism and patriarchy affects most nationalist polities. After the French Revolution,

> the code [of] Napoleon . . . declared that a French woman marrying a foreigner lost her citizenship, and an alien woman marrying a Frenchman automatically became French. . . . [A] French woman married to a Frenchman who expatriated himself, also was expatriated. The French government . . . regarded the woman's consent to marriage as her consent to the consequences. . . . Most nations followed the French example. (Sapiro 1984, 6, 7)

It has been a shared insight of many cultures throughout history that political rulership is family rulership writ large. But different notions of the family–state relation vie with each other in late-twentieth-century China. While politics will probably be decisive, it would be wrong to gainsay the impact of a growing popular privileging of energetic, independent females. It may promote a more open and tolerant political culture and weaken the appeal of patriarchal authoritarianism. The feminist insight of understanding the links between the two spheres—state and society, public and private, government and family—calls attention to how a culture promoting independent young women both discredits Confucian and Leninist repressiveness and also may advance the cause of constitutional democracy. Indeed it may even call attention to Confucian tendencies that highly value individual dignity and embrace law over the selfish whims of arbitrary rulers (de Bary 1994). A postmodern democratic nationalism now increasingly demands societal involvement dealing with everything from local instances of global environmental dangers to stopping police brutality. Local legislators in China have become ombudsmen on behalf of such matters.

As much feminist literature reminds us, the work of patriarchy in reducing women to an authoritarian and hierarchial private sphere is full of meaning for the public sphere, usually legitimating a dictatorial state as natural. Patriarchy is a refuge of authoritarians. As philosopher Immanuel Kant understood, paternalism is the cruelest of tyrannies.[18] Paternalism "undermines solidarity among the powerless by linking them as individuals to their oppressors" (Genovese 1976, 5).

Feminist history and theory inform us that women, and a people identifying with the plight of women, can find allies in their transgression of patriarchy. French revolutionaries of 1848 would not accept the misogynist stereotype of women in the public realm as Furies; in China's case, epigoni of a despised Jiang Qing. French women—as with Chinese at the end of the twentieth century— were imagined as young and beautiful and "not consecrated to obedience" (Strumingher 1993, 279). The courage of martyred women legitimated the autonomy of women. The alternative to independence for women was immoral enslavement by patriarchs. In France,

> a pure and honest girl [can] fall into the hands of a cheating rascal. And when the unfortunate· woman, now his wife, is provoked or encouraged by him to leave the path of honest living [i.e. to become a prostitute] . . . , does she owe him obedience? (Ibid., 278–79)

All cultures offer the possibility of a disruptive reinterpretation of the system of domination. That Chinese and French women would reinterpret culture similarly speaks to the robust explanatory power of paradigms addressed by the feminist discourse on *patria* and patriarchy.

China's Leninist dictatorship embodied a nationalistic authoritarianism of war-police mobilization against foreign enemies that rewarded young male toughs imbued with patriarchal biases against women, especially young ones (Friedman, Pickowicz, and Selden 1991). A similar phenomenon, as feminists have long pointed out, is encapsulated in Europe's early nationalism, with Rousseau the classic statement of how *patria* excludes the female from citizenship. The Communist Party's legitimating patriarchy in China similarly expected women to be pure, to stand by their men in the military, and to bear and rear patriots.[19]

In contrast to the Jacobin-Leninist tradition that Mao had embraced, and which Jean-Jacques Rousseau eloquently expressed, in which the natural woman is a breast-feeding mother who brings up sons to fight for the nation, the orientation highlighted in this chapter would subvert China's militarized state in part by supporting as a modal person the young girl who should be able fully to choose her destiny, premised on an awareness that young Chinese women have in fact not been the bedrock of the nation but its victims. Women, too, deserve human fulfillment. The poor, tough, loyal, conservative, northern peasant fighter is no longer idealized.

For the French thinker Jean-Jacques Rousseau, patriarchy was a morality that excluded women from the public sphere (Thomas 1991). In most cultures, power relations in the family tend to be presented as the larger political cosmos in miniature.[20] John Stuart Mill argued that family patriarchy was slavery and that at the state level, male and female should be equal citizens, that women should be given what men had. But even Mill's explicit argument could be dismissed;

just as Locke's defense of liberty against authoritarian patriarchy could seem, even to Locke, to have no liberating consequences for women, so presuppositionally entrenched is sexist patriarchy. Neither Mill nor Locke embraced the notion that fulfillment for young women was crucial to national salvation. In post-Mao China, however, women's autonomy has become a symbol of the effort against patriarchal authoritarianism and for democracy in both state and societal spheres.

China's socialist state engaged in "repressing sexuality, self, and all private emotions . . . while violence against women continued unabated throughout the decades after liberation" (Meng Yue 1993, 118). The writer Dai Qing found "that the state of women represented the state of the nation." She noted, "If you want to know how well this country's run, all you have to do is to look at the women at the bottom of society" (Wang Zheng 1993, 191). She found that the "condition of the women *is* the condition of the country at large. . . . If you want to know how wealthy a country is, how civilized or educated it is, just look at the women. . . . [T]he [official government] Women's Federation has . . . had serious negative effects" (ibid., 194). It opposed divorce if one partner wished the marriage to continue. The Shanghai writer Zhu Lin, a woman, finds "that of all the oppressions, the most brutal is the oppression of women" (ibid., 180). Her work is said to be especially popular among southern women (ibid., 186).

As with the Argentine mothers in the Plaza, males in power who are condescending sexists seldom take seriously or attack "mere" women, even as the patriarchal status hierarchy is disrupted by a potentially democratizing eruption of women, at least as symbol in the public sphere (Jelin 1990, 91, 92). Generalizing from Argentina (Jacquette 1989), a counterhegemonic project at first ridiculed as merely female can eventually become a potent and public embodiment of truth and life, of human rights and dignity, a major step toward democracy. My hypothesis is that this logic is already disrupting Chinese tyranny and perhaps preparing the ground for democratic liberties.

As captured in Liu Binyan's essay and Wu Ningkun's autobiography, the Mao-era discourse of protecting women was experienced as a fraud masking an actual intensification of the mistreatment of women. Ever more people in the post-Mao era feel that that was to be expected from rulers whose culture came from the ancient, northern, reactionary, Confucian heartland. The post-Mao privileging of China's historical south, represented by the ancient state of Chu, legitimates sexually independent females and discredits the logic of sexual purity. This anti-Confucian valorization has helped raise the prestige of the twentieth-century West Hunan writer Shen Congwen, who had been banned in the Mao era. Shen saw his rural region in China's south and his own familial roots as mixed with the blood of hill-region minorities, a vibrant, ribald people in opposition to stultifying Confucian repression that was continued during the Leninist era in Hunan's provincial capital, Changsha, by Mao's Leninist-Confucian heirs.

She Xuan (to put it anachronistically, China's Cinderella) is identified as southern, too. For Shen and his epigoni, Chu, the ancient kingdom of hibiscus in Hunan embodied the "triumph of 'healthy' untrammeled country love over Confucian restrictions," such that "There was nothing strange about a girl giving birth to an illegitimate child at her mother's home. A married woman could have a lover. The only criterion for a woman to take delight in a man was her consent." Prostitutes were simple, honest country girls, not subverters of a family ethic[21] (Kinkley 1989, 86).

The contemporary writer Can Xue (b. 1953) is also from Hunan in the south. In her *Dialogues in Paradise*, she too harks back to the Chu discourse "marginalized by Confucian canonization" (Jon Solomon 1993, 253), a supernatural world linked to Daoist symbolization. Her "stories are a form of uncompromising resistance to the hegemonistic position . . . an attack upon Confucianist tradition . . . designed to explode the straight-jacket of pathological monologism" (ibid., 257). But whereas the modern project in Western Europe championed reason against revelation, the post-Mao attempt to disturb the *ancien regime* of socialism champions passionate energies against stultifying repression. Against "the monologic sludge of post-Yan'an Maoism" (ibid., 259), Can Xue promotes a self that can dream. Against the repressed and hypocritically repressive patriarchs, she champions a woman's lyric joys of self. "Like Tu Fu, who was disillusioned with Confucianism and feared the looming threat of war, Can Xue reflects despair with the current disintegrating order" (Innes 1991, xiii). The new China will negate the dependent joylessness of the Mao world. Women will not play it safe and "marry . . . a worker. . . . [W]on't . . . get involved in politics. . . . [W]on't love" (Decker 1993, 295). Men will not abide by a loyalty that was a denial of self: "What he wanted to do, he was not allowed to accomplish; what he did not want to do, he didn't dare not to do" (ibid., 294–95). As with the final scene in the movie *Farewell My Concubine*, freedom for Chinese is the courage to be oneself, to not deny one's nature.

The mélange represented by "celebrating West Hunan as the 'last stand' of the culture of the ancient kingdom of Chu" seemed the better, lost soul of China's people (Kinkley 1993, 96). It was instinctive and holistic, at one with nature and the mundane joys of daily life such as festivals, religion, mores, songs, and crafts. Here was rich regional specificity, full of life, including the delights of local dialect, "a commitment to the south . . . at the expense of the north" (ibid., 105). It is a world that ridicules the Confucian female paragon of uncomplaining hard work, tightfistedness, self-sacrifice, and opposition to licentiousness; a repressed world that readily explodes into "evangelical hysteria, that is, a cause of the horrors of Mao's inhuman Cultural Revolution" (Lau 1993, 29). The valorized antithesis and negation of this hateful repression is the spirit of ancient Chu, "mystic, superstitious, uninhibited" (ibid., 27). The movie *Farewell My Concubine* celebrates Chu and identifies Mao's socialist state with the enemies of Chu.

Consequently, any continuing war on sexual urges or the autonomy of young women tends to be reimagined in the reform era as a counterproductive war on the hope of a better, happier, more fulfilled, and vibrant China. In so much post-Mao popular culture, the sensual young women, and not only of Chu, are superior to an immorally hypocritical, male-dominated ruling party of self-deception that actually raped and then scapegoated the victims. In contrast, natural young women, symbolic of all China, should give themselves freely, as moved by healthy passions. Demeaning dependence would give way to life-affirming, natural, spontaneous (Daoist) independence.

Dru Gladney's work helps us see that Mao-era Chinese anti-imperialists defined a homogenized, sacrificing, and disciplined Han national identity in part by imagining eroticized minorities who are happy and innocent, that is, backward, judged by steel-era production norms. But at the end of the twentieth century, in a quest for cultural freedom, including beauty, joy, and expressiveness, the repressive culture's dominant categories have been disrupted by finding the minorities as worthy of emulation. Gladney shows how post-Mao movies are pervaded by the counterhegemonic theme of taking supposedly sensually liberated minorities as models of humanness. Most of these are in the south, especially Yunnan. One goes to the southwest looking for nature and the natural, for color and life. Northerners look to such excursions as quests for authentic life.

The Confucian Leninists who previously insisted on individual sexual repression so that all could be saved by a proletarian ethos, represented by a male steel worker and female emulators, have been redefined as the antihuman other who repressed the people while hypocritically engaging in all the licentious misconduct they condemned. Dai Qing finds that one of the two major social issues China now confronts is sex. At "the bottom of society there is sexual repression and at the top sexual indulgence. That's unfair. It's an important part of injustice and inequality in China right now" (Wang Zheng 1993, 196). In addition, given popular changes in Chinese attitudes, "it just is no longer possible for the authorities to maintain sexual repression as they did before the GPCR" (ibid., 196).

Socialist patriarchy is re-experienced as sexual violence and fraud. The Party's language of protective posturing is taken as a cover for its raping. Freedom is signified by a woman's struggle or a movement in which some women take the lead. These include poets, characters in films, fiction writers such as Zhu Lin (King 1993), political analysts such as Dai Qing, and Democratic Movement leaders such as Chai Ling. Liberation of the young woman, the one whom historically patriarchal societies would most oppress and suppress, is the cause of human freedom.

People experience this symbolic south of freedom from patriarchy as a palpable reality. In the more open rural south China, young women tend to leave villages to obtain temporary employment in the factories of export-oriented light industry in cities such as Canton (Guangzhou) and then can return home with money-earning skills, including speaking Cantonese, increasingly the language of commerce. In contrast, in more conservative north China villages, men tend to leave the villages for good-paying jobs in construction and transportation, while young women stay locked in the village, mainly limited to weak earnings from basic crop production that the socialist state pays for at imposed low prices. In the northern cities, the men reconstitute a patriarchal subculture including drinking, brawling, and whoring. Most prostitution in China actually probably involves patriarchal northern males. Patriarchal authoritarianism defines the north, while freedom, openness, and mobility appear to legitimate a south where energetic young women work in a productive way, earn foreign exchange for the nation, and are in the vanguard of the future. The value struggle against authoritarian patriarchy is experienced as a struggle between a reactionary north and a progressive south in which young women are vital symbolic forces.[22]

This means that young Chinese women who are on the move are not that attracted by the regime's propaganda that they should emulate Japanese women, stay at home, and help educate their sons to save the nation. They do not embrace an identity based on suffering. As the conservative writer Wang Anyi would have it, in the language of the regime's pro-Confucian campaign,

> I think women's ability to endure is stronger than that of men. Especially Chinese women. Western women . . . suffer less. . . . Perhaps their endurance is not so great. . . . Oriental women have tremendous endurance, particularly Japanese women. (Wang Zheng 1993, 169)

Misleading propaganda about Confucianism as the secret of East Asian economic success has obscured East Asia's late-twentieth-century validation of women. From union and religious efforts on behalf of democracy in South Korea to electoral victories in Taiwan, women leaders have won great popular support. The 1993 loss of power by Japan's Liberal Democratic Party was, as Tetsuo Najita pointed out in his Association for Asian Studies 1993 presidential address, in no small part caused by opposition to the old conservatives by 80 percent of all voting-age women, an extraordinary gender gap. The new ruling coalition swiftly rewarded women with cabinet and other high-level posts.

Moreover, young Chinese grow up in the post-Mao era condescendingly and condemningly identifying women who stay at home as acting as do Japanese women. In fact, this regime's pro-Japanese propaganda seemed unpatriotic. It asks patriotic Chinese to take the nation's adversary and former aggressor, Japan, as a model to be emulated and embodied. To oppose an independent, public existence for Chinese women, to argue that they should stick to the domestic sphere, was to many to take the side of the Japanese who invaded China and raped Chinese women.[23] It reminded one that China's rulers had never forced Japan to pay reparations for its massive crimes in China. It helped further delegitimate the regime.

Not only are post-Mao rulers perceived as again selling out the people to make personally profitable deals with Japanese "moneybags," as they did when they previously did not insist on a proper indemnity to Chinese victims of Japanese rapists, but a highlighting of how the regime did not in fact protect Chinese women is a further reminder of the unpunished criminality that occurred when the Russian Red Army entered China at the end of the anti-Japan war. The Red Army was welcomed by China's Communists, although it raped as it came into China's northeast in 1945 (as it did in Poland, Austria, and Germany). This hitherto-buried story has somehow spread and further discredited the entrenched despotism.

This Russian raping created a problem for China's Communist journalists. They first solved it, one told me, by declaring that the Russians could not differentiate good Chinese from enemy Japanese. Next they argued that the crimes were committed by counter-revolutionaries, criminals freed from Siberian prisons because real Russian revolutionaries were in Europe, where they had been fighting Hitler. Suppressed facts such as the cover-up of the rape of Chinese by alien Communists and by Confucian Japanese invaders turn rulers pretending to be paternalists into apologists for foreign rapists. There is a loss of faith in the fable in which Confucian Leninists, exposed as rapists or protectors of criminal prostitution, could or would save the wounded people.

The literary critic Lydia Liu, in a 1991 paper presented to the annual meeting of the Association for Asian Studies, pointed out that the idea that anti-Japanese nationalism protected women from rape by Japanese soldiers hid the fact, revealed in the writings of Xiao Hong and Ding Ling, that women raped by Japanese soldiers were not embraced as heroes and martyrs by Chinese villagers. In fact, the Red Army did not save women so women could be free but rather to monopolize women for young peasant males, who were imbued with a violent patriarchal ideology. What the patriotic struggle offered Chinese males, author Xiao Jun recounted in *Village in August*, was that "After the revolution, you could get a wife without having to pay a penny" (Xiao 1954, 129).[24]

Consequently, ever more Chinese agree that for young women to live a decent life, they must be free of the hypocritical moralizations of the authoritarian patriarchs. If one wants to end the endless rape of China's young women, one must oppose Confucian Leninists.[25] Basic humanity, therefore, facilitates a discourse linking democracy, gender equality, and freed young women.

Authoritarian Patriarchy's Appeal

China's officially promoted literature of roots and nostalgia in defense of Confucianism could nonetheless provide a basis for military or strongman rule. But this would have to be in opposition to Leninism. Alexander Solzhenitsyn captures, in the language of authoritarian patriarchy, how Leninist socialism exploited women as part of a system destroying the people, leading to biological degeneration of the people . . . by the violent eradication of religion, by the suppression of every sign of culture, by a situation where drunkenness is the only form of freedom, where women are doubly exhausted (by working for the state on an equal footing with men and also in the home, without the aid of domestic appliances), and where the minds of its children are systematically deprived. (Solzhenitsyn 1980, 32, 58)

Such an experience can foster a view that the only way to save the people and restore the national culture to virile health is to restore women to their "natural" roles of wife and mother, so as to nourish the religion, civilize the men, nurture the children, and transmit the culture.

The patriarchal male fear of liberal equality as ending virtual ownership of women (*Minzhu Zhongguo* 1993, 93) is experienced as a virile need to preserve the culture's purity. This sexist theme is ubiquitous.[26] The conservative writer Wang Anyi is worried about men now doing things such as washing diapers. The "women of Shanghai have begun to . . . feel that Shanghai men lack masculinity" (Wang Zheng 1993, 169). " Shanghai men . . . really are wimps." They are "womanish men" (ibid., 170). "Chinese men have always been pampered . . . so they have very weak wills. Probably men are just weaker human beings than women are" (ibid., 171). Women, she insists, need men to be men.

Men who feel shamed for not having prevented the prior Leninist "rape" (Solzhenitsyn 1980, 31) could, in a post-Leninist world, seek to protect women and assume an authoritarian role illegitimately denied to them by the discredited tyranny and find support for this project among women. This perspective condemns as Western and antifamily an alternative of impersonal legal authority. Leninism and liberalism are then both presented as alien and cold. May Fourth values of science and democracy are interpreted as foreign. This discourse is not uniquely Chinese, though it is embraced by China's post-Mao conservatives.

The weak liberalism of Russia's February 1917 revolution is held responsible by Russian conservatives for the inability of the society to mobilize in October against the Bolshevik conquest of power when the West kept Russia fighting in World War I, the West thereby having left Russians vulnerable to Communist despotism. Deng Xiaoping may be preparing the political ground for such seeds when he insists that democracy would bring a chaos that would leave China weak, bloodied, and vulnerable. To protect one's own holy community, for conservatives, means rejecting the purportedly misleading message of an alien liberal democracy. The very survival of one's civilization is said to be at stake. It is a choice between us and them, an immoral and treacherous West.

In post-Leninist systems, conservative former Leninists tend to join with their traditionalist brothers in a crusade to keep women in or restore women to their supposed place, a reactionary crusade made somewhat popular and legitimate by the prior experience that Leninism was an assault on the family, with the immoral state stealing women and brainwashing children. But liberal democracy is seen by such people as no better than Leninism, because what the West really brings women is envisioned in terms of places such as Manila or Bangkok, which are treated as one's worst nightmare—innocent female children turned into prostitutes.[27]

Anxieties about the future of the family could provide fertile soil for militaristic, populist authoritarianism. It might find a warm response especially in China's more conservative northern countryside, where even in places where the Party is despised for cruelty and the government is hated for corruption, the military nonetheless retains an aura of legitimacy as an arena of moral discipline. But, as elsewhere, this authoritarian project would have to garb itself in anti-Communist and procommunalist outfits.

With almost a hundred million people uprooted in China, with the kidnapping, rape, sale, and forced prostitution of women palpably spreading, China may well provide fertile soil in which rightist authoritarianism could root itself.[28] With a quarter of a million women arrested for prostitution in 1992, Confucian Leninists depict prostitution and venereal disease as spreading. They portray innocent girls being attracted by money to go "to the south to engage in prostitution" (Central People's Radio 1993,). The southern city of "Shenzhen, which is nestled next to Hong Kong, is probably the richest city in China and is known for a freewheeling atmosphere in which prostitutes outnumber Communist party loyalists" (*New York Times* 1992). That is, northern conservatives reject and counter the discourse that makes China's south the source of a better future.

Southerners are stereotyped as too clever, as caring only about money, as willing even to sell the nation or its innocent girls. In contrast, northern conservatives present themselves as people of principle, family, and country. The human right that so-called advanced societies promoted for China was, to patriarchal authoritarians, the right to buy, sell, and abuse Chinese girls. The contest over national identity is suffused with a passionate discourse on gender.

Conservatives present sexual permissiveness as a threat to the sacred family. Homosexuality remains a criminal offense in China, punishable by years in prison. It is explained as a product of capitalism—although all Han Dynasty emperors had male lovers—that threatens the degeneration and destruction of the race by ending procreation and progeny. This immoral threat is said to flourish in south coastal cities most polluted by imperialism.

A patriarchal backlash has been unleashed in response to reforms in all Leninist states. The previously frozen system does not merely thaw, it also bubbles, boils, and steams. The sudden motion can cause moral vertigo. Certitude can be reassuring. Consequently, the old verities of authoritarian patriarchy can come to seem a stable mooring in a world awhirl and awash with incomprehensible change. In this political contest, woman as symbol is variously deployed.

Yet it has not been easy for China's patriarchal conservatives to establish an antiwoman politics in terms of a patriotic, integral defense of the sacred culture against supposedly Western values, especially to ward off so-called Western feminism, despite the illegitimacy of feminism. The common ploy of promoting an indigenous patriarchy as a non-Western feminism that truly respects woman's roles as wife, mother, and nurturer of the civilization has won little support in China. The truth, after all, is that the struggle against liberation for women virtually everywhere inspires a traditionalist backlash that defines itself as truly prowoman. This happens in all Western countries, too, usually as part of organized religion's effort. There is nothing peculiarly non-Western in the patriarchal discourse presented as supportive of women's natural strength and distinctive superiority. That conservative, patriarchal Confucians should act in China as their counterparts have within Islam, Judaism, Hinduism, Buddhism, and Christianity seems normal. Given all it has going for it, what is remarkable is the weakness of the popular response to the patriarchal appeal, so far.

Conclusion

To re-establish themselves, the dictators would relegitimate the repression of sex—a crushing of liberated young women—as natural, normal, and necessary. Hence the struggle for political freedom involves issues of gender, with women imagined by one side as the hitherto-martyred who deserve liberty. While behavior opposed to gender equality spreads, at a symbolic level the discourse that would liberate young women seems to dominate.

Given the force of pre-PRC Confucian patriarchy, its reinforcement by a Mao-era practices, and its official promotion by Leninist Confucians in the post-Mao era, what needs explaining is the popularity of assertive and independent women in the reform era as modal. With mushrooming sex consultation centers and more sex education in school, according to *China Daily*, the initiative seems to be with those who find a need for a more open approach to adolescent desires.

There is charm, however, in the nostalgic belief in safety and purity in an innocent place, represented by the traditional countryside. Even Hong Kong people into the 1990s, not having experienced Communist Party rule, often share Mao-era nostalgia for roots and warmth that makes it difficult to imagine a people in plural, open, and democratic terms. In Hong Kong, although people sang out "we don't want red nightmares" their self-vision as "loyal" "yellow faces" and "black eyes" orphaned by the rest of humanity nonetheless left many pining for some protective purity in a warm, familial, country world (Chow 1992).

Confucian Leninists contend that when young women went against nation and nature and sought some unnatural freedom, they ended up tragically as prostitutes. The discourse is reinforced by quotidian behavior that locks women up for safety, such as when only men drill wells (women as *yin* would guarantee failure) or when new mothers are kept indoors for a month so they do not pollute and neighbors and relatives come to feast at the end of that period of cleansing. Within this perverse conservative consciousness, the kidnapping and sale of women is proof that women need to be protected by a strong male. Because women are increasingly scarce and costly to marry legally, some men feel it just to resort to kidnapping and rape to secure the family that is needed for a moral life. Overpriced women made poor men immoral. The independent young woman is held culpable. Confucian Leninists parade as protectors and patriots.

The director of the Institute of Philosophy in Hungary's Academy of Sciences adds that an experience of the innocent indigenous community being "raped" by the West permits traditional authoritarians to reject democracy and the market as alien (often traders were minority ethnic groups), as threats to a people, requiring a purge of liberals and aliens (Tang 1993). If this backlash has turned out so far to be weaker in China, why? The problem for patriarchal authoritarians in power in China is that they appear as indistinguishable from Leninists who long ruined women. They seem so immoral that their charges reek of hypocrisy; their appeal is not heard.

The women whom the government in Beijing denounce as alien threats to Chinese values are less likely to be prostitutes than democrats. Thus two liberal women in the Hong Kong legislature, Christine Loh and Anna Wa, have been denounced by the Chinese press as "women with striking Western values and little feel for China and its ancient ways" (Holberton 1993).

What precisely is being negated matters. A population explosion in Mao-era China does not legitimate the notion of patriotism incarnate by promoting woman as baby-producers. The consensus is that population growth must be limited. In Albania and Romania, where the Leninist dictatorship kept abortion illegal, the post-Leninist successors won great support from women and the younger generation by making abortion legal. Even in Leninist states where abortion was legal in the socialist era, it was not meant to serve the autonomy of women. Indeed, it was seen by women as an unjust imposition by the patriarchy. Women lacked alternatives. That is, contraceptive devices were scarce. Sex education was unavailable. Males were not educated to share responsibility for impregnation. Because pregnancy out of wedlock could destroy a family, women often delayed telling anyone until past the first trimester. They then still needed illegal, back-alley abortions. Abortion thus was part of a system that endangered, demeaned, and controlled women. Leninist states that keep abortion legal are not seen as prowomen.

The democratic narrative, in contrast, includes a central role for independent young women. Such progress is imagined as part of a dynamic emanating from the south against a backward, archaic, and patriarchal north. This discourse has popular currency because the orthodox Leninist system was experienced by so many as a war on women and a surrender of national dignity to foreign interests.[29] Much in post-Mao popular culture is replete with depictions of Party power holders who abuse their authority through rape.

While women tend to want an end to the invasion of their privacy and an end to coerced abortion,[30] the consensus is that the 1.2 billion Chinese will not prosper if population growth is not constrained. The pressures for both ending coercive abortion and limiting population growth by permitting and facilitating abortion means that China would be better off if women were not defined by a need to stay home to bear and care for large numbers of children. So while feminism may seem alien in China, so does a renewed patriarchal cult premised on women staying at home. Legitimization of the transgression of patriarchy limits the appeal of Confucian Leninism and lends credibility to the promise of independent young women.

Facilitating the gender-equality agenda is the delegitimation of Mao-era anti-imperialism, which had privileged soldiers, autarky, and the north (Friedman 1994). In an anti-imperialist world that could treat tourism as subjugation, gender equality appeared to integral nationalists to be as an imperialist assault on a nation under siege, a nation needing patriotic women to pass on an ethos of self-sacrifice on behalf of national survival against the foreign onslaught.[31] That world, however, is gone.

In a time of reform away from command-economy rigidities, when much money—especially scarce and sought-after foreign exchange—could be garnered by state officials through insider dealing with alien outsiders, something decent folk could not do, the perception grew that the dictatorship had in fact joined with corrupt foreigners to demean ordinary, honest people who lacked personal ties to power, even alien power. The rulers seemed predators in league with corrupt foreigners. They certainly were not the sacrificing patriots they claimed to be.

A petty prostitute for foreign exchange, in contrast, seemed an honest victim who responded to an unjust situation created by the illegitimate rulers. This freelancer is but a small-time practitioner of arts that those in power are seen as using to cash in on big time.

Since "they" surely won't save "us," "we" must save ourselves. Author Dai Qing, in describing how socialist tyranny destroys dignity, explains that "The crux of the matter was the assassination of humanity and the invasion of the self" (Barmé 1991, 173). For a people seeking release from Leninist inhumanities, the individual subject is re-experienced as sacred and beyond the reach of any would-be interfering state. The overwhelming popularity of a need to accommodate sacred subjectivity for the young, the female, and the minority has limited the attraction of Confucian Leninism.

A felt need to end the rape of the nation and of the vulnerable women any decent nationalist would protect from rape was given the feel of palpable reality by a prior identification of the national cause as a fight to prevent the rape of the nation by alien invaders. But the Leninists, and not only in China, have turned out to seem alien—enemies of the culture. When they present themselves as Confucian in the post-Mao era, they do not win plaudits. Respect for elders instead is re-experienced as true human morality and not a particular Confucian contribution, or it is experienced as good Confucianism, while the rulers are frauds. In either case, other Confucian elements, such as the suppression of the young and female, can be targeted and negated. Because authoritarian communalists in China have failed to mobilize support premised on patriarchal values, because freedom for women makes good sense, antidemocratic forces seem far less potent in China.[32]

Still, one should not gainsay the prospect of a post-Leninist indigenous authoritarianism. Opinion is volatile. Missed democratic opportunities may not swiftly reappear. Authoritarian patriarchal behavior spreads.

So many new languages of validation barrage one simultaneously in Leninist systems undergoing basic reforms that it is most difficult for people to see that a profound pluralism that legitimates social space for diverse ultimate ethical projects is the only way to protect one's own moral life–world and not threaten that of others. Should political leaders emerge who hold the allegiance of various absolute ethical projects of wounded communities, it may not be easy to institutionalize a politics of compromise, coalition, and openness. It will just seem immoral or relativistic or subversive of firm ethical standards. Hence the equivalent of religious wars that so long traumatized the Netherlands and Britain and France before they could compromise and build a relatively pluralist democracy may be in the offing before many post-Leninist nations find value in and consensually institutionalize mutual understanding of, respectful compromise with, and confident openness to a civil society permitting associations committed to diverse ultimate ends.

And yet the delegitimation of Leninist rulers as hypocrites who did not protect women from rape is pervasive. So is the valorizing of young women, Buddhism, Chu, Daoism, the south, minorities, and other identities that negate the oppressiveness of the archaic Confucianism promoted by China's dictators. Chinese particularities may be with women and democracy.

Notes

Marion Smiley, Aili Tripp, and Marilyn Young generously critiqued a previous draft of this easay, an earlier draft of which was presented on February 25, 1994, at the University of California at Berkeley China Center Conference on Chinese Identity.

1. Consider the mother confronted by a child returning from kindergarten singing this song taught right after the June 4, 1989, massacre: "The army loves the people, the people love the army." The mother cannot say what she thinks for fear that her child might repeat it aloud at school.

2. "An outsider young woman was only 18 years old, . . . thin and small, like an unattractive 'ugly duckling.' . . . She entered a factory. . . . At the age of 25, she . . . went to work in Guangzhou. She now wore fashionable clothes, and became Westernized in behavior. Finally she got a divorce from her rural husband and married a person in Guangzhou." "Even more horrifying . . . foreign originated pornographic materials have become the catalysis of family fissions" (Su and Xu 1993, 35–36). Despite the overt condemnation, the hidden transcript seems to be a She Xuan (Cinderella) story of transcendence. Still, the notion that women's autonomy is a foreign threat to the Chinese family is not a Commu-

nist invention. Richard Wilson tells of a case in Taiwan in which a young wife sued for divorce from an adulterous husband who also abused her physically while his mother threatened her with murder. The judge advised the would-be divorcée, "The good wife should know how to cultivate forbearance—this is why the Chinese family system has endured for thousands of years. Westerners don't care about this and that is why their families are dying" (Wilson 1993, 112).

3. That "women should leave public life for men" is also the popular view in Poland, which had no Jiang Qing. Nonetheless, in Poland too men say, "Practice shows that whenever . . . a harem took power, the empire declined" (Simpson 1991, 24). Many Chinese particulars reflect general phenomena.

4. " [S]hortages of consumer goods and everyday services make household responsibilities especially onerous" (Lapidus 1992, 38).

5. Chinese men tend to agree that in the West males may be turned into henpecked husbands but that such emasculating unnaturalness will not be permitted in China. This insistence on keeping men virile and in charge is especially welcome among tough male peasants and soldiers. They see feminism as a treason that threatens national survival, a foreign subversion of what alone can keep China strong, harmonious, and ethical. This conservative authoritarianism seems a compelling morality in its opposition to young females seeking to destroy the Chinese essence, understood as the sacred nation, the holy family, and the common loyalty to a *patria* that unites state and society as a harmonious order of moral purpose.

6. "In the Soviet Union, woman's labor force attachment is increasingly blamed for a host of social ills, including juvenile delinquency, infant mortality, excessive abortion, and high divorce rates" (Moghadam 1992, 6).

7. Even in East Germany, where women were materially and socially better off than in any other Leninist state, in the March 1990 election, in which the conservative parties explicitly opposed prowoman policies, 46 percent of women voted conservative (Ferrel and Young 1992, 200).

8. In Russia a woman scholar at Moscow's Gender Center found, "The new catch phrase is 'Let's return women to their natural destiny' " (Cidylo 1993).

9. In the dominant northern European cultural prejudices in the United States, polluting sexuality similarly was walled off, first at the western frontier from Native American Indians, then from across the Rio Grande in Mexico, and throughout the country from African Americans on the other side of town.

10. Former President Jimmy Carter, on March 1, 1994, told an audience at the University of Wisconsin, Madison, that in working on the Atlanta project in poor areas of Atlanta, he was told by a junior high principal, on asking about teenage pregnancy, that the biggest problem was in the sixth grade, because men preferred very young girls, finding them more docile, cheaper, and far less likely to have AIDS.

11. In contrast, in the United States, paternalists were contradictorily comprehended as the essence of individualism. The restorationist South after the American Civil War still presented itself as the home of local liberty and self-governance.

12. While chatting with a young woman from a most conservative part of rural Anhui province, she explained that she decided to flee on a scorching summer day, when, to obtain a bit less discomfort, she opened the top button on her heavy, long-sleeved, all-season army shirt worn on top of a thick T-shirt that covered an elastic band holding in her breasts, only to hear elderly village women cursing her as a whore and tramp.

13. The sex trade is international. Prostitute purchasers from Southeast Asia trekked into the poorest parts of southwest China "carrying television sets to swap one per child" (Kempton 1992).

14. "[T]he treatment of 'the weaker sex' can be a sign that is used to enhance the image of a nation" (Sapiro 1984, 21–22).

15. *China Daily* reports that nearly 73 percent of women in cities and 81 percent in the rural areas believe that women should sacrifice for their husbands' success.

16. English readers will find this experiential truth making China's Communists as bad as Japan's imperialists—or even Hitler's Nazis—in Wu Yingkun's autobiography. The translation of William Shirer's *Rise and Fall of the Third Reich* in the early 1960s seems to have furthered this experience that Chinese were suffering precisely what Shirer described as Hitlerism. At least, that is how Chinese read it.

17. "The Chinese have paid dearly for the decades of 'saving the nation.' China may finally have stood up, but the Chinese have fallen down" (Li Ao 1992, 35).

18. This Kantian insight is one of the bases of Isaiah Berlin's liberal political philosophy.

19. In practice, male Party leaders could choose virtually any woman they wanted as a mate, and the young woman could hardly refuse.

20. In Britain, Rudyard Kipling (Curtis 1991) legitimated wealth-expanding imperialists as tough nationalists by presenting the male as needing to be free of women ("And a woman is only a woman, but a good cigar is a Smoke), free to struggle to liberate the nation from alien encirclement. Auden explained that Kipling would have British men overcome these obstacles to the *patria*, "the danger of encirclement" by the Picts beyond the Roman Wall, the Danes, the Dutch, the Huns, the "new caught sullen peoples half devil and half child, even the Female of the Species."

21. The popular image of a prostitute in the 1990s countryside is a temporary laborer saving the family by paying off her husband's gambling debts.

22. To be sure, women do work in urban factories in the north and men in the south do in fact do construction work in cities. But interviews in China suggest that the binary highlighted in this chapter is the one that defines experience.

23. If one accepted the notion that Japanese women could be held up as an ideal, then one argued against the regime's presentation of Japanese women as merely stay-at-home nurturer–educators. Instead, one pointed out that 40 percent of the Japanese workforce is female, that almost 66 percent of married Japanese women work, and that Japanese women are struggling for full equality (DPA 1994).

24. Likewise, in interviewing former Red Army soldiers in the north China plain at the end of the 1970s, I was startled to hear one explain that he had joined the Red Army because he had heard that the Japanese army raped Chinese women. Seeking clarification, I commented, "So you joined the army to protect Chinese women." The explanation, which began to sensitize me to the painful power of patriarchy within the armed resistance movement, was, "No, I could not afford marriage. Maybe I could get a woman by rape."

25. A bride-to-be, Kate Xiao Zhou reports, can still be publicly humiliated by a low bride price, proof to all that she is not "pure," if purity is decisive. Unmarried women in the reform era often still had to confess publicly to their immoral ways before being allowed to have an abortion. Dread of the ritual of degradation and the subsequent stigma probably were key reasons why unmarried women delayed abortions until late in the pregnancy.

26. It has also helped to define a male-female sexist discourse in the United States in communalist or racially related ways, especially the feeling that European women kidnapped by Native American men or raped by African-American men were better off dead.

27. The evidence does not support a contention that governments that most restrict foreign capital do best by women.

28. Moral revivalisms, from Protestant to Hindu fundamentalism, are appealing in part because they promise a stable family life for people threatened by family violence, unemployment, and criminality in an era when incomprehensible economic change dislocates some and threatens to uproot many more. Traditionalistic moral revivals are a global response to postmodern economic discombobulations.

29. There is little reason to believe that women in Leninist China in the Mao era did better than women in Leninist Hungary, where "Marital rape was not recognized by law, and only rarely were incidents of assault or wife-beating reported. Even less often were such crimes legally redressed." While the regime preached chastity, "every girl and woman has encountered sexual humiliation, molestation, rape, or abuse in some verbal or physical form—in school, at work, in the family, in the streets" (Bollobas 1993, 205).

30. In Poland in 1993, the democratic electorate abandoned the anti-Communists and embraced even the political party of former Communists when they supported women's goals, because the citizenry both sympathized with the plight of women and opposed any more statist intrusions in the private sphere. Consequently, Solidarity, which could not break with the church's patriarchal and conservative positions was, at least temporarily, discredited and lost badly (Singer 1993, 765). In other words, so important were the rights of young women and the inviolability of the private sphere that the people even supported ex- Communists who would preserve the rights of women.

31. Given a privileging of anti-imperialist preoccupations, men in Islamic societies could experience unveiling imposed by modernizers as a Western plot to leave native women naked and vulnerable. Even the revolutionary anti-imperialist Franz Fanon comprehended Western projects to free women, whether to end clitoridectomy in Africa or satti in Hindu India or foot binding in Confucian China or purdah in the Muslim world, as part of a plot to rape the nation by coercing women out of protective practices.

32. In contrast, Attila Agh, director of Hungary's Center of Democratic Studies, finds that extreme right-wing forces blame the political opening to democracy for all social and economic ills. They embrace instead an emotional, militant, antiliberal nationalism "interwoven with communism to become an ideology of the paternalistic state. . . . This combination of nationalism, populism, and right-wing extremism is the biggest threat to democracy" (Agh 1993, 207). Thus the issue of democracy is entangled with that of gender equality.

References

Agh, Attila. 1993. "The Premature Senility of the New Democracies." *PS* 26.2 (June), p. 307.
Bao Xiaolan. 1990. "Integrating Women Into Chinese History." *Chinese Historians* 3.2 (July).
Barmé, Geremie. 1991."Using the Past to Save the Present." *East Asian History*, No. 1 (1991), p. 173.
Bollobas, Eniko. 1993 " 'Totalitarian Lib': The Legacy of Communism for Hungarian Women." In Nanette Funk, ed., *Gender Politics and Post-Communism* (New York: Routledge), pp. 201–6.
Cai Yan. 1990. "Wealth of Sanitary Products Frees Women." *China Daily*, November 6.
Central People's Radio Broadcast (Beijing). 1993 (May 2). Translated in *Inside China Mainland*, July 1993, pp. 70–74.
Chan, Sylvia. 1989. "Chang Chiek's Fiction: In Search of Female Identity." *Issues and Studies* (September 1989), pp. 85–104.
Ching, Julia. 1990. *Probing China's Soul* (San Francisco: Harper and Row).
Chow Rey. 1992. "Between Colonizers: Hong Kong's Post-Colonial Self-Writing in the 1990s." *Diaspora* 2.2, pp. 151–70.
Chu, Godwin, and Yenan Ju. 1993. *The Great Wall in Ruins* (Albany: State University of New York Press).
Cidylo, Lori. 1993. "Russia's Women Face a New Reign of Fear." *Financial Times*, August 11–21.

Codrescu, Andrei. 1991. *A Hole in the Flag* (New York: Avon Books).
Curtis, Anthony. 1994. "Poet Laureate of the Politically Incorrect." *Financial Times*, January 22–23.
Dallas Morning News. 1993. April 19.
de Bary, W. T. 1994. "The Confucian Constitutionalism of Huang Tsung-hsi and Its Contemporary Significance." *State and Society in East Asia Network News Letter*, No. 3 (January), pp. 2–20.
Decker, Margaret. 1993. "Political Valuation and Revaluation in Contemporary Chinese Fiction." In Tami Barlow, ed., *Gender Politics in Modern China* (Durham, NC: Duke University Press), pp. 290–302.
Deng Xiaoping. 1992. "Gist of Speeches Made in Wuchang, Shenzhen, Zhuhai and Shanghai from January 18 to February 21, 1992." In *Beijing Review*, Nos. 6–7, February 7–20, 1994, pp. 9–20.
DPA Features. 1994. "Japanese Women Fight for Equal Pay." *China Daily* (February 19).
Duke, Michael. 1991. "Walking Toward the World." *World Literature Today* (Summer), pp. 389–94.
Einhorn, Barbara. 1992. "Concepts of Women's Rights." In Valentine Moghadam, ed., *Privatization and Democratization in Central and Eastern Europe and the Soviet Union: The Gender Dimension* (Helsinki: Wider), pp. 59–73.
Far Eastern Economic Review. 1993. (August 12), p. 56.
Fei Xiaotong. 1989. "Changes in Chinese Family Structure." In Chen Rinong et al., eds., *China: Landmarks of Reform* (Beijing: China Reconstructs Press), pp. 129–35.
Ferrel, Myra Marx. 1993. "The Rise and Fall of 'Mommy Politics'." *Feminist Studies* 19.1 (Spring), pp. 89–115.
Ferrel, Myra Marx, and Brigette Young. 1993. "Three Steps Back For Women." *PS* 26.2 (June), p. 200.
Fong, Monica, and Gillian Paul. 1992. "Eastern Europe." In Valentine Moghadam, ed., *Privatization and Democratization in Central and Eastern Europe and the Soviet Union: The Gender Dimension* (Helsinki: Wider), pp. 44–49.
Friedman, Edward. 1994. "Reconstructing China's National Identity." *The Journal of Asian Studies* (February).
Friedman, Edward, Paul Pickowicz, Mark Selden. 1991. *Chinese Village, Socialist State* (New Haven: Yale University Press).
Gao, Shijian. 1993. *Far Eastern Economic Review* (December 30), p. 71.
Genovese, Eugene. 1976. *Roll Jordan, Roll* (New York: Vintage).
Gilmartin, Christine. 1990. "Violence Against Women in Contemporary China." In Jonathan Lipman and Steven Harrell, eds., *Violence in China* (Albany: State University of New York Press).
Gladney, Dru. 1994. In *The Journal of Asian Studies* (February).
Hershatter, Gail. 1991. "Prostitution and the Market in Women in Early Twentieth Century China." In Rubie Watson and Patricia Buckley Ebrey, *Marriage and Inequality in Chinese Society* (Berkeley: University of California Press), pp. 256–85.
Heitlinger, Alena. 1993. "The Impact of the Transition from Communism on the Status of Women in the Czech and Slovak Republics." In Nanette Funk, ed., *Gender Politics and Post-Communism* (New York: Routledge), pp. 95–108.
Hildebrand, Reginald. 1993. "Some Persistent Doubts About Paternalistic Hegemony." *Contestation* 3.1 (Fall), pp. 67–76.
Hinton, William. 1993. In Carine, Theresa and Aileen Baviera, eds., *Black Cat, White Cat* (Manila: Philippine-China Development Resource Center).
Holberton, Simon. 1993. "Populism at War with Political Correctness." *Financial Times* (December 18–19).

Hom, Sharon, K. 1992. "Law, Ideology and Patriarchy in China." *International Review of Comparative Public Policy* 4.

Innes, Charlotte. 1991. Foreword to Can Xue, *Old Floating Cloud* (Evanston, IL: Northwestern University Press).

Jaquette, Jane, ed. 1989. *The Women's Movement in Latin America: Feminism and the Transition to Democracy* (Boston: Unwin Hyman).

Jelin, Elizabeth, ed. 1990. *Women and Social Change in Latin America* (Atlantic Heights, NJ: Zed).

Katzarova, Marina. 1993. "Opening the Door." *The Nation* (July 26–August 2), p. 149.

Kaye, Lincoln. 1993. "Reining in Erotica." *Far Eastern Economic Review of Books* (November 18), pp. 40–41.

Kempton, Murray. 1992. "A New Colonialism." *New York Review* (November 19).

King, Richard. 1993. "In the Translator's Eye." In Tami Barlow, ed., *Gender Politics in Modern China* (Durham: Duke University Press), pp. 209–14.

Kinkley, Jeffrey. 1993. "Shen Congwen's Legacy in Chinese Literature of the 1940s." In Ellen Widmer and David Wang, eds., *From May Fourth to June Fourth* (Cambridge, MA: Harvard University Press).

Kubin, Wolfgang. 1992. "Uniting With Your Body." In Tami Barlow, ed., *Gender Politics in Modern China* (Durham, NC: Duke University Press), pp. 137–50.

Lapidus, Gail. 1992. "The Soviet Union." In Valentine Moghadam, ed., *Privatization and Democratization in Central and Eastern Europe and the Soviet Union: The Gender Dimension* (Helsinki: Wider), pp. 37–43.

Lau, Joseph. 1993. "Variations of the Past in Han Shaogang's post-1985 Fiction," In Ellen Widmer and David Wan, eds., *From May Fourth to June Fourth* (Cambridge, MA: Harvard University Press).

Li, Ao. 1992. Translated in Geremie Barmé and Linda Jaivin, *New Ghosts, Old Dreams* (New York: Random House), p. 35.

Liu, Lydia H. 1991. "The Female Body and Nationalist Discourse." Paper presented to the Association for Asian Studies, April 14.

———. 1993. "Invention and Intervention." In Ellen Widmer and David Wang, eds., *From May Fourth to June Fourth* (Cambridge, MA: Harvard University Press).

Liu Xiaobo. 1993. September 23, 1992 interview with Wang Shuo. *Zhengming* (January 1). Translated in JPRS-CAR–93–015, March 5, p. 3.

Louie, Kam. 1989. *Between Fact and Fiction* (Broadway, Australia: Wild Peony).

Meng Yue. 1993. "Female Images and National Myth." In Tami Barlow, ed., *Gender Politics in Modern China* (Durham, NC: Duke University Press), pp. 118–36.

Minzhu Zhongguo [Democratic China, Hong Kong]. 1993. "Ethnic Arrogance and Self-Contempt." No. 18 (November), p. 93.

Mo Liren. 1993. "Chinese Adversity From Mind to Body." *Zhengming* (January 1). Translated in JPRS-CAR–93–015, March 5, 1993, pp. 3–5.

Moghadam, Valentine, ed. 1992. *Privatization and Democratization in Central and Eastern Europe and the Soviet Union: The Gender Dimension* (Helsinki: Wider).

New York Times. 1992. Hong Kong dispatch of March 31, 1992 (April 6).

Pickowicz, Paul. 1991. "The Theme of Spiritual Pollution in Chinese Films of the 1930s." *Modern China* 17.1 (January), pp. 38–75.

Rosen, Stanley. 1990. "Women's Education and Modernization in the People's Republic of China." In Ruth Hayhoe, ed., *Education in China's Modernization* (New York: Pergamon).

Sapiro, Virginia. 1984. "Women, Citizenship and Nationality." *Politics and Society* 13.1.

Simpson, Peggy. 1991. "No Liberation for Women." *The Progressive* (February) p. 24.

Singer, Daniel. 1993. "Of Lobsters and Poles." *The Nation* (December 20), p. 765.

Solomon, Andrew. 1993. "Their Irony, Humor (and Art) Can Save China." *New York Times Magazine* (December 19), pp. 42–51, 66, 70–72.

Solomon, Jon. 1993. "Taking Tiger Mountain." In Tami Barlow, ed., *Gender Politics in Modern China* (Durham: Duke University Press), pp. 238–65.

Solzhenitsyn, Alexander. 1980. *The Mortal Danger* (New York: Harper and Row).

Strumingher, Laura. 1993. "Looking Back." In Harriet Applewhite and Darline Levy, eds., *Women and Politics in the Age of the Democratic Revolution* (Ann Arbor: University of Michigan Press), pp. 259–85.

Su Haoliang and Xu Na. 1993. "The Divorce Phenomenon in Rich Rural Areas." *Fazhi Ribao* (August 6), p. 4. Translated in JPRS-CAR–93–073, September 30, 1993, pp. 35–36.

Sun, Lena. 1992. "In China, the Slave Market Includes Marriageable Women." *The Washington Post Weekly* (June 28–July 5), p. 18.

Tamas, G. M. 1992. "Socialism, Capitalism and Modernity." *Journal of Democracy*, 3.3 (October), pp. 60–81.

Tang Xiaobing. 1993. "Orientalism and the Question of Universality, The Language of Contemporary Chinese Literary Theory." *Positions* 1.2 (Fall), pp. 389–413.

Tanner, Harold. 1994. "Chinese Rape Law in Comparative Perspective." *The Australian Journal of Chinese Affairs* No. 31 (January), pp. 1–23.

Thomas, Paul. 1991. "Jean-Jacques Rousseau, Sexist?" *Feminist Studies* 17.2 (Summer), pp. 195–217.

Thompson, Julia. n.d. "Cuts and Culture in Kathmandu." Center for Nepal and Asian Studies, Tribhuvan University, Kathmandu.

Vanden Heuvel, Katrina. 1993. "Sex in the Time of Revolution." *The Nation* (June 21), p. 872.

Wang Jing. 1993. "The Mirage of Chinese Postmodernism." *Positions* 1.2 (Fall), p. 349.

Wang Rong. 1993. "Xie Champions Women's Rights." *China Daily* (October 11), p. 6.

Wang Yuejin. 1988. "Mixing Memory and Desire: *Red Sorghum* A Chinese Version of Masculinity and Femininity." *Public Culture* 2.1, pp. 31–53.

Wang Zheng. 1993. "Three Interviews: Wang Anyi, Zhu Lin, Dai Qing." In Tami Barlow, ed., *Gender Politics in Modern China* (Durham: Duke University Press), pp. 159–208.

Wilson, Richard. 1993. In Lowell Dittmer and Samuel Kim, eds., *China's Quest For National Identity* (Ithaca: Cornell University Press).

Wolf, Margery. 1985. *Revolution Postponed* (Stanford: Stanford University Press).

Wu Ningkun. 1993. *A Single Tear: A Family's Persecution, Love and Endurance in Communist China* (New York: Atlantic Monthly Press).

Xiao Jun. 1954. *Bayue de Xiangcun* [Village in August] (Beijing). Translation from Lydia Liu.

Zong Jie. 1994. "Novels Relive Love of Old China." *China Daily* (February 22).

Chapter 10

Is China a Model of
Reform Success?

Does rapid economic development in post-Mao China prove that reformers in Beijing have developed a wise strategy that will bring continuous growth with social stability, a strategy from which others should learn? The popular consensus seems to be that Russia was foolish to democratize before implementing economic reforms, because democratization created populist interests that then had to be mollified, interests that blocked reform. China's way, in this view, is better because a strong, centralized authoritarian state can impose needed reforms while a democracy cannot. The supposed lesson is that economic reforms toward marketi- zation should precede political reforms toward democratization. An American economist involved with World Bank aid to Russia pointed to Chile under Pinochet and China's rapidly growing southern province of Guangdong as successful transitions to world-market competition without foreign aid in just this way.

> The relevance of southern China for Russia is limited. Russia is no longer an autocratic state capable of embarking on a closely controlled, gradualist program of economic reform. Indeed, in a freshly democratic nation, one of . . . [the Prime Minister's] principal headache's is the ability of the industrial lobby to block the restructuring of state enterprises and sabotage monetary policy. (Prowse 1992)

U.S. Secretary of the Treasury Lloyd Bentsen returned from a trip to China and Russia invoking the same contrast.

> Russia is an experiment to see whether it is possible to build democratic political institutions before a functioning market economy is in place.

China is an experiment as to whether it is possible to develop a thriving free-market economy without democratic political reform. (Bentsen 1994, p. 6)

Or, as a top businessman in India put it:

Lee Kuan Yew was right and Mikhail Gorbachev wrong: *glasnost* (political openness) must take a back seat to *perestroika* (economic restructuring). (Dalmia 1994, 25)

American banker William Overholt likewise praised *The Rise of China: How Economic Reform Is Creating a New Superpower* (New York: Norton, 1993) in terms of the wisdom of "putting the horse of economic reform before the cart of political pluralism" (Manning 1994, 10).

While it is obviously true that a dictatorship can expand wealth, there in fact is no evidence—none—that authoritarian states perform better economically than do democracies (Helliwell 1993). Indeed, it is an obvious absurdity to argue that a dictatorship is required for wealth creation, even, as Stephen Haggard has detailed, in East Asia. To argue against the obvious fact that an East Asian democracy can grow rapidly, analysts must treat post–World War II Japan as if it were not a democracy. Actually Japanese land reform and the legalization of unions had created blocs of enfranchised farmers and laborers that had to be wooed by Japan's democratic politicians, groups whose rising living standards permitted the development of Japan's great high-quality consumer industries. Japan's economic miracle is almost inconceivable without democracy.

Even a weakened version of the hypothesis about some presumed superiority of authoritarianism—that successful economic reform requires an empowered and insulated technocracy and a strong executive—does not hold for China, where growth has come from political decentralization and has occurred despite an unreformed nomenklatura bureaucracy. There is no tripartite coordination of central technocracy, ruling politicians, and large business combines in China, as there was in Japan and Korea.

Of course, from the point of view of growth in a postmodern era in which change is so much more rapid and flexibility is decisive for success, the Japan–Korea model of centralized coordination may be too rigid and slow. It may impose long-term pacts where short-term adjustments are now required. China's post-Mao success is tied to small, nonfamous companies from Hong Kong and Taiwan. The success is linked to small, local enterprises in China, which may actually be far more competitive in the post-steel era than the old Japan–Korea model of superconcentration and centralization of power. Hence China's rapid growth is best understood in terms of how it is not copying increasingly outmoded aspects of the Japan model.

One might even conclude that China's rapid growth is related to the state center getting out of the way so that capital, domestic and foreign, could make

wise investment decisions in place of Mao-era economically irrational investments in hinterland areas. When China's dynastic era ended at the outset of the
twentieth century, there were "two Chinas—coastal and interior." Confronting
this "radical break between interior China (rural, bureaucratic, traditional) and
coastal China (cosmopolitan, enterprising, open to reform)" (Bergere 1984, 336),
Mao put China's money into the hinterland. Waste was high; returns were low;
the spread effect was nil. Post-Mao rulers instead allowed investment to flow
into the coast, where the payoff and spread effect were much larger. The shift
was made possible by an abandonment of an anti-imperialist ideology that
treated the coast as a hostage to foreign adversaries. A political shift away from
anti-imperialism as the essence of Mao-era regime legitimation has also permitted post-Mao China to earn billions from tourism, the world's largest industry,
whereas the prereform anti-imperialist ideology treated tourism as a return of
colonialism, reducing one's people to servants for foreigners.

If political ideology had not changed, post-Mao China could never have emulated the East Asian pattern of early industrial growth premised on the export of
cheap labor manufactures. Thus, in fact, from political decentralization to a
negation of anti-imperialist, antimarket ideology, China's economic success is
actually premised on the most basic political changes. Consequently, it is not
accurate to assert that China's success results from delaying political reform until
after economic reform. The conventional wisdom, which assumes that China has
carried out only economic reform. leads to dangerously misleading conclusions
about delaying political reform, when China in fact has carried out crucially
important political reforms.

The main propagandist for a successful model of East Asian authoritarianism
is Singapore's independence leader, Lee Kuan Yew. Mr. Lee's position is not
that others should do as East Asia has done, but that others cannot. That is, "East
Asian Authoritarianism–Lee Kuan Yew Thought" is a typical cultural chauvinism in which the very successful explain to others that the essence of the winner
explains the victory. The victor is so uniquely deserving as to be inimitable.

In patriarch Lee's view, the Philippines, lacking Confucian culture, cannot do
what Taiwan has done. Just compare East Asians, he avers, with Native Americans. The "stark reality," Lee insists, is that "if you start testing them, you find
that they are different, most particularly in their neurological development, and
their cultural values." Groups are not equal. Only Confucians, in the ideology of
East Asian Authoritarianism–Lee Kuan Yew Thought, are capable of "hard work
and thrift and deferment of present enjoyment for future gain" (Zakaria 1994,
117). Patriarch Lee, in addition, inveighs against the welfare state as a subverter
of the family, a system in which the society will "educate our women and they
become independent financially and no longer need to put up with unhappy
marriages" (ibid., 113). Confucian patriarchy is presented as the DNA of East
Asian success. Also, the "capricious young" should not count the same as a "man
over 40 who has a family" (ibid., 119). Confucianism's conservative authoritar-

ian patriarchal morality is portrayed as the basis of rapid growth with stability.

The ideology of East Asian Authoritarianism–Lee Kuan Yew Thought, Victor Mallet argues, is more political convenience than ethical Confucianism. Successful Malaysia and Thailand, after all, are not Confucian. Nor is rapidly rising Indonesia. How to ignore Shinto or Buddhism in discussing Japan, or Christianity in South Korea and Taiwan? What Mallet finds is senior leaders in China, Singapore, and Malaysia, who in their youth felt the pains of imperialism, trying in their senior years to justify the perpetuation of authoritarianism by presenting the West as arrogant, ignorant, decadent, and in decline, while the East is imagined as uniquely virtuous and singularly on the rise. East Asian Authoritarianism–Lee Kuan Yew Thought is as much an ideology as was Western racism, embraced in 1859 even by John Stuart Mill in *On Liberty*.

Mill then contended that Asians were infantile and therefore needed to be governed by rational, mature Europeans. In like manner, East Asian Authoritarianism–Lee Kuan Yew Thought is a rationalization and obfuscation of nasty self-interest. It is also a preconscious worldview. That is, when reform-oriented Chinese leaders experience the human rights resolutions of foreigners vis-à-vis Tibet as incomprehensible attempts to restore feudalism and slavery, when Tibetan culture is experienced as but "a living fossil," it is a view shared by most Chinese, as Mill's racist chauvinism was shared by most British. Yet it seems strange to find such an exoticizing and marginalizing of an indigenous culture still presuppositional so long after imperialism and colonialism have supposedly lost their hegemonic appeal and been exposed for what they were, except that well before pseudobiological racism was invented, hegemonic peoples had long ago invented numerous ways to define those they subordinated and peripheralized as barbarians, as uncultured subhumans.

Professor Susan Shirk does not buy the East Asian ideological justification. Her scholarly research does not reveal a Chinese economic formula of success. "No one has yet discovered a sure political formula for moving an economic system from command to market" (Shirk 1993, 350). In fact, "the Soviet Union probably did not have the option of taking the Chinese way" (ibid., 334). The difference in conditions in China and Russia is most obvious in the different factors that led most Chinese to seek market opportunities and led most Russians to refuse to leave their jobs in the former Soviet Union's market-disregarding state sector. Mao had locked over 80 percent of Chinese people in the countryside, where they were denied state-enterprise privileges. In the reform era, they fled their serf-like, bare-subsistence imprisonment on the land to grab any money-earning job available. In contrast, Stalin facilitated a hyperurbanization and a mammoth privileged heavy-industry sector that kept losing money. Workers feared losing their market-disregarding subsidies and did not race to embrace risky market opportunities (Sachs and Woo). The key difference comes from prereform histories that shaped very different policy possibilities.

If conditions are decisive, then one cannot accept the popular view that Deng

Xiaoping was wise and Mikhail Gorbachev was foolish. In fact, Gorbachev did try economic reform first. He did not adopt a policy of first democratizing the polity. The Soviet Russian entrenched apparatus, however, blocked efforts at economic transformation. So did the apparatchiks in China. But in China, because of Mao-era policies, the entrenched, centralized, top-down hierarchies were weaker. The gloomy, gray Brezhnev era of pervasive corruption had, in contrast, allowed the apparatchiks to grow unusually strong in the Soviet Union. Meanwhile, Mao initiated a series of blood-red campaigns against the Party apparatus, which resisted Mao's economically irrational attempts at even more "socialism" than that institutionalized by Stalin; for example, Mao's attempt to abolish even small, residual household plots whose produce could be marketed. Mao's continual wars against the Party bureaucracy and for economic rationality in the name of more socialism both weakened China's apparatus and also left many of its members understanding the economic inanities of Leninist socialism. Mao's monstrous mistakes had reshaped the political ideology of Chinese ruling groups. Thus Beijing reformers in the post-Mao era would have it far easier than Moscow's post-Brezhnev rulers in getting party bosses to accept reform policies. It was not that Beijing reformers were uniquely wise. Given the much bigger and far stronger obstacles to economic reform in Soviet Russia, Moscow had to use political reform to energize new political forces to oppose the entrenched status quo bureaucracy and their allied conservative or reactionary proletariat. The Beijing strategy could not work in the Soviet Union. Conditions were fundamentally different.

While post-Mao leaders were "humiliated to see that China lagged far behind even Japan and the newly industrialized countries of East Asia" (Shirk 1993, 35), East Asian location—understood as a time–space continuum—favored China in decisive ways. The locomotive of China's great export success was the southeast coast. That region, near Hong Kong and Southeast Asia and across the straits from the island of Taiwan, was home to over 40 million people who had migrated from mainland China and now lived in places that had done well in what had become the fastest-growing economic region on the planet. But because American policy after the two OPEC oil crises of the 1970s forced up the value of the currencies of this region, while their wages were rapidly rising, it made economic sense for these hardheaded people to invest their capital, technology, and market know-how in ancestral areas of China, where they often had reliable personal ties. They did so in order to hold American market shares in light industrial exports, taking advantage of poverty-stricken China's extraordinarily cheap labor that was inherited from Mao-era economic disasters that froze rural Chinese living standards at South Asian levels. Eighty to ninety percent of foreign investment in China came from ethnic Chinese in East and Southeast Asia.

Soviet Russia had no such opportunity. Also because of America's Cold War hostility to Russia, China, as an adversary of Russia, enjoyed most-favored-nation access to the American market, an advantage denied to Washington's

Cold War adversary in Moscow. Location in time and space gave China a unique opportunity at rapid export-oriented development. Gorbachev made even as brilliant as an Einstein still would have no similar policy options.

There was no economically dynamic group of neighbors looking to pour investment money into Soviet Russia to hold American market shares at the low end of industry. Soviet Russian workers, in addition, were already much better off than their Chinese counterparts. Worse yet, whatever large investment might possibly have flowed from West Germany into the USSR was negated by the extraordinary 1989 events that made it an imperative in German politics to first help the newly incorporated region of East Germany—at a price of about 100 billion dollars— while Americans preferred to work with Poles, Hungarians, and Czechs, whose economic reforms made investments and joint ventures easier. World developments left Russia out. In short, location—a combination of place and time—offered southeast coastal China an opportunity that simply did not exist for the Soviet Union.

To be sure, there are lessons here. A closed and market-disregarding economy will stagnate in an era of rapid global technical progress. An export orientation is required to take advantage of global opportunities for growth. If Russia were located where China is, could a Stalinist Russia have succeeded on the basis of post-Mao reform policies?

If one looks inside China at regions that, as in the Soviet Union, were dominated by unprofitable, subsidized state enterprises of heavy industry, those Chinese regions also could not take advantage of the new international economic opportunities. Relatively speaking, exports from China's Stalinist economy regions stagnated or declined, as did their counterparts in Russia.

But China's obstructive burden from heavy megaindustries, employing huge numbers whose production was uncompetitive and wasteful, was far smaller than Soviet Russia's. As the nerve center of the Community for Mutual Economic Assistance (COMECON, CMEA), Soviet Russia produced heavy-industry goods to exchange with all other CMEA members. Consequently, in place of world-competitive exports, Russia sent out a very high percentage of noncompetitive products that were accepted by CMEA members because they could not escape the Moscow-imposed, Soviet-dominated CMEA, which was in fact a political empire, not a wealth-expanding economic common market.

In contrast, already by 1960–61, China had to seek export markets based on competitiveness to get around a U.S.-led embargo among the industrialized democracies joined by a new Soviet-led CMEA embargo. The result was that while Russia depended on primary products such as energy resources and gold for foreign exchange, both of which were limited because of increasing cost and decreasing earning power by the 1980s, China, even in the Mao era, learned how to sell light industrial products from bicycles to canned goods abroad. The result was that a move toward export-oriented marketization in Soviet Russia would engender massive unemployment in a huge and noncompetitive heavy-industry sector, as would not be the case in a China whose economy was structured very differently.

In addition, because Mao had mistrusted the centralized economic apparatuses headed by his political adversaries, he could self-interestedly promote a policy that kept the command-economy center weak and promoted instead the growth of smaller industries at regional levels. Mao's policy was far more wasteful in terms of economic results than Stalin's mobilizational centralization, but from a political perspective, it left post-Mao rulers who lacked Mao's unique capacity for charismatic mobilization (Dittmer 1987) far weaker against regional entities. Thus reform in China could more easily avoid obstruction by a smaller and weaker central apparatus, whose continuing waste, in addition, was far less costly. Reformers in Beijing could even choose to carry the cost of this wasteful but much smaller heavy-industry sector as a perhaps bearable price of political stability. Reform in Russia, in contrast, could not avoid challenging, frightening, and causing a tremendous antireform backlash reaction from the gargantuan and entrenched command-economy, heavy-industry, state-enterprise system that was tied to networks of political loyalty to the central state apparatus. In China, a region away from the center could and would readily and self-interestedly choose exports and market-oriented reforms using mobile rural labor when given the opportunity. A similar possibility simply did not exist in Russia. The political acumen of Gorbachev versus Deng has little or nothing to do with choices available.

China was also better situated to benefit from reform because of unexpected consequences of prior policies. Mao-era war communism in China was premised on not leaving China's east coast region vulnerable to an expected foreign invasion. Hence new heavy industries were not located on the coast. In fact, many heavy industries that were on the coast even moved inland during the quarter-century when Mao ruled China. Consequently, the heavy industry–state enterprise apparatus that blocked reform in Russia and would not take advantage of reform in China was weakest along China's east coast, across from Cold War enemies South Korea, Japan, the Ryukyus, Diaoyutai, and Taiwan. Thus antireform political interests were smallest on China's east coast. Reform politics could most easily be institutionalized here. It is most misleading to ignore the actual political base of China's economic gains.

Another advantage that post-Mao reform leaders inherited in China was a far smaller threat that a turn to marketization would explode into almost uncontrollable inflation. In Russia, as the pun had it, "we pretend to work and they pretend to pay us." That is, people in the prereform era were paid in currency that bought nothing because desired consumer goods were unavailable and basic food, clothing, and shelter were subsidized. People built up huge stores of worthless rubles that flooded into the market and bid prices way up once marketization began. In China, on the other hand, because Mao hated and tried to destroy money, the 80-plus percent of rural dwellers living beyond vegetable-farming suburbs had virtually no cash. Chinese peasant households lacked the means to bid prices high as soon as consumer goods began to appear. Consequently, inflation-engendering marketization in Russia, but not China, threatened millions of veterans, retirees, widows, and others on fixed incomes. It produced an immediate and powerful political backlash against reform in Russia as soon as reform started. No similar antireform political force was generated in China. Therefore, the politics of building a winning proreform coalition, the focus of two excellent studies of China's political economy by Susan Shirk and Dorothy Solinger, was much more easily achieved in China.

This suggests that not only could Moscow not succeed by reform policies that worked for Beijing but that it also makes no sense to look for a pure economic model of success. There was a political structure in southeast China that could shape interests that would want to grab the opportunity when Beijing carried out the key political reforms, devolving economic and political power to the regions, allowing physical and factor mobility, and negating the ideology of militarized anti-imperialism.

In other words, it is not true that China did not carry out any political reform and merely promoted economic reform. Without political reform, the east coast, reform-oriented provincial leaderships and new small enterprises that could link up with overseas Chinese investments for exports could not even have existed. The truth is that the priority of political reform was decisive. Given the centrality of political factors to reform success, it is crucial to understand the debate among specialists such as professors Susan Shirk and Dorothy Solinger on the conflictful politics of Chinese economic reform, especially in terms of why Stalinist institutions could not quite block the reform thrust in China. Nonetheless, conservative interests have obstructed privatization; prevented full decollectivization; impeded the creation of a real banking system; and stopped price, tax, and banking reforms. In short, it is not yet even true to claim that China is an instance of reform success. Again, inherited differences between China and Russia obscure what should be obvious.

Consider the monumental difference between the countryside in the Soviet Union that Gorbachev had to work with and the countryside in China with which Deng Xiaoping had to work. In the conventional wisdom, China's Deng brilliantly carried out an economic policy of decollectivization that increased food supplies to the cities and raised living standards for the countryside, while Gorbachev stupidly pursued political liberalization. This misleading contrast gets everything wrong at the causal level, although it is a fact that in China the quantity and quality of urban food improved tremendously and rural living standards likewise soared.

There was no way China's rural reforms could work in Soviet Russia. Almost as soon as the Bolsheviks conquered state power, Lenin sent out armed teams of the urban poor to seize the grain in the countryside to serve the purposes of war and revolution, a synthesis of coerced mobilization for leveling subsistence and rationing known as war communism. That policy launched a two-generation-long war of the socialist state against the peasantry (Conquest 1986). The peasantry was mortally wounded. In addition, Stalin's heavy industrialization drive welcomed into the cities migrants from the countryside who accepted as progress even miserable urban working conditions because almost anything was better than suffering the stagnant cruelties of the countryside. Over two generations, the young fled the Russian countryside, while those left behind—no longer peasant household economies—survived in an economy of dependent fawning (plus spurts of energy on small household plots). When Gorbachev in 1988 offered Russian collective farm laborers free land, six out of seven households rejected the land. They were afraid of responsibility and independence.

It is inconceivable that post-Mao era Chinese peasants would have turned down free land. China could benefit from decollectivization in 1978–79 because entrepreneurial, market-oriented peasant households survived in China to grab with extraordinary energy the opportunity of a transition away from antipeasant policies that had privileged heavy industry. Peasants survived because China only had collectivized in 1956. In contrast, Russia's two-generation (1918–88) war on the peasantry had obliterated peoples, and the Soviet onslaught had broken religious bonds of meaning; in addition, both of these had combined with hyperurbanization. Mao, on the other hand, locked up China's various peasantries in their villages, full of local bonds of meaning. Deng Xiaoping then unlocked the collective system in 1978–79, while the first generation of peasants who had lost the land of land reform was still alive and anxious to take advantage of the opportunities offered by mobility and marketization. Russia lacked such human capital when Gorbachev attempted to privatize agriculture. The peasantry had been wiped out in Russia. Moscow could not do what Beijing did.

It is not even true that the post-Mao leadership implemented a wise, popular, and productive policy of decollectivization after Mao's death, as the conventional wisdom wrongly has it. Instead, Mao's conservative successor, Hua Guofeng, fought to hold on to the Stalinist system. Even in the mid-1990s decollectivization is far from complete in China. Land is not alienable. It cannot be freely bought, sold, rented, or inherited. The center still can order and impose quotas and low prices that alienate peasant households and keep poor those still locked into grain production. In fact, reactionaries and Stalinists (that is, so-called Maoist revolutionaries and antimarket, anti-private-property leftists) continue to argue the singular virtues of large-scale production, collective labor, and statist "rationality" and keep pumped up numerous Potemkin-village collectives, hoping one day for a Stalinist comeback. These reactionary forces in the Party were so strong that the original 1978–79 decollectivization initiative was but partial, tentative, and experimental.

Nonetheless, poor peasants pushed through the little opening offered and began to dynamize China's stagnant economy despite the weakness of reform policies. Society was ahead of the state. The center then was faced with a choice of reversing what had proven enriching or allowing wealth-expanding labor and factor mobility to continue in the direction they had self-interestedly chosen. Against the wishes of reactionaries who wanted to continue the czarist-Stalinist apartheid system of internal passports that kept peasants locked on land they did not own and could not legally leave without the permission of feudal-like party lords, the peasantry gradually has been freeing itself from the party–state, subverting restrictions, and creating wealth despite a Party power structure so tilted in the conservative direction that it would not welcome freedom and progress for the peasantry. As Kate Xiao Zhou details in her 1994 Princeton political science dissertation, China's peasantry should receive most of the credit for this reform success.

Villagers able to flee the enserfing collective system were often at first popularly called "freed people" (zi liu ren), a play on the term for the only land in the collective era that households could sow as they saw fit—so-called private plots, actually "land retained for the self" (zi liu di). People who were now retained for their own purposes in the reform era were experienced as, and referred to as, freed people, those escaping the peonage-slavery of the collective system. Comprehending economically irrational collectivization as refeudalization is a popular experience, not an outsider's label.

Even in the mid-1990s, villagers are not yet certain that they are free; they still fear they may again be imprisoned on collectives. Consequently, they have been trying to grab wealth as quickly as possible (even if it means destroying the land by the overuse of chemical fertilizers or weaking long-term productivity by refusing to invest in water conservation or the education of their children) and turn it into consumables (for example, a new and better house) that the state could not take back from freed households, even should the socialist state again move against the freeing of the peasantry. The Chinese countryside is, consequently, a very tense and potentially explosive place. Contrary to the view of an authoritarian polity as a speedy, efficient policy maker, in fact, the factional struggle in China actually has led to stalemate and delay such that many things— such as decollectivization—are never quite decided, such that unresolved tensions could yet explode.

> The secretary-general of the State Council complained, "Many problems remain unsolved for a long time because of the objection from a minority. . . . Too many people exercise veto in our public organs." (Shirk 1993, 118)

No evidence supports the myth that tyrannies act with the speed of lightning. As the president of the National Committee on United States–China Relations put it:

> [T]he principal danger facing China is interminable policy gridlock resulting from elite conflict and uncertainty, autonomous local authorities who resist

> needed moves, and a populace . . . unwilling to make the short-term sacrifices
> that will lead to a better future. As a result, mounting . . . problems will not be
> addressed effectively. (ibid., 67)

In sum, the political struggle over reform continues in China. To understand how China has gotten as far as it has, but only so far, one should ask political questions and see China not as a land with lessons of success but as a nation still caught in a potentially explosive struggle with a still-fragile political economy. This is what both Shirk and Solinger so brilliantly do. Both make excellent use of social science approaches to study how reformers have built coalitions and compromises to get as far as they have despite opposition from conservatives. As Shirk puts it, reform

> reflects a political logic . . . [reformers] pushed against the stone wall of the
> Chinese bureaucracy. Where they found loose stones, they pushed through;
> when stones would not move, they did not waste energy pushing. . . . Not all
> the Maoist feudal, patriarchal ways . . . were actually eliminated. (ibid., 6, 9)

Shirk offers a principal-agent, neoinstitutional analysis of how reformers were aided by a Chinese Leninist system that was "more decentralized and less institutionalized than it had been in the Soviet Union" (ibid., 12). She finds that Gorbachev lacked the conditions to do what Deng did. The rigid Soviet system and lack of authority available to third-generation Russian leaders precluded taking the Chinese reform road, which was built on utilizing inherited possibilities from "institutional flexibility and authority" (ibid., 22) of an original revolutionary generation of leaders. The serious question that comes out of this kind of analysis, a question that Chinese themselves anxiously worry about, is—have reforms built new institutions, shaped new interests, and legitimated new ideas such that the reform agenda away from Stalinist-Maoism cannot be reversed?

This means, does further success require transforming those elements of the conservative Leninist system that were compromised with and left in place in order to build the political coalitions that have taken China just so far? This refers to things such as a dual-track price system; remnants of the internal passport system that locks up villagers in the countryside; soft budget criteria to bail out profitless state enterprises and, along with urban subsidies, engender growing budget deficits that could yet lead to hyperinflation; and no real banking or tax system based on money values that could be used to manage these problems. In sum, China is not an instance of successful reform but a case of a "hybrid partially reformed system" (ibid., 196). But is it a stable, long-lasting hybrid?

Shirk suggests that those who run the unreformed state-owned economy— already producing less of the national income than do some state sectors in democratic Europe (ibid., 48)—are ever less weighty and increasingly persuaded that survival of their reduced power and reduced personal networks involved with these socialist remnants requires accepting and acting by the logic of reform. Should they resist reform, then inflation and income polarization could engender oppositional forces that would overthrow the system they benefit from and could even scapegoat them. In 1994 according to China's Party Secretary, if the regime proves incapable of further reform to deliver continuing economic results, then, after Deng and the first generation of leaders are gone, an experience of economic failure could destroy the last supports of the system. With his highest official position honorary president of the bridge society, Deng has not institutionalized a new system of power but has only used his personal position to get around the entrenched Stalinist institutions. It is not obvious therefore how the Chinese polity will perform when Deng goes. It is much too soon to dub the impressive results to date a certain success.

Conservatives in the late 1980s insisted that a reform notion of joining the great international circle of the world economy meant subordination to world capitalism. Their nationalism and power interests led them to try to reverse reforms. Conservatives blamed China's trade deficit and corruption on decentralizing power to local personnel. Conservatives wooed hinterland provinces to oppose an emphasis on coastal progress. But privileging the hinterland, as Mao had, would not deliver growth, foreign exchange, technological progress, or product-cycle upgrading. Mere euphemistic changes were imposed to mollify conservatives. The policy of joining the international circle was renamed coastal development, with the hinterland contributing raw materials. Still, conservatives could preclude the alienation of rural property, make a priority of dealing with inflation fears by turning off the capital flow to rural enterprises, and maintain an antipeasant policy of forced grain quotas at low prices. This set of antipeasant policies has built up more political dynamite in the countryside and hastened rural migration to the cities.

Reforms stressing the coastal provinces and rural entrepreneurs were needed to create jobs and wealth. Also, a patriotic desire not to stay behind while the rest of East Asia raced ahead hastened a re-establishment of economic realism. However much reform policies subverted the control of the northern conservatives, regime legitimacy required wealth expansion based on continued privileging of regions, people, and forces that were most opposed to the northern conservatives (Yang 1991). Conservatives could still join with military chauvinists on an anti-American (or anti-Western) or antitraitor line to try to block further reform and more openness. In sum, China's great success is not the consequence of a wise strategy by clever leaders, who in fact have been split and stalemated.

If one concludes that China's rapid development has not emulated the means used by Japan except for aggressively pursuing market-oriented export expansion, does that mean China's transition should be understood as a unique achievement in contrast to other command-economy systems? A senior economist at the Asian Development Bank does just that and congratulates China for gradualism and sequencing. Instead of a big bang of privatizing the heavy-industry sector and rationalizing prices, purportedly the counterproductive path of Eastern Europe, Beijing, supposedly, first cleverly reformed agriculture and then freed up light industry (Rana 1994, 4). But, as explained above, conditions were so different that (1) Russia could not similarly reform agriculture, and (2) Russia's and Eastern Europe's heavy-industry sectors were so much weightier than China's that those countries could not afford not to tackle that problem or they would risk a continuing drain that could destroy the currency and produce hyperinflation. Indeed, to the large extent that those vested interests in Russia have blocked such reforms, they do seem to have hastened economic disaster. Besides, as Shirk shows, Beijing did not cleverly sequence reforms; rather it pushed ahead where there was least resistance. No doubt China benefited tremendously from agricultural commercialization, but Russia lacked a peasantry, the human capital on which such a reform could ride to success. In fact, agricultural commercialization is far from complete in China. Conservatives have fought a rearguard action against rural marketization that continues to threaten peasant gains. Since 1984–85 many of rural China's tillers have actually fallen behind (Chen 1993, 52), as income has been withheld and taxes have skyrocketed.

> First, purchasing funds for the fall 1992 grain and cotton harvest were short 63.5 billion yuan, because some localities used their funds for fixed asset investment. Second, the increase in the burdens of peasants exceed[ed] the rate of their income growth. From 1985 to June 1991, the per capita increase in peasant income was 10 percent, but rural tax revenues increased by 16.9 percent, per capita collective burden increased by 11 percent, and direct rural household burden increased by 17.5 percent. (Wu 1933, 3)

The first wise step for which China's rulers are congratulated in fact has yet to be completed. As anthropologist Myron Cohen has noted, the spending patterns of villagers reveals them as in no way grateful to the regime for its reform policies. Rather, villagers spend ever more money on ever more magnificent homes because they believe that even if or when policy reverts to full collectivization, the home will not be confiscated by the unpopular, unaccountable, and illegitimate state.

Not wealth-expanding reform, but their own power position within the old system, is what China's leaders concentrate on. The Beijing government's priority has been not alienating the state-enterprise system, fearing that price rationalization and privatization would create in China the forces that made for the Solidarity movement in Poland. Beijing so far seems incapable of ending huge subsidies to money-losing state enterprises or of stopping a relative decrease in central revenues. Consequently, Beijing keeps ending up making farmers pay the price. Burdens pile up on peasant backs. The rulers therefore have to fear rural explosions such as that led by a popular army veteran which occurred in Renshou and was supported by students in the Sichuan provincial capital in the first half of 1993.

What made the farmers in Renshou see red this spring was not poverty per se or the unfair gap that has arisen between the farmers and nouveau riche in the cities. It was the yoke of new taxes and fees and "voluntary contributions" that the local authorities have come up with at shorter and shorter intervals—and then collected with a brutality reminiscent of an old-fashioned bailiff. (Moller 1993, 1)

So, more villagers are allowed to flee to cities. More pressure grows to close money-losing state enterprises. But the cost of ending inflation and freeing up rural dwellers could be, as in Russia, urban unrest. Fear of layoffs is already leading to unofficial labor organization (Kaye 1993, 13). The regime fears society organizing in its own interests and therefore backs village Party leaders who repress protesting villagers. It arrests and tortures and executes labor organizers.

Are China's reform-era leaders buying time until development spreads sufficiently to tamp down angers or are the rulers adding fuel to a fire that will soon be nipping at their heels? Whatever the answer, this crucial, open question suggests that it is an error to premise research on the post-Mao economic transition as a quest for a secret of success that others should emulate. The transition is incomplete. While wealth accumulates, so do angers and tensions.

Solinger's language suggests that she, too, is uncertain whether the compromises forged by Beijing in the post-Mao era will suffice as a long-term basis for continued stability and growth. She finds in her most insightful study of state-enterprise reform in Wuhan that the reformers have broken open former command-economy rigidities (Solinger 1993, 141) in a way that has strengthened the state, which is the purpose of the ruling group. They have, she finds, achieved these goals by creating a dependent business class.

But Solinger also finds that the result is "stasis" and a "limit on full-fledged reform" (ibid., 79). This partially reformed China is not capable of Japanese-style indicative planning (ibid., 113–14). The logic of the system instead remains trapped within an economics of scarcity and a politics of bureaucratic bargaining (ibid., 103). China has not transited out of command-economy dilemmas. In fact, the political struggle between conservatives and reformers, centralizers and decentralizers, may be growing more intense because conservative centralizers cannot stop powers from going "to the lower levels of administration" (ibid., 51). The center has lost control over resource allocation and raw materials (ibid., 115, 116). The center increasingly lacks the resources to subsidize its urban, command-economy, heavy-industry base because such pouring in of money threatens to cause hyperinflation and urban discontent. When it steals money from elsewhere to pay urban subsidies, it makes urban–rural relations ever more "competitive and hostile" (ibid., 220). The whole thing seems grossly unfair.

So, while the economy grows, the political system remains "much as it always has" been (ibid., 154), except that regionalism is growing (ibid., 164). While reform has reached an impasse, the southeast coastal regions have found a way to fund themselves (ibid., 258), such that it may become "capable of smashing the monolith" (ibid., 270). Meanwhile, the old system continues and keeps bailing out the northeast region with its Stalinist economic formation. In sum, the conflict over reform is still inconclusive (ibid., 260). China in the early 1990s looks to Solinger much like China just before the 1911 republican revolution of enlightened provincial forces against the discredited *ancien régime*. It hardly seems a model of success. Solinger's wise and data-rich argument makes great sense to me. More important, increasingly Chinese see it just the way Solinger describes it, a conflict between an absolutist *ancien régime* and progressive provinces.

Shirk, on the other hand, finds that the reformers at the center have successfully aligned with the dynamic regions to avoid conservatives at the center and maintain stability and growth based on this political coalition. Already the percentage of industry controlled by the central state is less than in Austria. Already the percentage of national income generated by the state is less than France. Why cannot growth continue in this direction, with the center maintaining order? To be sure, this keeps the Leninist despotism entrenched in power, but Shirk concludes, this "while distasteful in moral terms, may be the best short-term political strategy of economic reform" (Shirk 1993, 350).

Minxin Pei agrees for the very short term. But he sees the state weakening and problems intensifying such that it could yet turn out that Russia will suffer "lower *total* transitional costs" (Pei 1994, 209). "The ultimate—and most critical —test for the Chinese model," he concludes, is whether China can hold together or whether China is accumulating political dynamite "for a nationalist revolution similar to that which dismembered the former Soviet Union" (ibid., 210). China is not yet a success to be emulated.

I read Shirk's brilliantly accumulated data throughout her excellent book as suggesting just this most dangerous possibility and her optimistic concluding argument on the last couple of pages as an add-on. Her shrewdly obtained, weighty evidence persuades me that China's reform success does not even guarantee that China will not break apart and fall into bloody chaos. To be sure, happier outcomes are also possible.

Solinger's and Shirk's hardheaded descriptions of where reform is actually at are quite similar. Shirk agrees that reformist price rationalizers have been "unable to push through the stone wall of the Chinese bureaucracy" (Shirk 1993, 265). Indeed, it is "impossible to achieve genuine reform within the framework of the traditional system" (ibid., 249). This reads much like Solinger's brilliantly articulated description of "stasis." Reform, Shirk concludes also, has "stalled halfway down the road" (ibid., 335).

The question is, since Deng-era reformers "made an end run around the central planners and industrial bureaucrats . . . by appealing to . . . local officials" (ibid., 36), since the Mao-era system was already "regionally based" (ibid., 29), with provincial leaders of higher rank than in the Soviet Union (ibid., 94), will China suffer a fate similar to Ethiopia, the German Democratic Republic,

Czechoslovakia, Yugoslavia, and the Soviet Union, a change in national structure and national identity? After all, China has devolved financial autonomy as did Yugoslavia (ibid., 149).

Although Shirk finds that "parochialism and regional conflict" have intensified (ibid., 50) and an ever higher percentage of resources is in the hands of provincial administrators, the center, for her, nonetheless maintains the authority to prevent provinces from acting in their own interests (ibid., 84) because regional officials remain accountable to "an elite selectorate" (ibid., 90, 185) and "China is a unitary state" (ibid., 182). She may yet prove right on the outcome. The future remains open. But so often do central leaders express fear of disunion that she is not quite persuasive in stating that "the center has little reason to fear . . . a loss of central control or national disintegration" (ibid., 149–50). As Pei concluded, it is in fact the big unresolved question. It cannot be dismissed out of hand.

There already "is a considerable degree of de facto delegation of authority and resources to the provinces" (ibid., 112). When coastal Guangdong province is allowed to pay a market price for inputs, that is, a higher price than the state would pay, "all the goods produced in neighboring regions flowed to Guangdong" (ibid., 144). Since Beijing faces a continuing budget crisis and, an insufficiency of resources, while the provinces "assume proprietary financial rights" over enterprises and can treat resources "as entitlements," Beijing "was in the position of a medieval king who . . . had to extract funds from feudatories" (ibid., 151, 161). "The provinces were expected to bail out the center" (ibid., 173). This sounds like a basis for a Magna Carta, or a potential federal constitutional republic, or wars among regions for the throne, which is what Solinger concluded when she saw the gerontocratic regime as similar to the old Manchu Dynasty on its last legs, facing provincial power ready to make a republican revolution as in 1911.

Shirk's data supports Solinger's conclusion. Already "the feudatories sat in the council that selected the king" (ibid., 162). Already there is "Balkanization of the market" with "each locality walling itself off like a feudal manor" (ibid., 186). Indeed the provincial representatives are becoming the strongest group in the Central Committee (ibid., 151). Provincial advocates already have "held up American federalism as the model to emulate" (ibid., 165). The provinces already compete for foreign investment, much as do the states in the United States (ibid., 182). The centralizing Ministry of Finance's "fiscal conservatism rarely prevails" (ibid., 237). Provinces have already been enfranchised to participate in a newly invented set of secret work meetings where policy is actually decided (ibid., 150). Already "Beijing, Shanghai and Tianjin" have "reserved permanent seats" in the Party Politburo (ibid., 195). Provinces have been "able to win increasingly generous revenue-sharing contract terms" (ibid., 152). Already the regions have more control over their administration and more ties to the military than was the case in the former Soviet Union. Local patronage machines have expanded and been strengthened. "[F]iscal decentralization and enterprise profit

retention" have eroded the power of the center (ibid., 238). Local officials identify with the fate of their domains (p. 189). Recentralization is impossible (ibid.,
156). Indeed, in any bargaining, the provinces keep winning (p. 169). The center
keeps surrendering more power to the provinces (ibid., 173). The conservative
strategy cannot reverse this trend. Conservatives are merely keeping faith with
antireform allies by further subsidizing provinces, such as Liaoning, with Stalin-
ist-economy, money-wasting interests (ibid., 193).

There is a regional split between loss-generating old state enterprises in the
west and northeast and profitable new enterprises "on the coast" (ibid., 269). The
fast-moving provinces see the conservative center exploiting them—"beating the
fastest oxen" (ibid., 290–91)—to subsidize the inefficient system that is the
political support of losers. The officials from the money-losing state enterprises
rank high "on the center's nomenklatura list" (ibid., 285). That is, a split leadership has permited decisions that "protect[ed] the backward" (ibid., 277) and
"punished the advanced." It is the backward, the failures, whose political logic
prevails (ibid., 282). This is not reform success. The "hard-liners . . . would
never go along with dismantling state ownership" (ibid., 313). Surely one option
that successful reform provinces must consider is a political system where they
no longer have to subsidize useless parasites that hold China back. But what does
that mean for political continuity or stability?

So much does real power increasingly lie in the regions "that the allure of
national position has faded, [and] the center has lost some leverage" (ibid., 189).
With China divided by language regions, the danger is officials perceived to
speak their regional language but not the Beijing dialect (ibid., 207, 223). In fact,
already provincial officials are acting as if people in the provinces will soon be
voters, "gambling on a change in the political system occurring in the future"
(ibid., 189).

A key reason that China's reforms may not sustain the traditional Leninist
socialist political system is because of the intensifying popular experience of a
corrupt and unjust division of rewards. The system seems inequitable in the
extreme. This is in direct contrast to East Asia developmental states, which
produced the most equitable growth ever witnessed on the planet.

It is odd that this equity is not at the center of the understanding of East Asian
success. This equitable sharing of income gains permitted the government to
leverage high savings. All could feel that sacrifice today would be fairly rewarded tomorrow. Japanese business intellectual Shijuro Ogato explained that
the basis of Japan's social stability has been "the relatively equal distribution of
income and the upward social mobility of labor" (Bartley et al. 1993, 49). In East
Asia, "growth . . . was . . . above all, quite equitable" (Papanek 1988, 29). But
this is not what has been happening in China.

> Singapore, Taiwan and South Korea (and Japan as well) managed to raise
> living standards for nearly all their people at roughly the same pace, thus

achieving a remarkable degree of economic equality. China, by contrast, has seen a rapidly widening gap between haves and have-nots, accompanied by debilitating corruption and abuse of power (Isaacs, 1993, 23).[1]

The equity in East Asian growth in the generation after World War II was real, but it was not a planned outcome. It instead was an unintended product of many distinct factors; a land reform that undermined the power of rural lords; an experience of national crisis that led all economic sectors, especially powerful ones, to accept limits on their income gains in order to guarantee the stable success of the whole system; a merit, career, professional civil service of basic integrity; and a universal education system tied to merit exams and promotion from school to work based on performance. This combination of factors produced an experience of system equity.

Other than the long-term effects of the 1948–52 land reform, China in the post-Mao era lacks these factors and instead suffers from a profound experience of intensifying inequities. For some Chinese, that injustice even produces nostalgia for the Cold War era, when foreign threats fostered an atmosphere of shared sacrifice. But that era is gone. Institutions are decisive. Unreformed institutions in China, ironically, discredit the reform project.

Thus the tensions that exploded in urban Beijing in spring 1989 and in rural Renshou in early 1993 seem to be intensifying in China, even while wealth expands rapidly and the poorest of the poor rise out of Mao-era stagnant poverty. China is an economic success. The speed of growth in the early 1990s was truly mind-boggling. But it is not obvious that the political deals put together to achieve that economic dynamism can long sustain a unitary centralized system dominated by conservatives, who are experienced as treating everyone, especially the more successful, most unfairly. The center weakens; the regions strengthen. To be sure, phenomenal economic growth premised on the peasant household economy, labor mobility, and plugging into East Asian export-oriented economic dynamism could yet win the regime the time to buy off the intensifying tensions that bedevil the system. But surely China cannot yet be deemed a model of reform success if it is not a foregone political conclusion that this center can long hold firm.

Notes

1. In Europe, socialists tend to accept the view of East Asian dynamism offered by Lee Kuan Yew, what I call East Asian Authoritarianism–Lee Kuan Yew Thought. That is, instead of learning from how East Asian economies have moved up the value-added, high-technology ladder in ways that have permitted great equity, all they see is political repression and economic exploitation of cheap labor, dressed up in Confucian language. It is Veblen's view of Japan's success at the start of the twentieth century; Schumpeter's view of the rise of imperial Germany. Greek socialist Prime Minister Andreas Papandreou explained that in the new global economic battle,

the troops are the legions of low-wage workers in places like East Asia. What globalization of the market has thus meant is a transfer of poverty from East to West.... Spain's 22 percent unemployment rate is linked to Asia's rising standard of living. (Papandreou 1994, 51)

Actually, Singapore workers earn more than British, Japanese more than Americans. As East Asia subcontracts into cheap-labor China, so do Europe and America. There are good reasons why East Asian leaders see leaders in the democratic West as whiners. Nonetheless, Papandreou's erroneous description of East Asia in general may, at least for the early reform era, be not so inaccurate for China.

References

Bartley, Robert et al. 1993. *Democracy and Capitalism* (Singapore: Institute of Southeast Asian Studies).

Bentsen, Lloyd. 1994. "Economic Revolution." *New York Times* business section (January 23), pp. 1, 6.

Bergere, Marie-Claire. 1984. "On the Historical Origins of Chinese Underdevelopment." *Theory and Society* 13.3 (May), p. 336.

Chen Xiwen. (1993). "Improving Rural Reform Based on Market Requirements." *Gaige* [Reform] (May 20), pp. 60–65. Translated in JPRS-CAR–93–064, September 1, 1993, pp. 51–56.

Cohen, Myron. 1991. "Being Chinese." *Daedalus* 120.2 (Spring).

Conquest, Robert. 1986. *The Harvest of Sorrow* (New York: Oxford University Press).

Dalmia, Gauray. (1994). "The Price of Liberty." *Far Eastern Economic Review* (March 3), p. 25.

Dittmer, Lowell. 1987. *China's Continuing Revolution* (Berkeley: University of California Press).

Friedman, Edward. 1990. "Deng Versus the Peasantry." *Problems of Communism.* (September–October), pp. 30–43.

Haggard, Stephen. 1990. *Pathways from the Periphery* (Ithaca: Cornell University Press).

Helliwell, John. 1993. Working Paper 4066, National Bureau of Economic Research. Summarized in Edward Balls, "Can Yeltsin be a Democrat and a Reformer?" *Financial Times* (October 11).

Isaacs, Arnold. 1993. "China Inc." *New York Times Book Review* (November 28), p. 23.

Kaye, Lincoln. 1993. "The Price of Reform." *Far Eastern Economic Review* (November 4), pp. 12–13.

Lampton, David. 1992, "China's Biggest Problem." In Joint Economic Committee, Congress of the United States, eds., *China's Economic Dilemmas in the 1990's* (Armonk, NY: M. E. Sharpe), pp. 65–69.

Moller, Gregers. 1993. *Berlingske Tidende* (July 15, 25). Translated in JPRS-CAR–93–066, September 13, 1993, pp. 1–4.

Mallet, Victor. 1994. "Confucius or Convenience?" *Financial Times* (March 5–6).

Manning, Robert. 1994. "The Great Leap Upward." *Far Eastern Economic Review* (March 10), p. 10.

Papandreou, Andreas. 1994. "Europe Turns Left." *New Perspectives Quarterly* (Winter), pp. 50–53.

Papanek, Gustav. 1988. "The New Asian Capitalism." In Peter Berger and Hsin-Huang Michael Hsiao, eds., *In Search of An East Asian Development Model* (New Brunswick, NJ: Transaction Books), pp. 27–80.

Pei Minxin. 1994. *From Reform to Revolution: The Demise of Communism in China and the Soviet Union* (Cambridge, MA: Harvard University Press).
Prowse, Michael. 1992. *Financial Times* (August 14), editorial page.
Rana, Pradumna. 1994. "Word Games." *Far Eastern Economic Review* (January 13), p. 4.
Sachs, Jeffrey, and Wing Thye Woo. Forthcoming. "Structural Factors in the Economic Reforms of China, Eastern Europe and the Former Soviet Union."
Schumpeter, Joseph. 1955. "The Sociology of Imperialism." In *Social Classes/Imperialism* (New York: Meridian), pp. 1–98.
Shirk, Susan. 1993. *The Political Logic of Economic Reform in China* (Berkeley: University of California Press).
Solinger, Dorothy. 1993. *China's Transition From Socialism* (Armonk, NY: M. E. Sharpe).
Woo, Wing Thye. Forthcoming. "The Art of Reforming Centrally Planned Economies: Comparing China, Poland and Russia."
Wu Shangmin et al. 1993. "Determining, Analyzing and Devising Countermeasures for China's Current Economic Situation." *Gaige* [Reform], (May 20). Translated in JPRS-CAR–93–064, September 1, 1993, pp. 2–7.
Yang Dali. 1991. "China's Adjustment to the World Economy." *Pacific Affairs* 64.1 (1991), pp. 42–64.
Zakaria, Fareed. 1994. "An Interview with Lee Kuan Yew." *Foreign Affairs* 73.2 (March–April).

Chapter 11

Was Mao Zedong a Revolutionary?

Even to raise the question "Was Mao Zedong a revolutionary?" seems perverse. Virtually all his political life Mao self-consciously pursued revolution. He is universally recognized as a leading revolutionary, both as a theorist and an activist. Mao asked his colleagues on August 15, 1959, "Please take a look at which is better, the Chinese revolution or the Paris Commune? And how to compare the Chinese revolution with the Russian revolution of the 1905 era? Or the 1958–59 construction of socialism in China with Lenin's Russia of 1919, 1921? Which is better?"[1] Mao's goal was to be the most revolutionary and the most Communist, taking Lenin's war communism and Marx's momentary utopian mulling on the Paris Commune as the essence of communism. In each case, both with the Paris Commune and Bolshevik Russia, the moment given universal import was a mobilization for war in which survival, not prosperity or human decency or human fulfillment, was of foremost concern to Mao. His communism was war communism.

Mao carried forward war communism in the Great Leap Forward.[2] War communism originates in Robespierre's mobilization of France for war and was emulated by both Lenin and Stalin in the 1920s. War communism institutionalizes a terror that ruins the peasantry. Economic historian Vasili Seliunin explains, "It wasn't the famine that caused the grain requisitions, but rather the opposite; it was the mass requisitions (ordered by Lenin) that caused the famine. The evidence clearly points to the fact that the mass liquidation of kulaks took place precisely in the years of 'war communism' and not in the early 1930s."[3] S. A. Nickolsky in 1990 published a Russian-language study of war communism that details how it "was not necessitated by any economic reasons" but by a military model of the economy that treated the peasantry as "a disappearing

Originally published in *Issues and Studies* (Taiwan), August 1990. Reprinted with permission of the Institute for International Relations, Mucha, Taipei, Taiwan.

class."[4] Mao was correct in his insistence that his class-struggle war mobilization was in the orthodox tradition of Lenin and Stalin. This cruel reality, containing a strong potential for genocide against the peasantry, is missed by analysts misled by Trotsky's insistence that Stalin's path was a bureaucratic degeneration. Leninist states do not build rationalizing bureaucracies of the Weberian kind. Rather, they negate capitalism. Liu Guoguang, in the November 1986 issue of *Zhongguo Shehui Kexue*, pointed out that even before seizing power, the Bolsheviks aimed to eliminate currency and commodity exchange. Recalling this, Bukharin said, "we did not regard war communism as . . . a system made necessary by a particular stage in the civil war. . . . [W]e saw it as a policy that the proletariat should extensively adopt in the wake of victory."[5]

Mao's policy in China is Lenin's war communism.[6] The locus classicus of war communism is probably Plutarch's life of Lycurgus as translated by Rousseau into his ideal of a militarized Sparta and then among the Jacobins in their ideal, spartan republic. This militarization, mistakenly conceived of as revolution, legitimates a continuing secret police war against opponents of the regime and a politics of extreme nationalism. Even in the late-twentieth-century Soviet Union, the prevalence of war communism ideology continued with post-Stalin rulers. "For them, the victory in the war confirmed the value of the system. That was socialism. . . . The advancement of technology to them meant the nuclear bomb and modern means of delivering it. They were the true heirs of a military empire; their minds had been formed in the years of 'war communism,' and that was the only guidepost they knew."[7] War communism, not bureaucratic rule, is the essence of the Lenin–Stalin state system.[8]

Conceptualizing Revolution

Even if the results of Mao's war communism project were deemed economically irrational and monstrously inhuman, surely it was a revolutionary quest. After all, it is Mao who synthesized the tactics of protracted guerrilla war such that peasant wars stopped being dead-end defeatism and became instead victorious wars of national liberation. And it was Mao who, after seizing state power, captured the imagination of the world by seeking to continue the revolution after the armed revolution ended in a policy of continuous revolution known as the Cultural Revolution. Pol Pot's genocidal Khmer Rouge won Mao's congratulations and support for going yet further with this effort.[9] The murderous Sendero Luminoso in Peru pursued the Maoist project in the 1990s.[10] Even if one finds Mao's project cruel and evil, can one doubt that Mao was a revolutionary?

But what is a revolutionary? Both parts of Mao's struggle, the conquest of state power and the policies pursued in power, must be scrutinized. Why should a violent, military seizure of state power be seen as a revolution? Must not a revolution contain some progressive and liberating content? Genghis Khan's conquests brought fundamental changes in the social structure of Russia, but few historians of Russia consider this large, rapid, coerced change of state and society to be revolutionary. Most Russian historians find that this rapid seizure of power and total societal change actually retarded progress. There are numerous military coups and putsches that are seldom dubbed revolution. The Bolshevik Revolution, as with Leninist seizures of power in the 1970s in Ethiopia and Afghanistan, was a military putsch. A revolution is neither a violent seizure of power nor a big or sudden social change, or even both combined. Brutal conquests by imperialists are not labeled revolutions. If the Confederacy had won the American Civil War and extended a system of slavery, that would not have been revolutionary. It seems nonsense to denote the basic changes imposed by Hitler as revolution.

One must address the actual consequence of the actions and events. In Iran, was the early-1950s government led by nationalizing patriot Mossadegh a revolutionary one? By the modernizing Shah who replaced Mossadegh? By the anti-imperialist Khomeini who, at the end of the 1970s, followed the Shah to power? While each has been styled revolutionary, can each actually be revolutionary if each is antithetical to the others? The meanings ascribed to revolution require analysis.

For Marxist-Leninists, who conceive of revolution as abolishing private property, money, and trade and as throwing out imperialists, Pol Pot may be a revolutionary. But the Maoist Pol Pot was a mass murderer.[11] Writing of the failed consequences of Bolshevik-style revolutions, including those of Mao and Pol Pot, Boris Kagarlitsky concludes, "The failure of the revolution as a democratic revolution ominously foreboded its future failure as a social revolution."[12] The Bolshevik Revolution, even to Russians, increasingly seems an "unmitigated tragedy." Per capita consumption of meat in the 1980s was less than prior to World War I.[13] Russia, the world's seventh-ranking nation when the czar fell in 1917, was seventy-seventh in per capita income when Gorbachev came to power. The dilapidated, ugly buildings of Moscow led its leading architect to conclude that the Communist Party had done worse destruction to the capital than had the hated, reactionary Mongols. If the result of Lenin's work was stagnation or destruction, can the cause be revolutionary?

Kagarlitsky conceives of revolution in the tradition of Hannah Arendt,[14] a tradition focusing on the creation and institutionalization of political spaces for democratic political exploration and participation. In this tradition, the supposed revolutions of Lenin, Mao, and Pol Pot, all heirs of Robespierre's French Terror, are suspect because their project precluded the real work of revolution: the expansion of political space for free citizen action. A recent analysis of "40 Years of PRC" by M. Titarenko finds the most important historical lesson of the Chinese revolution, based on a claimed need to defend the revolution, to be "an enormous influence of the French Revolution," understood as "the idealization of the role of revolutionary violence."[15] In Arendt's perspective, to build on Robespierre's terror negates revolution and betrays freedom.

There are, however, other traditions of revolutionary analysis. The notion of revolution is contested. Barrington Moore, Jr., finds violence essential to the revolutionary project.[16] So do Marx and Lenin and many others. From Edward Bulwer-Lytton's observation that "Revolutions are not made with rosewater," to Mao's similar comment that "Revolution is not a dinner party," much of the study of revolution revolves around the violent road to seizing and holding power, a reality embodied in Madame Roland's conclusion that humanity "can be regenerated through blood alone." This chapter, however, abandons the usual focus on the who and how of violence, instead to engage systematically in an inquiry into the diverse consequences and content of revolution, a matter of great moment that is too often slighted in a popular and scholarly fascination with "blood alone."

By analyzing Mao's record in terms of the five major traditions of revolutionary outcomes, this chapter will clarify why Mao was a revolutionary only from a certain theoretical perspective, but not others. Like Kagarlitsky, Adam Michnik, a theorist of the Polish revolution of Solidarity in the 1980s, finds that the Bolshevik project Mao embraced was the child of the crimes and errors of the Jacobin terror of the French Revolution. It could not liberate people, as Arendt shows revolution should, but instead brought servility and stagnation.[17] Yet Mao once seemed most revolutionary. To comprehend Mao as revolutionary, the consequence of Mao's efforts can be measured against the five major theoretical notions of revolution, one premodern, four modern.

In the traditional notion, in which human life was lived as a great cycle, revolutions were actions that began the cycle yet again, permitting a fresh beginning. Revolution was a new start, but not a breakthrough, because society would inevitably be corrupted and so degenerate over time, requiring yet another revolution —and another, and again another, in endless repetitive cycles.[18] This European notion of revolution harmonizes with other traditional ontologies and cosmologies, such as the Chinese view of yin and yang and of dynastic cycles. Quite typically for revolutionaries, the victors in China's 1911 republican revolution started counting life afresh with year 1, not 1912. Aristotle fought against the historically inevitable process of degeneration and renewal by seeking a permanent balance of forces that could maintain a proper constitution to preclude the chaos and destruction inherent in the traditional revolutionary cycle.

Modern thinkers broke with the traditional concept of revolution as cyclical renewal by the seventeenth and eighteenth centuries because they saw life as progressive and purposeful. Economic, technical, medical, scientific, and other changes held out the promise that humans could break out of the ancient cycles and fetters and conquer higher ground. In addition, these new creations could be intended. Goal-oriented humans could purposively choose reasonable ends and find means to obtain their goals. The prospect of achieving a project of progress and reason was the new promise of revolution.[19] Revolution no longer was conceived of as a traditional cycle allowing humans a fresh start that would then, inevitably, be corrupted and degenerate. Rather, revolution was a permanent and planned achievement.

But what this revolutionary achievement actually has been is disputed. There are four competing analytic approaches, with each supposedly singularly capturing the essentials of modern revolutionary achievement. These conceptual schemes can be identified with four major theorists—Tocqueville,[20] Braudel, Marx, and Arendt. The conflicting notions of revolution are: building a modern state, creating a new nation, overthrowing a reactionary social class by a more progressive class, and expanding and institutionalizing political freedom. Each is seen as a genuine breakthrough, not an ephemeral start to be lost in subsequent decline.

Mao's project seems to seek the first three achievements. A renewed nation would inaugurate a state that would build socialism and defeat reactionary classes and their imperialist backers. Yet when one examines Mao's actual impact, one finds that the state he created cannot deal with modern challenges; the nation he left behind threatens to disintegrate; and the social group that took power and institutionalized itself in the Mao era, 1957–77, established another cycle of feudal-like rule and misrule. As a modern revolutionary, Mao's work failed. At best, he is a traditional revolutionary wasting an opportunity for a fresh start. (Since Mao rejected the idea of revolution as freedom, dismissing it in the Marxist-Leninist manner as a sham obscuring the reality of a bourgeois dictatorship, Mao's work was not intended to advance the cause of democratic freedom.) Let us then look at the three approaches to modern revolution that Mao embraced, starting with state building.

Revolution as State Building

Tocqueville identified the French Revolution not with political events such as the calling of the National Assembly in 1789, the Constitution, Declaration of Rights, or the subsequent execution of the king, but with a long process during which many generations built a centralized state, thereby enhancing the capacity to conquer the blessings of modernity. In 1979, Theda Skocpol analyzed Mao's revolution in the Tocqueville manner,[21] as a deep, historical process, culminating in a restructuring of power and in the making of a strong centralized state capable of delivering the blessings of the modern world—security from foreign enemies and prosperity for the people of the revolutionized state. (This chapter will bracket the thesis that a politics bringing as much inhumanity, terror, and death as Stalin, Mao, or Pol Pot brought cannot be legitimated by any measure of other achievement.)

Barrington Moore, Jr., was the original theorist who found that all revolutions —fascist, communist, or democratic—violently win a breakthrough to modernity. As with Perry Anderson's subsequent analysis,[22] the finding is that movements such as Mao's help destroy the obstructive social forces and bases that otherwise block a breakthrough to a modernizing centralized state. However, by the end of the twentieth century, it was obvious that China, as other Leninist states, had failed to create a basis for continuous modernization and instead institutionalized an inflexible and feudal-like system incapable of winning for the citizenry the material blessings of the modern world.[23] Skocpol took China's failed modernization as an instance of successful modernization.

In Skocpol's state-building approach, the Chinese revolution begins with the breakdown of the Manchu Dynasty, because the Manchus were incapable of defending the nation against imperialism or of mobilizing financial resources to modernize the state. The revolutionary struggle continues, according to Skocpol, after 1911 until China's Communist Party builds a state with the capacity to extract resources and deploy them so as to defend the nation against imperialism and create administrative organizations that incorporate previously excluded popular sectors—in China, especially the peasantry.[24] The Chinese state established by Mao was one of "national autonomy,"[25] that is, one that broke free of exploitative capitalist imperialism.

The main feature of a victorious revolution, for Skocpol, is the institutionalization of a Weberian-style bureaucracy with a national capacity. "In Weber's view, revolutions function ... to further bureaucratic domination, all the more inevitably to the extent that they establish state controls over the economy. . . . The Chinese Revolution gave rise ... to a much larger, more powerful, and more bureaucratic new political regime." Skocpol comprehends revolution in a Weberian manner. "More leadership positions in society ... become formal salaried offices within organizational hierarchies. . . . [They are] impersonally defined . . . offices in organizations with specific goals ... separated from private interests. . . . No longer could officials ... combine their family ... with ... the state or party."[26]

This analysis misleadingly ignores the neotraditional essence and actual dynamics of Leninist states.[27] Leninist Stalinism selects and promotes to official posts a nomenklatura based on connections of personal loyalty.[28] The state becomes a private arena. Jobs, statuses, and offices are inherited. The whole system, as accurately described in Liu Binyan's *A Higher Kind of Loyalty*,[29] is personalistic and corrupt. Merit, professionalism, and technical criteria are slighted. And Mao worsened the inherent Leninist-state tendency to minimize recruitment by competence, producing a system incapable of delivering to the Chinese people the blessings of wealth from the permanent revolution in technology and science.

Skocpol analyzes revolution to "explain the autonomous power ... of states as administrative and coercive machineries embedded in a militarized international state system."[30] A state defends the nation and mobilizes its resources. Skocpol's work reflects mid-nineteenth-century categories and concerns and combines them with the misunderstandings of dependency theory, an insistence that state building succeeds only by delinking from the world market. She is silent on global developments since the era of Tocqueville and Marx. It is as if the steel technologies of the mid-nineteenth century were the end-all and be-all of development. Hence Leninist-state power holders need not concern themselves with innovation, science, world-market competitiveness, skilled labor, managerial know-how, or the flexibility to adapt to changes in technology and economy.

What actually is institutionalized by Leninist-Stalinist states is a form of autarkic war communism incapable of leading in the above-listed tasks. Mao's major innovation, probably premised on seeing the Spanish Revolution fail in the 1930s in its defense of Madrid (as the Chinese failed at Wuhan against Japan) and of seeing Stalin's regime survive the Nazis by a retreat of military industry to the Ural Mountains (similar to Chiang Kai-shek's strategic retreat from Japanese invaders and to Mao's retreat from Chiang's forces), was to premise his war communism, as embodied in the 1964 and after policies of the third front, on a defense in depth by an armed population. That economically irrational priority, a particular form of war communism, weakened yet further the capacity of China's Leninist system to win the resources needed to keep up with the permanent technological revolution of a continuously modernizing world. The historical record suggests that Leninist states are not flexible or capable enough to succeed in that revolution. Leninist states require a political revolution to smash the outmoded personalistic state apparatuses that fetter human minds and energies and the forces of production. The Chinese revolution, from the Tocqueville perspective of state building, has yet to happen. The Leninist system built by Mao after conquering state power is an obstacle to that revolution. By the standard of state building, Mao was not a successful revolutionary.

Revolution as Nation Building

In a second notion of revolution, as stated by Stanley Hoffman, "the great question addressed by the Revolution [is]: How does one establish this nation? How does one create the modern citizen?"[31] The major contemporary theorist in this tradition, François Furet,[32] at one with Fernand Braudel's 1986 study of the long history making for *The Identity of France*, interprets revolution as the emergence of a nation. A long history "of origins,"[33] creates a common identity, a sense of a shared fate. (If revolution is a history of building national identity, then did revolution in China—as elsewhere in Asia—succeed millennia ago? Is Mao's work superfluous to the project?)

As does Eugene Weber's great study of *Peasants Into Frenchmen*, Furet focuses on the "integration of villages and peasant culture into the . . . nation." The claim of Marxists is that bourgeois dictators stole and monopolized "the victory of the people." For Marxists, only a socialist revolution can be authentically national. In contrast, Furet claims that revolution becomes truly national when even Marxists accept the democratic republic. A revolution, in overthrowing "the aristocratic principle in society," establishes a nation of equal citizens.[34]

In this sense, the national revolution is yet to happen in China, because the Leninist state structurally denies the notion of equal citizens and instead builds top-down statuses of caste and locale. Leninists insist that the Party elite deserves unique and permanent power and privilege above others. "The leadership of the Communist Party is . . . granted . . . by the countless revolutionary martyrs who . . . shed blood and sacrificed themselves."[35] This notion of a permanent dispensation permitting the dead to rule the living is precisely the feudal excrescence that, according to Thomas Paine, a modern republic was to end as it allowed all the living—not only the heirs of military conquerors—to decide their own destiny, to change the laws and rulers, and even to amend the constitution.[36] A system that negates equal justice for all is not yet one nation. The Leninist state remains an embodiment of the aristocratic principle. "The idea of the feudal system is inseparable from the idea of privilege. As such, it is incompatible with the concept of law which presupposes universality, hence equality of individuals before a common law."[37] In Leninism, the law privileges the Party, further privileges the nomenklatura within the Party, and yet more highly privileges the highest strata within the nomenklatura. The system does not offer equal justice for all.

A national revolution is the seizure by civil society of "space for development" for all the diverse individuals and groups to have room to act. But Leninists insist instead on their omniscient state imposing on ignorant society a unified, centralized will. Maoism, indeed the Jacobin notion of revolution, takes this imposition to the Rousseauist extreme of trying to remove all intermediary bodies so that the state finds no barriers in compelling society to move precisely as the rulers wish.[38] That privileged autocracy precludes the reality of a modern republican nation—equal, initiating citizens.[39]

In Leninism, all opponents of the state's will are traitors and counter-revolutionaries,[40] and, therefore, some imagined pure nation would be better off without them. (In fact, a pervasive police apparatus is celebrated to seek out enemies. The regime annually calls on the people to love the public security force.) Whereas the nation or republic is inclusive of all people, Leninist rule tends toward the removal of all autonomous groups or opinions treated as subversive. The crimes of Stalin, Mao, and Pol Pot, as well as attacks on peasant, ethnic, regional, and religious identities, all embody the logic of the Leninist perversion of the notion of nation, a logic of privileging pure red revolutionary blood. It is a blood theory of class or caste.[41]

Furet invites one to look at national holidays to see if the nation is symbolically celebrated. Did the new people in power make holidays of the great days symbolizing the successful struggle against the feudal monarchy and imperialism, or did they commemorate days of national humiliation—days such as, in China, October 10, May 4, September 18, December 9, July 7, August 15? Or do the rulers celebrate their own aristocratic privilege—July 1, 1921; August 21, 1927; October 1, 1949? Does the new state celebrate the struggle of the people for constitutional freedoms and control over taxation against the monarchy, or does it treat the popular struggle as a fraud?

The effort of democrats on China's mainland in the 1980s to claim the mantle of the 1898 and 1911 struggles against the reactionary Manchu Dynasty and to equate Mao and the post-Mao dictators with the old-fashioned, antireform, anti-republican tyrants, the Empress Dowager and Yuan Shihkai, is laden with symbolic contestation over the meaning and content of the nation. That struggle informs us that for all his superpatriotism, Mao was not authentically national.

> A century has gone by since the Reform Movement of 1898, and it seems we are still stuck at the starting line, trying to change our old ways and make our country strong. I seem to see Tan Sitong, the vanguard of reform, who "drew his sword and sent his laughter into the sky," raising his arms and calling out to this generation, "Burst through the net!"[42]
> Enough! Today's China is not the China of the Yuan family's warlord rule. It is not the China of Empress Dowager Cixi either. We absolutely will not let him go on sitting in the palanquin of the emperor who has "abdicated."[43]

What is revealed here is that this notion of revolution as nation building, as the other comprehensions of revolution analyzed herein, is not an imposition by outside analysts. Rather these notions of revolution illuminate the living, continuing struggle to win the revolution Chinese want, a national revolution. Whereas Mao had claimed at the inauguration of the People's Republic that a new nation existed because "the Chinese people had stood up," the demonstrators, in contrast, found that their spines were ever more bent from dependent groveling before arbitrary power and that the patriotic democratic movement was the opportunity when "All of the Chinese people should stand up." Having originated in commemorations of the Mukden incident, when Japan began to occupy China's northeastern provinces of Manchuria, and in remembrance of the December 9, 1935, movement against Japanese conquest, the demonstrators were true patriots. Insulted that the privileged parasites who used power for their own private purposes dared question their nationalism, the demonstrators insisted that theirs was the "largest patriotic movement in the last seventy years," distinguishing "my China," the people's true China, from that of the feudal-like rulers, their false China. "For the people, for China, we should work together as one." The people seemed one as taxi drivers drove demonstrators for free, vendors kept prices down despite shortages, and even thieves stopped stealing. Willing to sacrifice their blood to awaken the nation, the citizenry responded to songwriter Hou Dejian's lyrics to "Descendents of the Dragon," identifying the Chinese nation, the dragon's descendants, with the hope of their shared culture, not with the Communist Party, socialism, Marxism-Leninism, or the dictatorship of the proletariat. "There is a dragon in the ancient Far East, /It is called the Middle Kingdom, / . . . /Black eyes, black hair, yellow face, /A descendent of the dragon forever. / . . . /Wipe your eyes giant dragon, /See clearly forever."[44]

Whereas Chinese increasingly complain that under Leninism things are worse than under the Japanese or than under the Nationalist Party, or, astoundingly, than even under the Manchus, Leninist rulers contend that they have won the people the blessings of the national revolution. University of Hong Kong vice chancellor Wang Gungwu subscribes to the regime's own perspective of "the 1949 Revolution" as a "culmination of the process . . . restoring China to greatness."[45] This greatness has been defined by the ideologues of the People's Republic in anti-imperialist and military terms. Foreign control of the economy ended, industry was nationalized. A united, independent nation was formed. China built intercontinental missiles and nuclear weapons and stood up with armed might against the United States, the Soviet Union, India, and Vietnam. Voting as one of but five veto-wielding nations in the United Nations, China is, since Mao conquered power, recognized as one of the world's few great powers.

But China was granted that United Nations veto power even during the chaos of civil war. It was not a position won by Mao's conquest of power. The world recognized the reality of a great Chinese nation before Mao's rise.

The building of military might through a continuous Mao-inspired effort to institutionalize war communism actually debilitated the economy of the country and weakened the nation. Besides, it was not Mao's armies that defeated Japanese invaders and threw them out of China. To mask the lie in the claim that Communists embody the independence struggle, Party historiography magnifies the role of Stalin's armies in defeating Japan. America's role in World War II's Pacific war against Japan is slighted.

Constant propaganda about success in terms of nuclear weapons and ballistic missiles and a need for continuing resistance to an imperialism supposedly threatening to reverse socialism hides a basic contradiction of the Leninist regime. Lacking any authentic cultural identity to lend dignity to the people, and fearful of the consequences of fully entering the world community and world market, Leninist rulers keep the nation locked in ignorance, militarism, and hate of foreigners. This is a perversion of nationalism.

In addition, it is not obvious why state control of the economy should be a matter of national success. Many weak, corrupt, and unpopular ruling groups have nationalized foreign enterprises. In Leninist states, however, as Kornai has shown, soft budget criteria of the command economy guarantee that nationalization debilitates the economy and weakens the nation. When Mao died, he bequeathed China a stagnant command economy and a demoralized, albeit chauvinistic, people. Leninist anticapitalism cum anti-imperialism cannot permit itself to understand the importance of international openness or money and finance as positive factors in the creation of national wealth. The contradiction is embodied in the post–Beijing massacre regime of Deng Xiaoping begging for investment or cheap aid while denouncing materialism and money.

Despite repeated chauvinist appeals from on high, a common national identification of a shared fate has declined since the inauguration of the People's Republic. All sectors of Chinese society felt exploited and abused by Mao-era policies. Consequently it is not easy for post-Mao reformers to forge a national equity pact with an experientially fair distribution system (taxes, wages, profits). People in Shanghai, Jiangsu, Zhejiang, Guangdong, and Fujian believe they should be allowed to retain their earnings. They see new housing in the nation's capital or the imported cars chauffeuring the rulers as proof of theft from the people by a self-serving, privileged stratum. The state center insists on taking more than relatively flourishing regions wish to surrender. As in other Leninist systems, the onset of reform joins local particularistic identities with economic self-interest and a delegitimation of the corrupt and incompetent state rulers to the point that these regional forces threaten to rend the national fabric. Mao did not build a united nation with a lasting common identity. As with other Leninist states, China too could come apart. The nation could disintegrate. The revolutionary achievement of national unity is far from consolidated. Indeed the Leninist system makes success unlikely.

Prolonged rule by a Leninist-Stalinist system turns notions of nationalism upside down. This is best understood not by focusing singularly on minorities or regions that, as in Yugoslavia or the USSR, would break away from the center, but rather by analyzing how the center itself eventually rejects the regime's chauvinist notion of the nation. The regime tries, at first with success, to discredit opponents and emigrants as traitors. But eventually, and sometimes suddenly, repression and stagnation make heroes of those who fled. Traitors are transformed into patriots. If one focuses on the Soviet Union restoring citizenship to dissidents who had fled abroad, or on East Germany being totally undermined by emigrants, or on Russia seceding from the Soviet Union, one then attains a clearer understanding of what is at stake. The change is seen in post-Mao China among people who begin to insist that the nation was better off in some prior era.

The issue is deeper than historical fact. The issue is personal political identity. Patriotism is redefined in popular consciousness because people cannot accept the idea that the incompetent parasites holding state power represent the nation. The more the rulers are discredited as greedy, self-aggrandizing individuals using power for private purposes, the more likely is a popular quest for other sources of identifying what makes a person a patriot.

A sign that China has reached this turning point in national self-identification is the spreading experience that the various semi-independent networks of the Party act as a mafia, a private, criminal network taking care of those in the small family but excluding the ordinary citizenry in the big family. The Party is seen as a means only of personal advancement. The political police are seen as a gang of private thugs serving the corrupt individuals in power. In sum, the state is exposed as a private realm. Consequently it has no claim to people's nationalistic loyalties. People must look elsewhere for a nation.

While Deng Xiaoping looks forward to visiting a Chinese-run Hong Kong and makes off-and-on threatening gestures toward Taiwan, the foundation of the nation tends toward fracture or collapse. It is not obvious that Mao Zedong's conquest of power in 1949 institutionalized a great and united nation. The incapacities, stratification, state–society gap, and particularisms of a Leninist system contradict the modern nationalist project. The kindest verdict history can render to Mao's revolution, taken as nation building, is that all the evidence is not in.

In the post-Mao era, Mao has been linked to reactionary Ming Dynasty chauvinistic policies of cutting China off from the world. A truly modern nationalism has yet to be created. The cuts and fissures that became apparent in the anti-Manchu struggle have not bound and healed. In June 1989 Beijing residents learned that they could be as badly treated as Tibetans. The same fate threatens Fujianese, Cantonese, Shanghaiese, and others in China. Locales throw up barriers to a national market. Region is pitted against region. If the Leninist regime has failed even in its attempt to impose a nationwide absolutist mercantilism, then it has not built a modern nation. From the perspective of nationalism, Mao's revolution may be an utter failure.

Mao's policy of politics in command actually alienates society from the state rather than building a united nation. Indeed, even according to Marx, Thermidor is "the reassertion of real society over the *illusion of politics.*"[46] If Mao, who put politics in command, fought against Thermidor, the natural assertions of society, he actually opposed the nation's various wills, the real revolution seeking space to express itself. The post-Mao Deng Xiaoping regime, in continuing Mao's struggle against society (against revisionism, bourgeois liberalism, civic will, etc.), continues Mao's counter-revolutionary project, the repression and suppression of civil society. The ideologues around Deng are aware of this antipopular impact, so whereas Mao tried to build an artificial, new, Communist culture, the post-Mao dictators try to co-opt and resurrect a sanitized, apolitical tradition of the old, things like the Dragon Boat Festival and the Beijing Opera. Neither Mao's artificial culture nor the post-Mao traditionalism can build a common, modern, authentic national identity.

Rather than embodying revolutionary nationalism, the mainland of China at the end of the twentieth century looks like France on the verge of the overthrow of its *ancien régime.* Revolutionary dynamite is piling up that could explode the *ancien régime.* The peasantry hates the local representatives of the state, a vast peasant proletariat flees the village, the ruling order is discredited, society knows that it is the loyal nation and that the rulers are the parasitic and privileged. The rulers are increasingly seen as a group that has stolen state power for its private purposes. If "Revolution can be considered a vast process of socio-cultural integration, achieved through . . . anti-feudal patriotism,"[47] then one must conclude that the Mao regime did not achieve that integration because it established yet another premodern order. Like the monarchical centralizers of late absolutist Europe, the Leninist state tries to swallow society[48] but ends up merely seizing and redistributing wealth, not releasing the societal forces that can create wealth and expand the reach of equal justice to all of the nation. Even when power holders in such a system see a need for "unifying the national market, nationalizing production and exchange, breaking up the old agrarian communities based on autarky," they still stop the reform success because they are even "more concerned" with upholding the Leninist distinctions that legitimate and preserve their power[49] but that undercut the imperatives of a flourishing nation. The rulers need peaceful international economic exchanges with the world for national prosperity, but to hold power they need foreigners as threats to and enemies of the nation. "[W]ar meant revolution and peace meant counter- revolution."[50] The Leninist regime is caught on the horns of a dilemma it is constitutionally incapable of solving. It needs peace, but peace delegitimates the regime. Eventually, inevitably, the perversion that equates revolution with a permanent war against enemies foreign and domestic will end. It is an open question whether the forthcoming modern revolution will culminate in a rejoining of a secure and dignified Chinese nation within the world community and world market or in the splitting of the nation into nations. In either case, the evidence suggests that Mao's revolutionary project will have failed to create a modern Chinese nation.

Overthrowing a Reactionary Ruling Class

The third notion of revolution that Mao's China would embrace is the overthrow of reactionary classes by a more progressive class or classes. This is the classic Marxist legitimation. In socialism, the proletariat replaces the bourgeoisie. Of course, Leninism distorts Marx in substituting a party (or its leaders or leader) for the progressive class, claiming that the class cannot represent itself. This party, which legitimates itself as embodying the interests of the most progressive and liberating future, has turned out to reflect a form of reactionary chiliasm. That is, it infuses a nineteenth-century moment with ancient utopian content.

Furet asks of Marx: "Whence came his absurd conclusion in 1871 that the state was nearing its end?"[51] Marxism takes the moment of steel technologies and British free-trade imperialism as the culmination of precommunist progress. When the world market instead developed, expanded, and changed, Lenin in the early twentieth century then described a new final stage—finance monopoly capitalism—focusing on how Germany caught up to Britain through the state's coordination of banks and industry. It was another reactionary chiliasm. Lenin missed the creative and productive function of money and financial discipline. He missed the importance of skilled labor and scientific innovation and export performance in the rise of Germany. He missed the permanent revolution of science and technology, production, exchange, and finance. In power, Lenin took the moment of Fordist mass production as modern progress as such, and even expanded Fordist techniques of assembly-line production using unskilled labor. This entrenchment of a historical moment mistaken for a final solution added to gargantuan Fordism and Bismarckianism, the statist implementation of Marx's idea of a centralized administration of everything from big steel to farming made big. The result is a monstrosity, the rigid and outmoded Leninist systems that fall ever further behind new techniques to produce wealth that require flexible adaptation to new scientific revolutions. Leninist regimes entrench the historic moment of big steel, big state, and big mass production with unskilled labor.

While the Leninist command economy continues to serve the narrow purposes of war communism and the privileged Party and its nomenklatura in the secret police and other state apparatuses, there is no economic mechanism in the Leninist system for continuous innovation, productive efficiency, export competitiveness, consumer satisfaction, or financial lever utilization. The system entrenches an anachronistic moment of stratified privilege and outmoded production techniques, and hence falls ever farther behind advanced technology. Chinese democrats describe the regime as feudal; that is, not even as progressive as bourgeois democracy. "I see the forces of conservatism trying their utmost to drag our nation back," declared prisoner of conscience Liu Qing.[52]

Rather than finding the ruling group to be progressive or revolutionary, it is commonplace for Chinese to dismiss the discredited Leninist regime, experienced as holding China back and backward, as merely feudal. As early as 1986 thousands of students marched in Hefei shouting, "Down with feudal dictatorship!" "We want democracy!"[53] At the same time, at Beijing University, a wall poster declared, "This is our political system . . . [which is] identical to the most tyrannical feudal despotisms we've had."[54] As Liu Binyan saw it, "upper level political life in the Central Committee is very much like court politics in feudal China."[55] Leading intellectuals in Beijing on May 16, 1989, joined to call for an end to "feudal-style special privileges,"[56] adding the following day, "Seventy-six years have passed since the Qing dynasty fell. Yet China continues to have an emperor, though without that title—an elderly, doddery dictator."[57] Hunger strikers swore an oath that "under no condition should we . . . yield to autocracy and bow to the emperor of China in the 1980s."[58] In trying to woo and win soldiers to their side, democracy activists mocked the feudal nature of the regime: "Now, our Crown Prince Deng Pufeng . . . flies into the Northeast. . . . The Heilongjiang Province leadership, upon hearing of his lordship's arrival waste no time in taking him on a grand tour. . . . Prince Deng is delighted."[59] As Shen Tong explained it, the Democracy Movement's goal was "to break out of the dynastic cycle."[60] A Beijing University student described the regime's policies as "not unlike the doctrines of the Catholic Church in medieval Europe that the earth was the center of the universe."[61] A teacher at People's University noted that the system was based on "obedient subordinates," "loyalty and flattery," because "this power structure is essentially the same as that of feudal Chinese society."[62]

It was a commonplace to describe the regime, as did a youth from Liaoning: "In the past we overthrew the old emperor; today new emperors live within Zhongnanhai."[63] Student organizations that served the state were ridiculed as "the royal tool."[64] A declaration of a final hunger strike at the start of June 1989, perhaps penned by Liu Xiaobo, explained, "For thousands of years, Chinese society has experienced a malicious cycle of overthrowing old emperors and then putting up new emperors. . . . What we want is not a perfect God but a sound democratic system."[65] Consequently the isolated 1979 appeal of Wei Jingsheng to overthrow China's twentieth-century Bastille[66] was by 1989 a premise of popular consciousness as democracy activists moved to "seize state power by means of storming the Bastille."[67] Apparently aware of the French Revolution–like possibility, Deng Xiaoping dramatically warned his colleagues that if they lost, their heads would roll.

One could contend that the popular perception of the regime as feudal-like, however widespread, is erroneous. One could argue that the Leninist regime is progressive because the state nationalizes the economy and guarantees minimums to ordinary people, thereby providing a more humane life than would a system that relied on a private economy and the market. (Of course, the matter at issue is not state versus market, but what kind of state.) This is the long-discredited argument of feudalism against liberal democracies. Guaranteed minimums are valued above wealth-expanding forces. The feudal corvée permitted road building. Guilds guaranteed work. Church parishes guaranteed charitable minimums. But, for Marx, that which stifles the forces of production is reactionary.

The defense of Leninism as socialism is likewise similar to the defense made by nineteenth-century American slaveholders against the free labor of the industrializing north. Slavery provided guaranteed minimums and full employment. So do a host of late-twentieth-century oil-rich states in West Asia that are usually called feudal or military or repressive. There is nothing emancipatory in projects that deny humans space for individuals or groups of common identity or interest to act in their own behalf. Leninist defenses of socialism are based on a shriveled and backward notion of humanity that in no way embodies a progressive project. Leninism actually builds on historical continuity with the institutional forms of czarist Russia, once known as the most reactionary empire in Christendom. The nomenklatura, the state-swallowing society, the mistrust of the individual, the pervasive police, and the big state-run industries are all extensions of czarist Russian forms. There is meaning in the analogy of Leninist socialism with late feudal mercantilist absolutism.[68] It is difficult to avoid the conclusion of late-twentieth-century groups that overthrew Leninism, finding it a reactionary system, an obstacle to human progress.

To the extent that Maoism goes further than even traditional Stalinism in this feudal-like Leninist direction of defining groups by inherited statuses and privileging people by closeness to the sovereign, leaving little place for criteria of merit, competence, and technical proficiency, Mao's China is a major obstacle to an emancipatory project. From the perspective of class analysis, Mao Zedong then was not a revolutionary. He held back progress, entrenching a ruling group more backward then those found in liberal democracies. Liu Binyan suggests as a description of the ruling party terms like "a fascist organization" or "a mafia."[69] Given how often Leninist China makes sense when analogized with feudal systems, slave societies, and even the stagnant Asiatic mode of production, it is difficult to equate Leninist dynamics with emancipatory projects such as revolution.[70]

Defenders of Maoism as continuing the revolution after the revolution, as avoiding both the exploitation of capitalism and a bureaucratism into which Leninism could degenerate, still insist on the revolutionary essence of Maoism. But although the war communism inherent in the Leninist-Stalinist project does not lead to Weberian bureaucracy, it produces something far worse—inordinate arbitrary power over individuals and groups. This project would annihilate all identities or bodies that interpose themselves between the will of all-powerful rulers and totally vulnerable members of society. Hence the tyranny of Leninism is the basis for a subsequent backlash based on experientially primordial identities such as race, religion, or ethnicity.

A measure of the despotic, counter-revolutionary content of Leninism is its extreme patriarchy. Liu Binyan notes that, as reflected in its exploitation of gender power, Mao's Leninist state looks less like a progressive entity and more like "a social throwback" to "slave society." With people "dependent on government subsidies" as "a matter of life and death," "the Party secretary could pick and choose any girl from destitute families to sleep with him, in return for food subsidies, a practice not tolerated even under feudalism."[71]

What cries out for explanation is not just that Leninism is not revolutionary, but how an expansion of its war-communism notion of revolution pulls society in an ever more inhuman direction. What was purportedly more "left," turned out actually to be more "right." The confusion of the categories inherited from French Revolution Jacobinism is obvious in the oxymoron of students of China that "the leftists were the conservatives." The confusion is obvious in the contrast between Mao's concern that Khrushchev was taking the capitalist road and the fact that what Khrushchev was actually doing—and what led to Khrushchev's undoing—was undermining the corrupt privileges of the nomenklatura and taking the first small halting steps in a democratic direction. To Mao, anything that limited the power of purported representatives of the proletariat was attacked as taking the capitalist road. A society most exposed to the power of the proletarian dictatorship was, for Mao, the best.

To understand why Mao's revolutionary quest in fact kept China a brutal and backward tyranny, the concepts of left and right have to be re-examined. Mao explained leftism as moving faster toward communism than conditions permitted. Rightism was what held back movement toward communism. Therefore, whatever extirpated obstacles to communism—the market, religion, foreign influences, the household, money, material incentives, or individualism—was considered left. Society itself was the enemy target to be bombarded by Mao.

From a Marxist point of view, in which communism is meant to free individuals to be their truly human selves, a war on individualism and on multiple identities is not progressive. Mao's project of nativistic collectivism resembles fascism. Hence when Mao dismisses as rightist everything in harmony with democracy, universal human rights, autonomous spheres, and competence, Mao in fact embraces an organismic notion of politics that actually tends toward fascism.

Liu Binyan writes that he noticed in 1957 that Mao's idea of left and right reversed their meaning. During China's Hundred Flowers liberalization, Liu complained, "those who support progress and oppose bureaucratism and conservatism [i.e., the traditional Stalinist model] should be classified as 'leftist.' Why then are they labeled 'rightist' while those who oppose reform and want to continue with the old [Stalinist] ways are honored as 'leftist'? Why this strange inversion?"[72]

In the post-Mao era, Liu clarified the reason for "this strange inversion." A so-called leftist accepted the Leninist-Stalinist system that privileged the stratified ruling groups. A so-called "rightist," concerned with democracy and human rights, with protecting the autonomy of family and religion, and with developing an economy that delivered the goods that people wanted, threatened the centralized, monolithic tyranny. Hence "the leftists . . . were never treated by [the rulers] as enemies, and the battle [with leftists] was always treated as a family matter."[73]

But it is the inversion that requires explanation. Why, as Liu finds, had Leninists "in the name of revolution . . . brought about . . . colossal disaster?"[74] Why did the rulers achieve "the opposite of their slogans and promises?"[75] One answer was that "the ladder upward had been climbed with the help of toadyism accompanied by 'revolutionary' activities—that is to say, ultra left excesses."[76] Consequently, the struggle between right and left was actually a struggle "between those who were more humane and more devoted to public interests . . . and political opportunists seeking personal or group [i.e., state power network] interests on the other."[77] In short, the system rewarded and promoted people who attacked defenders of democracy, human rights, religion, the market, authentic culture, incentives, learning from the world community, etc. More communism, moving to the so-called left, was an invitation to more inhumanity and irrationality, to nativistic, autocratic know-nothingism. The invitation to move left toward communism guaranteed instead "fascist rule in the name of the 'dictatorship of the proletariat.'"[78]

This inversion, in which left ends up meaning fascist, reactionary, and nativistic, should be compared with the original notion of left and its historical development. Left is the term applied to those in the National Assembly during the French Revolution who voted both to execute the king and to prevent any check on the national legislature's supremacy. They mistrusted federalist solutions as diluting the concentrated power of a revolutionary center, as surrendering revolutionary power to local, feudal, and counter-revolutionary remnants.

This concentration of power is not yet Leninism. Legislators in the revolutionary republic are chosen in contested elections. Decisions are made with open, public debate and voting. Nonetheless, it is also clear how, once the Jacobins impose war communism, for example, a seizure of grain for distribution at a below-market price, thus treating those engaging in market sales of grain as traitors tied to foreign counter-revolutionaries, then the logic of Leninist war communism has been unleashed. Any obstacle to the imposition of the concentrated will of the state center mobilized for war is treated as subversive and, therefore, unacceptable.

Yet Leninism is more than a monolithism that concentrates force and rejects multiple representations of autonomous interests. It is also, as Jerry Hough has detailed, a kind of fundamentalism, in what he calls the Khomeini manner; that is, it experiences both international market forces and individual reason as the devil's work. Its major enemy is the liberal republic. Hence Leninism embodies a reactionary content that it places in the centralized forms of monolithism that emerge from the French Revolution. These are given the aura of war communism because it is believed that unless all particular interests sacrifice themselves to the omniscient and omnipotent center, then the alliance of foreign counter-revolutionaries and local traitors will destroy all that the revolution promises. However, the international market, foreign sources of knowledge, and local initiative and control are all required for development and democracy. Instead, the Jacobin project, the enemy of all these progressive forces, has been defined from the war-communism moment of France between 1792 and 1794 in a manner that will be cruelly repressive and nonprogressive. It will be nativistic and fundamentalist. The logic that Robespierre borrowed from Rousseau's idealization of Lycurgus's Sparta becomes in Lenin's politics a top-down, oppressive, all-encompassing, military superpatriotism. It is more Khomeini than Marx, since Marx, of course, never embraced Robespierre's terror. Marx never believed political force could substitute for genuine human development.

Building on Robespierre's attempt to solve problems, however, leads to a violent, permanent quest for enemies sabotaging supposed revolutionary progress. Conceiving things in the Jacobin way blocks realization by would-be revolutionaries that it is their war communism, a fundamentalist project, that is inherently antipeople, antidevelopment, antidemocracy, in sum, counter-revolutionary.[79] Left has been inverted. It actually is rightist, reactionary, and inhuman. Mao and his inversion of left and right, therefore, were not peculiar products of China. Rather they were the natural heirs of a particular world-historical tradition that privileged purity of concentrated will against society. Consequently, the Leninist system committed to Maoist fundamentalism entrenches a counter-revolutionary reality resplendent with huzzahs to a purportedly true revolution. Hal Draper, examining Karl Kautsky's notion that the history of (Leninist) socialism went back to Lycurgus, which was collectivism "as a permanent disciplined garrison in a state of seige," plus "the terroristic regime imposed over the helots (slaves)," found that what claimed to be socialism was, in fact, as also in Edward

Bellamy's utopia in *Looking Backwards* (1887), its opposite, a society organized or an "army . . . regimented, hierarchically ruled by an elite," in fact "a forerunner of fascism."[80] From its origins, the actual internal logic of the war-communism system was the inverse of its propagandistic categories of progress, democracy, and liberation. Agents of this tradition cannot bring a progressive project into practice. Mao's Leninist project negates the hope of the third meaning of revolution.

Revolution as Freedom

There is no need to expand upon the fourth notion of revolution, revolution as freedom, since Mao rejected it. Yet Hannah Arendt's analysis is relevant in the post-Mao era. In fact, social forces propel progressive democrats in precisely the manner explicated by Arendt. Freedom as revolution is not only analyzed in the theoretical writings of Hannah Arendt or in the tradition of Thomas Paine, but it is comprehended in real life among democratic opponents of Leninism, such as Poland's Solidarity theorist Adam Michnik. The Jacobin-Leninist tradition of "left" as liberating has been emptied of meaning.

> Revolutionary terror has always been justified by a vision of an ideal society. . . . Society [i.e., Solidarity] has never had a vision of ideal society. It wants to live and let live. . . . [T]he conflict between the right and the left belongs to the past. . . . "[W]e are neither from the left camp nor from the right camp, we are from the concentration camp."[81]

To read Arendt's description of the great Hungarian revolution of 1956 is also to be introduced to anti-Leninist revolutions a generation earlier.

> If there ever was such a thing as Rosa Luxemburg's "spontaneous revolution" —this sudden uprising of an oppressed people for the sake of freedom and hardly anything else, without the demoralizing chaos of military defeat preceding it, without coup d'etat techniques, without a closely knit apparatus of organizers and conspirators, without the undermining propaganda of a revolutionary party . . . we had the privilege to witness it.[82]

The world witnessed this spontaneous eruption against tyranny again at the end of the 1980s in Eastern and Central Europe, and also in China. Chinese democrats were so self-consciously committed to their political purpose that they debated rejecting the participation of workers with economistic demands lest the revolution be seen as narrowly self-interested.[83] As Arendt described it a generation earlier:

> [T]he people were aroused only by open words, . . . in breaking the deadly spell of impotent apathy. . . .
> [T]he rebellion . . . started with intellectuals and university students . . . [n]ot the underprivileged. . . . [T]heir motive was . . . exclusively Freedom and

Truth. . . . The voice . . . speaking so plainly and simply of freedom and truth sounded like an ultimate affirmation that human nature is unchangeable. . . . [A] yearning for freedom and truth will rise out of man's heart and mind forever.

Total domination succeeds to the extent that it succeeds in interrupting all channels of communication . . . [as] long as terror is not supplemented by the ideological compulsion from within. . . .

[O]ppression . . . is felt for what it is and freedom is demanded.

The . . . people . . . knew that they were "living amidst lies" . . .

[F]reedom resides in the human capacities of action and thought, and not in labor and earning a living.[84]

In like manner, members of China's Democracy Movement put forth virtually no selfish economic claims, instead acting out of a willingness to sacrifice even their lives to win equal (not privileged) citizenship for all in an open public realm of knowledge. Freedom required truth, political space, and equality. The democrats in embracing basic values such as truth share their knowledge that the Leninist system is premised on inhuman lies. For Arendt, the Marxist project is inherently incapable of emancipating society. Its premises are misguided.[85] Hence it is easy to see that Marxism in Leninist guise leads to a less than modern or liberating project and can survive only by censorship, charisma, chiliasm, and chauvinism. If the 1989 events in China signify that these illusions are disappearing,[86] that the regime is revealed as a parasitic and reactionary tyranny imposing a life of palpable hypocrisy on the Chinese people, then China is ripe for revolution, modern revolution. Mao's quest, building on Jacobin war communism and systems similar to those of czarist Russia that Lenin expanded into an anachronistic, absolutist, feudal-like system of state power, was not that of a modern revolutionary. A capable state, a united nation, an emancipatory project of democratic freedoms, the real work of modern revolution, this is China's better future. The analyses and slogans of China's spring 1989 Democracy Movement are the discourse of freedom as previously illuminated by Arendt.

[We] see a country rotting in decline, in which the people are not masters of their own lives, in which the press has no freedom. . . . [W]e have waited patiently. . . . Should we have to wait interminably and futilely? . . .

The greatest hope for progress in China is an awakened citizenry that strongly demands political participation. Whoever claims to represent the people's interest must . . . enter into a dialogue with the people.[87]

Academic credits are truly valuable, a degree worth even more; but without democracy we don't want either.[88]

Their democratic goal was "transparency," ending a government that was private and secret by making it open and public. They demanded press freedom and public disclosure of the incomes of officials.

"We want opposition parties to criticize the government, and newspapers to criticize the government—just like they have now in Hungary."

"Down with Dictatorship." "Long Live Freedom."

"The main problem China has today is the lack of democracy."

"The ten meter long banner of white cloth ... [in whose] center was a single black square. 'It means we have a mouth ... but we have no voice.' "

"People's Daily, People's Daily/ ... Alway printing lies, always printing lies."

"Xinhua tells lies. It should get rid of the habit." "The news media should tell the truth."

"Long live journalists with a conscience."

"We would like to have more *glasnost* so that more dirty linen could be thrashed out."

"*Beijing Daily* tells lies."

"I love life, I need food, but I'd rather die without democracy."[89]

This was not Mao Zedong's project. When Mao took power, China had a fresh start. But it was wasted. Decline swiftly set in. The system degenerated, became pervasively corrupt, and deligitimated itself. Increasingly, people in China express a need for another fresh start, but not another traditional revolutionary cycle; perhaps, not even much violence. China has yet to have a revolution to win a real breakthrough, a truly modern revolution. Mao Zedong was a revolutionary, but of the traditional sort.

Notes

1. *Mao Zedong sixiang wansui* (Beijing, 1967), p. 309.
2. Edward Friedman, Pickowicz, Paul; and Selden, Mark, *Chinese Village, Socialist State* (New Haven: Yale University Press, 1991).
3. Cited by A. Brumberg, "Moscow: The Struggle for Reform," *The New York Review of Books*, March 30, 1989, p. 39.
4. For an analysis of war communism, see Wladzimerz Brus, "Utopianism and Realism in the Evolution of the Soviet System," *Soviet Studies* 40.3 (July 1988), pp. 434–43, and the sources Brus cites.
5. This is explicated in *People's Daily*, January 2, 1987, p. 5.
6. Translated in JPRS-CEA–87–018, March 13, 1987, p. 2.
7. Dusko Doder and Louise Bramson, *Gorbachev* (New York: Viking, 1990), p. 34.
8. Nikolai Shmeler and Poper, Valdimir, *Revitalizing the Soviet Economy* (New York: Doubleday, 1990), p. 5.
9. For an analysis of Pol Pot taking Maoism further, see Edward Friedman, "After Mao," *Telos*, Fall 1985, pp. 23–46.

10. One of the signs that it is Maoism is its self-understanding that it builds so as to be able to survive a worldwide nuclear war.

11. The legitimation of revolutionary terror, going back to the Jacobins, is that the revolutionaries are cruel so that others may live kindly, that the blood they shed removes the sources of yet greater bloodshed. What we learn actually is that all lives are valuable, each person deserves due process, and when human rights are abused and the abuses excused, then the society's future is yet more terror and bloodshed.

12. Boris Kagarlitsky, *The Thinking Reed* (London: Verso, 1988).

13. Brumberg, "Moscow," p. 37.

14. Arendt, *On Revolution* (New York: Viking, 1963).

15. *Far Eastern Affairs* (Moscow), No. 1 (1990), p. 73.

16. Moore, *Social Origins of Dictatorship and Democracy* (Boston: Beacon, 1966).

17. Adam Michnik, *Letters from Prison* (Berkeley: University of California Press, 1985).

18. Karl Griewank, "Emergence of the Concept of Revolution," in *Revolution: A Reader*, ed. Bruce Mazlish et al., (New York: Macmillan, 1971), pp. 13–18.

19. Herbert Marcuse, *Reason and Revolution* (New York: Oxford, 1941).

20. Alexis de Tocqueville, *The Old Regime and the French Revolution* (New York: Doubleday, 1955).

21. Skocpol, *States and Social Revolutions* (New York: Cambridge University Press, 1979).

22. Anderson, *Lineages of the Absolute State* (London: New Left Books, 1974).

23. Edward Friedman, "Permanent Technological Revolution and China's Tortuous Path to Democratizing Leninism," in *Reform and Reaction in Post-Mao China*, ed. Richard Baum (New York: Routledge, 1991).

24. Skocpol argues that the particular state created by Mao was uniquely participatarian and egalitarian. Going to publication just before post-Mao revelations made obvious the catastrophe Mao imposed on China's rural poor, indeed, on all China's people, Skocpol gives credence to the entire panoply of Cultural Revolution propaganda as if the lies were facts. Some would discredit Skocpol's work for this error. This chapter, however, will bracket this major factual mistake on her part. It leads to silence on the secret police and the state-terror apparatus (she is silent on the Emergency Salvation Campaign of 1943, the slaughter in the 1946–48 land reform, the slave labor system, the antirightist campaign, etc.) and to silence on how the rural poor were locked into their poverty (she chooses not to discuss the Great Leap famine and offers not a word on the impact of antimarket policies, of monopoly purchase of grain at state-imposed low prices, of campaigns to cut capitalist tails or to stress grain production to the detriment of economic crops, etc.)

25. Skocpol, *States and Social Revolutions*, p. 287.

26. Ibid., pp. 286, 263, 264.

27. Consider, for example, the works of Kenneth Jowitt and Andrew Walder.

28. Michael Voslensky, *Nomenklatura* (Garden City, NY: Doubleday, 1984). In an August 18, 1980 speech, Deng Xiaoping described how "when someone got to the top even his dogs and chickens got there too; likewise, when someone got into trouble, even his distant relations were dragged down with him" (*China Daily*, July 1, 1987, p. 4).

29. Liu, *A Higher Kind of Loyalty* (New York: Random House, 1990).

30. Skocpol, *States and Social Revolutions*, p. 292.

31. Hoffman, "A Note on the French Revolution and the Language of Violence," *Daedalus* 116.2 (Spring 1987), pp. 149–56. Also see Murray Forsyth, *Reason and Revolution: The Political Thought of the Abbe Sieyes* (New York: Holmes and Meier, 1987), esp. ch. 3, "The Revolutionary Principle: The Nation Repossess Itself."

32. Furet, *Interpreting the French Revolution* (New York: Cambridge University Press, 1981).

33. Ibid., p. 3.

34. Ibid., pp. 4, 7, 10, 15.

35. Wang Zhen, quoted in Orville Schell, *Discos and Democracy* (New York: Doubleday, 1988), p. 235.

36. Paine, *The Rights of Man.*

37. François Furet and Ozouf, Mona, eds., *A Critical Dictionary of the French Revolution* (Cambridge, MA: Belknap Press, 1989), p. 690.

38. Furet, *Interpreting*, pp. 24, 31.

39. Ibid., p. 25.

40. Ibid., p. 27.

41. The blood theory of class was eloquently analyzed in the Cultural Revolution by the martyred Yu Luoke.

42. Han Minzhu [pseud.], *Cries for Democracy* (Princeton: Princeton University Press, 1990), p. 170.

43. Ibid., pp. 333–34. However accurate this analysis of Chinese politics being the source of Chinese backwardness is, it permits the regime to appeal to chauvinistic emotions, accusing the reformers of whitewashing imperialists when they declare, "in the 1860s and 1870s, Japan's Ito Hirobumi and China's Yan Fu studied in Britain and returned home with aspirations to save their countries through modernization. . . . Ito became prime minister in charge of the Meiji reformation, while . . . Yan Fu witnessed . . . the failure of the 1898 Reform Movement. Making use of existing opportunities, Japan rose . . . and China, losing the opportunity, landed itself in greater catastrophe" (Luo Rongxing and Cao Huanrong, "The Historical Position of China's Reform," *People's Daily*, October 7, 1987, p. 6 translated in JPRS-CAR–87–056, November 9, 1987, p. 11). There may be great staying power to antireform chauvinism when combined with censorship, repression, guaranteed minimums, and privileged organs of coercion, especially if the capitalist world market collapses or new technologies are more in harmony with Fordism rather than horizontal and immediate ties among skilled, highly educated workers.

44. Scott Simmie and Bob Nixon, *Tienanmen Square* (Vancouver, BC: Douglas and McIntyre, 1989), pp. 2, 8, 41, 71, 74, 83, 114, 131, 132, 143, 150, 155, 165, 166, 168, 169.

45. Wang, "Outside the Chinese Revolution," *The Australian Journal of Chinese Affairs*, No. 23 (January 1990), p. 35.

46. Furet, *Interpreting*, p. 58.

47. Ibid., p. 99.

48. Ibid., p. 104.

49. Ibid., p. 110.

50. Ibid., p. 127.

51. Furet and Ozouf, *Dictionary*, p. 979.

52. In *Seeds of Fire: Chinese Voices of Conscience*, ed. Geremie Barmé and Minford, John (New York: Hill and Wang, 1988), p. 303.

53. Donald Morrison, ed., *Massacre in Beijing: China's Struggle for Democracy* (New York: Time Inc. Books, 1989), p. 125.

54. Schell, *Discos and Democracy*, p. 237.

55. Liu Binyan, with Ruan Ming and Xu Gang, *"Tell the World"* (New York: Pantheon, 1989), p. 96.

56. Yi Mu and Mark [pseud.] Thompson, eds., *Crisis at Tienanmen: Reform and Reality in Modern China* (San Francisco: China Books, 1989), p. 165.

57. Ibid., p. 167.

58. Ibid., p. 222.

59. Han, *Cries for Democracy*, p. 28. For a brilliant satire of the politics of Leninist systems written as an Aesopian parable of the feudal-emperor system of Haile Salassie, see Ryszard Kapucinski, *The Emperor* (New York: Vintage, 1984).

60. Han, *Cries for Democracy*, p. 379.

61. Ibid., p. 163. To make this point, in 1979 Brecht's play *Galileo* was performed.

62. Ibid., p. 153.

63. Ibid., p. 139,

64. Ibid., p. 74.

65. Simmie and Nixon, *Tienanmen Square*, p. 167.

66. Barmé and Minford, *Seeds of Fire*, pp. 279–89.

67. Yi and Thompson, *Crisis at Tienanmen*, p. 223.

68. Hernando DeSoto, *The Other Path: The Invisible Revolution in the Third World* (New York: Harper and Row, 1989).

69. Liu, *A Higher Kind of Loyalty*, p. 269. That the unaccountable, delegitimated party turns into a "mafia-type local party" is also reported for the Soviet Union. (Doder and Bramson, *Gorbachev*, p. 126).

70. G. Batishcher found that " 'barracks-Communism' is even worse than capitalism, since it expressed the attitude of those individuals and classes who, in Marx's words, have 'not only failed to go beyond private property, but [have] not yet even reached it.' . . . 'barracks-Communism' is 'reactionary, being oriented on patently pre-bourgeois forms, and re-establishing the Asiatic Mode of Production.' " Similarly, Tsipko concludes, "utopian collectivism becomes in practice . . . worse in many ways than slavery" (Kagarlitsky, *The Thinking Reed*, pp. 275, 287).

71. Liu, *A Higher Kind of Loyalty*, p. 138. The notion of revolution as class liberation slights and suppresses peasantry, race, ethnicity, and gender. Should the notion of revolution not include the concern of both the Shah of Iran (not the Ayatollah Khomeini) and the Leninist regime in Afghanistan (not the mujahadin) for gender equality? What is revolutionary about subordinating half of humanity? (See Valentine Moghadam, "Revolution Engendered," paper presented to the Twelfth World Congress of Sociology, July 1990, Madrid, Spain).

72. Liu, *A Higher Kind of Loyalty*, p. 80.

73. Ibid., p. 154. Also see, pp. 269, 153.

74. Ibid., p. 131.

75. Ibid., p. 137.

76. Ibid., pp. 132, 152.

77. Ibid., p. 187.

78. Ibid., p. 145.

79. Gorbachev was the first ruler of the Soviet Union who "rejected . . . anti-intellectualism, anticlericalism, and the fear of the West that had characterized the Bolshevik era. He sought to rescue communist doctrine from fundamentalism and revive its relevance to the modern world" (Doder and Bramson, *Gorbachev*, p. 72).

80. Hal Draper, "The Two Souls of Socialism," 1965, reprinted in *New Politics* 3.1 (Summer 1990), pp. 131, 145. Sparta was not a model for supporters of the French Revolution who embraced liberty, the arts, and peace. Mary Wollstonecraft found that "Rousseau celebrates barbarism. . . . [H]e exalts . . . the brutal Spartans who . . . sacrificed . . . the slaves who had shown themselves heroes. . . . [Why] banish the arts of peace, and almost carry us back to Spartan discipline?" (*A Vindication of the Rights of Women* [New York: Norton, 1967], pp. 43, 57).

81. Michnik, *Letters from Prison*, pp. 88, 91.

82. Hannah Arendt, *The Origins of Totalitarianism*, epilogue.

83. This discourse of democracy is often misunderstood as an elitist and condescending attitude toward workers. Adam Michnik finds that because Leninism fosters a demoralized and privatized people, opposition politics must take an antipolitical form. In China, the sacrifice unto death of the hunger strike was that pure apolitical act that galvanized the citizenry out of their demoralized and privatized routines. Chai Lin saw China's democracy struggle as "a war between love and hatred" (Simmie and Nixon, *Tienanmen Square*, p. 176).

84. Simmie and Nixon, *Tienanmen Square*. This is not to deny that there were a large number of economic and social discontents. Nonetheless, they took a pure political form, a demand for true and honest democracy.

85. A graduate student in the Law Department of Beijing University put it this way in May 1989: "In 1825, European capitalism came down with malaria which, from then on, came every eight or ten years. A Jewish doctor hastened to take the patient's pulse, and jumped to the conclusion that the disease was incurable. In the prescription he made in 1848 [in the *Communist Manifesto*], he claimed that capitalism was surely doomed, and just as surely, the final victor would be socialism . . . . More than a century has passed . . . all the patients for whom this doctor had pronounced the death sentence have turned out to be the embodiment of vigor and the spirit of life. Meanwhile, the primitives who had taken hold of the doctor's magic elixir and gulped it down . . . are feeling listless and sick to the marrow of their bones . . . ." (Han, *Cries for Democracy*, p. 167). Before the crackdown on democratic reformers, even *People's Daily* (September 19, 1986), p. 5, quoted Engels stating in 1884 about "The Outline of the Critique of Political Economy" that "It has now become completely outmoded . . . !"; about "The Condition of the English Working Class," as seen in 1886, "The conditions described . . . have become things of the past"; and of 1848, when it seemed that the proletariat would defeat the bourgeoisie, "our views . . . were nothing but an illusion" (translated in JPRS-CPS–86–085, December 12, 1986, pp. 10–13).

86. The major continuing illusion is that Chinese culture blocks a democratizing project. Taiwan's politics give the lie to that understanding. Still, to the extent that the Leninist system creates dependent people who feel a lack of self-confidence and find no independent civil institutions such as churches to build on, it is possible to conceive of a democratizing Chinese mainland, as with East Germany, welcoming in at some point the political parties of a democratic Taiwan.

87. Han, *Cries For Democracy*, pp. 86–87. Democratizers such as Yu Haocheng had even learned to cite the democrat Marx. "Marx said, 'Without press freedom, all other freedoms become illusions' " (*Xin Guancha*, August 25, 1986, translated in JPRS-CRS–86–081, November 6, 1986, p. 45).

88. Han, *Cries for Democracy*, p. 67.

89. Simmie and Nixon, *Tienanmen Square*, pp. 22, 26, 29, 32, 66, 71, 72, 74, 75, 78, 86, 88, 89, 95–96, 145, 163.

Part Four

Democratic Prospects

Chapter 12

Is Democracy a Universal Ethical Standard?

The presupposition of this chapter is that an international movement to promote human rights is a proven and pragmatic instrument that can advance the cause of democratization. The Germans proved this in the 1970s in Spain. The United States did likewise in the 1970s in Argentina. Throughout the former Soviet Union and in the Leninist states of Eastern Europe, the human rights movement that was legitimated by the Helsinki Accords succeeded in the 1980s. Democracy has shown itself to be a pan-human potential that can be promoted through international efforts. Such efforts are realism personified, the advancement of an ethical good with no risk of war.

Japan has not been a leading actor in this international effort. This chapter explores some of the reasons why the West has been so little perturbed at Japan's inaction, some reasons why there has been so little pressure in Japan for an active human rights policy, and some reasons why Japan could yet become a leader in the international efforts on behalf of human rights. At issue is whether Japan can and should do more to promote democratization in places such as Myanmar (Burma), China, and North Korea.

Why do so many people accept the notion that the concept of human rights is misleadingly universalized and attribute it instead to the peculiar and culturally specific Western European tradition of sacred individual souls and missionary religions, such that Asia in general and Japan (or so-called Confucian societies) in particular are assumed to find the concept of universal human rights to be absolutely alien? In the West, this Europe–Asia binary opposition pervades thinking, from abstract philosophy to the popular media. The idea of a culturally unique and democratic West, however, is a dangerous, antidemocratic construct.

Originally published in *Moral Education III* (1993), pp. 49–62. Reprinted by permission of the Carnegie Council on Ethics and International Affairs.

At the end of the twentieth century, unconsciously reflecting this historically structured antidemocratic discourse, the German human rights advocate–philosopher Jurgen Habermas concluded that after the defeat of Nazism, the new Federal Republic of Germany "was founded in the spirit of the occidental understanding of freedom, responsibility and self-determination."[1] Ernst Nolte, Habermas's adversary in the German debate over the origins of the inhumanities of the Hitler era, also assumed the cultural superiority of the Occident, and argued within the same anti-Asian polarizing binary logic that stigmatizes Asia as barbaric. He held that "the Nazis . . . carried out an 'Asiatic' deed only because they regarded themselves . . . as potential . . . victims of an 'Asiatic' deed."[2] That is, fear of the imposition of Leninism-Stalinism's barbaric terror and police-state "gulag" practices led Germans to use Asian fire to fight Asian fire. Europe is conceived as pure and good.

These oppositional categories of good, democratic Europe and evil, tyrannical Asia pervaded the analysis of the Bolshevik Revolution even at its origin. Emma Goldman, a great anarchist human rights activist, whose work on behalf of political prisoners of conscience subsequently helped create Amnesty International and led to the international human rights movement, immediately found Lenin "a shrewd Asiatic" who brought forth "Asiatic barbarism." The English anarchist journal, *Freedom*, in January 1922 summarized the repression, terror, and cruelties in the new Leninist dictatorship as "the most revolting Asiatic form of a war of extermination," a horror in which "the spirit of the Asiatic regime was revived."[3]

The conservative Russian Slavophiles in the former czarist empire who threw in with the Bolsheviks did so understanding the revolution as the victory of true Russia, that of its Asian traditions against Western liberal individualism.[4] And when the Bolsheviks fell, Lenin was depicted by democratic victors as not Russian but Mongol. Paintings made his facial features seem East Asian. The European-Asian binary appears deeply rooted in the European subconscious, a notion whose sources go back millennia to a multicentury Christian European nightmare experience of holding off Muslims, Mongols, and Ottoman invaders who would otherwise destroy Europe's civilization.

In the European philosophy of Hegel, despotism is represented by the Asian regime, with history as the march of freedom into the West, abandoning the supposedly vegetative despotism of the East. Montesquieu had explained that this Asian despotism was natural and peculiar, a consequence of contrasting European and Asian climate and geography. Marx continued this stigmatizing of the East with his notion of Asiatic despotism based on a uniquely Asiatic mode of production that lacked any civilizing, progressive dynamic. Such presuppositional binaries that have for so many centuries been assumed to be obviously true pervade and infuse Western thinking from left to right. The binary is assumed even among the most anti-Marxist Western analysts. Carl Friedrich and Zbigniew Brzezinski found that "the inroads of totalitarianism into the Orient, where despotic forms of government have been the rule for thousands of years . . . , preempt any too optimistic estimate of the totalitarians' lack of capacity for survival."[5]

And John King Fairbank, America's preeminent organizer of China studies in the post–World War II generation, argued, without challenge, that a great civilization could arise in north China, but not in the heavily populated, rice-growing south, because the north was similar to Western Europe. The presuppositional binary logic pitting a universal West against a peripheralized East denied the East any progressive, liberating human potency.

Thinkers who suffered under Soviet tyranny in Europe, such as Milan Kundera, described that despotism as a war of "Russian civilization" on "Western culture."[6] Czech president Vaclav Havel is typical of spokesmen for democracy in the former Soviet empire in seeing democratization as a rejoining of Europe, an abandonment of Asia. This popular view is reinforced at the academic level. There is a long and continuing tradition, represented in American political science by the influential work of Harvard University professor Samuel Huntington, that finds democracy to be the outcome of a uniquely West European cultural process.[7] Even in the 1990s, Huntington explains democratization in the Philippines and Korea in terms of a Western Christian influence and despotism in China in terms of Confucian continuities.[8] As the brilliant European scholar George Lichtheim put it:

> The fundamental fact about the American Revolution surely is that it occurred in a Protestant country with an Anglo-Saxon tradition. . . . No Protestant population could ever have been beaten down to the French (or Spanish or Latin American) level. Even the serfs of Prussia were not reduced to quite the existence of the peasant helotry of neighboring Catholic Poland. . . . In present-day [1964] Europe, the two largest Communist parties are those of France and Italy. . . . Hitlerism arose in Catholic Austria and Bavaria, not in Lutheran Prussia. . . . The modern age . . . begins with the Reformation. . . . [T]he Dutch Rebellion and the English Civil War set the stage for the American Revolution. . . . Holland . . . is the cradle of the modern world.[9]

This privileging of religious political culture in Reformation Europe as the key to democracy, in addition to ignoring contributions to European success from openness to the rest of the world, skips over the large flaws in the argument.[10] It would be easier to argue that because the Protestant definition of democracy in early modern England precluded including Irish Catholics, Jews, and non-Europeans from the West Indies and the Indian subcontinent, the democratization of the United Kingdom of Great Britain was delayed or damaged (and may yet explode). A subsequent grant of civil rights to Catholics and, yet later, Britain's international leadership of efforts to end the trade in enslaved Africans, permitted a retrospective reconsidering of English Protestant history that omitted the genocidal war against Catholic Ireland and the English wealth drawn from West Indian slave plantations, not acts of Protestant universal humanism. American president-elect Abraham Lincoln was painfully aware of the hypocrisy and fraud inherent in the self-serving English notion of Anglo-Saxon Protestants as uniquely and essentially tolerant, humane, and democratic. He ridiculed it, knowing of the racist parochialism of all too many American Protestants.

> As a nation, we began by declaring that "all men are created equal." We now practically read it "all men are created equal, except negroes." When the Know-Nothings get control, it will read "all men are created equally except negroes, and foreigners, and Catholics." When it comes to this I should prefer emigrating to some country where they made no pretense of loving liberty—to Russia, for instance, where despotism can be taken . . . without the base alloy of hypocrisy.[11]

What cries out for explanation and explosion is the continuation of the anti-democratic myth that finds in English Protestant culture alone the social and value prerequisites of democracy.[12] Entering the 1990s, with Muslim Albania democratic, with Buddhist Mongolia democratic, with Buddhist Tibetans hoping for democracy, with Buddhist Thailand a fledgling democracy, with Hindu/Muslim India's post–World War II democracy having survived vicissitudes that most analysts assumed would readily swamp a supposedly weak democratic culture, with Confucian Taiwan and Confucian South Korea making great democratic strides, with numerous South Pacific animistic island republics and Africa's Botswana stable democracies since independence, and with Buddhist-Confucian-Shinto Japan democratic, surely no sensible person would any longer give voice to the Eurocentric presupposition of a uniquely humane and democratic Europe versus a uniquely despotic and inhuman Asia.

Yet the wisest of American analysts of democracy still treat the stigmatizing binary of democratic Europe and despotic Asia as if it embodied profound historical wisdom. The political culture of democracy is still presented as peculiarly Protestant or Christian in the works of senior American political scientists. Seymour Martin Lipset still insisted in 1990 "that the correlation of democracy with Protestantism and a post-British connection point up the importance of cultural factors." The history of the West is presented as an emergence from an Athenian democratic essence that respects freedom and individual worth. The West is imagined as democratic in a deep structural sense.[13]

Actually the modern nation-state is a rather recent invention. And the Athenian myth of deep structural origins of European democracy is an even more recent creation. Athens did not stimulate emulation in the early republics of Holland, England, or France. Even at the end of the eighteenth century, Enlightenment thinkers tended to see ancient Athens as a negative example, a place supposedly made unstable, chaotic, and vulnerable by the entrance of the mob into politics. It was militaristic, protofascist, militarily strong Sparta that was touted as the Greek model for a Western Europe having to unite in ascetic strength to make sure that it was no longer vulnerable to alien invaders.

One reason the West invented Athenian origins was because it was difficult to legitimate democracy as superior merely because the moderns were supposedly superior to the ancients in Europe. Even the grand rise of early modern Europe did not produce easy victory for the moderns who tried to discredit defenders of ancient European greatness. As in the rest of the world, Europeans, too, cherished their ancient heritage. The narrative of an ancient democratic heritage passed on to modern Europeans was more appealing than the notion that democracy was the result of a modern rupture.

Of course, it is not unusual for a people to imagine their history to congratulate their supposed cultural essence for their present-day success. It is a way of saying "we earned it." It is a pervasive tendency. Americans credited American success to Yankee ingenuity; British credited British success to socialization on the playing fields of Eton. Japanese, too, engage in this self-serving culturalism when they explain how Japanese history or Japanese culture or Japanese values naturally make Japan economically successful. Many Japanese who will not welcome democracy as the product of an American-made constitution, a rupture after defeat in World War II, will be satisfied to believe that the constitution was a Japanese product put over on the Americans, or that individual freedom already flourished in the Taisho era. However and wherever democratizing communities struggle and progress, the democratic is indigenized.

If a past is conceived of as singularly anti-individual and antidemocratic, ignoring the rich diversity of possibilities that are manifest in all cultures, then self-congratulatory essentialism can take on a malign character, since the idea of good versus evil then becomes readily attractive to chauvinistic nativists who, since the late nineteenth century, appeal to a racist social Darwinism as science. The Italian Nazi group of the 1990s, with swastikas shaved on their heads and anti-alien violence in their agenda, calling themselves The Western Political Movement, is a reminder of the latent horrors in these polarizing binaries that can make all others subhuman, a problem violently apparent in so much of the post–Cold War European world, and in Japanese culture, too.

In post-Leninist Russia, the protofascist right imagines a multicentury war between the holy people and soil of Russia against the satanic forces of the West, the Enlightenment, individual values, and material progress.[14] The Communist despotism is experienced as the poisoned fruit of a misconceived liberal project (the too-weak February 1917 democracy).[15] Consequently, in an era of turmoil and decline, there is ever more support for a true, pure, moral Russian autocracy. The war-prone forces in such antidemocratic particularism are well known. Any Japanese, therefore, should be able to see that a peaceful global project is made easier within the political discourse of democratic universalism. That is, Japan, even from a narrow perspective of self-interest, has a major stake in a peaceful democratic Asia.

There are those who insist, however, that Japan is incapable of treating Asians as potentially democratic. In this perspective, Japanese are the most parochial and chauvinistic people. Japanese are said to believe that while they can understand all others, no other can understand Japanese. And Japanese are so contemptuously condescending toward others in this understanding that when a Japanese speaks of Asia, taken as an object of analysis, he tends to exclude from Asia the subject of Japan, taken as an observer and mover. In this understanding, Japanese, more than all others, are incapable of democratic universalism.[16] But if people, whether generally Western, or particularly Protestant or British, could only see themselves as others see them, it would be obvious, as revealed in self-serving oppositional binaries, that parochial chauvinism, sadly, is quite widespread, maybe even shared among all the peoples of the world. As Japanese readily see through Western self-congratulations, and as Westerners see through similar Japanese foibles, the real point is that all peoples both suffer from these parochial disabilities and enjoy democratic possibilities.

The political question is, what happens when chauvinism conflicts with self-interest; that is, what if Japan would do better in the world if it could imagine itself as part of an Asian democratic project? It is not obviously in the interests of the Japanese people to embrace the particularistic pole in the binary opposition. In fact, one might well expect in this debate that Japanese interested in preserving a world of peaceful progress through interdependence would be on the other side, the side of democratic human potential. After all, they suffered the consequences of their own autocratic, purist particularism. And Shinto-Buddhist-Confucian Japan is now a democracy. Nonetheless, Japanese are still compelled to be treated elsewhere in Asia as a nation where Shinto, emperor-worshiping militarism could yet again emerge. It is in Japan's interest to put that ghost to rest. Therefore it seems odd that even cosmopolitan, wise Japanese tend to add their voices to a dangerous chorus whose words tell of an almost infinite number of European peculiarities and preconditions that somehow make East Asians unsuited for democracy, ignoring the fact that all political democracies, including those in the West, are compelled to grapple with their own authoritarian political culture.

The contrasting responses to the brutal crushing of China's 1989 democratic movement—with Japan seeking to maintain normal relations with China's rulers and with America condemning the tragic end of China's Democracy Movement in the Beijing massacre—permitted Japanese to mock America's democratic crusade. While it would be most unfair to homogenize the diversity of Japanese reactions, the dominant tendency was a ridiculing of supposed American naivete. The "Japanese have a different concept of democracy." "The Japanese view American diplomats as overly moralistic, unnecessarily blunt and often suckers for any sob story on CNN." A Japanese analyst dismissed Western "exaggerated expectations about China's possibility of positive change consonant with Western values,"[17] finding of China rather that the sheer size of the country, poor traffic and communications networks, huge and ever increasing population, limited resources, stagnating standard of living and low literacy must inevitably limit the pace and scope of political democratization. Under these conditions, the leadership insists that precipitous political democratization can only lead to chaos. . . . What makes this case different and difficult is the differences about values which is most basic. (To be precise, the term "people," or "*renmin*" in Chinese, tends to have an aggregative connotation; in the West the term is almost synonymous with individual.)[18]

Actually, "people" is aggregative in English, too. Of course, Westerners who think their culture uniquely individualistic make similar outrageous claims as the Japanese one above. No culture has a monopoly on pompous, hypocritical claims that are on their face patently absurd or narrowly self-serving. One wise Western theorist of democracy exemplified this absurdity in claiming that "Democratic politics arise only in post-traditional societies" because of "the tremendous importance of individualism and the individual in democratic politics," with individualism realized by "get[ting] the state out of people's beds; . . . that one's private life . . . is one's own business," such that abortion is not an arena in which people "pass criminal judgment on what goes on in other people's sexual lives."[19] But despite this proud trumpeting about American individualism, everyone knows that by such a standard that equates tolerance for choice on abortion with individualism, in fact Americans are far less individualistic than Japanese or members of other Confucian societies. Facts, however, do not readily subvert proud cultural chauvinism. The myth of unique Western individualistic prerequisites of democracy neither describes actual Western history nor serves the purposes of democratization elsewhere, since it allows chauvinistic despots to present themselves as the preservers of the cherished culture against hated alien values.

Arguments for unique political cultural emergences ignore the reality that a potential for the entire spectrum of good and evil abides in all humanity. Once democratic republics had been built in the Atlantic basin from Britain to Buenos Aires, however, any people, no matter how hierarchical their culture, could learn from and institutionalize democratic structures and practices. A democratic culture could follow as democratic institutions, ideas, and interests reshaped some of the culture.[20]

Cultural uniqueness and cultural prerequisite claims, however, seem true because they appeal to unquestioned popular prejudices of the moment. They are circular arguments. When the moment of the prejudice has passed, as with the supposed late-nineteenth-century wisdom that the feudal Japanese were culturally incapable of savings, hard work, or business sense, then the truism is revealed as patent nonsense. Cultural narratives of particularistic, antidemocratic uniqueness are just such self-defeating truisms in China today or Japan yesterday. In fact, Japanese historians, in contrast to the prejudiced consensus, tend to find that imperial China had a less despotic notion of the emperor than did Japan and that China enjoyed far more societal openness. In short, Chinese culture could be said to be richer in prerequisites of democracy than is Japan's, a culture that turns out to be quite compatible with democratization.

Hence, one should dismiss out of hand the notion that American foreign policy is uniquely and unrealistically moralistic and missionary-driven in pursuing democracy, while Japanese foreign policy is pragmatic and businesslike. This contention, explaining away Japanese inattention to democracy and human rights as a cultural artifact—even when argued in its weakened form, claiming merely that a Japanese government dominated by a conservative ruling party tied to business interests is naturally realistic—is not an explanation to be taken seriously. In fact, Japan's G-7 industrialized democratic partners, who promoted Ostpolitik and the Helsinki Accords on human rights, were also conservative, business-oriented, and very realistic, yet also committed to democracy and human rights.

The difference in policy orientation on human rights and democracy between Germany and Japan does not emerge from contrasting inherited cultures. Why then does Germany's ruling conservative party have a strong commitment to democracy and human rights, while Japan's does not? A cultural answer might point to an alleged lack of guilt in Japanese culture, a built-in tendency to always blame the alien other, such that Japan, in contrast to Germany, has never come to grips with its own painful horrors of the World War II era, even, at times, acting as if Japan were the victim of a war that somehow almost began with the nuclear hell brought by the Americans to the people of Hiroshima, a view that pretends that bloody hands are clean and causes many uncompensated Asia victims of Japanese militarism almost to cheer for the devastation of Hiroshima.

But the source of the Germany–Japan difference lies in politics, not culture. The Cold War as played out in Europe and Asia was asymmetric. That is, democratic Germany allied against the Sino-Soviet bloc of Leninist tyrannies by joining with democratic equals—France, Great Britain, Italy et al. In contrast, democratic Japan allied against the Sino-Soviet bloc of Leninist tyrannies by joining with lesser military tyrants in Asia—Rhee in Korea, Jiang in Taiwan. In Japan, consequently, it was not obvious that it was freedom that opposed Leninist despotism. Many conservative Japanese, therefore, could even see America, which after 1945 was willing to ally with anti-Communist dictatorships, as having revealed it had erred in siding with China against Japan's anti-Communist dictatorship in World War II and then conclude that America's anti-Communist war in Vietnam would not have been necessary if America had backed anti-Communist Japan earlier. In democratic Germany after World War II, in contrast, it was obvious that the country had been split and the east temporarily lost to inhuman communism because of Germany's own historic crimes and errors. A profoundly asymmetrical experience of political friends and enemies made for different policy orientations on democracy and human rights in Germany and Japan. For Cold War Japan to have promoted human rights would have embarrassed Cold War despotic allies. Only in Asia, of all world regions, did a human rights regime not grow.

If the causes of Japan's lack of concern for democracy and human rights are merely historical, essentially political, then they can change. Indeed, a civil and human rights movement is beginning to grow in Japan. A full civil rights revolution in Japan—as occurred in America in the 1960s—might make it seem natural for Japanese to embrace democracy and human rights as a norm, as happened in America starting only in the mid-1970s, not before. Americans, contrary to the myth, did not always make democracy and human rights a top priority.

On the other hand, Japan's party politics could become more electorally competitive. One party or group could embarrass the other by accusing it of only supporting murderous despots in Beijing or elsewhere who eventually will lose popular support and proceed to produce turmoil and perhaps even a successor regime that is an anti-Japanese government. Or politicians could point out that the fragile Chinese tyranny, legitimated mainly by chauvinism, could seek survival through adventurism or great-power ambitions, dangerous war-prone tendencies that flow easily from militaristic tyrants. Clearly that is the policy direction of China's present nativist faction. Thus, if Japan cares about peace and stability in Asia, it might begin to question a policy of embracing chauvinistic, war-prone tyrants and look instead to democratic norms. But Japanese ask, how can Japanese promote human rights in China when Chinese see Japanese as lacking any human rights qualifications? That is, Japanese are seen as having blood on their hands as a result of a long aggression in China.

Surely backing a Chinese government with blood on its hands cannot be defended as a way of cleansing Japan in the eyes of the Chinese people. It is the oppressed Chinese people who remain victims of a lack of Chinese human rights practices by their despotic government.

I will sketch a possible answer to Japan's human rights dilemma, not as a policy suggestion but as a way of showing that Japan can easily act on human rights should it but make the commitment to do so. A Japanese human rights policy toward China could be preceded by a resolution of the compensation issue by direct payments to victims of worst-case atrocities (e.g., "comfort women," medical experiments, and the people of Nanjing); by imposing a general human rights policy that does not single out China; by fostering the creation of private, international human rights societies for all East, South, and Southeast Asia in countries that have high prestige and can take the lead on human rights (e.g., democratic India and prodemocracy groups in Korea, Taiwan, and Thailand); by informing public opinion and pressuring Asian governments from international society on human rights; and by reassuring the victimized people of China who seek maximum openness to and interaction with the world that the goal of Japan is not to end policies of expanding exchanges with China in culture, education, science, investment, and trade, but to actually further more open and authentic international exchange.

Indeed, it should be clear that human rights improvements by Beijing will win more such benefits for the Chinese people; that is, that benefits denied by conditioning aid to oppressors will be restored once the oppressors are gone. In this regard, then, Japan might first look to deal with Myanmar and North Korea as worst-case violators and as places where Japanese trade and investment are minimal, and to act on human rights in league with regional and international bodies so that the policies do not seem merely Japanese policies and international principles of human rights action are regionally legitimated.

In addition, these new international human rights initiatives will be best received if they are experienced as part of a larger set of enlightened, mutually beneficial international initiatives. These can deal with disease (e.g., AIDS) research and control, environment and ecology, drugs, and crime (including forced prostitution). That is, the new initiative could include cooperatively grappling with generally recognized Asian problems and moving aggressively on human rights violations at home in Japan, including quality-of-life issues and racial and gender equality, as well as civil and criminal rights. In short, the best way to promote human rights in China is not by having a policy that singles out human rights violations in China—which would indeed stir Chinese nationalist resentment—but by implementing a major, general policy attuned more toward human rights in general, at home and abroad. This is merely a hypothetical sketch. Any Japanese grappling with human rights in Asia will be far more sensitive, surefooted, and successful than the jejune project just outlined.

In fact, the February 1992 Draft Report of the ruling party's Special Study Group on Japan's Role in the International Community has already acknowledged the universality of freedom and democracy. With Japan seeking a world of peaceful progress in Pacific Asia and with democracy the only political process that guarantees peaceful succession, it is quite natural that a Japan seeking particular policies in harmony with its growing responsibilities and strength would, as in the Draft Report, cite Japan's constitution, which declares, "We desire to occupy a honored place in an international society striving for the preservation of peace, and the banishment of tyranny and slavery, oppression and intolerance for all times from the earth. . . . We believe that no nation is responsible to itself alone, but that laws of political morality are universal; and that obedience to such laws is incumbent upon all nations." Yet in Asia, where Japan could take real political initiatives on democracy and human rights vis-à-vis Myanmar, China, North Korea, etc., the Draft Report is silent, suggesting mainly economic aid.

In short, despite movement in the direction of democratic norms, all the practical problems of politics will remain in Japan, as elsewhere. The politics of human rights in a consumer-oriented democracy of proud patriots is no easy matter. It is not always easy for democratic Japanese to answer politely when cruel neighboring tyrants who care not a jot for the human rights of their own people insist that Japan pay for prior Japanese human rights violations of a previous generation and of a nondemocratic Japan that has long since been superseded. And yet the long-run interests of Japan in Pacific Asia will be advanced by establishing the legitimacy of an Asian human rights regime. Acting in terms of Japan's long-term interests requires a painful grappling with ongoing consequences of past evils, many of which do not seem fair to this generation of generous economic-aid-granting, democratic Japanese.

As all peoples, Japanese, when confronted by demands for reparations and contrition and then probably again for more economic aid, will experience them selves as innocent, even offended, surely mistreated, when paying billions today while getting neither the prestige nor the standing in international bodies that Japan's actual contribution merits. The American language of universality on human rights and democracy will seem hypocrisy to many in Japan, since Japanese will naturally focus on the hypocrisy in America's past record and in the Asian recipient's present posturing. In other words, if Japan is to take policy steps in a normative direction, it will have to be for powerful Japanese reasons, based on a Japanese political logic, one that advances Japanese interests.

My guess is that Japan will move in a policy direction of human rights and democratic internationalism, not because it sees that the argument about a peculiarly democratic Western culture is a myth, which it is; not because its allies urge such a course, which they do; but because it is both in Japan's narrow interest and also its enlightened long-term interest to become a partner in the international effort to advance human rights and democracy. A peaceful policy of principled international action of that sort does not directly confront the explosive topic in Japanese politics of troops overseas, yet it advances Japan's interest in a stable and peaceful Asian region. It establishes Japan as a moral leader, one that is deserving of international prestige. It makes more likely a happy East Asian future of peace, stability, and internationally interdependent economies. An unstable, Leninist despotic regime in China suffering a permanent succession crisis will not automatically evolve into democracy because it gets richer, any more than did Bismarck's Germany or Meiji Japan, the models that China's post-Mao tyrants emulate in the 1990s. Those model authoritarian regimes became militarily expansionist. Consequently, Japan's concern for peace and prosperity in Asia will be promoted by acting as a leading participant in human rights.

Therefore, despite all the Japanese realists who dismiss supposed naive American moralism and who claim that they know better how to deal with Asian tyrants, Japan, for its own reasons, will eventually make itself a leader of democracy and human rights in East Asia. To be a leader in today's world on the side of peace and progress compels promotion of democracy and human rights.

Notes

1. Habermas, *The New Conservatism* (Cambridge, MA: MIT Press, 1992), p. 240.
2. Ibid., p. 212.

3. Cited in Alice Wexler, *Emma Goldman in Exile: From the Russian Revolution to the Spanish Civil War* (Boston: Beacon Press, 1989), pp. 27, 62, 102.

4. Jane Burbank, *Intelligentsia and Revolution: Russian Views of Bolshevism, 1917–1922* (New York: Oxford University Press, 1986), ch. 5.

5. Carl Friedrich and Zbigniew Brzezinski, *Totalitarian Dictatorship and Autocracy* (1956; reprint ed., New York: Praeger, 1961), p. 29.

6. Cited in Thomas Pangle, *The Ennobling of Democracy* (Baltimore, MD: Johns Hopkins University Press, 1992), p. 14.

7. Samuel Huntington, *Political Order in Changing Societies* (New Haven: Yale University Press, 1968).

8. Samuel Huntington, *The Third Wave* (Norman: University of Oklahoma Press, 1991).

9. George Lichtheim, "Varieties of Revolutionary Experience," *Partisan Review*, Summer 1964, p. 434.

10. William H. McNeill, *The Pursuit of Power* (Chicago: University of Chicago Press, 1982).

11. Cited in David B. Davis, *Revolutions* (Cambridge, MA: Harvard University Press, 1990), p. 45.

12. Not only is the crucial role of the Dutch slighted in Anglocentric histories, but Catholic contributions, such as the establishment in St. Mary's, Maryland, of the first tolerant religious community, is ignored in histories focused singularly on Protestant contributions.

13. Seymour Martin Lipset, "The Centrality of Political Culture," *Journal of Democracy*, Fall 1990, p. 82. In contrast, African analyses of African cultural inheritance that facilitate democratization stress that two-thirds of the people in Athens were slaves, more than many African societies that are stigmatized as slave societies.

14. See Alexander Yanov, *The Russian New Right* (Berkeley: Institute of International Studies, 1978) and *The Russian Challenge and the Year 2000* (New York: Basil Blackwell, 1987).

15. See the works of Alexander Solzhenistyn, especially *The Mortal Danger* (New York: Harper and Row, 1980) and *From Under the Rubble* (Washington, DC: Regenry Gateway, 1974).

16. J. T. Wixted, "Reverse Orientalism," *Sino-Japanese Studies*, December 1989, pp. 17–27.

17. Thomas Friedman, "America's Japan Policy," *The New York Times Magazine*, June 30, 1992, p. 52.

18. Asai Motofumi, "Japan's China Policy—A Pattern of Consistency," in George Hicks, ed., *The Broken Mirror: China After Tiananmen* (Chicago: St. James Press, 1990), pp. 307, 306.

19. Eli Sagan, *The Honey and the Hemlock* (New York: Basic Books, 1991), pp. 81, 82.

20. Edward Friedman, ed., *The Politics of Democratization* (Boulder, CO: Westview Press, 1993).

Chapter 13

Consolidating Democratic Breakthroughs in Leninist States

When the Berlin Wall fell and democracy danced on the rubble of crumbling tyranny, ecstasy was tempered by the knowledge that a breakthrough in the confining bonds of despotism does not automatically guarantee a successful consolidation of democracy. When the walls of tyranny tumble, forces surface from beneath the smelly heap whose resultant foul winds are not friendly to freedom. Wise voices warn that a nasty fate may still await the celebrants who have triumphed over the inhuman Leninist party-state. They decry "a nationalism that readily slides into an exclusive, aggressive, xenophobic chauvinism . . . drawing on the most backward and reactionary interpretations of religion."[1] Emerging from the garbage of Leninism, a "social Pandora's box; . . . a Hobbesian *bellum omnium contra omnes* of ethnic, corporatist, nationalist, etc., interests"[2] can spread "some of the most sordid aspects of traditional culture,"[3] motivating "a populace so ignorant that the main alternative to communism itself seems to be . . . vicious bigotry."[4] These latent, divisive responses to the brutally divisive rule of Leninism include the delegitimation of the prior nationalism of Leninist anti-imperialism and, consequently, a need for a new national identity, even for the dominant ethnic group.[5] This nationalist need may complicate the building of a democracy, or it may make the democratization of a Leninist system more complex than the democratization of many other kinds of dictatorships.

The Difficult Political Geography of Democratization

How then should a polity craft a democracy so that it will become institutionalized such that the gains from consolidating political freedom out of Leninist

Reprinted from M. L. Nugent, ed., *From Leninism to Freedom* (Boulder, CO: Westview Press, 1992), by permission of Westview Press.

dictatorship last through the generations? The late-twentieth-century emergence of democracy in Latin America has led to an insightful, generalizable, and political approach to the crafting of democracies.[6] Based on the notion that democracy can be politically crafted, practice and theory suggest that democracy can even be engineered in as seemingly unlikely political soil as that of a much- divided South Africa.[7] The continuation of India's struggle to devise political institutions and social policies to keep its democracy viable[8] and new attention to the fledgling democracies of most of the post-Leninist world (Ethiopia, Mongolia, Nicaragua, Cambodia, Angola, Poland, Hungary, Czechoslovakia et al.) provide rich data for drawing policy lessons on how to analyze and solve political problems in order to consolidate democracy in the post-Leninist world.[9]

Yet some of the conclusions from a political approach to crafting democracy are less than cheering. From whatever despotic origins come a democratic people, the harsh truth is that simple and safe evolutions from despotism to democracy are most rare. So frequently were democracies superseded by some other political form in ancient Greece, that democracy seemed but a moment in a continuous cycle. In contrast, in the age of modern nation-states, democracies have been frequently institutionalized for centuries such that they often seem a uniquely stable form of politics. However daunting is the task of democratization, the outcome is well worth the effort.

When the provinces of the Netherlands first united in the sixteenth century, the beginning of an age of modern nation-states, the alliance between Catholics and Protestants, and between south and north, would not hold, eventually unleashing more years of wanton slaughter, civil war, and chaos before the would-be Dutch republic split and the north formed the United Provinces of the Netherlands. When the democratic Netherlands "became the first in the history of modern Europe to retain power and found a durable regime,"[10] it did so only after many false starts, much bloodshed and destruction, and a permanent surrender of the region most opposed to democracy. It took quite a while before a political consensus could be formed that could hold together and deal with issues that had to be dealt with. While democratic openings may be frequent, consolidations of democracy are rare. One secret of successfully consolidating democracy, already apparent with the Netherlands, is limiting the scope of government. That is, by reserving a large role for societal, nonpolitical spheres, the burden of responsibility, and therefore the potential blame of democratic government is reduced.

The vicissitudes of democratization in the Netherlands were not unique. The thirteen American colonies, which in 1781 won their independence from Great Britain, drew up Articles of Confederation that did not achieve the advantages of union, that failed to hold the thirteen constituent parts together in a shared quest for freedom and prosperity. After much trauma and loss, a new Constitution was implemented in 1789 aimed at perfecting the union. But, as with the first construction of a United Netherlands, the regional political compromises of conflicting political identities involved in crafting a consensus in support of the new Constitution augured eventual bloodshed and potential national disintegration.

The Constitution of the American nation included the legalization of slavery, a form of domination absolutely incompatible with liberty or democracy. The Constitution, a flawed pact with the devil, carried fiendish fuel for a fiery Civil War that, almost a century after independence, ended slavery at a cost in lives greater than all other American wars, past and subsequent. Generalizing from the Dutch and American experiences suggests that consolidating a democratic breakthrough is a long-term, multistage, complex, and potentially explosive political task.[11] Post-Leninist democratization may prove more formidable. As will be explicated below, the regional and communalist forces that must be conciliated in the wake of a Leninist opening to democracy tend to be peculiarly obdurate.

Still, the original Dutch and American political compromises that made possible the constitutional compact embody general lessons. All the compacting units had to be persuaded that there was a fairness in how power was apportioned between center and regions, between bigger and smaller states. There is a craftable political geography at the base of democratization. Going back to ancient Athens, political divisions for choosing representatives had to be carefully drawn to make most likely an outcome that would keep the polity united but not dominated by a predictable special interest.[12] Since all potentially democratic states have their own histories, regional splits, economic interests, and communal divisions, these political rules have to be devised to suit each nation-state to keep the compact viable and flexible so as to meet changing conditions. While reality puts a limit on what can be theorized at a general level about democratization, no state, no matter how much it fools itself about being homogeneous, can avoid the nettlesome task of forging a geographical compact to choose representatives to avoid experiential injustices that would lead some major entity to find its interests irreconcilable to the democratic pact.

Even early democratic consolidation—the 1688 limited constitutional republic in Britain—confronted obdurate obstacles of political geography that left a festering, conquered Ireland to haunt the dreamers of permanent peaceful progress in a liberal democracy. Time and again history reveals that succeeding in democratic consolidation after a popular, legitimate democratic opening is far from guaranteed.

German Weimar democracy failed. So did the February 1917 democratic revolution in Russia. And why the 1789 liberal breakthrough in France could not be consolidated for almost a century bedeviled many generations of the French. The ubiquitous failure of democratic breakthroughs in Latin America led analysts of that region to see the swing to democracy from dictatorship and then back as a historically given, deeply driven, almost permanent feature of politics. It seemed impossible to consolidate democracy.

In Asia, China's 1911 republican breakthrough to democracy was lost in less than two years. Similarly, Japan's 1920s Taisho-era opening to democracy was soon harshly clamped closed by military dictatorship. The 1961 popular democratic revolution in Korea was also swiftly reversed by a military coup. Liberal democratic African regimes established at independence from European colonial rule had a similar sad, short life. Democratic openings could not be consolidated.[13] The post-Leninist problems of legitimating a new nationalism and conciliating regional communalisms make the usually difficult consolidations yet more problematical.

In every region of the world, in Europe, the Americas, Africa, and Asia, democratic openings were not peacefully, easily, and immediately consolidated. American political science is replete with attempts to explain why it is so difficult to consolidate democracy. Studies of revolution, such as Crane Brinton's conservative classic, *Anatomy of Revolution*, find that revolutions cannot consolidate an initial liberal republican state form but must move on to a radical terror.[14] The approach to democratization from the perspective of political crafting, cited above, instead would ask what was wrong in the French political pacts of 1789 and 1792 or Russia's of February 1917 that facilitated the demise of those democratic republics. Political scientists try to draw meaning from past democratic failures so that political wisdom can overcome political obstacles that would otherwise obstruct democratization. As Western political philosophy distinguishes between the roles of *fortuna* and *virtu*, so the role of political knowledge is to expand the force of *virtu*; that is, to learn better how to craft democratic systems that will not be fated to fail because of contingent, social inheritances of geographical divisions and communal differences among diverse peoples and interests.

The Challenge of Leninism to Democratization

Most of post–World War II American social theory, however, has found that *fortuna* tends to be decisive, that the social inheritance is stronger than the will and wisdom of democratization. The dominant hypothesis has been that stable democracy requires a democratic civic culture and a society dominated by urban middle classes, neither of which purported democratic preconditions obtains in most of the world. Hence the policy advice of post–World War II American political science hastened to favor supporting so-called military modernizers over a supposedly impossible democratic project. Department of State Policy Planning Director George Kennan noted in 1948:

> We should cease to talk about . . . human rights . . . and democratization. . . .
> [W]e should not hesitate before police repression by the local government.
> This is not shameful since the Communists are essentially traitors. . . . It is
> better to have a strong regime in power than a liberal government if it is
> indulgent and relaxed and penetrated by Communists.[15]

Along these lines, in his famous study, *Political Order in Changing Societies*, Samuel Huntington, writing in 1968, offered an explanation of why the "attempt to establish some sort of liberal, democratic, constitutional state . . . frequently" fails and the democrats

> are swept from power. Their failure stems . . . from their inability to deal with . . . political mobilization. . . . [T]hey lack the drive and ruthlessness [requiring concentration of power] to stop the mobilization of new groups. . . . [T]hey lack the radicalism to lead it. . . . [T]he liberals are brushed away either by counter revolutionaries who perform the first or by more extreme revolutionaries who perform the second.[16]

Nothing in Huntington, with his emphasis on mobilization and ruthlessness, gives hope for a broad expansion of democracy. Almost nothing in the political science of democratic crafting builds on Huntington's hypotheses. His perspective seems a product of the assumptions of a short historical moment. Beyond Cold War rationalization of policy preferences, and beyond not being able to imagine that a democratic pact can be created for almost any society,[17] Huntington's basic social science error lies in his theoretical premise, the presupposition of modernization theorists (which includes analysts with very different political orientations such as Barrington Moore and Theda Skocpol)[18] that all political systems must undergo a once-and-for-all painful transformation to a state system dubbed modern. The evanescent nature of what is thought of as the modern world is, in actuality, more a permanent social crisis of change outpacing consciousness than a problem with a solution definable as "political order," as Huntington wrongly had it.[19] Democracy's superiority includes its ability to be open to the conflicts of continuous change and to adapt flexibly. Because those who choose a communalist alternative to the uncertainties of democratization do so out of fear of the openness of democracy in a post-Leninist world, democracy should be crafted so that it can grapple with this modern dilemma of permanent change that threatens communalist identities.

Post-Leninist Obstacles to Democratization

Still, whatever the flaws in his analysis, Huntington called attention to both the historical difficulty of consolidating liberal democratic breakthroughs and a major institutional cause of that difficulty, a recalcitrant military. Post-Leninist democratizers also must confront this difficulty. The works on crafting democracy cited above offer precise suggestions for taming the antidemocratic tendencies of powerful military institutions.

In addition, consolidating a democratic breakthrough from a Leninist dictatorship may be particularly difficult.[20] First, the usual obstacles are unusually strong. The coercive apparatuses usually include vicious, politically loyal, army-like security forces that have so much blood on their hands that they may well fight against an opening to democracy. In addition, the pervasiveness of the Leninist secret police apparatus and the complicity of so many with it means that to reveal the truth and to do justice in a democratizing era may threaten so many as to add greatly to the recalcitrants who will try to reverse the democratic breakthrough. To decrease the likelihood of success for the antidemocratic forces, democrats should study the lessons detailed in Wechsler's (book cited in note 15) on forgiving even torturers and exposing the truth of worse criminals as a way of decreasing any future likelihood of a reversion to a brutal Leninist police state. Caution and mercy are needed to decrease the numbers opposed to democracy. Since breakthroughs to democracy are lost more often than they are consolidated, democratizers should act prudently to preclude worst-case reversals.

The 1989–90 breakthroughs to democracy are but initial steps in a prolonged political struggle. Openings to democracy in Leninist systems were nastily and swiftly slammed shut before 1989–90. That history contains a warning for the future. The great 1956 democratic Hungarian revolution was crushed at its birth by the Soviet Union. The 1967–68 democratic opening in Czechoslovakia to "socialism with a human face" was quickly repressed by Soviet-led Warsaw Pact forces. The democratic opening won in 1980 by Solidarity in Poland suffered a cruel defeat a couple of years later when a Polish martial-law regime imposed itself. Democratic forces in the early Bolshevik Party were readily quashed by the secret police. Mao easily sent off to forced labor people who sought democracy in response to his 1956–57 liberalization campaign that invited people to point out flaws in the system. The militaries in Romania and China both seem to have sealed off democratic openings. In Mongolia, democratic leaders feared a military reimposition of Leninist dictatorship. Whereas some people contend that with Moscow no longer opposing democratization, the process will be smooth sailing, in fact, the complexities of the struggle to consolidate a democratic opening in a Leninist state are not mere matters of whether or not a people were or were not included in the Soviet orbit.[21] The same complex processes are at work in Russia as in Hungary; in Mongolia, China, and Yugoslavia as in Czechoslovakia. Internal forces are decisive. And even beyond the potential opposition of those in the institutions of coercion and of those who are complicitous, there are many people who prefer a different kind of dictatorship to democracy.

For clues to the yet more painful problems for democratizers wrought by Leninism, greater attention should be given to Yugoslavia. Already in 1953, Yugoslavia specifically committed itself to negating Stalinism and institutionalizing decentralist political reforms. Yugoslavia should not be treated as distinct from all other Leninist countries because of ethnonationalist features supposedly peculiar to Yugoslavia. Perhaps the mainstream social science proposition explicated so lucidly by Huntington, that Leninist political institutions have to be successful, has long led, misleadingly, to treating Leninist failures as anomalies.

The persistence of antidemocratic forces in Yugoslavia, rather, may in crucial ways be paradigmatic. Yugoslavia is the Leninist polity that has for the longest time pursued policies of agricultural decollectivization, world-market openness (including lots of travel to democratic Western Europe), and great economic reforms in order to construct a competitive, modern economy. Yet forty years of such seemingly enlightened, anti-Stalinist policies did not consolidate democracy. All actual democratic breakthroughs were quickly suppressed. The causes are not peculiar to Yugoslavia.

To the large extent that Leninism is a conservative militarist chauvinism (anti-imperialism), its beneficiaries could, in a post-Leninist era, ally with conservative communalists who also experience freedom as foreign pollution. One serious problem in post-Leninist democratization is that Leninist rule can engender a new, tough nationalism tied to a dominant ethnic group, the old military, or the secret police and then identify its opposition to liberty, individualism, or the secular with a national project of unity, size, prestige, order, and keeping out foreign ways depicted as subverters of all that is good and healthy in the historical heritage. Understanding Leninist states as similar to traditional or feudal ones may help explain similar proclivities when the old system breaks down, tendencies toward order through "populist, usually military, dictatorship."[22] The vicissitudes of post-Leninist democratic consolidation resemble France in the century after the Bastille fell, a century in which cries for military order often won out over constitutional liberty. Clearly, the general difficulties of democratization when compounded by the peculiarly difficult consequences of Leninism suggest that consolidating an original breakthrough from Leninism to democracy is no simple matter.

All the wise economic reforms, starting in 1958, that brought the people in Hungary, as in Yugoslavia—and, after 1978, in post-Mao China—great economic progress not only do not automatically evolve into democracy, they in fact give purpose to those who feel a stake in the political system and who therefore oppose democratization. But at the same time, the reforms also actually further delegitimate the ruling group, thus increasing the likelihood of a bloody clash between recalcitrant polar forces; democratic consolidation, in contrast, requires a broad middling consensus. This perceived intensifying of all the divisive forces in the society makes it seem to many that only a dictatorship can keep the nation from disintegrating. With a renewed communalist nationalism legitimate, and with chaos the seeming alternative, many prefer the superficial security of communalist dictatorship to the untried risks of democracy. Coercion, charisma, co-optation, fear of chaos, and chauvinism may, in sum, permit the old ruling group to hang on to power, but at the price of a political paralysis and a further poisoning of group reconciliation. Chaos and division may seem the price of abandoning Leninist despotism for a democratic experiment, such that extreme nationalistic despotism seems a preferable option to many.

The problem and promise of democracy will therefore be most attractive if it offers a loose confederation with negotiated equities that hold the prospect of a continuing yet more just nation avoiding worst-case outcomes. Democrats will do best if they can enter the political fray with a means to meet the demands of communities and social equity. The problem for democrats is how to get this message out and how to make it persuasive. This issue of democratic union or bloody alternatives (civil war, cruel repression, communalist strife) is central because the first moves away from Leninism tend to intensify many of the evils of the system that foster loyalties other than the democratic kind.

Leninist reforms worsen societal cuts and sores, turning them into life-threatening wounds because, fearing cleansing open air, Leninists cover up the splitting sores, guaranteeing that, beneath the surface, not only does no healing occur, but that poisonous scapegoating and political mistrust become ever more presuppositional to politics, making it painfully difficult to build broad coalitions based on a shared national identity that could permit a swift and peaceful evolution into, and consolidation of, democracy.[23] To the extent that Leninist states foster tough chauvinistic militaries, state/society polarization, and powerful and conflictful, yet ultimately, subnational communalist identities, Leninism obstructs a consolidation of democracy that

> requires a disenchantment with central authority in general, an army too weak or demoralized to impose its will on society, and a broad alliance between elites and popular groups in defense of individual [and communal] freedoms.[24]

To consolidate a democratic opening in a post-Leninist world therefore requires dealing with a national and nationalist legitimation crisis in a peculiarly sharp and explosive form, perhaps worse than is the case in a transition from other kinds of tyrannies. The intensity of this difficulty occurs because Leninist states not only freeze prior regional, ethnic, and religious divisions but also because Leninism worsens the communalist contradiction, since all groups are kept to a territory and frozen into place—no market, mobility, individualism, or growth of cross-cutting cleavages to cushion primordial conflict. All communities are made to feel the victim of the dominant group, while the dominant group blames all others. The result is a pervasive, poisoned pattern of "nation blaming nation."[25] An elite from the dominant community can then appeal to renewed chauvinism to maintain national unity. The smaller groups, in opposition to the central community, tend to reflect populist nationalisms.

A problem for crafting democracy in a post-Leninist order is whether to accept division or bring peoples (many? all?) together in a federation. Usually the task of the democratizers will be easier if they do not seem the enemies of popular patriotism. Some new glue must replace the desiccated and deadly bond of chauvinistic Leninist anti-imperialism. This requires legitimating a new national identity and establishing political institutions that will both support that new national center and also seem fair to all the diverse regional communities. It is not easy.

Hence the relation between center and region is crucial to potential stability. Political compromise and civil freedoms are required to guarantee cultural authenticities. The democracy's lines and rules should build in incentives to trans-communalist coalitions.

But the political center in an economically reformist but still Leninist political system that is based on a command economy with powerful central ministries and money-losing state enterprises can only offer minor concessions to federalism. The center remains self-interestedly economically irrational. Regions therefore lack any large incentive to compromise with a reforming Leninist center that still holds on to the central ministries and heavy-industry enterprises of a politico economic formation that fears devolution, market, and democracy as death. That old Leninist system is based on pricing and distribution that hurt the regions. The burdensome Leninist command economy is also a political machine of incompetents. Its costly, oppressive institutions are overstaffed, parasitic, massively polluting, extraordinarily wasteful, and mammoth. No area or community outside of that privileged, useless economy wishes to see its hard-earned money go to taxes to support the devouring dinosaur of the outmoded Leninist center. A new stability based on compromise and coalition is unlikely if all divisions of the tax take seem inherently arbitrary and illegitimate. The center must concede, an imperative that can seem to threaten national unity. The contradictions are explosive. The economically illegitimate can seem politically legitimate. Two potential forces—national disintegration and an unaccountable and thievingly heavy, outmoded central economy—are in absolute conflict. That makes consolidating democracy in a post-Leninist world peculiarly difficult because early reform strengthens local power, undercuts the center's tax take, and makes the struggle over regional or federal power seem all or nothing,[26] whereas democracy requires a broad compromise consensus. Post-Leninist forces tend to run counter to the imperatives of compromise and consensus. Thus a section of the Leninist old guard, especially if it experiences itself as chauvinistic, can act with military and secret police hard-liners, presenting themselves as the only alternative to disintegration and chaos. The regions or communities in opposition to the tyrannical, parasitical center may then feel compelled to opt for disunion. These forces of polarization greatly complicate post-Leninist democratization.

The Inevitability of the Democratic Option

The same general tendencies apply in China as elsewhere. The crisis of dictatorship or disunion as seeming political alternatives surfaces after the original Leninist anti-imperialist leaders disappear and as time erodes popular illusions about the possibility of a reforming socialism resolving historically deep conflicts that are intensified by the politics of Leninism. Given the particularities of the ruling group or chronological moment, one cannot predict how long illusions last that Leninism can be a basis for a new stable compromise. Eventually the old rulers will split. But given the power of antidemocratic alternatives, reformers and democratic stability will do best if the democrats can ally with opposition moderates swiftly to craft a consensual democracy. Given regional and communalist divisions, as well as nationalist passions, plus outrage at earlier Leninist inhumanities, such a coalition of compromise and consensus is not guaranteed. It is not easy. It has a higher likelihood the more it succeeds in some post-Leninist system, the more it seems a legitimate and successful post-Leninist option. Clearly an alternative to dictatorship and disunion should be so welcome that the democratic path can seem imperative, the only salvation of nation, equity, and ordered progress.

Yet every place has its peculiarities. The old guard in Beijing wins time and political latitude because it has delivered the economic goods. Chinese openness to the world economy benefits from China's economic geography, its proximity to the world's most dynamic economic region. Decollectivization is a success in China because of the survival of the peasant household whose economic actions permit speedy rural development. Finally, the traditionalism of the Chinese regime seems legitimate to many because Mao's prior locking up of villagers in the countryside for a generation has allowed regime fundamentalists, in a post-Mao reform and mobility era, to appeal both to protofascist rural dwellers anxious over rapid change, experienced as foreign and individualistic, and to urban status anxiety, based on fear of an influx of lower-paid rural workers. These Chinese particularities can perpetuate chauvinist Leninism in China. Still, Leninism in China, too, is threatened by the eventual limits on growth inherent in the system. The system itself inevitably gets experienced popularly as an illegitimate, selfish, and private realm that stands in opposition to popular needs. The Leninist system creates similar delegitimating forces in China, Cuba, or Czechoslovakia.

All the usual questions of consolidating democracy apply then to each and all—with the added caveat of the need to confront the peculiar issues of Leninist democratization: nationalist legitimation, regional disintegration, and the ending of the burdens of a command economy. Still, in general, when the first generation of rulers is gone, with an acknowledged need for market-oriented world openness, some group within the regime seems likely one day to try to build bridges to the broad, moderate voice of the excluded citizenry so as to peripheralize both antidemocratic recalcitrants within the old order and also vengeful oppositionists seeking justice for innumerable, extraordinary crimes. The imperative of making democracy succeed is almost inevitably going to appear on the political agenda. Consequently, it is worthwhile even for democratic opponents in a still-Leninist state to begin to contemplate how they would consolidate a democratic breakthrough, how they would quell the fears of those who could be attracted to alternatives to democracy.

Surely it will help make the transition more peaceful and stable if it is clear that democrats can, after a democratic opening, craft institutions that truly consolidate the breakthrough. How does one defang the secret services, reduce and professionalize the military, turn the nomenklatura apparatus into a meritocratic civil service, etc? The literature on crafting democracy already addresses all of these questions. Whatever the particulars, in general the answer is: by crafting a political framework of reconciliation that protects diversity, promotes consensus, and civilizes conflict. An early attempt to figure out solutions to the problem of consolidation permits democratizers to appear more in command of the forces to be grappled with, appeal to latent nationalisms, and soothe those anxious over potential chaos. The democratic alternative can be made into a political imperative.

An Economic Pact for Social Equity

But those goals are not easily achieved in a post-Leninist world. With debt and budget crises compounded by the wasteful, parasitic, command economy, there is little money to buy off—or buy in—so many groups. And swift solutions may be needed to hold the nation together, since Leninism's nasty inheritance leaves little popular faith in half measures, given the mistrust and hate of angry and long-suffering communalist groupings that have run out of patience and trust. Given the need to persuade so many that they will not be economically or communally destroyed, it is no solution to suggest that the market is all the answer needed, although at the same time, no solution is possible until market-oriented dynamics are basic to the system. Ways compatible with a market orientation that also seem equitable to numerous outraged communities must be devised. That need requires an economically active state center. While the literature on crafting democracy already addresses equity, including matters of making the civil service open and professional, it tends to abjure the requirements of state action in the economic realm.

Each nation, of course, must resolve equity problems within its peculiar set of conflicting social forces. There is, however, a major danger of heeding the conventional wisdom that tends to come from generalizing from the transition to democracy in Latin America and other regions where American intervention seems divisive. This is because Latin Americanists, explainers of anti-Yankee sentiment to the people of the United States, tend to see the United States as only a problem in building democracy, since ties to the Yankees may easily discredit one's nationalism in Latin America. Actually, the United States and other democracies can have a large influence in helping fledgling democracies consolidate political freedom, especially in the economic realm.[27]

Latin Americanists, however, tend to be ignorant of Leninist realities. Not understanding the pervasive corruption and economic irrationality of the Leninist apparatus, seeing their own region's murderous right-wing military dictatorships as the worst evil, a Latin Americanist wrongly comments that "the prospects for democratization look better in the post-socialist nations than in military dominated dictatorships . . . [because the former] have a better bedrock of professional public institutions upon which to build than with authoritarian regimes which have been corrupted by personalism and parasitism."[28] In addition, Di Palma contends that in comparison to Latin America, where American power could still disrupt the fledgling democratic effort, Eastern European peoples in post-Leninist systems are fortunate because Russia simply got out of the way and allowed the people's democratic urges to rise and win—surely not a description of Gorbachev's actions toward Honecker. More importantly, this analysis misses both the economic pact needed to consolidate a fledgling democracy and the great impact international economic aid can have in making that economic pact work. International help matters, as democrats in post-Leninist democracies deeply appreciate. Democrats in Russia and Eastern Europe have consequently been contributing to the democratic cause in Tibet. It is worth generalizing from these post-Leninist tendencies of international cooperation and social equity.

The writings of Gillespie, Di Palma, and other students of democratization in Latin America and Southern Europe insufficiently appreciate the major points made in this chapter about the extraordinary obstacles to democratization in post-Leninist or reforming Leninist systems. They do not see the daunting nature of economic reform. In addition, given the centrality of world-market competitiveness to expanding wealth since World War II, the peculiar weakness of the Leninist system in this regard makes it less likely that internally generated resources will, in a post-Leninist era, swiftly be sufficient to meet the pent-up demands of various subnational communities. If the economy contracts, all communities can experience themselves as victims. Therefore, the fledgling democracy seeks foreign aid on almost any terms. That weakness can make the fragile democracy seem a dependent traitor to the patriotic cause. This weak, post-Leninist political economy entering the world market is profoundly threatened by seeming dependence on the nearby hegemon (Germany for Poland, Japan for North Korea or China), a matter that further complicates the democratizers' need and attempt to win nationalist legitimation, because the economics of survival could also seem a politics of losing the nationalist mantle.[29]

An issue that cries out for more attention in any analysis seeking ways to make it more likely that an opening to democracy will lead to a true consolidation of democracy in post-Leninist states—an issue overlooked in the present literature on democratic crafting—is that of the international economic realm, including finance, trade, and production. In the post–Bretton Woods world, democratization would be greatly facilitated—and the likelihood of vengeful chauvinistic backlash lessened—if international economic institutions and richer nations had ways of providing an economic package to facilitate and cushion the related, traumatic economic transitions concomitant to the political transition. These costly and painful economic transitions are not necessarily required or traumatic in transitions from non-Leninist despotisms to democracy. The fragile post-Leninist democracy is less likely to shatter if it can seem a new center fair to all communities, if it can preclude an all-out war of region against region that strengthens communalist identities as orders of exclusive meaning that increase the forces tending toward group hatred, nonreconciliation, and even civil war.[30]

In this area of reconciliation, the conventional wisdom, premised on non-Leninist experience, about the political institutions facilitating a successful transition from despotism to democracy, slights the importance of creating a shared economic interest in the democratic process. Analysts of democratization in non-Leninist states tend to see consolidation as a building of a broad coalition, a matter of conciliation and ending fears of worst-case treatment by the new state so that there is a shrinkage and peripheralization of antidemocratic recalcitrants among both elites and challengers. In addition, the state is less likely to be a target of outrage if it is able to surrender much of the economic burden to private arenas. This means weakening the state and sharing power. For such purposes a parliamentary system with proportional representation is promoted as superior because it helps prevent a winner-take-all outcome that might overly concentrate the fruits of victory and thus undermine the ties holding various suspicious groups in the fragile democratic coalition. There is some obvious wisdom in this approach.

But a post-Leninist state, as part of democratization, needs to legitimate a new nationalism and prove that all now will be treated fairly. It needs to guarantee an equity pact among regions and communities. These needs may make superior a presidential system with a program agenda that includes a social-equity pact. Because of the profoundly alienating experience during the age of Leninism of inordinate unfairness to all groups, the tendency of those generalizing from Latin America and Southern Europe to focus singularly on the importance of fair rules of one central political game and to decry as dangerous the seeking of *any* particular socioeconomic outcome misses the imperative in a post-Leninist world in trying to consolidate a democratic polity, of re-establishing the notion that the system is equitable to various regions and peoples, that there are numerous political games at work, and that they have to be coordinated from one political entity. The new polity must engineer an institutional consensus with a weaker political center in many realms, yet one strong in the realm of economic coordination, as is the European Economic Community.

To maintain stability and build legitimacy in post-Leninist democratization, it may be worth learning from the examples of social equity in post–World War II Japan, South Korea, and Taiwan in knitting together a common national enterprise in which the state center began as quite illegitimate to most people, as in the post-Leninist world. Unfortunately, the conventional wisdom, with its focus on the lessons of Latin America and Southern Europe, has tended, misleadingly, to treat East Asia as an anomaly or a miracle.[31] Without an East Asian–style legitimately interventionist state in the realm of socioeconomic justice and coordination, the tendencies of reforming Leninist states to intensify regionalism can be multiplied by immediate losses of groups and regions from sudden marketization and competitive criteria that can short-circuit any attempt to institutionalize an experience of fairness in the political networks of democracy.

Growth without equity can keep a regime illegitimate. This has been the experience of South Korea, since the mid-1960s the world's most rapidly developing nation. Yet its political center throughout the 1980s enjoyed little popular legitimacy for a number of reasons, including caring for rich cronies while ordinary people were told to tighten their belts, changing the rules of entrance to schools, and not making entrance to the civil service sufficiently competitive by exam. A legitimate central economic capacity is needed to make the overall pattern of benefits seem fair and equitable. Consequently, to enhance the likelihood of successfully consolidating a post-Leninist democracy, mere privatization and marketization will not do. A balance must be created between state intervention for growth and equity and central state disentanglement in so many other realms, so that the central government is not the target of all economic frustrations and so that local groups can be assured that their most sacred interests will be protected.

Conclusion

Atul Kohli, in *Democracy and Its Discontents*, finds that an inability to achieve this balance is a major cause of disintegrative tendencies in India, a state that long tried to combine features of both political democracy and a closed, Leninist-style command economy in a nation divided by numerous communalist identities threatening national disintegration.[32] Kohli concludes that facilitating stable national parties to run the state increases national identity, since party and political programs help maintain a precarious balance and can prevent disintegration, and even consolidate democracy. This means that in crafting the original breakthrough to democracy, it is worth worrying about how to avoid a proliferation of parties that will preclude a needed national consensus.

In sum, the failure of democratization is usefully seen as a political failure, as an inability of political elites and democratic challengers to concern themselves with, imagine, and build institutions, rules, expectations, coalitions, and balances suitable to consolidating an original breakthrough. Guidelines for consolidating post-Leninist democracies cannot simply repeat the lessons of Latin America. Lessons from democratic struggles in South Korea and India seem far more relevant. Most relevant are the struggles of democrats in reform Leninist regimes. These already manifest the issues and changes described above. They highlight the imperatives of political reconciliation, communalist confederation, and social equity.

The political problematique of democratization is never easy. Leninism makes it particularly difficult. But because the problem is political, and therefore in a realm of action open to creative human intervention, there should be political solutions to get past the obstacles to consolidating democracy in post-Leninist states. This chapter sketches and summarizes hopeful political crafting that constructs political bridges to surmount these obstacles and enhance the likelihood of success in consolidating democracy.

Notes

1. Ralph Miliband, "What Comes After Marxist Regimes?" in Ralph Miliband et al., eds., *Communist Regimes: The Aftermath* (London: Merlin Press, 1991), p. 324.
2. *Telos*, No. 81, p. 148.
3. Harry Harding, *China's Second Revolution* (Washington, DC: Brookings Institution, 1987), p. 29.
4. Letter, *New York Times Magazine*, February 25, 1990, p. 10.
5. See Edward Friedman, "Ethnic Identity and the Denationalization and Democratization of Leninist States," in M. Crawford Young, ed., *The Rising Tide of Cultural Pluralism* (Madison: University of Wisconsin Press, 1993). People who think China uniquely resistant to democratization because its Leninism had nationalist legitimacy ignore national Leninism in Albania, Mongolia, Yugoslavia, Soviet Russia, Ethiopia, Mozambique, Angola, and even Czechoslovakia and East Germany. Those who see Eastern Europe's democratization as a simple nationalist response to Russian colonialism ignore potent subnational divisiveness (e.g., Czechs versus Slovaks). In fact, the cruel contradictions of Leninist dynamics impel decentralist and democratic forces and struggles everywhere in the Leninist world.
6. Giuseppe Di Palma, *To Craft Democracies* (Berkeley: University of California Press, 1991).
7. Donald L. Horowitz, *A Democratic South Africa: Constitutional Engineering in a Divided Society* (Berkeley: University of California Press, 1991).
8. Atul Kohli, *Democracy and Its Discontents* (Cambridge: Cambridge University Press, 1991).
9. The rich literature on the democratization of formerly Leninist states grows larger by the day. A good place to begin is the work on Poland by shrewd analysts such as Adam Michnik, Roman Laba, and David Ost.
10. Perez Zagorin, *Rebels and Rulers 1500–1660*, Vol. II (New York: Cambridge University Press, 1982), p. 127.
11. Barrington Moore, Jr., *Social Origins of Dictatorship and Democracy* (Boston: Beacon, 1966), contends that the American democratic revolution should be conceived as including the Civil War because without the defeat of feudal-like, military-oriented, old-fashioned plantation owners, the antidemocratic forces in the United States could have precluded the consolidation of a successfully industrializing democratic polity.
12. For an introduction to political crafters in democratic Athens, see the following books and their sources: M. I. Finley, *Politics in the Ancient World* (Cambridge: Cambridge University Press, 1983); Eli Sagan, *The Honey and the Hemlock* (New York: Basic Books, 1991).
13. An exception is Botswana. See John Holm and Patrick Molutsi, eds., *Democracy in Botswana* (Athens: Ohio University Press, 1989).
14. Brinton, *Anatomy of Revolution* (New York: Vintage, 1957).
15. Cited in Lawrence Weschler, *A Miracle, A Universe: Settling Accounts with Torturers* (New York: Penguin, 1990), pp. 115, 116.
16. Huntington, *Political Order in Changing Societies* (New Haven: Yale University Press, 1968), pp. 268, 269.
17. Democracies persist not only in Botswana, but also in Hindu India, Buddhist Sri

Lanka, Shinto Japan, Jewish Israel, Catholic Latin America, and the animist South Seas, and have begun in Confucian, Lamaist, and Islamic nations.

18. Skocpol, *States and Social Revolution* (New York: Cambridge University Press, 1979).

19. For a discussion of the inappropriateness of Leninism to post–mass production technologies, see Edward Friedman, "Permanent Technological Revolution and China's Tortuous Path to Democratizing Leninism," in Richard Baum, ed., *Reform and Reaction in Post-Mao China* (New York: Routledge, 1991).

20. See Edward Friedman, "Theorizing the Democratization of China's Leninist State," in Arif Dirlik and Maurice Meisner, eds., *Marxism and the Chinese Experience* (Armonk, NY: M. E. Sharpe, 1989), pp. 171–89.

21. In contrast, Su Shaozhi finds the distinction between imposed and indigenous Leninism to be decisive. In M. L. Nugent, ed., *From Leninism to Freedom* (Boulder, CO: Westview Press).

22. Jack Goldstone, *Revolution and Rebellion in the Early Modern World* (Berkeley: University of California Press, 1991), p. 499.

23. For a shrewd analysis of democratization in these terms, see Di Palma, *To Craft Democracies.*

24. Goldstone, *Revolution and Rebellion*, p. 480.

25. Sonja Licht, "Pluralism or Nationalism," *East European Reporter*, reprinted in *CADDY Bulletin*, No. 65 (June 1991), p. 20.

26. This chapter will not discuss the economic issues associated with dismantling the rigid command economy since so much good work already exists on that subject.

27. See Barbara Stallings and Robert Kaufman, eds., *Debt and Democracy in Latin America* (Boulder, CO: Westview Press, 1989).

28. Charles Gillespie, "Di Palma on Democratization," *San Francisco Review of Books* (Spring 1991), p. 36. Informed people would know that Kiev, in the czarist era, suffered pogroms against Jews, but usually only specialists would know that a rich Jewish culture in Kiev of around 200 synagogues continued and was reduced to only one in the Leninist era of thoroughgoing repression.

29. In China, because the conservative reformers so fear opening up to the democratic world, an over-reliance on Japan—seen as not caring about human rights—could lose the surviving patriotic credentials of the Leninist remnant. See Edward Friedman, "The Foreign Policy of the Li Peng Group," *Asian Outlook* 26.4 (May–June 1991).

30. Actually, as suggested earlier, the political coalition consolidating democracy can involve compromises that inadvertently yet rigidly institutionalize certain rules to the exclusion of certain people, and thus increase the likelihood of future implosions of the democracy if changes are not made. No rules of the game, however democratic, can be considered finally appropriate or fair.

31. Edward Friedman, "Democratization: Generalizing the East Asian Experience," in Friedman, ed., *The Politics of Democratization*, (Boulder, CO: Westview Press, 1994).

32. Atul Kohli, *Democracy and Its Discontents.*

Chapter 14

Permanent Technological Revolution and China's Tortuous Path to Democratizing Leninism

Prior to the 1989–90 political transformations in Eastern and Central Europe, many analysts found it inconceivable that Leninist states could become democratic.[1] This chapter argues not only that democratization is possible, but that in an era of rapid and continuous global technological revolution, democratization can facilitate the modernization of Leninist systems. Unlike early theories of once-and-for-all modernity, which ordained a singular transition to universalistic values and thereby condemned the familistic Confucian societies of East Asia to perpetual backwardness,[2] this chapter views modernization as an ongoing process of institutional adaptation to technological change—change that periodically produces new economic lead sectors and shifting world-market logics.[3]

Viewed in this perspective, the contemporary drive for basic reform in Leninist states emerges as a consequence of the declining efficacy of the centralized command economy's hierarchical mass-production system, which was originally designed to compete with the great steel-based economies of Germany and America at the start of the twentieth century. This system was supported by an inordinately rigid institutional framework unsuited to an international era that demanded increasingly flexible institutions and competitive trade as conditions of economic progress.[4]

Social theorists in Leninist states speak to the same point when they find that late-twentieth-century developments in science and technology cannot be exploited by Leninist-Stalinist institutions developed for an earlier age of steam,

Reprinted from Richard Baum, ed., *Reform and Reaction in Post-Mao China* (New York: Routledge, 1991), by permission of Routledge.

railroads, and heavy steel. Leninism, they argue, is increasingly incompatible with the imperatives of poststeel modernization.[5] This outdatedness opens (or reopens) the question of democracy as an integral part of a particular historical moment in the ongoing process of technological revolution.

The Crisis of Leninism

Once the original charismatic, state-building leader of a Leninist system dies or is discredited, the regime, which cannot deliver on its promise of poststeel modernity, requires a new mode of legitimation. Democratization, as a response to systemic crisis, is an attempt to relegitimate the system and its temporary need for shared sacrifice in order to retool economically.[6] Such illegitimacy is explained in Leninist systems in terms of a generally accepted finding that the country is more backward than democratic market societies, leading to a Marxist labeling of the Leninist system as feudal, that is, precapitalist—and thence to a (misdirected) attack on traditional culture as a presumed source of continuing backwardness.

In focusing primarily on the issue of a ruling group's capacity to deliver the material blessings of a changing form of modernity, no slight is intended to the notion that democracy is a human potential. It is well known that from ancient China to precolonial Africa, diverse societies have embraced elements of civil rights and community participation. That the theory and practice of democracy developed most fully in the West does not make democracy a culturally peculiar Western product any more than the fact that penicillin was discovered in Britain means that it cannot be used in Beijing or Moscow.[7] The desire to have institutions that reduce the likelihood of arbitrary power and human degradation is not a passion unique to a rising bourgeoisie. People in Leninist systems suffer the daily humiliations of fawning before the powerful and dissembling in front of their children. A healthy polity is democratic. As science, medicine, and technology are generalizable human achievements, so are toleration, human rights, and democracy.

Nonetheless, democracy has spread most rapidly at particular moments in history. Certain challenges to state power more readily facilitate democracy as a solution. Democracy first rose in Western Europe as an open, participatory response to a crisis of late medieval absolutism and religious intolerance when trade and technology expanded to offer new wealth-creating opportunities.[8] Absolutist, mercantilist states with their narrow monopolies came to be seen as corrupt and privileged parasites, denying to too many people the blessings offered by new economic opportunities.[9] It is possible that in the poststeel world of rapidly changing technologies, global forces act in a similar way to discredit privileged, statist, mercantilist dictatorships of the Leninist type that fail to win or spread the benefits of new technological and international economic opportunities. In China the Leninist party dictatorship was (albeit unofficially) blamed for leaving the Chinese people ever farther behind their East Asian neighbors.[10]

Democrats in Leninist states challenge the very legitimacy of the system in their redefinition of self-styled advanced socialist states as relatively backward, feudalistic, or traditional entities. The hidden corruption of the ruling groups, who channel foreign exchange to their friends and families for purchase of foreign cars, delicacies, and electronic goods, is experienced in much the same way as a venal monarchy monopolizing all economic benefits for itself and its courtiers—at the expense of the country. In a world of nationalism, the economic polarization of Leninism, pitting state against society, redefines the rulers as parasites. Their unearned, sometimes secret, always readily gossiped-about privileges discredit the ruling groups as less than modern.

There are major social science traditions that take seriously Stalin's identification with the earlier and only partially successful Russian modernizers, such as Peter the Great, and that understand the dynamics of Leninist systems as more traditional than rational, in the Weberian sense of modernization.[11] Analytic categories that conceptualize Leninist systems as based on traditions of fealty and hierarchy, rather than competence and contract,[12] have been utilized by social scientists to decode the political language of China as feudal,[13] neofeudal,[14] or neotraditional.[15] Nonetheless, rulers in the Soviet Union, as in China and other Leninist systems, did—as in modernizing Japan—put in place institutions designed to improve on the impressive economic record of Bismarck's nineteenth-century, rapidly rising Germany in protecting steel and grain and delivering military autarky, state strength, and national power.

Lenin and the German Experience

Like Japan's Meiji oligarchs, Lenin and his colleagues looked to the most rapidly industrializing countries of the West for clues as to how to build a yet stronger, more prosperous nation. In 1920, Lenin found Germany to be "a country that is able to set gigantic productive forces in motion. . . . Her technical level [in electrification] is even higher than America's."[16] For Lenin, "The electrical industry is the most typical of the modern technical achievements of capitalism."[17]

Lenin was deeply impressed by "the younger and stronger" Germany.[18] He found that "Bismarck accomplished a progressive historical task. . . . Bismarck promoted economic development."[19] In *State and Revolution*, Lenin cited Engels to argue that what socialists must do is to change the political logic of Bismarck's achievement so that the wealth produced would serve socialist purposes (by raising the great mass of people), rather than serve purportedly capitalist purposes (by only enriching the few wealthiest exploiters). In short, Lenin argued that Bismarck's " 'revolution from above' . . . must not be reversed, but supplemented by a 'movement from below.' "[20]

In his essay *Imperialism*, Lenin described contemporary Germany as the epitome of modern development. No longer was it "a miserable, insignificant country."[21] By concentrating economic power in the few largest monopolies, trusts, and cartels—a concentration that permitted coordination among banks, industries, and government so that large investments "can accelerate technical progress in a way that cannot possibly be compared with the past"[22]—Germany emerged "younger, stronger and better organized." Finding that those new economic organizations that concentrated and centralized command of the economy must dominate modern life "regardless of the form of government,"[23] Lenin argued that "[t]he result is immense progress in the socialization of production. . . . Production becomes social, but appropriation remains private."[24] Capitalism thus paves the way for socialism, since "state-monopoly capitalism is a complete material preparation for socialism . . . a rung in the ladder of history between which [it] and the rung called socialism there are no intermediate rungs."[25] Calling Germany the "most concrete example of state capitalism," Lenin referred to the German experiment as the " 'last word' in modern large-scale capitalist engineering and planned organization. . . . [Substitute] a proletarian state, and you will have the sum total of the conditions necessary for socialism."[26]

Just "remove the top" of the German system so that it serves "the interests of the whole people" and, for Lenin, the result would be a modern socialist state.[27] History, for Lenin, had constructed in Germany and his Bolshevik party "two unconnected halves of socialism." "Germany and Russia had become the most striking embodiment of, on the one hand, the economic, the productive, and the socio-economic conditions for socialism, and, on the other hand, the political conditions."[28]

In Japan, the Meiji oligarchs found other lessons in the rise of Germany and the West. They focused on how private savings could be increased and institutions could funnel funds into industrial investments; how universal and technical education facilitated advanced technology and salable products; how crucial were protected home markets turning out exportable products that earned foreign exchange; how the state helped private businesses stay profitable if they proved internationally competitive; and how a militarily won colonial empire over the backward peoples was a prerequisite of joining the advanced nations. In contrast to Lenin and the Bolsheviks, the Meiji oligarchs institutionalized the expansion of wealth inherent in technological dynamism and trade expansion.

Both Lenin and the Meiji oligarchs saw agriculture as a weakness in Germany. Japan would end that weakness through imperialism: taking rice from Korea, soybeans from Manchuria, wheat from North China, and fruit and sugar from Taiwan. Lenin believed that capitalism's successes were unbalanced and inhuman, causing a disparity between success in steel and failure in agriculture. "The privileged position of the most highly cartelised industry, so-called *heavy* industry, especially coal and iron, causes 'a still greater lack of concerted organization' " in agriculture.[29] While other agricultural policies were, in theory, possible for socialists, in practice—building on Marx's condemnation of the French peasantry under capitalism as counter-revolutionary, his declaration of a need to industrialize agriculture, and Lenin's commitment to a "concerted organization" of producers in a statist manner to permit a mobilization for war against counter-revolutionaries—Stalin's class-struggle justification of coerced collectivization[30] was one logical, catastrophic consequence of a Leninist understanding of the lessons of capitalist agricultural development. It was, moreover, one not easily reversed.[31]

"Fordism" and Soviet Gigantomania

Seeing the large, the organized, and the statist as progressive, while seeing the small, the spontaneous, and the market-based as backward, ruling groups in the Soviet Union pressed forward with a gargantuan centralized form of modernity. Whereas Japan adapted a flexible, somewhat decentralized approach to production that stressed technical education,[32] in the Soviet Union Henry Ford's mass-production techniques were praised, imported, and expanded. The result was a Leninist-Stalinist caricature of late-nineteenth- and early-twentieth-century Germany and America, acknowledged as the world's two most economically advanced societies. Assembly lines were set up with deskilled tasks so the jobs could be filled by peasant illiterates. But lacking the discipline of competitive markets, Stalin carried Fordist principles of mass production and an unskilled division of labor far beyond the point of economic irrationality (a point at which the Ford Motor Company virtually became bankrupted in the 1930s, in the face of competition from General Motors[33]). With innovation impossibly expensive because of oversized units of production, and with no spur from international competitiveness because of his preference for autarky, Stalin's gargantuan, heavy-steel, mass-production Fordism stagnated technologically. These obstacles to technological innovation were intensified by a secret police apparatus and a nomenklatura system for cadre selection and promotion that rewarded the loyal and obsequious and penalized the creative and innovative.

The successful space flight of the Soviet *Sputnik* in 1957 called attention away from Hungary's 1956 democratic revolution and obscured the fact that a rapid spread of innovations in science, technology, communications, finance, and trade were rendering Stalin's unchanging Bismarck–Ford model ever more wasteful and ever further behind new, fast-moving lead technologies. While Americans argued about the alleged Soviet missile gap, the Soviets in the 1960s tried to use spies to steal computers and information technology.[34] The humiliating fact for the Soviet Union was that the Leninist state—with its command economy, collectivized agriculture, maximization of import substitution and self-reliance; with its secret police, closed society, and appointments premised on networks of political loyalty rather than competence—was becoming ever further outmoded, yet ever more deeply entrenched.

The Democratic Impulse

It was so obvious to Soviet physicist Andrei Sakharov that Soviet-type systems would stagnate and decline if they did not open up and democratize that (watching President Lyndon Johnson act on his Great Society agenda) Sakharov predicted that capitalist societies would emulate socialist ones in guaranteeing all citizens basic minimums and that Leninist dictatorships would go democratic, as had the West. The two worlds would converge.[35] Détente and democracy were predictable because inevitable.[36] If the Soviet Union did not open up, encourage creativity, rely on professionals, democratize, allow public mobility and freedom of information, then the economy would stagnate, incomes would fall, morality would decline, alcoholism, crime, and drugs would spread, and the Soviet Union would "fall behind the capitalist countries in the course of the second industrial revolution and be gradually transformed into a second-rate provincial power."[37]

A similar anxiety has motivated nationalistic reformers among ruling groups in post-Mao China.[38] In their view, either China modernizes or it will stagnate as a second-rate power and continue to lose legitimacy among an increasingly cynical and privatized population. While modernization requires democratic openness, virtually no democratic theorist in China or any other Leninist state has in recent times imagined democratization in terms of harmonies with the dominant thrust of the politics of Mao Zedong or the writings of Karl Marx. For Mao, democratization had little to do with legal due process, civil liberties, the right of an opposition to organize and win state power in competitive elections, or checks on arbitrary power. For Mao, true democracy meant using state power to smash the sources of class distinction. While he could mobilize people to attack hated officials, the result of what Mao called class struggle—as with Stalin's purges—was the use of state coercion and terror against factional and personal opponents at all levels of society.[39] Nothing democratic was achieved.

Strikingly, democrats in reforming Leninist systems do not hark back to Marx's notion of all power to the associated laborers. While there is among Chinese reformers some interest in codetermination in the workplace, and while there has been some discussion of worker-owned enterprises and democratized labor unions, there is virtually no theorizing about workers seizing power. Mao inadvertently discredited that Marxist notion in the Cultural Revolution's vigilante brutalities against technocrats, managers, and professionals—indeed, against all educated people.

In Leninist states, a major factor delegitimating the notion of democratization as power to manual laborers is the perception that in order to move up the technological ladder, to improve economic efficiency, and to become competitive in the world economy, it is necessary to rely on knowledge, not brawn; on white-collar, not blue-collar, workers; on the skilled, not the unskilled; on leaders who understand modern technology, not on political hacks.[40] The proletariat as a vanguard class (not as powerless individual workers) is experienced as being at one with the parasitic party–state officials who serve themselves first and thereby force the powerless within the nation—and the nation within the world economy—to fall further behind.

Openness to the international world of advanced science and technology is a prerequisite of democracy and development in general. And for China, it is also a prerequisite of integration in, competition with, and growth within the dynamic Pacific Rim.[41] Such international openness cannot be long sustained without a concurrent opening to democratization. As Franco's Spain opened to democracy when it gradually integrated with a democratic European Economic Community,[42] similar tendencies will predictably be unleashed in Leninist states as they seek to become integrated into a world market dominated by political democracies.[43]

Theoretical Perspectives on the Democratic Prospect

Democratization of Leninist regimes has suddenly emerged as an issue—seemingly from nowhere—because the three major contending approaches to Leninist systems essentially precluded the prospect of democratization. In totalitarian theory, which highlights the inhumanities inherent in Soviet-style regimes, there are no internal, dynamic contradictions that permit transcendence or transformation of tyranny.[44] From the theoretical perspective of orthodox Leninist-Stalinism, on the other hand, the nominally socialist state is already a functioning democracy—albeit a "people's democracy."[45] Finally, in the third major approach to Leninist systems, which stresses analysis of factions, interest groups, and bureaucratic politics, considerable insight is generated into key short-run issues—much as neoclassical economics sheds light on the relationships among prices, wages, and interest rates; however, the approach does not lend itself to addressing long-run questions about regime change—just as neoclassical economists cannot foresee changes in technological lead sectors and hegemons.

Many theories of modernization similarly tend to bracket the issue of democratization. Neither of the two dominant modernist schools, the Marxist and the Weberian, conceives of democracy as part of the solution to the postfeudal crisis.[46] Instead, solutions are sought in terms of negating the evils of capitalism or building efficient organizations or mobilizing the masses behind charismatic leadership. In both the Marxist and Weberian traditions, democracy is at best epiphenomenal and more likely an obstacle to progress. Indeed, even at the end of the 1980s, Leninist rulers who thought in Marxist terms about emulating Pacific Rim economies assumed that all that was needed was economic readjustment. Analysts in the Weberian tradition conceived of Pacific Rim success in terms of the efficient institutional adaptations of soft, authoritarian developmental states.[47] In neither case was democracy part of the solution.[48] The categories of established social scientific comprehension slighted the democratic agenda.

There are, of course, ways to think of the rise of the East Asian economies that do focus on the issue of democracy. Japan's post–World War II success was made possible by the legalization of unions and the legitimation of interest groups and competitive parties. This constrained Japanese planners to pay careful attention to rising socioeconomic expectations at home—which became the basis of Japan's successful export drive. Democratization and development were similarly facilitated by land reform, which destroyed concentrated landlord power. As the cases of England, Sweden, and post–World War II Japan demonstrate, democratization is more solid when based on a broad alliance that includes an independent commercialized peasantry.[49] Decollectivizing the Leninist system may thus be seen as a prerequisite of democratization.

Authoritarian industrialization, wherein labor cannot demand a fair share and capital is not democratically competitive, invariably rests on a fragile and volatile foundation, as revealed in the cases of South Korea in the 1970s, prewar Japan, and Bismarck's Germany.[50] While authoritarian industrialization involving great popular sacrifice is no doubt possible, equitably shared sacrifice—made easier by democracy—can best provide the necessary social tranquility and successful path through the painful retooling and restructuring of the economy, both requisites for modernization in the poststeel era.[51]

Recent theories of political change, rather than taking a long and comparative view of large-scale democratization in earlier eras, tend to focus narrowly on the present moment.[52] Attracted by an extraordinary series of post-1973 political developments from Greece to Argentina, much of the current writing on democratization treats the process as one of redemocratization. Tellingly, this category comfortably includes a democratizing Czechoslovakia (conquered by Soviet forces in 1948 and crushed by those same forces in 1968), but excludes a China that has never known democracy and has never gone through Renaissance, Reformation, or Enlightenment.

Restructuring the Leninist Leviathan

An issue that is missing in a focus on redemocratization is how aging, steel-based, uncompetitive, gargantuan, labor-intensive industries such as Poland's Lenin Shipyard must be restructured as part of a larger undoing of the command economy,[53] accompanied by a redoing of the Leninist system to replace the nomenklatura with competitively elected officials and professional civil servants; replacing the lawless, pervasive police with an independent judiciary and individual rights; and replacing the party's monopoly on truth with a democratic equity pact.

To theorize about democracy in terms of the discrediting of a feudal-like state incapable of managing a more modern economy, as this chapter does, leads to a focus on the earlier democratizations of Holland and England rather than on Greece and Argentina in the late twentieth century. This approach directs attention to the striking similarities between contemporary Leninist state quandaries and those experienced in an earlier democratizing epoch.

China's modernization process will undoubtedly find its own particular way of negating its premodern inheritance, just as the Netherlands, England, and France were shaped by their rooted particularities. Cultural norms have been reinforced by Leninist forms. The key point, as stated by China's noted democratic writer Liu Binyan, is that not only had China's initial May Fourth (1919) drive to win democracy by destroying feudalism failed, but that the Leninist system, far from burying the corpse of feudalism, had carried on its spirit and breathed into it new life.[54] Its "management principles modeled on the feudal patriarchal system are a step backward from capitalism."[55] Its use of marriage as a way of cementing political obligations and networks made in-law relationships "twice as important as they ever were in feudal society."[56] The result of the system was that a leader, "though he lives in a socialist society in ... the twentieth century, dreams the dreams of an eighteenth century feudal monarch."[57] So manifest and palpable is the analogy with the vicissitudes of reform in the late absolutist monarchies of Europe that the government of China in the early 1980s censored all writings premised on this analogy.

Even in the cases of the Netherlands and Britain, historians tend to agree that political democracy is not the immediate consequence of a rising bourgeoisie and its revolution. Instead, democratization reflects a political seizure of opportunities and openings, a grasping of particular contingencies and conjunctions— as, for example, when the need to raise taxes for public purposes or to mobilize for war constrains elites to permit greater political access on the part of a larger portion of the citizenry. As part of the costly restructuring of wasteful and inefficient Leninist systems, the challenge of shared sacrifice to meet contemporary global, technical, and economic competition may offer just such a conjunctural possibility. In a situation of systemic crisis, Leninist ruling groups cannot succeed with halfway reforms; the center loses money, taxes seem inequitable (if not corrupt), and the only alternative to democracy is more inflation. In order to mobilize popular action or sacrifice from citizens, Leninist elites, acting in their own interest, may thus be compelled to consider including the citizenry in the political process.[58]

Reactionary Alternatives to Democratization

Yet it is possible for reactionary Leninist rulers, in their desire to maintain power at any price, to substitute a populist, ersatz democracy of nativistic scapegoating for the real thing—as was done by the German kaiser and the Russian czar. The implicit nativism of Chinese leaders, who treated violent student riots against Africans in December of 1988 much more gently than they treated peaceful demonstrations for democracy a few months later, offers an instructive comparison. Something dangerous is at work when frustrated male Chinese students and young male workers in Nanjing, anxious about marriage, money, and housing, become enraged at the sight of supposedly inferior Africans, amply supplied by the Chinese government with money and living space, also dating Chinese women. The whole system seems illegitimate when native virtue goes unrewarded while foreigners cavort at Chinese government expense.

Chinese tell stories of their officials allowing African students to get away with bullying, berating, or beating up Chinese. They view Chinese women involved with African men not as dates but as prostitutes lacking patriotic dignity, selling out national pride for a fistful of money.

Patriarchy and patriotism, gender chauvinism, and national chauvinism are emotional forces that fuel explosive passions. The scarcities and inequities of daily life in China, while foreigners are pampered in luxury hotels and air-conditioned buses, serve to reinforce a militant chauvinist perception that foreigners routinely exploit Chinese—who must then fight back to regain their dignity. Perceptions of repeated humiliation at the hands of foreigners fan the flames of populist xenophobia. When Indonesia, Vietnam, and Albania turned against China in the 1960s and 1970s after having been recipients of Chinese foreign aid, it reinforced the experience of many ordinary Chinese that their country's leaders had rewarded undeserving foreigners and slighted long-suffering Chinese. In a similar vein, student demonstrators in 1986 ridiculed China's rulers for failing to take the Diaoyutai Islands back from Japan,[59] and in 1988 criticized those same rulers for failing to block the continued separate existence of a rival "Republic of China" on Taiwan.[60]

Populist scapegoating hurts the democratic cause. While prodemocratic activists have sought to mobilize popular sentiments to discredit the excessive patriotism of China's rulers, opponents of reform have found it convenient to turn populist xenophobia against reformers, accusing them of selling out the nation to "polluting" foreigners.[61] Reformers usually retreat in the face of such scapegoating tactics, thus further legitimating a reactionary chauvinism that threatens to undermine reform, openness, and democracy. Democracy demonstrators in Beijing in spring 1989 almost never identified themselves that way. Instead, they called their struggle a patriotic movement. The same populist nativism that presents the disease AIDS as yet another evil foreign import that kills innocent Chinese also renders it extremely difficult to challenge the view that excessive permissiveness and liberalization are the root causes of pro-independence riots in an ungrateful Tibet, requiring harsh martial law. Chauvinism pervades China.

Populist Movements and the Search for Dignity

As they struggle to regain their lost dignity, the Chinese people find little evidence—except in the military sphere—that they have actually stood up, as Mao claimed at the time of the founding of the People's Republic.[62] The perception that China's Leninist state system has not permitted the people to stand up is strikingly put in Zhang Jie's novella, *The Ark*. She writes:

It has started all over again, this life of pleading and begging. Whether you wanted to get a divorce, an apartment to live in or a suitable job, it always involved grovelling at the feet of others in the hope that they would show pity and understanding. What was so extraordinary about such requests? They were not asking for more than their fair share. When would Liu Quan at last know what it felt like to stand up proud and straight? She was not yet old, but she felt as if her back had been bent for a whole long lifetime.[63]

In the months preceding the Tiananmen crisis of 1989, people gossiped openly about a corrupt and hypocritical elite that feathered its own nest at the expense of the bent-over people. Tales spread of children of rulers residing in cushy foreign posts or growing rich as middlemen in trading companies, grabbing superprofits without contributing any real productive labor and thereby contributing to spiraling retail prices paid by hard-working, innocent Chinese on the supposedly "free" market. In 1988, Deng Xiaoping, China's paramount leader, had to reprimand his own son, who was running a firm said to be imposing monopoly prices on imported television sets.

The Nanjing anti-African riots of December 1988 showed the explosiveness of the conflict between Leninist rulers who refuse to concede to genuine democratic demands and an outraged people who insist on a right to articulate their own interests. Mistrust of government officials helped spark the outburst in Nanjing. Similar frustrations had earlier fueled a riotous celebration in Beijing after the defeat of Japan's volleyball team[64] and an angry riot in Beijing upon China's being defeated by Hong Kong in soccer.

In 1985 and 1986, populist xenophobia took a more political turn. Demonstrations against Japanese merchants, portrayed as venal, dishonest, and corrupting of Chinese officials, provided a thin mask for naked contempt toward hypocritical, parasitical power holders, conceived as betraying their own people by imposing high prices while grabbing unearned, speculative profits for themselves through foreign connections.[65] This widespread contempt for corrupt, self-serving officials erupted briefly—but powerfully—in the massive antigovernment demonstrations of April and May 1989. This contempt has deep roots and long branches.

Viewing the democratic reform movement through the prism of their own struggles, in 1986 democratic intellectuals sought to memorialize the victims of the cruel, massive purge of educated people in 1957, only to find their path blocked by Deng Xiaoping, who had played a key role in the 1957 repression. As a sign of his displeasure, Deng assented to a purge of reformist Party Secretary Hu Yaobang and launched a campaign against bourgeois liberalization, threatening to spill the blood of future proponents of democracy.

The Democracy Movement of 1989

In the light of such events, China's democrats concluded by the spring of 1989 that if they did not act to change China's direction, then, as had been the case for generations, once again reactionary rulers would drag the Chinese people away from the changes required to win them the blessing of the modern world. Among educated people, this feeling was intensified by a series of debates in 1988–89. Party General Secretary Zhao Ziyang made a desperate attempt to woo paramount leader Deng Xiaoping away from reactionary Party elders by embracing the notion of a neoauthoritarian transition to modernity which did not require democratic political reforms and which could be built on the foundation of China's Confucian culture—much as (supposedly) had occurred in Japan, South Korea, Taiwan, and Singapore. The Chinese gerontocracy remained unmoved, however. Represented by General Wang Zhen, who reportedly prided himself on his illiteracy, they led the successful campaign against reform leader Hu Yaobang, banned the television series *River Elegy*, which traced China's downfall as a world power to its nativistic ancient culture, and put the brakes on all further structural reform.[66]

Muckraking journalists like Liu Binyan were silenced when they wrote that nationalism had to be tempered. Democratizers who called attention to the privilege, corruption, and tyranny of the conservative military were likewise silenced.[67] Meanwhile, China's post-Mao rulers continued to embrace as supreme symbols of legitimation successes with atomic bombs, hydrogen bombs, and intercontinental missiles.[68]

By early 1989 students and democrats realized that immediate action was needed to reverse a reactionary chauvinism pulling the Chinese people back toward the nineteenth century instead of pushing them forward to the twenty-first. A nascent civil society emerged as citizens began to organize in their own interest. Official preparations for the celebration of the seventieth anniversary of the May Fourth Movement, which had in 1919 embraced democracy and science, produced convoluted claims by conservative Party propagandists that victory had already been won and that therefore people who attacked feudalism today were actually traitors demeaning China's glorious culture. This direct, frontal challenge provoked many more students to openly embrace democratic values as practiced elsewhere. They ridiculed the Confucianism of senior leaders as a self-serving national betrayal similar to that of earlier reactionary rulers such as Yuan Shikai and the Empress Dowager. And they concluded that China needed a more powerful May Fourth student/citizen movement for democracy. With reactionary rulers fearful of losing everything and democrats believing that all would be lost if they did not risk themselves, the two forces moved inexorably toward a clash.

Much remains unknown about top-level maneuverings and divisions within the Party and military during the spring 1989 flowering of democracy. It seems that Deng himself, as in 1957, played a key role in carrying out the conservative agenda. One wonders what might have happened had some top Politburo leaders been willing to oppose Deng and his senior allies publicly, or had Party Secretary Zhao Ziyang early on turned to embrace the hundreds of thousands of demonstrators. Perhaps a democratic opening might have been won. But the Leninist system which kept those higher-ups in power would have had to go. For whatever reason, reform leaders within the Party, government, and military vacillated at the critical moment, allowing Deng to unite with the reactionary gerontocrats and their allies within the government and military to kill the flower of democracy.

Conclusion: The Future of Leninism

Notwithstanding the brutal Chinese crackdown of June 1989, the crisis of the permanent technological revolution cannot be solved by reactionary Leninism. There are some remaining state leaders whose hands are not bloodied who could seize another opportunity to join the citizenry against the delegitimized Leninist state. Meanwhile, Deng and his allies can appeal to superpatriotism and historic values to woo those harmed or placed under stress by the effects of modernizing reforms. There are in contemporary Leninist states large numbers of people who, as in late feudal times, fear losing their small guild protections. The transition from a rigid, feudal-style autocracy to a dynamic society capable of technologically competing in the world market inevitably causes painful stresses, losses, and frictions. Without genuine democratization, Leninist rulers face an increasingly difficult and complex political problem—how to hold on to the levers of power while continuing modernizing reforms. Enlightenment aristocrats in late-eighteenth-century France failed; revolution ensued. Bismarck in late-nineteenth-century Germany succeeded in holding on to power and continuing with modernization—but only by not alienating traditional rural and military bases of power, that is, by not continuing with political reforms. Instead, Bismarck and his conservative successors displayed military toughness abroad while conceding to racist populism at home by scapegoating some of the new domestic rich as not real Germans.

Similar historical dynamics are at work in China. Caught on the sharp horns of an insoluble dilemma, China's rulers—like Bismarck in Germany—have embraced much that is reactionary and chauvinistic. It is a dangerous path. The crisis is systemic but the question of which way to turn is clearly political. The struggle continues between revolutionary democracy and reactionary Leninism.

As with post-Bismarck Germany, Taisho Japan, or post-1905 Russia, what the crisis of Leninism reveals is not that democracy *must* win, but that it *may* win. Economic challenges offer an opening. Politics determine if the opening will evolve into democratic political forms. Consequently, as in post–French Revolution Europe, conservatives may win for a while. Likewise, military force may temporarily gain the upper hand. As demonstrated at Tiananmen and Timisoara, naked coercion can be employed to suppress democrats. Neighboring countries may suffer. Nonetheless, the historical forces that gave rise to the democratic impulse are undiminished; and the issue of democratization cannot but remain high on a basic and continuing political agenda.[69]

Notes

1. William H. Luers, "Don't Humiliate Gorbachev," New York Times, January 30, 1989; Shaomin Li, "The Road to Freedom: Can Communist Societies Evolve into Democracies," Issues and Studies (Taiwan) 24, No. 6 (June 1988), pp. 92–104. The scholarly editors of a three-volume study of democratization decided not to include any Communist countries because "there is little prospect among them of a transition to democracy" (Larry Diamond, Juan Linz, and Seymour Martin Lipset, eds., Democracy in Developing Countries: Asia [Boulder, CO: Lynne Rienner, 1989], p. xix). A classic statement of the view that Leninist states cannot be democratized from within is in Jeane Kirkpatrick, Dictatorships and Double-Standards (New York: Simon and Schuster, 1982).

2. In the late 1940s, it was generally assumed that Confucianism blocked modernization; by the 1980s, however, the common view was that Confucianism facilitated modernization. The British historian Maitland has described cultural explanation of historical outcomes as "a sort of deus ex machina, which is invoked to settle any problems which cannot readily be solved by ordinary methods of rational investigation." Cited in Peter Geyl, Debates with Historians (New York: Meridian Books, 1958), p. 212.

3. Influential theorists adopting this perspective include Schumpeter, Kuznets, Vernon, Rostow, and Kondratieff. That a permanent technological revolution was in place by the eighteenth century and contributed to democratization is argued in Roy Porter and Mikulas Teich, eds., Revolution in History (Cambridge: Cambridge University Press, 1986).

4. For a history and theory of flexible production as superior to Fordist production, see Michael Piore and Charles Sabel, The Second Industrial Divide (New York: Basic Books, 1984). For an argument that flexible production facilitates democratization in Leninist states, see Edward Friedman, "Theorizing the Democratization of China's Leninist State," in Arif Dirlik and Maurice Meisner, eds., Marxism and the Chinese Experience (Armonk, NY: M. E. Sharpe, 1989). The relevant problem for Leninist systems is not that mass production is outdated but that a system solely defined by that logic is anachronistic.

5. See Elizabeth Valkenier, The Soviet Union and the Third World (New York: Praeger, 1983), pp. 90 ff.; and Richard P. Suttmeier, "Science, Technology and China's Political Future," in Denis Simon and Merle Goldman, eds., Science and Technology in the Post-Mao Era (Cambridge, MA: Harvard University Council on East Asian Studies, 1989), pp. 375–96.

6. Hungarian democratic leader Janos Kis finds that "[R]uling parties are seeking to make room in the power structure for a legal opposition with the design of using its authority to legitimize austerity measures and demobilize social resistance" (J. Kis, "Poland and Hungary in Transition," Journal of Democracy 1, No. 1 [Winter 1990], p. 76). Similarly, Vladimir Bukovsky finds democracy the best way to solve "the problem of converting an extensive and inefficient economy into an 'intensive' and productive one" (V. Bukovsky, "Squaring the Circle," Journal of Democracy 1, No. 1 [Winter 1990], p. 87). Barrington Moore, Jr., highlights the importance of social compact or equity pact among groups as being essential to the democratic route to modernity. See his Social Origins of Dictatorship and Democracy (Boston: Beacon Press, 1966), p. 415. For an application of Moore's theory to East Europe, see Gale Stokes, "The Social Origins of East European Politics," Eastern European Politics and Societies 1, No. 1 (1987), pp. 30–74.

7. The Chinese democrat Fang Lizhi makes this point: "Just as in the case of making the atomic bomb, the first scientist to make one got the Nobel Prize, but now any student of high-energy physics understands the principles. . . . It is not too difficult to repeat what someone else has done" (*Ming Bao*, July 1988, translated in *Joint Publications Research Service* [hereafter *JPRS*] CAR–88–061, October 3, 1988, p. 4).

8. There is much persuasive data on the long crisis of the sixteenth and seventeenth centuries that served to facilitate popular movements—such as creation of the democratic Netherlands—against wasteful courts incapable of organizing for wealth expansion, food delivery, and legitimate taxation. See Geoffrey Parker and Lesley Smith, eds., *The General Crisis of the Seventeenth Century* (London: Routledge and Kegan Paul, 1978).

9. Hernando De Soto, *The Other Path: The Invisible Revolution in the Third World* (New York: Harper and Row, 1989), spells out this historical analogy between the mercantilist states of old and today. The scriptwriters of the Chinese television series *River Elegy* are also well aware of this similarity when they speak of "officially sanctioned monopoly rights and a privileged stratum having authority over the distribution of commodities." (The script is translated in JPRS-CAR–88–002-L, December 6, 1988. They equate the promise of China's opening to the world in the late twentieth century with that earlier opening. "The ships that began to sail the open seas in the fifteenth century . . . carried the hope of science and democracy," p. 34.)

10. This experience was consciously heightened in the immediate post-Mao era by the Deng Xiaoping group, which circulated to schools, enterprises, and government agencies videocassettes of travelogues from Taiwan and other similar material. The contrast with Japan is made in the television series *River Elegy*, in which it is noted that whereas at the start of Mao's Great Leap "China's gross national product was about the same as Japan's, by 1985 it was only one-fifth of Japan's" (*JPRS*, note 9, p. 24).

11. Alec Nove, *Political Economy and Soviet Socialism* (London: George Allen and Unwin, 1979), ch. 2; Robert C. Tucker, "Stalinism as Revolution from Above," in Robert C. Tucker, ed., *Stalinism* (New York: W. W. Norton, 1977), esp. pp. 97–100. A classic statement of this equivalence of Leninist socialism with backward, feudal absolutism is Ryszard Kapuscinski, *Emperor* (New York: Vintage Books, 1983 [1978]).

12. Kenneth Jowett, *The Leninist Response to National Dependency* (Berkeley: Institute of International Studies, 1978).

13. Tang Tsou, *The Cultural Revolution and Post-Mao Reforms* (Chicago: University of Chicago Press, 1986), ch. 5. Chinese political philosopher Wang Ruoshui argues that the habit of blaming corrupt, arbitrary power and privilege on class enemies, so common in the Maoist era, made sense to Chinese because feudal culture led Chinese to assume that democracy meant benevolent despots rather than public servants: "Due to the deep influence of feudal ideology, our discussion of democracy has been limited to how leaders should understand the people. An upright feudal official and a good emperor could be democratic if they accepted others' advice. . . . We have to correct this misunderstanding. First, democracy is the system of a country under which the people have the right not only to criticize but also to supervise, vote, recall, etc." (Wang Ruoshui, *Wei rendaozhuyi bianhu* [Beijing: Sanlien Publishers, 1983], in JPRS-CAR–88–056, September 19, 1988, p. 15). Earlier moments in this democratic critique of socialist feudalism are explicated in Edward Friedman, "The Social Obstacle to China's Socialist Transition: State Capitalism or Feudal Fascism?" in Victor Nee and David Mozingo, eds., *State and Society in Contemporary China* (Ithaca: Cornell University Press, 1983), pp. 148–71.

14. Lowell Dittmer, *China's Continuous Revolution* (Berkeley: University of California Press, 1987), pp. 58, 79, 245.

15. Andrew Walder, *Communist Neo-Traditionalism* (Berkeley: University of California Press, 1986).

16. Included in Robert C. Tucker, ed., *The Lenin Anthology* (New York: W. W. Norton, 1975), p. 632. Nikolai Schmeleve and Vladimir Popov similarly cite Lenin's concept of socialism as, "Soviet power plus the Prussian railway system plus American technology and organization of trusts plus American public education" Schmeleve and Popov, *Revitalizing the Soviet Economy* (New York: Doubleday, 1989), p. 4.

17. V. I. Lenin, *Imperialism* (New York: International Publishers, 1939), p. 68.

18. Tucker, *Lenin*, p. 187.

19. Ibid., p. 199.

20. Ibid., p. 361.

21. Lenin, *Imperialism*, p. 119.

22. Ibid., p. 39.

23. Ibid., p. 58.

24. Ibid., p. 25.

25. Cited in Ulysses Santamaria and Alain Manville, "Lenin and the Problem of the Transition," Telos 27 (Spring 1976), p. 80.

26. Ibid., p. 81.

27. Ibid., p. 83.

28. Ibid., p. 82. It was democratic socialists in Germany, arguing for an electoral path to power, who first contended that given the socialized economy created by state capitalism, their party's democratic conquest of state power would guarantee the full victory of socialism.

29. Lenin, *Imperialism*, p. 28.

30. Robert Conquest, *The Harvest of Sorrow* (New York: Oxford University Press, 1986). Schmeleve and Popov, *Revitalizing*, find war mobilization to be the essence of the Leninist system.

31. See Edward Friedman, "Decollectivization and Democratization in China," *Problems of Communism* 38, No. 5 (September–October 1989), pp. 103–7. This centralized "war communism" attack on the peasantry was carried yet further, first by Mao and then by Pol Pot. See Friedman, "After Mao," *Telos* 65 (Fall 1985), pp. 23–46.

32. David Friedman, *The Misunderstood Miracle* (Ithaca: Cornell University Press, 1988).

33. David Halberstam, *The Reckoning* (New York: Avon Books, 1986) ch. 5.

34. Jay Tuck, *The T Directorate* (New York: St. Martin's Press, 1986). KGB defector Stanislav Levchenko reports the organization's mission in Japan as "getting our hands on as many high technology items as possible" (*On the Wrong Side* [New York: Pergamon-Brassey's, 1988], p. 102).

35. Andrei Sakharov, *Sakharov Speaks* (New York: Vintage Books, 1974), pp. 54, 105.

36. Ibid., p. 100.

37. Ibid., p. 132. In contrast, C. B. McPherson (*The Real World of Democracy* [New York: Oxford University Press, 1972], p. 17) found Soviet rulers "within sight of their goal of a classless society."

38. Edward Friedman, "Maoist and Post-Mao Conceptualizations of World Capitalism: Opportunities and/or Dangers," in Samuel Kim, ed., *China and the World*, 2d ed. (Boulder, CO: Westview Press, 1989).

39. J. Arthur Getty, *Origins of the Great Purges* (Cambridge: Cambridge University Press, 1985), argues that Stalin predated Mao in unleashing the rank and file against the established bureaucracy in the name of political purity, democracy, and the rights of the party rank and file (pp. 242, 105, 195, 206). Only in the subsequent wartime need of the Soviet Union for national unity did Stalin protect the corrupt, privileged bureaucracy and become the precursor of the Brezhnev era.

40. The script for *River Elegy* reflects this view in its comment: " 'Those who operate on skulls make less than those who shave heads, and those who play the piano make less than those who move pianos.' Payment for mental labor and physical labor is turned upside down" (*JPRS*, note 9, p. 24).

41. In this perspective, the key citation from Karl Marx is the following: "The Pacific Ocean will have the same role as the Atlantic has now and the Mediterranean had in antiquity and in the Middle Ages—that of the great water highway of world commerce; and the Atlantic will decline to the status of an inland sea, like the Mediterranean nowadays." (Cited in B. Klyuchnikov, "The Soviet Far East in the Pacific Century," *Far Eastern Affairs* 4 [1988], p. 7).

42. See Edward Malefakis, "Spain and Its Francoist Heritage," in John Herz, ed., *From Dictatorship to Democracy* (Westport, CT.: Greenwood Press, 1982), pp. 215–30.

43. Democrats in Taiwan and Hong Kong have long argued this larger significance for their local efforts. Deng Xiaoping and his allies condemn the conspiracy of democratic reformers in China and world market integrationists in the industrialized democracies for trying to roll back communism. The threat to China's dictatorship from the new moment in modernization is palpable.

44. Consequently, many analysts have focused on the Hungarian revolution of 1956 as if it were mainly a nationalistic struggle. General Bela Kiraly, leader of Hungary's freedom fighters, responded that their struggle was "*for* democracy" and "against the secret police." The goal was "reform within the Party . . . [and] internal democracy in the Communist Party" (Michael Charlton, *The Eagle and the Small Birds* [Chicago: University of Chicago Press, 1984], pp. 124, 125).

45. It is symbolic of the delegitimation of this tradition that Samir Amin writes, "The dogma of a single and monolithic party is, therefore, antithetical to socialist democracy." The "absence of even bourgeois democracy signals that the Soviet state is oppressive and exploitive." "Democracy, which is an historical product of the bourgeois revolutions in the West, represents a decisively progressive step in the evolution of human society" (*The Future of Maoism* [New York: Monthly Review Press, 1981], pp. 121, 99, 98).

46. Ira J. Cohen, "The Underemphasis on Democracy in Marx and Weber," in Robert Antonio and Ronald Glassman, eds., *A Weber–Marx Dialogue* (St. Lawrence, KS: University Press of Kansas, 1985), pp. 274–95.

47. Koji Taira, "Japan's Modern Economic Growth: Capitalist Development Under Absolutism," in Harry Wray and Hilary Conroy, eds., *Japan Examined* (Honolulu: University of Hawaii Press, 1983), pp. 34–41; Chalmers Johnson, "Political Institutions and Economic Performance," in Frederick Deyo, ed., *The Political Economy of the New Asian Industrialism* (Ithaca: Cornell University Press, 1987), pp. 136–64. For the social science literature on whether dictatorial states facilitate economic development, see E. William Dick, "Authoritarian Versus Nonauthoritarian Approaches to Economic Development," *Journal of Political Economy*, July–August 1974, pp. 817–28; Erich Weede, "The Impact of Democracy on Economic Growth," *Kylos* 36 (1983), pp. 21–39.

48. But since, as David Friedman (note 32) shows, militarist Japan's economy was one of flexible production, one cannot argue that in itself flexible production leads to democracy. The poststeel new technologies, which require instantaneous, horizontal communication and coordination, help erode dictatorship. But political action is still required at the state center. Barrington Moore, Jr., concludes that with respect to both freedom and prosperity, "it was the atomic bomb and MacArthur's occupation . . . that broke the shackles of Japan's ancient regime" ("Japanese Peasant Protests and Revolts in Comparative Perspective," *International Review of Social History* 33 [1988], pp. 327, 328).

49. See Joseph Femia, "Barrington Moore and the Preconditions for Democracy," *British Journal of Political Science* 2, No. 1 (January 1972), pp. 21–46; Jonathan Tumin,

"The Theory of Democratic Development," *Theory and Society* 11 (1982), pp. 143–64; D. A. Rustow, "Transitions to Democracy," *Comparative Politics* 2 (1970), pp. 337–363; Franklin Castles, "Barrington Moore's Thesis and Swedish Political Development," *Government and Oppositions* 8, No. 3 (1973), pp. 313–31.

50. Rahl Dahrendorf, *Society and Democracy in Germany* (New York: W. W. Norton, 1979). Antidemocrats in both the Soviet Union and China romanticize South Korea's experience as an iron fist or neoauthoritarian path to wealth and power, ignoring the explosive fragility of Korea in the 1970s.

51. The problem for noninsulated rulers is that mutually beneficial international openness can appear to vulnerable sectors of the society as betrayal and sellout of the nation to foreigners.

52. See Guillermo O'Donnell et al., eds., *Transitions from Authoritarian Rule* (Baltimore: The Johns Hopkins University Press, 1986).

53. This is argued in detail in Roman Laba's Ph.D. dissertation on Poland's Solidarity (University of Wisconsin, Department of Political Science, 1989), to be published by Princeton University Press.

54. Personal conversation, December 1988.

55. Liu Binyan, *People or Monsters* (Bloomington: Indiana University Press, 1983), p. 8.

56. Ibid., p. 52.

57. Ibid., p. 61.

58. David Mason, cited in Gregory Flynn, "Problems in Paradigm," *Foreign Policy* 74 (Spring 1989), p. 67. Cf. the articles by Kis and Bukovsky, note 6.

59. Allen S. Whiting, "The Politics of Sino-Japanese Relations," in June Teufel Dreyer and Ilpyong J. Kim, eds., *Chinese Defense and Foreign Policy* (New York: Professors World Peace Academy, 1989), p. 143.

60. Personal report from Nanjing.

61. Since the Communist Party's official historians of the Mao era denounced reformers as traitors, reform democrats in the post-Mao era not only legitimate earlier reformers such as Yan Fu and Liang Qichao who struggled for "civil rights," "ruler . . . chosen by the public and dismissed by the public," and "constitutionalism," but these democrats also equate today's opponents of reform with earlier reactionaries protecting vested interests. (See Li Honglin, "Looking at the Reform Movement of 1898 Ninety Years Afterward," *Xin Guancha*, November 25, 1988, in JPRS-CAR–89–014, February 15, 1989, pp. 7–9.)

62. Patriotic Chinese take pleasure therefore in selling expensive weapons to foreign nations to the displeasure of U.S. government officials.

63. Zhang Jie, *Love Must Not Be Forgotten* (Beijing: Panda Books, 1986), p. 159.

64. On anti-Japanese sentiment, see Whiting, "Politics," pp. 135–65.

65. Debates in China on Japanese brutality are explosive. Writer Bai Hua said of the Nanjing massacre, "Nanjing had a defense force two and a half times the size of the Japanese army. . . . [But] the commander-in-chief . . . panicked and fled; the people were left without a leader and Nanjing was lost. Within six weeks, the Japanese took 300,000 lives. Even the Japanese could not believe it. Once 135 Japanese soldiers even managed to capture 13,000 Chinese soldiers, and tied them up, ten to a bundle . . . and slaughtered them all. Just by sheer number of bodies, these 13,000 men could have overwhelmed the Japanese, but they were full of cowardly hope, and nobody resisted. In the end, they were all killed." Bai Hua's point is that a narrow, materialistic, and fatalistic culture of survival, as in the days of Japan's occupation, still threatens China today, when rulers "resemble serf owners," because people still try to get by rather than sacrifice themselves for democracy (*Jiushi Niandai*, November 1988, in JPRS-CAR–89–005, January 13, 1989, pp. 59, 60).

Bai Hua's vision of a culture which leads Chinese to be "thankful for being able to survive for one more hour" was criticized as an apology for the murderous Japanese, equivalent to a Jew apologizing for Nazi genocide (*Jiushi Niandai*, January 1989, in JPRS-CAR–89–014, February 15, 1989, pp. 51–53).

66. For a study which focuses on the reactionary role of the gerentocracy, see Liu Binyan, *Tell The World* (New York: Pantheon, 1989).

67. These exposés of the military include: "What If I Were Real?" in Perry Link, ed., *Stubborn Weeds* (Bloomington: Indiana University Press, 1983), pp. 198–250; "General, You Can't Do This!" in Helen Siu and Zelda Stern, eds., *Mao's Harvest* (New York: Oxford University Press, 1983), pp. 158–71.

68. See John Wilson Lewis and Xue Litai, *China Builds the Bomb* (Stanford: Stanford University Press, 1988).

69. With the Leninist-Stalinist path to modernity discredited, the clash between traditionalist chauvinists and democratic reformers resembles similar struggles in the era before World War I and the Bolshevik Revolution, whose outcomes were not invariably favorable to the democrats. See, e.g., Ervand Abrahamian, *Iran Between Two Revolutions* (Princeton: Princeton University Press, 1982).

Chapter 15

Democracy and "Mao Fever"

In the hearts of many, Mao Zedong is still a mysterious figure, a 'god' that appears only once every 500 years[1]

In an interview celebrating the centennial of Mao Zedong's birth, Chinese leader Bo Yibo acknowledged that "how to evaluate Mao's thought and his historical position has been a very complex and sensitive problem." Bo simply explained Mao's failures in harmony with the official line that Mao's errors began "in the latter half of 1957." Bo chalked it up "to an overestimation of both international and domestic class struggle and a cocky and impatient urging for success."[2] A college student put the official contrast between the good early Mao and the bad late Mao more pointedly. "He liberated China, saving 400 million people. He mobilized the Cultural Revolution, ruining 800 million citizens."[3]

The American Marxist journal *Monthly Review*, in contrast to the official line in China, unabashedly celebrated Mao for his later efforts. The Mao of the antirightist movement, the Great Leap, the Third Front, and the Cultural Revolution was embraced as the primary mover against conservatives and capitalist roaders in the Party. He "believed that coping effectively with China's fundamental problems would be possible only in a socialist society in which the real interests of people, long-suffering and desperately poor, would be paramount."[4] Anticapitalists and revolutionaries should build on Mao's supposed great achievement. Increasingly, *Monthly Review* has described the Maoist Sendero Luminoso, an annihilationist group in Peru, as carrying forward the Maoist mission.

In opposition to *Monthly Review*'s praise of Mao, the Western media has enjoyed poking fun at China's Mao fever, as in the March 21, 1994, *Nation* magazine story, "China Goes Pop; Mao Meets Muzak." Visitors notice that

---

Originally published in *The Journal of Contemporary China*, No. 6 (Summer 1994). Reprinted with permission.

millions in the city who drive use his image as insurance against accident, while many tens of millions of gamblers in China's countryside pray to his icon for good luck before they wager. Visitors find humor in China's Mao fever.

> At Shaoshan . . . where Mao was born . . . an oriental Jerusalem has emerged complete with rows of stalls selling trinkets. The only god is *mammon*.
> In . . . Yanan, . . . Karaoke bars . . . include an up-tempo version of *The East Is Red*, mock the austere "spirit of Yanan."[5]

In Beijing's Xidan district, a restaurant called "The Remember Bitterness, Imagine Sweetness Restaurant" opened in October 1993. It celebrates a *nouveau riche* conquest of poverty, offering a nostalgic and rustic atmosphere and exotic insect dishes served with the strongest machismo alcohol, not the inedible fare of the actual "remember bitterness" meals of the Cultural Revolution era. The exotic restaurant meal is followed by a free ride home by human-drawn pedicab. As perceived by Western reporters, Mao fever mocked Mao.

Elsewhere in Beijing, Tang Ruiren serves Shaoshan food in the "Mao Family Restaurant," which prominently displays a picture of Mao back home in Shaoshan thirty-plus years earlier with local people, Mrs. Tang, babe in arms, prominent among them. The reporter comments:

> Mao would turn in his crystal sarcophagus if he could see the . . . karaoke room complete with flashing disco lights, a bar, an illuminated dance floor, and drinking booths lit by a soft red glow.

One customer insisted that rather than being nostalgic for Mao, the Mao Family Restaurant reflected a contemporary quest for anything and everything new and different. "[Y]ou could open a restaurant called Hitler's and people would go to it."[6]

In contrast to this ridiculing of Mao fever, China's fundamentalists have made use of the Mao fever.

> Under the guise of reviving patriotic education and remembering Chairman Mao, the Propaganda Department has reinstated a large number of products of the Cultural Revolution, including "model revolutionary" operas and songs favored by the Gang of Four.[7]

Legitimating intensified repression, the Mao fever is not a laughing matter.

My own approach is to take Mao very seriously and try to situate him in his Leninist intellectual tradition. To be sure, no single approach can capture all the multifaceted aspects of Mao. But Mao Zedong's political project is best understood as a descendent of the Jacobin heritage that moved out of France through Babeuf, Bounorotti, Blanqui, Lavrov, and Lenin. This antimarket and superpatriotic Jacobin mobilization, which legitimates a terroristic tyranny in the name of

Enlightenment ideals, commandeers basic foods for rations at below-market prices and privileges the army and its support network and deploys a pervasive police network to search out and destroy counter-revolutionaries and traitors while rewarding the superloyal.

The tradition that China's Communists institutionalized was Lenin's continual struggle to avoid the fate of the defeated Jacobins, whose heads were chopped off in the French Revolution's Thermidor. Lenin made use of Stalin's analysis of the nationalities problem to privilege the dominant national group as truly proletarian, a project that in fact led to a war not only against the culture of all minorities but also to a war against so-called nonproletarian elements of the dominant nationality's culture as part of an effort to discredit and suppress all authentic societal forces.

A life-or-death effort to consolidate state power against enemies real, potential, or imagined required an all-out mobilizing of a "permanent and irreconcilable war with the outside world,"[8] with their own people treated "as building material for fantastic structures designed by men who know no peace."[9] Lenin erroneously believed that "the Jacobins' catastrophic economic policy had brought magnificent results, but having imitated it during the period of so-called 'war communism,' Lenin realized that the country was on the brink of an abyss and ordered the retreat early enough not to share the fate of Robespierre."[10] Thus, because the Jacobin project is inherently self-defeating, its progenitors inevitably compromise with it to survive. They promote market-oriented New Economic Policies (NEP), thereby inviting back in the forces that supposedly continue to threaten it, again legitimating a total and cruel mobilization against all enemies, foreign or domestic. After his Great Leap famine, Mao conceded to reformers, only to resume war-communism mobilization with various campaigns from 1964–65 to 1971–72, legitimated by the war mobilization known as the Third Front.

To those who inquire why China and Russia were so susceptible to the appeals of the Jacobin project, Barrington Moore, Jr., in 1966 found that similar absolutist, centralized, bureaucratic state histories facilitated similar policy preferences in postrevolutionary Russia and China. "Tsarist Russia had already predisposed bureaucrats, intellectuals and the mass of the people to accept the notion that the state should take the leading role in mobilizing the resources of society and was entitled to carry out any changes it considered appropriate to that end, whatever the human cost."[11] Other explanations for the appeal of Jacobinism are possible.

Statist Jacobin Leninism involved combining nationalist and anti-imperialist appeals (aimed at putting "an end to imperialism, fascism and war"[12]) with a war on peasant household farming and marketing so that the center could seize the produce of agriculture and use it to guarantee subsistence for the ruling apparatus, the armed forces, and urban dwellers (thereby inadvertently but inevitably "assuring the destruction of the country's agriculture").[13] Integral to this effort in the twentieth century, Leninism included an all-out drive to build up steel-related military industries.

Mao Zedong was a Communist leader who continued this Leninist-Stalinist tradition of Jacobinism yet further, paving the way for the subsequent murderous work of the Khmer Rouge, Sendero Luminoso, the Naxalites, and White Flags. This comprehension of Maoist dynamics in terms of a Jacobin legacy is obvious to many Chinese analysts. For Jin Yaoji (Chin Yao-chi, Ambrose Y. C. King), China's anti-imperialist nationalism took a tragic and "pathological twist, the Jacobinism that fused nationalism, moralistic thinking, and absolute power."[14]

The democratic theorist Yan Jiaqi explains that

> during France's Jacobin dictatorship, Paris lay under a pall of revolutionary terror. Laws and procedures were thrown by the wayside, as in China's Cultural Revolution, in order to destroy the enemies of the revolution. The prevailing principle was this: "all enemies of the people are criminals, all of them should be put to death." Not only the blood of Royalists was spilled at the guillotines, but also the blood of revolutionaries and countless innocent men.... Camile Desmoulin inveighed against the reign of terror ... : "In those days, a mere conversation could be a conspiracy ... a simple glance, a pang of sorrow or sympathy, a sigh, or even silence was tantamount to a crime.... [T]o save one's own skin, one was forced to express pleasure at the death of relatives and friends ... even expressing fear might be construed as a crime...." Camile Desmoulin was eventually sent to the guillotine for publishing these writings. During the Cultural Revolution, too, countless people ... met a fate similar to Camile Desmoulin's.[15]

Any student of both the French and Chinese revolutions can find numerous harmonies between the two Jacobin projects. The French Jacobins, for example, changed chess pieces so feudal king, queen, bishop, knight, and castle would no longer be superior to democratic foot soldiers, mere pawns in feudal chess. Likewise, the high cards in card games were renamed. People wore the poorest and most patched clothes as a sign of virtue. Any student of China can list the mirror-image happenings in Mao's Cultural Revolution.

For Chinese Communist conservatives, the post-Mao policy rupture is meant to combine authoritarian Confucian values and pragmatic economics to break with the Jacobin-Leninist project. The conservatives treat both Mao-era "ultraleftists" and post-Mao democrats as equally alien Jacobin fanatic dangers to practical indigenous rule and real benefit for *our* people. A militarized, traditionalist, authoritarian communalism equates both Mao's Red Guards and post-Mao democrats with the Jacobins. Since Mao's death, China's Leninist ruling groups have been dominated by pro-NEP people. For the conservatives who insist on political continuity, Deng Xiaoping is an authoritarian leader who at long last has learned how to implement wealth-expanding and popular NEP reforms to promote the economy while maintaining a stable polity. Singapore patriarch Lee Kuan Yew is the most renowned exponent of this conservative

286 NATIONAL IDENTITY AND DEMOCRATIC PROSPECTS

Confucian evaluation that celebrates the worth of an authentic strong man.

Chinese neoconservatives refer often to the anti–French Revolution wisdom of Edmund Burke. They seem well aware that the official Beijing definition of Jacobinism as "radical democracy" omits the Jacobin synthesis of the Reign of Virtue and the Reign of Terror. In China's misleading official historiography, the major sin of the Jacobins was losing power, Marx was their all-out supporter, and Lenin fulfilled the promise of Robespierre's revolution as carried forward in the Paris Commune, also supposedly embraced by Marx.

The neoconservative Party opposition to Jacobinism in China, however, is also a coded opposition to contemporary democratizers. Both cultural revolutionaries and contemporary political liberalizers who favor open, competitive politics are seen as utopian and abstract ideologists of miraculousness, the belief that some system solves all problems and that all opponents of the utopian transformation are to be treated as enemies to be destroyed. In this neoconservative framework, today's democrats and yesterday's hated Gang of Four both suffer from the diseases of Jacobinism, an illness that China must avoid to stave off chaos and civil strife.[16]

Conservatives in the West who are suspicious of democracy do indeed take the same position.

> What would the sage of Beaconsfield [Edmund Burke] have made out of recent events [the crushing of the spring 1989 Democracy Movement] in China? . . . [H]e warns . . . against picking sides on ideological grounds. . . .
>
> Mao Tse-Tung, the founder of the Chinese regime, would certainly have answered to Burke's idea of a Jacobin. . . . But over the origins of any system of government, says Burke, we must "draw a decent veil.". . . Deng Xiaoping began his rule as a reformer and liberaliser of Mao's system. . . . There is no . . . democratic past. . . . Deng's China . . . qualifies . . . as an *ancien régime* . . . open to the charge that he is only reforming in order to preserve something essentially benighted and evil, while his opponent will make a brave new start based on enlightenment and correct principles. . . .
>
> Deng's student critics . . . were ideologues without any practical experience of politics, much less government. Ah, we may say, but their ideology was sound. . . . [T]hey even erected a statue of liberty. . . . [I]t was to the statue of liberty in the *Place de La Revolution* that Madame Manon Roland, on the way to the guillotine, addressed her famous remark, "Liberty, what crimes are committed in your name!"
>
> [T]he students . . . held no elections, even among themselves, and their leaders conducted purges on points of doctrine . . . just as the Jacobin club did 200 years earlier. . . . Wu'er Kaixi, the students' unelected "charismatic" leader, wanted to "try the guilty leadership before the masses.". . .
>
> We can only guess how the Chinese students might have behaved in power . . . whether they had among them the heirs of Milton and Mill or of Saint-Just and Robespierre. As to how Burke might have viewed their suppression, here he is on a regicide he had no reason to like. "Cromwell had delivered England from anarchy. His government, though military and despotic, had been regular

and orderly. Under the iron, and under the yoke, the soil yielded its produce."
Burke urges us to judge by results, and . . . Chinese agricultural production has
certainly improved under Deng Xiaoping.[17]

In other words, depending on who and what emerges in the succession crisis
in post-Deng China, Mao will be differently evaluated. If military-based authoritarian Confucians will win out, then the present Chinese conservative view that
equates 1980s democracy activists with 1960s Red Guards could also win out.
Both Jacobin Leninism and liberal democracy would then equally be condemned
and dismissed as unsuitable foreign projects.[18]

But whatever the evaluation, in the 1990s Chinese still generally celebrate
Mao Zedong. The position of democratic theorist Xu Liangying that "China
shouldn't commemorate Mao. No one in the [former] Soviet Union commemo-
rates Stalin,"[19] has little support in China.

Democratic critics see Deng as faced with an impossible task, since the ruling
groups can no longer appeal to the discredited ideals of war communism and
anti-imperialism. As a result, as Chinese democrats see it, no amount of economic reform success can attract a people who now comprehend the rulers as
greedy, parasitic, and useless. It is only a matter of time, in this view, before the
Chinese regime, as other Jacobin-Leninist states, is toppled. Democratic theorist
Wei Jingsheng found of Mao,

> He dragged practically all of China onto a road of brutality, treachery, and
> poverty, indirectly causing a hundred million people to starve to death and
> forcing another hundred million to leave home and wander as beggars. Be-
> cause of Mao Zedong, as many as a million people were persecuted politically
> and tortured physically and mentally for years on end. Mao Zedong's crimes
> were too numerous to mention. He outdid the worst despots in the world.[20]

As Hu Jiwei put it, "The dictatorship-based socialism that Stalin implemented
was totally wrong. Such socialism, which also encompasses Mao Zedong's dictatorship-based socialism is fascist socialism, to which I am opposed."[21]

This democratic perspective on Mao is increasingly presuppositional outside
of China among those who experience the end of the twentieth century as the era
when democracy triumphed and authoritarian ideologues were revealed as cruel
monsters. In 1994, Cold War historian John Lewis Gaddis found Mao and Stalin
to be "brutal romantics."

> They were, like Hitler, murderous idealists, driven to apply all of the energies
> they and the countries they ruled could command in an effort to implement a
> set of concepts that were ill-conceived, half-baked and ultimately unworkable.
> They believed that, by sheer force of will, all forces could be overcome, and
> they were willing to [have others] pay whichever price was necessary in lives
> to overcome them.[22]

The two words inserted in brackets, "have others," are in keeping both with Gaddis's point of view and with Immanuel Kant's understanding that dictatorships are more readily war prone and care less about cruel consequences than do democratic republics precisely because dictatorial ruling groups do not bear the burdens they impose on the nation. What would make the inserted words misleading for the present would be a Chinese nationalistic understanding of Mao, that is, an appreciation of Mao as a patriot who identified with the fate of the nation, with its pain also being his pain. In fact, that seems to be the dominant view of Mao in China today. He is a great patriot. That experience is opaque to most outside analysts, who therefore misunderstand the dominant Chinese appreciation of Mao.

If there is a consensus position on Mao in the 1990s in China, it is that whatever else Mao may or may not have been, Chinese tend to believe that Mao was a dedicated nationalist. Of course, Jacobins are superpatriots.

The problem is a post-Mao crisis of national identity. What is a Chinese nationalist in the 1990s? Chinese national identity is now being contested and, therefore, Mao as a symbol is under contestation in terms of contrasting national narratives. People committed to different political futures for China imagine different Mao Zedongs.

When Party General Secretary Jiang Zemin praised Mao at the celebration of the 100th anniversary of Mao's birth, Jiang held Mao up as "a great patriot and national hero" because Mao had established the present political system, which Jiang declared could not merely solve its own contradictions but could also provide the only system that "could save and develop China."[23] The party-state embodies the nation. From the narrow, self-serving perspective of today's ruling groups, China's Foreign Ministry spokesman Wu Jianmin denounced Jeremy Bennett's BBC television biography of the secret life of Mao Zedong, which portrayed Mao as a womanizing, power-hungry, mass murderer as "vicious slanders."[24]

From the popular perspective in China, Wu's denunciation was unnecessary. Mao is genuinely popular in most of China. It therefore may be centuries before the Chinese people will see that Mao was in fact a Jacobin disaster.[25] It took the French some two hundred years before that consensus could be reached on Robespierre's group. For that long the terror seemed too tied to patriotism and the creation of a modern nation. And as the one who restored the nation's dignity, Mao was and is far more charismatically popular in China than Robespierre ever was in France. It is possible to imagine Chinese, therefore, as not historically and emotionally capable of reaching this negative consensus on Mao for a much longer period, say five hundred years.

For most Chinese in the 1990s, Mao, a great man, threw out foreign exploiters, restored national self-respect, and gave the poor a better chance in life. It is not just the elderly who experienced the horrors of pre-1949 war, chaos, and famine who admire Mao as the negator of a hellish past. With the regime illegitimate and national identity contested, the symbol of Mao can also be deployed against today's rulers.

It is therefore even possible that Mao's popularly received critique of a selfish Communist Party state at the start of the Cultural Revolution could become popular yet again. Many educated urban youth read Mao's 1960s words and find insight in their critique of Party people in power today who are serving only themselves. Reactionaries try to take advantage of this popularity.[26]

Some Chinese editorial writers offered a historical basis for focusing on Mao as a protodemocrat. They celebrated the 100th anniversary of Mao's birth by highlighting the promise of the era of the New Democracy, praising Mao "for the quick and complete success of the Chinese democratic revolution, that is, the overthrow of the feudalism, imperialism and bureaucratic capitalism in China."[27] New democracy is made legitimate. In other words, if post-Mao China is again bureaucratic capitalism, as Maurice Meisner and others argue it is, then Mao may again legitimate a new democratic revolution. More attention is being given to the Mao of the New Democracy era, when he was genuinely open to constitutional democracy. If Mao is popular, then democrats may win popularity by embracing Mao, reimagined as a democrat.

There is a historical debate over what happened with Mao in the era of the New Democracy. A researcher at the Chinese Academy of Social Sciences, Wang Haibo, celebrated Mao's birth centennial with an analysis of Mao's views on the new democratic society.[28] Building on the work of the Marxist theorist Yu Guangyuan, Wang found that Mao's theory was a great achievement of universal significance for colonial and semicolonial peoples. China's losses came only after it "prematurely ended the new democratic society in 1952." China wrongly abandoned Mao's great creation and instead acted on Lenin's irrelevant notion of destroying capitalist classes in a transition from capitalism to socialism, although China actually had never built a capitalist society. Had China acted on Mao's "epoch-making development," which recognized that China still had to fulfill the political, social, and economic tasks of a new democratic society as it emerged from semifeudalism and semicolonialism, China would have been doing since 1952 what it had been doing in the post-Mao era, only it would not have had to face the difficult task of dealing with the overcentralized, command-economy state that was built with a mobilizational, vigilante capacity after 1952 to destroy purported enemy classes.

During the Cultural Revolution, Mao's number-one political target, President Liu Shaoqi, who was persecuted to death, was called a "right opportunist" for having sincerely supported democratization in early 1946. President Liu indeed did then say,

> China is on its way to democratization. We consider that the new stage for peaceful democratic reconstruction has already begun. . . . [T]he main task [now] is drafting the constitution through which a parliamentary and cabinet

system of government akin to that of the United States and Great Britain will be adopted.[29]

The dirty little secret, according to the most up-to-date scholarship, is that

> there is no doubt that inside the leadership it was Mao himself who most clearly visualized "a new democratic era" and led the campaign to prepare the party for new forms of political activity.[30]

Whereas the antidemocratic, conservative post-Mao leadership in China labels proponents of democracy as Westernizers who do not understand the Chinese people, in 1946, in the New Democracy era, the leader who took that reactionary position and exploded the attempt to craft a constitutional democracy mediated by the American George C. Marshall was Chiang Kai-shek (Jiang Jieshi). Chiang opposed parliamentary democracy, saying that "most of the people are irresolute, uneducated and inexperienced. . . . Marshall does not understand the different conditions in our country."[31] In other words, the Deng-era Communist Party antidemocratic leadership has gone over to the position of the reactionary leader Chiang Kai-shek. Against such reactionaries, Chinese can align with Mao's and China's own true democratic heritage.

In this manner of praising Mao the democrat, democratic theorist Yu Haocheng, publishing in Hong Kong, cited Mao of the New Democracy era as on the side of furthering human rights.

> Mao Zedong . . . said . . . in his October 10, 1937, letter to Lei Jingtian that Huang Kegong's shooting and killing Liu Xi represented "the renouncing of the revolutionary stand and the renouncing of the human stand," thereby affirming the existence of human rights of a universal nature.[32]

Democratic theorist Guo Luoji sees Mao as good when he supported the New Democracy but bad when he "personally cast aside that concept" and denounced as "right deviationists" those in the Party who wished to continue the New Democracy. When Mao "cast aside" the New Democracy, democratic theorist Guo Luoji finds, Mao then "called himself the Qin Emperor." Mao became "a traitor to the people" (that is, an opponent of the peasant rebellion led against Qin by Chen Sheng and Wu Guang).[33] The question of autocracy versus democracy becomes a matter of the bad Mao versus the good Mao, the autocratic Mao who would be a Qin emperor against the democratic Mao who would empower the long-suffering Chinese people.

"In the 1990s," democrat Wei Jingsheng asks, "has a verdict been returned on Mao Zedong as a historical figure? No. Because he is still playing a role in real life."[34] The predominant desire among Chinese is to imagine Mao symbolically as good and as a patriot. If Qin-Han is now bad, then Mao cannot be a Qin-Han tyrant. In Chinese popular consciousness, the alternative to despotic Qin-Han, understood as the entrenched Leninist despotism, is Chu and an open south. If Mao would be negated by finding him a man of Qin-Han made backward, ignorant, and tyrannical by his exposure to north China peasants, then a good Mao, one presumed to be a Chinese patriot, has to be re-envisioned as the enemy of Qin-Han, as a true southerner, an heir of Chu, someone rooted in the Hunan locale. Such a Mao has begun to appear in the Chinese media.

Mao's home in Hunan in the south becomes a "childhood paradise." "That paradise . . . was his maternal grandmother's home in Tangjiage, where he spent most of his childhood and teenage years with her big family." This good Mao in 1956 contributed 500 yuan "to repair the house's main hall." For his Hunan relatives, the real Mao is defined by his "local accent, laugh, sense of humor, and knowledge of familiar topics."[35] A cousin whom Mao addressed as "ninth brother" in 1949, on meeting him for the first time since 1927, remembers that meeting:

> The younger Mao said that it was Mao's pure local accent "which immediately brought together the chairman and him.". . .
> All townsfolk who had met Mao were impressed by his unadulterated accent. Although the government had long promoted *putonghua* or standard mandarin, Mao himself never mastered the "official speech" [*guan hua?*] as local people call it. His strong accent touched his townsfolk, although it sometimes caused difficulties for his colleagues and especially his interpreters.[36]

In the 1990s, with the language politics of the post-1949 north experienced as part of an illegitimate, selfish, northern-based despotism,[37] Mao could become seen as one of us rather than one of them, a good locally rooted southerner, not an alienated bureaucrat at a parasitic northern capital, not an Emperor of Qin. This Mao then could be popularly worshiped as one of the people, incorruptible and non-nepotistic, in contrast to the post-Mao rulers, who are dismissed as greedily and narrowly concerned only with their own. Mao, one of whose sons died in the Korean War and none of whose children rose to wealth and power, can be redefined as at one with the people, meaning real and rooted, suffering local folk like us, not the alien, Mandarin-speaking nomenclature headquartered in Beijing. Mao Zedong's son, Mao Anqing, and daughter-in-law, Shao Hua, are chief editors of a series of works published by the Hunan People's Publishing House marking the centenary of Mao's birth with a host of books celebrating Mao's deep concern for the people of Hunan. With national identity contested and up for grabs, it is even possible to imagine this Mao of Chu, the enemy of the centralized tyranny of Qin-Han, combining with the New Democratic Mao to help legitimate a federal democratic project.

Thus, in Chinese politics, one may ask, which Mao will win? None of the many contemporary appraisals of Mao is *the* truth. People differ greatly on the significance of Mao's 1990s popularity. It is Mao as a symbol that is being deployed in Chinese politics. Mao really is dead. It is a living politics that will decide the fate and fame of a dead Mao Zedong.

What is extraordinary is how wide open the struggle is to associate Mao with such different national projects. The array of possibilities is as broad and diverse as the multistranded Chinese political spectrum. Thus in addition to the attempt to co-opt Mao as a good southerner who never would speak standard Mandarin, the lying dialect of bureaucratic propaganda, the opposite tendency also is alive and has to be confronted. The bad Mao, the Emperor of Qin, however, can be imagined and condemned as alien. Instead of rooting Mao as authentically Chinese, that Mao can be peripheralized as not really Chinese. To be sure, this notion of Mao as not really Chinese is a minority tendency in an era of "Mao fever."

Still, China's media announced early in 1993 that recent research had discovered that Mao's lineage was Hakka. The family had moved into Hunan province from the north in the Ming Dynasty. Should Chinese topple the Communist Party regime, Chinese then could, as Russians already have done, discover that the Communist leaders (manipulators) were not even "us." The Communists were aliens, "them." The party-state could be redefined as essentially Hakka, not even Chinese. In just this way, Russians see Lenin as Asian, not Russian. Mao could even become a Hakka who was at war with southern Chinese peasants, as in fact he was.

In the political combat of today's China, and in the concomitant struggle to legitimate diverse symbols of national identity, Mao can represent all sides: the south, the north, and even the alien. The variety of strongly held views of Mao competing in China suggests that Mao will continue to be reappraised for many generations to come. His importance and his myth seem so weighty that it could take a very long time before Mao is recognized for what he was, a destructive Jacobin-Leninist who wasted the blood, treasure, and precious time of the Chinese people. Until then, ever-changing reappraisals of Mao will continue to serve as significant counters in an ongoing political contest.

Democrats can embrace as the real Mao the Mao of the New Democracy and the popular leader who refused to be corrupted by the language of the Mandarins, while slighting the false Mao, the antipeople Emperor of Qin, and the non-Chinese Hakka. Democrats might do best by not describing Mao as the Jacobin he really was.

I said in an essay written at Mao's death that people in China "will re-create and reinterpret Mao to fit their eventual needs of the moment. The Mao who was is yet to be."[38] Now almost twenty years later, I am confident enough to be a bit more precise, but only a bit. Given Mao fever, that is, if Mao is "still a mysterious figure, a 'god' that appears only once every five hundred years,"[39] then it could take five hundred years, maybe, before Mao would be just another useless Jacobin-Leninist. But it need not take that long for China to democratize. France democratized long before it came to terms with the Jacobins. So it could be, too, with the Chinese, democracy, and Mao.

Notes

1. Chen Jianxiang and Zhao Hong, "What Do the 'New Collegians' Know About Mao Zedong?" *Daxuesheng*, No. 12 (December 10, 1993), pp. 20–22, translated in JPRS-CAR–94–013, February 24, 1994, p. 5.
2. Bo Yibo, "Commemorating Mao Zedong," *Chinafrica*, December 1993, p. 7.
3. Chen and Zhao, "Mao Zedong," p. 5.
4. *Monthly Review* (MR), "Notes from the Editors," 45.8 (January 1994), inside back cover.
5. Tony Walker, "Making Money Out of Mao," *Financial Times*, December 24, 1993.
6. Catherine Sampson, "The Remembering Bitterness, Thinking of Sweet Things Restaurant," *Wall Street Journal*, February 2, 1994.
7. Willy Wo-lap Lam, "Intellectuals Suffer in Silence," *South China Morning Post*, January 12, 1994, p. 19.
8. Michael Howard, "The Vast Detour," *Times Literary Supplement*, November 6, 1992, p. 6.
9. Richard Pipes, "The Great October Revolution as a Clandestine Coup d'etat," *Times Literary Supplement*, November 6, 1992, p. 4.
10. Leszek Kolakowski, "A Calamitous Accident," *Times Literary Supplement*, November 6, 1992, p. 8.
11. Geoffrey Hosking, "Heirs of the Tsarist Empire," *Times Literary Supplement*, November 6, 1992, p. 6.
12. Adam Ulam, "Myths of Leninism," *Times Literary Supplement*, November 6, 1992, p. 8.
13. Robert Conquest, "The Party in the Dock," *Times Literary Supplement*, November 6, 1992, p. 7.
14. Ambrose Y. C. King, *Zhongguo Shehui yu wenhua* [Chinese Society and Culture] (Hong Kong: Oxford University Press, 1992), p. 193, cited in Thomas Metzgar, "The Sociological Imagination in China," *Journal of Asian Studies* 52.4 (November 1993), p. 942.
15. Yan Jiaqi, *Toward a Democratic China* (Honolulu: University of Hawaii Press, 1992), p. 215.
16. Michael Sullivan, "The Impact of Western Political Thought on Chinese Political Discourse on Transitions from Leninism, 1986–1992," *World Affairs* (Summer 1994).
17. Murray Sayle, "After the Revolution," *The Spectator*, September 22, 1990, p. 11.
18. If one credits Harvard political scientist Samuel Huntington's understanding of why conservative third world authoritarian regimes can be more stable than democratic experiments, this conservative, authoritarian view of both Mao and democracy as alien could well predominate in some near future.
19. *Far Eastern Economic Review* (FEER), January 13, 1994, p. 11.
20. Wei Jingsheng, "The Best Lesson Mao Zedong Taught Us," *Kaifang*, November 18, 1993, translated in JPRS-CAR–94–007, January 27, 1994, p. 15.
21. Zhang Weiguo, "Discussing Democracy and Journalistic Freedom with Hu Jiwei," *Zhengming*, August 1, 1993, pp. 62–65, translated in JPRS-CAR–93–065, September 3, 1993, p. 40.
22. John Lewis Gaddis, "The Tragedy of Cold War History," *Foreign Affairs*, January/February 1994, p. 151.
23. *China Daily* (*CD*), December 28, 1993.
24. *China Daily* (*CD*), December 24, 1993.
25. Frank Ching has argued that the censorship and condemnation backfired and

called attention to the film, increasing the number of people who would see it and perhaps believe it as the hidden truth. Rulers can shoot themselves in the foot. Anxious and arrogant Leninist rulers could inadvertently hasten the democratization that they actually wish to thwart.

26. Deng Liqun's antireform group tries to capitalize on this popularity. It celebrated Mao's 100th birthday in Hunan by attacking Deng Xiaoping's policies of openness and reform (Lu Geng, "Deng Liqun a Time-Bomb," *Baixing*, February 11, 1994, pp. 10–11).

27. *China Daily (CD)*, editorial, "Mao's Legacy," December 24, 1993.

28. Wang Haibo, "A Study of Mao Zedong's 'On the New Democracy,'" *Jingji yanjiu*, No. 12 (December 20, 1993), pp. 16–25, translated in JPRS-CAR–94–011, February 16, 1994, pp. 3–10.

29. Odd Arne Westad, *Cold War and Revolution* (New York: Columbia University Press, 1993), p. 149.

30. Ibid.

31. Ibid., p. 150.

32. Yu Haocheng, "On Human Rights and the Corresponding Legal Safeguards," *Dangdai*, August 15, 1993, pp. 94–96, translated in JPRS-CAR–93–086, December 3, 1993, pp. 1–3.

33. Guo Luoji, "Use Democratic Means to Implement the Democratic Goal of Democratization," *Ming Bao*, September 1993, pp. 124–33, translated in JPRS-CAR–93–086, December 3, 1993, pp. 3–11.

34. Wei, "Best Lesson," p. 15.

35. *China Daily*, "Mao's Days in Paradise," *December 29, 1993*.

36. *China Daily (CD)*, December 13, 1993.

37. Edward Friedman, "Reconstructing China's National Identity," *Journal of Asian Studies*, February 1994.

38. Edward Friedman, "The Innovator," in Dick Wilson, ed., *Mao Tse-Tung in the Scales of History* (Cambridge: Cambridge University Press, 1977), p. 303.

39. Chen and Zhao, "Mao Zedong," p. 5.

Chapter 16

The Oppositional Decoding of China's Leninist Media

As recent critical scholarship known as the "reader/response school" informs analysts that authorial intent and reader response need have little or nothing in common, similarly, nonwritten popular culture cannot be taken at face value in an effort to comprehend popular oppositional possibilities. This is true of all societies and times. Throughout history, Chinese were well versed in attack by innuendo (*hansha sheying*). Symbols, even those made out of cement, are plastic in their meaning. In the American depression of the 1930s, when banks seemed unjustly to foreclose unpaid mortgages and seize the land of virtuous, hard-working farmers, popular consciousness turned even the sadistic robber-killers Bonnie and Clyde into popular and protected social bandits who supposedly robbed the unjust banks and helped poor people. In retrospect, popular mythologizing served to indicate support that could come to a reform leader who would oppose the financial moguls, as Franklin Roosevelt did. Consequently, decoding popular mythologies can offer a methodology that provides clues to prospects for a democratic or reform opposition even in the particular situation of contemporary China.

In Leninist dictatorships,[1] public opinion is inordinately volatile because people must manufacture a good conscience, the result of their daily complicity with an oppressive system required to protect and advance family interests.[2] Typical of this opinion volatility, a poll of people in the Ukraine in the last year of the Soviet Union showed 90 percent in favor of staying in the Union, whereas only eleven months after free speech and press began, over 90 percent voted for an independent Ukraine. With opinion so volatile and much of Leninist conscious-

Reprinted from Chin-Chuan Lee, ed., *China's Media, Media's China* (Boulder, CO: Westview Press, 1994), by permission of Westview Press.

ness very superficial and transient, a scholar needs clues to deeper realities. Decoding popular response in Leninist China is most useful if it pays less attention to the momentary and manifest, which merely gives good conscience to compelled complicity, and instead probes the latent meaning of popular response in a search for underlying trends, as is done in the scholarship on political symbolism in the work of Murray Edelman.[3]

In mid-1986 the old guard of elder rulers in China was moving against a weakened and isolated leader of expansive reforms, Hu Yaobang. After Party General Secretary Hu was not seen in public for a few days, a rumor spread that he was preparing to flee to the Soviet Union. People gossiped that Moscow was threatening China's antireform elders with nuclear attack should the reactionaries try to block the progressive Hu's escape. Although unsupported, this rumor spread a myth that ruling reactionaries would someday, somehow, be defeated by the forces of good. Symptomatically, Chinese readers flocked to tales of good conquering evil, or chivalry and swordsmanship based on China's fabulous outlaw-heroes and knights-errant.

Also in the 1980s, tales were recounted about the massively corrupt behavior of the nonaccountable children of the senior leadership. A story spread that a son of China's paramount leader was in cahoots with officials in the northwestern city of Xian, making gobs of ill-begotten wealth by illegally cornering a monopoly on grossly marked-up, high-priced luxury television sets. Amazingly, the son cut his ties to the firm, which was disbanded. This dialogue and reaction occurred with no muckraking exposures in the official press, with the discourse occurring at the level of rumor and gossip. Political reality lies beyond the printed word.

Discrediting Oppressors

Outsiders who only read the official story cannot hear the words in the minds of reader respondents that give meaning to symbols, turning cement into moldable plastic. Throughout the universe of Leninist nations, people who have been fooled and cheated in the past read subsequent official stories to protect themselves from being played again for chumps. Once nationals in Leninist states know that the regime is split, they read the media seeking signs of support for their worldview. Starting right after the establishment of the People's Republic in 1949, Mao Zedong launched one attack after another against an allegedly hidden opposition which supposedly used the popular media to undermine what Mao called socialism. Mao's group found, revealed, and denounced essays, books, and movies full of antiregime messages. Chinese consequently could presume that even the official media were replete with Aesopian or hidden messages on the side of the people. Chinese became expert decoders, eagerly believing that a sculptor had depicted Mao as a Buddha with one eye slightly open because he wanted to see who did not worship him.

On a university campus where a statue of Mao Zedong, the leader of the Great Leap Forward and the Cultural Revolution—the one responsible for massive famine and pervasive oppression—remained standing, passersby in 1991 did not comment that a hero was being celebrated, but that a culprit was finally being punished. People said, "In the summer, he burns; in the winter, he freezes; year-round, birds shit all over him."

Throughout history, in all parts of the world, outraged people find similar ways to turn a discredited regime's propaganda against itself. The issue here is not Mao himself. At the very same moment that some cursed Mao, other Chinese could put up pictures of Mao as a way of saying that even Mao—whose son died in the Korean War—was better than the post-Mao crowd whose sons were getting rich in foreign deals. What was shared, rather, was a popular response that turned a legitimizing symbol for the regime into one that opposed the dictators. The very nature of being human, of seeking some dignity, limits the capacity of repression and propaganda to fill people's heads with the ideas, categories, and worldview of discredited despots.

Another extraordinary instance of decoding and recoding occurred in a political prison on the outskirts of the capital right after the Beijing massacre of June 4, 1989. The authorities' tactics, in using their control of information for reprogramming democratic opponents of the Leninist dictatorship, included playing the national anthem and compelling prisoners to stand and sing that hymn to the regime. But the prisoners sang it with enthusiasm. The prisoners sang with gusto. "Arise! Refuse to be enslaved! . . . The Chinese nation has reached its most crucial hour. . . . Arise! Arise! Arise! . . . Onward! In the face of the enemies' fire, Onward! Onward! Onward!" They believed that this song, composed during the patriotic resistance to Japan, also expressed their patriotic resolve against armed tyrants who had enslaved the people. The authorities dropped their ritual of disciplining degradation. The decoders had prevailed, even in prison.

Hegemony Questioned

Popular, oppositional decoding may run counter to the expectations of those who accept the work on ideological hegemony of the powerful Italian Leninist theorist Antonio Gramsci.[4] This is because Gramsci's entire problematique is misconceived. He wrote in an era when and a nation where liberal democracy seemed to turn into police-state fascism when challenged from below. He wrote to legitimate Leninism. He assumed that democracy was a deception masking a bourgeois dictatorship and that there was something false in the consciousness of industrial workers that kept the proletariat from finding the goals of Leninist Marxism attractive and compelling. Gramsci concluded that ideological presuppositions of the dominant capitalist class project so pervaded consciousness as to be hegemonic, that is, the rulers' ideology precluded the people from critically comprehending their plight and the creation of an oppositional mind-set.

298 NATIONAL IDENTITY AND DEMOCRATIC PROSPECTS

Yet in retrospect, it makes more sense to ask why Gramsci was misled by the actualities of the Leninist project. Given the economic disaster and political barbarism embedded in the Leninist project from Albania to Angola, it seems more sensible to ask what is wrong with the minds of Leninist intellectuals who are still attracted to that inhuman Leninist project. Why can't misguided intellectuals free themselves more readily from Marxist-Leninist ideological hegemony? In contrast to the ideological blinders of such elites, people outside of the ruling culture tend to construct an oppositional culture.

As James Scott has shown in two superb studies,[5] subordinated groups, in contrast to misled Leninist intellectuals, have little trouble turning the ideologies of oppressive rulers against the tyrants. Stories abound in China about how audiences in darkened movie houses and live theaters applaud at the inauspicious moment—inauspicious as defined by regime propaganda. So people applaud on hearing "What if the Nationalist Party came back?" before an answer with a negative assessment can be given in the film. People delight in recounting how such films had to be withdrawn for better editing or how runs of plays were cut short. Despite the repressive dictatorship, people recount instances when their will prevailed. The Gramscian notion of hegemony and Marxist false consciousness are approaches that underestimate the power of people to see through the camouflage of dictators.

In autumn 1991, for example, the dictatorship in Beijing sought to relegitimate itself by appealing to the symbolism of Mao Zedong, who also had struggled to prevent democratization. Students at Beijing University, seeing through the veil of deception, immediately plastered the campus with portraits of Mao. Students decoded the message as victims of despots, manipulating a symbol in their own oppositional interest rather than in support of Mao and in opposition to democracy. The portrait represented the students' cry against today's despots and put Mao in a relatively favorable light. To embrace Mao, for the popular opposition, meant delegitimating the regime. Chauffeurs hung a small image of Mao from the rearview mirror seeking good fortune, as gamblers prayed to him hoping that their numbers would turn up. Mao, who inveighed against superstition, became the god of the superstitious.

This ordinary mode of oppositional decoding or silent resistance reflects the impossibility of ideological hegemony. Gramsci had everything virtually backward. China's oppositional decoders, who readily reject the hegemonic project of those who monopolize the media, thereby convey a hopeful message about the human capacity to resist the self-serving myths of an intended ideological hegemony and struggle for something better.

Two stories spread after the crushing of the 1989 Democracy Movement, both of which testified to the isolated and transient character of the Leninist dictatorship. One story centered on Cui Guozhen, a peasant-soldier said to have been burned, crucified, and tortured by the demonstrators. Such a corpse existed. It was publicly displayed in Beijing as proof of the injustice of the Democracy

Movement. But in the story that spread, when Cui's father was offered a sizable monetary reward by President Yang Shangkun, believed to be one of the architects of the massacre, the father refused the money, worrying out loud that he feared what might happen when the verdict on the democracy struggle was reversed and Cui was no longer a martyr. Indeed, Cui's father was said to have insisted that, given the unrecognizable corpse, he believed his son was still alive. It was supposedly soon discovered (and covered up by the authorities) that Cui was indeed alive and well, home in Jilin province, where he had been transferred just prior to the Tiananmen Square incident. Thus there was, at least in popular mythology, no martyr of opposition to the democratic struggle.

Another story told of the fate of a junior officer at a military academy in Shanghai who wanted to send the central authorities a telegram saying that the enemies of the people were those declaring martial law. His commander promised to protect this outraged officer, but beseeched him not to send the cable. Instead, the junior officer sent his declaration of support for the democratizers to Shanghai's Fudan University democrats, who then transferred it to Beijing. Although higher authorities decided to arrest and try the officer, his local unit won approval for a two-year sentence to be served in their lockup, the equivalent of a nice hotel. Subsequently, the officer was given a cushy job supervising Shanghai nightclubs, while Beijing was told that the culprit had been mustered out of the military. The premise of the story was that popular unity would win eventual victory for the democrats. Putting the two stories together creates an oppositional mythos in which the real Chinese army is with the democratic cause of the people that will ultimately triumph.

Popular Cynicism

This demythologizing and remythologizing, however, is often misleadingly idealized. In fact, the decoding does not guarantee that the popular opposition either gets the facts straight or organizes reinterpreted information in its own political best interest. The consequences of popular cynicism should not be romanticized. Despite social-bandit mythology, Bonnie and Clyde, after all, were only vicious criminals who were no help to the poor.

Oppressed people incapable of political action often grow cynical about all political views and actors. Hence, if they hear a propaganda lie from Beijing and a different story on the Voice of America, they often assume that the truth must be somewhere in the middle. Consequently, cynical consciousness unintentionally lends some credit to the regime's lies. Cynical, powerless, and outraged people tend to believe the worst about all political actors, including potential friends within the divided ruling groups. Thus China's 1989 Democracy Movement condemned Party General Secretary Zhao Ziyang for the corruption of his offspring, thereby furthering a dismissive popular attitude that obstructed any mass politics of reaching out from movement democrats to ally with regime reformers. As with a similar condemnation of Deng Xiaoping's physically handicapped son, pure moral outrage and cynicism self-defeatingly precluded accepting a broad alliance of popular democrats and regime reformers that might have replaced the Leninist dictatorship.

The focus of this chapter, however, is not on the creation of politically useful truth for a democratic movement, but on the limits of propaganda effectiveness by the dictatorship. Hsiao Ching-chang and Yang Mei-rong report that people treat

> a story in the newspaper saying, "the students' patriotism is running high in the universities, and the Anti-Bourgeois Liberalization campaign had obtained vital achievements". . . [to mean] that students have lost confidence in the leadership of the Communist Party and yearn for democracy and freedom.[6]

In other words, because the people have their defenses, the regime cannot act in a hegemonic manner. It is therefore worth decoding the oppositional culture for clues about future Chinese politics.

The crushing of the Democracy Movement in 1989 and the subsequent purge of twenty-four of twenty-five section heads of the *People's Daily* were not part of a process of unrestrained tyranny in which a ruling group had unlimited power to impose its will and policies on a hapless population. Such a description would incorrectly describe the state system as totalitarian, one in which the political elites have all the power. That analysis leads to a projection of no end to the discredited dictatorship.

But because China's rulers lack legitimacy, the alienated citizenry decode government propaganda to harmonize it with popular oppositional presuppositions. There are such contradictions within the system, and between power holders and the people, that to classify the state system as totalitarian obscures potentially powerful popular opposition. An idea of a society's ability to defend itself against the Leninist system can come from looking at a realm of state secrecy and apparent total state control—foreign policy. This examination reveals great limits on Leninist power and potential for a transformation of the system.

If the rulers did control a totalitarian system, they would be able to manage information and passions so that a manipulated people applauded the purported heroics of leaders who claimed to protect the people against dangerous enemies at home and abroad. In reality, policy is experienced by most politically conscious Chinese outside the ruling group as antipeople, almost despite any of its particulars.

The regime tries to woo public opinion by propagandizing a policy the populace should like, while executing a contradictory policy of hidden purposes defined only in the cloakrooms of power. The regime fears to make its true aims known, but it reiterates the slogan of "openness" as the essence of its foreign policy. It is silent on its goal of relegitimating its power by siding with all remaining Leninist dictatorships.[7] Its priority foreign policy goal is not to serve citizen needs but to hold on to power. Consequently, the government attempts to rigidly control the media in order to persuade the public, while hiding a deep policy direction that is inherently objectionable to a politically conscious citizenry that seeks economic exchanges to improve living conditions.

A foreign policy priority of China's rulers, in the wake of the democratization of Leninist systems from East Germany to Mongolia, is to help surviving Leninist-type dictatorships that resist political reform. What do Chinese think of such friends? It is absurd to believe that Chinese support the mass murderers who rule the miserable nation of Myanmar (Burma). It is likewise inconceivable that ties to North Korea win applause. In fact, stories spread in China of North Korea as an ingrate that would be poverty-stricken if not for Chinese aid. Normalization of relations with Vietnam will persuade Chinese, including the military, that sending Chinese to die there in 1979 was an unnecessary sacrifice of life, thus further undermining the regime's nationalistic legitimacy. With the rulers perceived to be narrowly self-serving, citizens decode the media to ferret out the hidden truth from the media, in advance of any real facts, as to how the rulers sacrifice the people.

The government acts as if public opinion mattered, that the media are powerful shapers of public opinion, and that the media as powerful shapers of public opinion cannot be allowed to reveal the regime's actual foreign policy purposes. Popular oppositional presuppositions, however, impose limits on the capacity of the dictators to carry out a "nonpropagandized" foreign policy that mainly serves their closed, corporate power interests. Having seen journalists and broadcasters in the 1989 Democracy Movement demonstrate behind such slogans as "Don't force us to lie," regime opponents assume that "the vast majority of CCP news workers ... have not been content with the CCP's obliteration of press freedom."[8] Viewers and readers, therefore, assume that media workers will find ways to provide data that actually subvert the illegitimate, hidden purposes and policies of the supersecretive Leninist system. Despite propaganda, censorship, control, and manipulation, the media are also experienced by alienated Chinese as an instrument of truth, delegitimation, and even democratization.

At times, journalists do plant Aesopian messages against the dictatorship. There is no doubt that the diagonal reading of one poem in the overseas edition of *People's Daily* did indeed say "Down with Li Peng." With the 1989 Democracy Movement having shown the isolation of the rulers, ever more people assume that all good people only pay lip service to the state, while actually thinking for themselves. Consequently, there is a virtual mass movement to decode the Aesopian antiregime messages that people assume must be hidden in the mere lip service to the regime. This attitude of decoding the antiregime content of propaganda is a contagion that even spreads to non-native readers of Chinese who stay in the country for any length of time.

Democratic Potential

One reason Chinese so often interpret media events to prove that the media reveal the truth about the regime, despite censorship and severe punishment for media democrats, is Chinese culture. Far from being uniformly antidemocratic, Chinese culture contains democratic potential. Chinese culture teaches that an ethical, educated Chinese must stand up for justice and the people even at the cost of career or life. When Wang Ruoshui was removed as managing editor of the *People's Daily* for his revelations of exploitation, many young people showed up at his office the day he had to move out.[9] One told me that Wang was surprised to see them and asked, "Don't you know I have been criticized and punished by the Party?" Someone answered that that was precisely why the people were there to help him. In like manner, right after Liu Binyan was booted out of the Party and attacked in the press in 1987, a stream of visitors went to see Liu and a torrent of signed letters poured in despite secret police surveillance. Rather than being cowed by the 1989 martial law crackdown, politically aware people found that very few people informed for the authorities. Consequently, people speak freely to friends in ever larger numbers.

The illegitimacy of the regime and a change in values cause people to decode regime lies and thereby reveal unspoken truths. With regime ideologist He Xin a laughingstock and regime spokesman Yuan Mu a target of cursing, people often assume that the real truth is probably closer to the opposite of what the regime claims. Because a discredited ruling group is seen as selling out the people for private gain, while people who know how to buy and sell get wealthy outside the state sector, southerners can even revel in a northern pun aimed against them. People understand the attack in a way that defuses it. Hence southerners laughingly repeat the canard, "Northerners love the country; southerners sell the country," implying that the northern-based regime, in fact, is but a group of hypocrites, while southerners have the ability to make money and survive in the competitive world economy. I overheard gossip about how southern anti-Communist leader Chiang Kai-shek knew how to get money from the rich Americans, a trick the discredited regime in the north cannot perform.

Heroes and Victims

When the regime attacks a muckraking writer, Liu Binyan, or a courageous democrat, Fang Lizhi, Chinese who read the attacks understand them as attempts by the media to publicize the antiregime ideas of those under attack. The citations of the words of those under attack are treated as the hidden and real message. The metaphysical presupposition of the decoding ontology is that China's cultural heroes are bravely standing with an unjustly victimized people against selfish and outmoded rulers. Given the way the people insist on understanding the media and their messages, the regime is damned whether or not it censors and punishes. Insiders assert that the rulers have decided not to attack hidden messages for fear it will make them seem weak and out of control. The media are consequently seen as doing their best to reveal the hidden truth. Hence, similar to a Rorschach test, people project what they want to see—the Chinese people and their media standing up against an unjust order.

Consequently, press censorship cannot achieve its purposes. The regime gave great publicity to flooding in the summer of 1991 in order to trumpet relief funds from Taiwan and Hong Kong to enhance the image of rulers in Beijing as the respected leaders of all Chinese. Chinese, however, noted that the stories hid both the human suffering and the culpability of rulers for the floods. Hence, stories of people in Taiwan and Hong Kong helping the victims were taken as proof that even outsiders cared more about mainland Chinese than their rulers.

This popular decoding makes the rules seem destined to fall. People say that when heads of military units give lectures, they comment that their unit was not in Beijing during the June 1989 massacre. The evidence of popular decoding suggests that the military, to prosper as a proud and patriotic institution, already distances itself from the perpetrators of the Beijing massacre and insists that it never would have used such tactics on its own. The ridiculous and meretricious official interpretation of the massacre will eventually be corrected formally, culminating in the targeting of a few worst culprits and an acknowledgment of the patriotism of the demonstrators. History, people think, is not on the side of the rulers.

The issue, however, is not the June 4 massacre or any other single event. As mentioned earlier, public opinion is inordinately volatile in Leninist systems. Even June 4 can quickly pass from popular consciousness. What continues is a discredited system that forces people to live complicitous, two-faced existences that outrage people because the regime has lost its legitimacy. Chinese, refusing to be made fools of again by government propaganda, assume that the official story is the big lie. This belief puts a limit on the regime's ability to legitimate policy.

Thus one could have known in advance that the Chinese people would not believe that disaster relief from Taiwan and Hong Kong was a manifestation of respect for rulers in Beijing, as the media claimed. Media propaganda on the flood changed rapidly, as if in a silent dialogue with regime critics. At first, the flood was said to prove the need for more power to collectives. Later, it was used as evidence that the army, in charge of flood relief, loves the people. By the fall, however, the new media line on the flood, to counter the daily gossip by a distrustful populace about the disaster having had political causes, was that disasters *also* have natural causes. Once again, oppositional decoding was so loud and clear that ruling groups felt a need to respond.

Patriotism, Chaos, and Nativism

Is there any popular credibility for the accounts in the press of the happiness of scholars and scientists who have returned from abroad, presented as proof that the better future is in China? People usually consider the returnees crazy and mock such stories. Do Chinese believe the accounts of life in America in terms of crime, drugs, homelessness, AIDs, racism, and unemployment? While a few may believe such accounts, a story that spread in China during the Gulf War reflects different thinking among Chinese. Chinese rulers condemned a hegemonic United States for picking on Iraq, portrayed as a small, oppressed third world nation. Ordinary Chinese, on the other hand, volunteered to fight on the American side in Kuwait. This reflects a profound split in the military and in society in general, whereby the young see their elders as hurting China's national dignity by acting on irrational Maoist categories of bad big and good small states. A craving for a new, true, and pure patriotism results.

This does not mean that Chinese automatically embrace democracy—a patriotism of the Constitution—as a superior alternative. They tend, rather, to identify with American strength crushing weak Iraq. They seem to long for similar Chinese strength. Such popular tendencies could be satisfied by nativistic, ascetic militarism in China. The younger military officers know that China's Maoists isolated China from advanced science, technology, and weaponry, thus making China weaker. Propaganda is reinterpreted to harmonize with the popular presupposition that an *ancien régime* is out of touch with China's future needs. Whether the preferred alternative will be open democracy, nativistic militarism, or something worse remains unknown. Oppositional decoding, however, suggests a lot of popular tendencies in the antidemocratic direction.

Importantly, this decoding suggests that despite extraordinary economic growth in the post-Mao era, Chinese remain disenchanted with the Leninist rulers, even in the countryside, where the economic boom is mind-boggling. The rural Party tends to be corrupt and hated. Economic success is experienced by ordinary villagers as occurring *despite the system*—as success in *getting around the system*. Villagers do not credit the rulers in Beijing for post-Mao economic gains. Change is assumed to be needed in Beijing's power holders and policies regardless of the specifics surrounding the June 4 massacre.

Has the constant media barrage indicating that democratization in other Leninist states has resulted in chaos, decline, and division served the rulers' purpose of legitimizing the antidemocratic Chinese regime? Do Chinese believe that they are fortunate to enjoy a Leninist system that delivers both stability and economic growth, a combination said to make China the envy of frightened, suffering people in post-Leninist states all around the world? In China there *is* great fear of chaos and making things worse by premature or ill-conceived attempts at political reform. This anxiety, however, surrounds the death of the ruling elders; it does not credit the Leninist system for China's recent economic success. Indicatively, politically conscious Chinese citizens, in contrast to the ruling elders, celebrated the fall of Ceauşescu in Romania and the failure of the coup orchestrated by the old guard in Russia. None tout other surviving Leninist regimes in Havana, Pyongyang, and Hanoi as models for the future. Leninist dictatorship seems an anachronism.

Chinese benefited greatly from the openness and partial decollectivization that accompanied post-Mao reforms, just as did people in Yugoslavia and Hungary in the 1950s and 1960s. But reform within Leninist state institutions is limited. The Chinese Leninist state guarantees polarization between people and rulers, an intensifying budget crisis, economic viability moving outside of the control of wasteful and misguided central ministries, worsening corruption, and the existence of useless—and, therefore, experientially hypocritical—state enterprises. The regime continues to be legitimated while regional identities strengthen. Alienated citizens are not grateful for Leninist rule in China, even when faced with post-Leninist chaos elsewhere. The continuation of a counterproductive Leninist system in China is taken to block progress and even make a regression possible. In short, people decode regime propaganda in ways that can legitimate and activate future antiregime action.

Fear of chaos, disorder, and disintegration could in the future serve the demagogic interests of a tough, anticorruption military despotism that would appeal also to nativistic sentiments. In 1992, I heard numerous individuals mock patriotism and then, in the next breath, long for a regime they could be proud of, such as an America whose rulers smashed Iraq and supposedly proved their concern for the American people by crushing rioters in Los Angeles. Such supposed goodness is contrasted with betrayal of the people by rulers in Beijing, alleged to allow African blacks in China to run riot over Chinese. This methodology of decoding reveals some strong antidemocratic nativism in the opposition. Perhaps this comes from Chinese thinking as antiregime patriots, trying to believe the regime's chauvinistic propaganda but interpreting the material against the regime.

Reinterpreting Regime Propaganda

Many Chinese do accept some regime propaganda as partially true, but do so to discredit the regime. The people tend to add on what they know from experience —overseas Chinese come from places doing much better than people in China, students who return from abroad are treated as carriers of truths that are unavailable in China, and people who stand up to the regime are regarded as heroes. Thus the regime's propaganda lies are, by and large, irrelevant. Chinese who read official newspapers seriously are mocked for wasting their time. Chinese who pass on news from foreign sources such as Voice of America, BBC, Taiwan, and other foreign sources are treated as purveyors of truth. At times word spreads that a particular journal—the English-language *China Daily* or a paper covering the international economy—can be read for hard information. A combination of quotidian daily experience, the corrupt and false system, and the deep personal desire not to be fooled induces people to construct "truth" from preferred, nonofficial sources that discredit the system.

One of the most twisted outcomes of reinterpreting government propaganda occurred in the Nanjing race riots of December 1988.[10] Chinese students, having read endless denunciations by their leaders of America's antiblack racism, experienced blacks from Africa as part of the undeserving privileged in China. The official Chinese media, which decried American racism against blacks, were discredited. The Chinese, therefore, assumed that white American students, as representatives of a system which properly treated blacks with contempt, would naturally join Chinese students in their outrage at the Chinese government's unfair privileging of African students, at "humiliating" ties between Chinese women and African men, and at a rumored unpunished murder of a Chinese by an African. Chinese student demonstrators perceived a common goal with white Americans: rewarding merit by punishing the undeserving. The Chinese anti-African mob displayed especial anger toward an American teacher in Nanjing who condemned the Chinese students, seeing him as a dupe, fink, and apologist for a tyranny that privileges the incompetent. Popular decoding reveals a receptiveness to meritocratic and democratic values replacing the regime's privileging of political loyalty. Concomitantly, however, a powerful, ongoing dispute between a primordial "us" and the regime could reinforce nasty communalist tendencies, as developments in other post-Leninist states have already shown.

Still, people try to counter what they assume are regime lies. Regime propaganda on foreign policy and popular desires, moreover, is taken to be in conflict. People tie southern China, Shenzhen, Hong Kong, Taiwan, and the United States to a happier future. The rulers, however, warn that cultural pollution and bourgeois liberalization come from these places, far from the supposed good, solid northern loess soil that sprouted the Confucian Chinese values of mutuality and self-discipline. Popular decoders, however, see a ruling group whose children are set up in cushy southern jobs, given a foreign education, and provided lucrative foreign trade contracts.

In the permanent succession crisis that shapes the politics of Leninist states, large sectors of the governing apparatuses begin to wonder about their careers once the elders are gone. What should they as individuals, family members, and corporate entities do to survive and prosper? The military has to worry about its corporate prestige. Its junior officer corps is well aware that the 1979 intervention in Vietnam, wars on the Chinese people by the military in various Cultural Revolution campaigns starting in 1966, and the June 1989 massacre have turned public opinion somewhat against them. More actions are not seen as in the military's long-term corporate interest.

Remembering when Albania was China's only ally, officers tend to see the embrace of the few remaining, weak Leninist dictatorships—scoffed at by the Chinese people—as an indication that China's elders are trying to live outside of international norms. Because membership in the international scientific and technological communities benefits China economically, politically aware people reject regime policies that threaten China with international censure. The military and citizenry in general, therefore, tend not to support the current regime's nuclear proliferation and missile sales policies, which threaten China's access to the global economy and international prestige. Readers of the press, noting the headlining of pro-China praise by minor officials in a small African state, cannot help but get the message that the regime has painfully isolated China from happier global possibilities by ignoring international norms. The endless declarations that China has friends all over the world often seems an attempt to obscure the regime's self-imposed isolation. Even Chinese in official sectors have learned to decode meaning into media propaganda that discredits the regime and could legitimate a process of political reform into democracy or a tough, military authoritarianism.

The frightened ruling clique in post-Mao China focuses great attention on public opinion, thereby tacitly accepting the power of democratic legitimation while subverting the Leninist doctrine that the vanguard leadership knows the way to the future. Apparent quiet and stability, therefore, are false clues of a momentary hiatus in political action that call attention away from decoding evidence that a crisis of legitimation defines the Chinese political system. Unseen and unheard, China's people share musings about alternatives to what is detested.

Chinese media heroes have contributed mightily to this new potential; Chinese cultural creators have furthered despotism's delegitimation. Journalists such as Deng Tuo, Wang Ruoshui, and Liu Binyan have tried to tell the truth about Mao's irrationality, the inhuman essence of the Leninist socialist system, and the outmoded, feudal nature of the party-state. The editors and staff of the *World Economic Herald* in Shanghai, including the renowned Qin Benli, also contributed greatly to letting truth into China. Viewers were captivated by the six-part television series "River Elegy" that frontally attacked the worldview of elders who opposed Zhao Ziyang's attempt to push much further with reforms. People experience a daily struggle against censors in all areas of reporting in China, from movie makers to fiction writers and journalists.

Creating Oppositional Symbols

People seek and find hidden truths in media headlines or story juxtapositions and then spread the "true" story to undermine the regime's lies. For example, a story spread about the symbol of the 1990 Asian Games hosted in China (Figure 16.1). The symbol was said to be an *A* (for Asia) on its side, the better to look like an open, welcoming Great Wall. But is that an *A*? Looked at sideways, taxi drivers in Beijing told me that it contained a commemoration to the democratic martyrs of June 4, 1989, or 6–4–89, as it is put in Chinese. One can see from the right side a distinct 6 and on the left, a distinct 4. From a left side view of the symbol, one can see the whole as a distinct 8 and the left side as 9, hence 6–4–89.

Did the creator of the symbol intend this, or did people read antiregime decoding into a neutral sign? What then is the regime to do? If it tears down the Asian Games posters, it reveals it was tricked and displays weakness. If it lets the posters stay up, then the story of a successful popular revolt spreads. Rumors

Figure 16.1 **Symbol of the 1990 Asian Games**

consequently spread with details of the creator of the symbol and his successful flight from regime police, gossip that further ridicules regime ineptness and isolation.

In like manner, the regime banned the *V* for victory symbol of the democratic protesters. When a television advertisement ran for a product that highlighted two of something—symbolized by a jutting out of the same two fingers that make the *V*, people merely mentioned the product instead of making the sign.

Delegitimation is such that even media repression and censorship further delegitimate the rulers. T-shirts with totally apolitical slogans, such as the English word "bored," were banned as subversive. A story spread of a cartoon in which three people were sitting. Balloons above their heads carried their repressed conversation:

Person One: Sigh.

Person Two: Sigh.

Person Three: Stop that bourgeois liberalization propaganda.

Even when the regime tries to be one with popular meanings, its efforts are mocked. A story spread of paramount leader Deng Xiaoping reading a televised speech in which he tried to appeal to cultural pride by using an ancient slogan once forbidden. It was said that he was so new to the historically valued idiom that he said the old phrase backward and had to return to the television studio to retape the talk. People swore that a close view of the tape proved the fraud and indicated that the regime was not at one with the Chinese people.

Surface Tranquility, Volcanic Eruption

Chinese are creating space in society where the truth may get through. People talk and visit and share truths they claim to have garnered from the media, thereby breaking what Hannah Arendt labeled "the deadly spell of impotent apathy." A burgeoning literature on the growth of civil society in late Leninist regimes explores this topic.[11] Thus, regardless of recent economic gains and stepped-up appeals to chauvinism, people insist on the truth and put freedom on their political agenda when they know they are living amidst lies.[12] That, of course, was the agenda of the spring 1989 Democracy Movement that seemed impossible to those who had believed that surface tranquility reflected success for regime propaganda and economic reform. In fact, decoding reveals that the surface tranquility hides volcanic forces seeking an outlet through which to transform the political landscape.

What then is the true foreign policy of the Chinese government—as understood by politically conscious Chinese who look for hidden, delegitimating, decoded messages? It is neither the proclaimed purpose of openness to the world market nor the hidden purpose of allying with other Leninist regimes in the hope that China and socialism can save one another. Rather, the hidden foreign policy of the rulers is taken to be selling the fruit of the people's hard work for the private benefit of the isolated regime and its friends.

In 1988–89, new Mercedes-Benzes in Beijing were taken as the essence of China's foreign policy. The people's work won foreign exchange which was then monopolized by the ruling strata. Aid from and trade with Japan are taken to demonstrate that rulers are selling out China to the Japanese for the private benefit of the elite. Arms sales by firms led by the family members of the ruling group are not seen as winning foreign exchange for China's modernization or pridefully circumventing American attempts to limit military escalation, but as seizing corrupt opportunities for the highest members of the feudal monarchy's court to enjoy personally the most expensive luxuries of a corrupt life at the people's expense. China's foreign policy is decoded as a crime, almost treason.

None of this means that a popular uprising will soon topple the Leninist dictatorship and build a popular, liberal democracy. It does not even mean that people clearly see or now know how to act against the discredited dictatorship. What the decoding means is that, over time, the dynamics of the Leninist dictatorship alienate most of the people and persuade them that they can see through the propaganda of a corrupt, incompetent, and unconscionable regime. This combines with a Chinese historical tradition that expects courageous ethical acts by the intellectuals who work in cultural spheres such as journalism, fiction, movies, and television and creates an extraordinary antiregime, oppositional potential in China.

Still, the existence of that potential does not guarantee victory, let alone democracy. Inertia, anxiety, and the discrediting of all politics can maintain the status quo. Moreover, a strong antiregime tendency that is quite antidemocratic also exists.

Yet there is more: democratization—the danger that Leninist rulers define as "peaceful evolution." It is supposed to undermine a moral socialism. The rulers endlessly inveigh against peaceful evolution. Yet virtually all Chinese I have talked with in China about that slogan ironically see "peaceful evolution" as the regime's actual policy and only worthy legitimation. When the regime invokes peaceful evolution it boasts that, in contrast to post-Leninist transitions elsewhere that have led to violence and chaos, China's rulers are moving China gradually into a market-oriented economy, a merit-based society, and as people decode the message, a democratic policy, but that Chinese are doing so without disorder or decline. The regime is popularly praised for democratization by evolution, the policy direction it most fears and attacks. Chinese experience their media and their cultural heroes as contributing to the democratic evolution that so terrifies many of China's Leninist power holders. Propaganda is turned against the propagandists. What Chinese insist on decoding from their media is a message and a hope, a portent that Chinese, too, many one day know freedom.

Notes

1. A Leninist dictatorship combines four institutional networks: a secret, hierarchical, and militarized party; a command economy; a pervasive police; and a nomenklatura system of appointments and promotions by political loyalty.

2. The writings of Vaclav Havel are an excellent critical introduction to this complicitous mentality.

3. See Edelman, *Politics as Symbolic Action* (Chicago: Markham, 1971). For insight on "the kind of code breaker we need," see Salman Rushdie, *Imaginary Homelands* (London: Granta Books, 1991), pp. 203–6. For an application to China, see Jeffery Wasserstrom and Elizabeth Perry, eds., *Popular Protest and Political Culture in Modern China* (Boulder, CO: Westview Press, 1992).

4. For a good critique of Gramsci, see James Scott, *Domination and the Arts of Resistance* (New Haven: Yale University Press, 1990), pp. 90 ff.; and Leszek Kolakowski, *Main Currents of Marxism*, Vol. 3 (New York: Oxford University Press, 1978), pp. 240–44.

5. James Scott, *Weapons of the Weak* (New Haven: Yale University Press, 1988) and *Domination and the Arts of Resistance*.

6. Hsiao Ching-chang and Yang Mei-rong, "American Press Coverage of the Cultural Revolution," paper delivered at China Times Center Conference, "Voices of China: Ambiguities and Contradictions in China Reporting and Scholarship," Minneapolis, Minnesota, October 4–6, 1991.

7. Thus it gives friendship aid to Cuba.

8. Political philosopher Hannah Arendt found that this insistence on truth eventually undermines and explodes Leninist states that impose a hypocritical existence on people. For an application of Arendt's insights into China's Democracy Movement, see Edward Friedman, "Was Mao Zedong a Revolutionary?" in Bih-jaw Lin, ed., *The Aftermath of the 1989 Tiananmen Crisis in Mainland China* (Boulder, CO: Westview Press, 1992), pp. 39–66.

9. Wang Ruoshui, *In Defense of Humanism* (Beijing: Joint Publications, 1986).

10. The following material is from Michael Sullivan, whose article on the Nanjing riot appears in the 1994 *China Quarterly*, but who wrote a longer and more detailed version, from which this paragraph also draws.

11. See Lawrence Sullivan, "The Emergence of Civil Society in China," in Tony Saich, ed., *The Chinese People's Movement* (Armonk, NY: M. E. Sharpe, 1990), pp. 126–44; Barrett McCormick, Su Shaozhi, and Xiao Xiaoming, "The 1989 Democracy Movement: A Review of the Prospects for Civil Society in China," *Pacific Affairs* 65, No. 2 (Summer 1992), pp. 182–202.

12. Hannah Arendt, "Reflections on the Hungarian Revolution," *Journal of Politics* 20 (1958), pp. 5–43.

Part Five

Conclusion

Chapter 17

Some Continuities
Are Radical Ruptures

With democracy increasingly institutionalized in Korea, Taiwan, and Japan, and only external forces preventing a similar outcome in Hong Kong in 1997, it is apparent that Sinic or Confucian culture, however hierarchial or authoritarian, does not block democratization (Friedman 1994).[1] Of course, all democratic societies —not least, those in Western Europe and North America—have to grapple continually with the intolerant tendencies in their cultures. Doing so is an inescapable and political task. There is no reason Chinese cannot do so, too. Historian Roger Des Forges shows that premodern China in fact had as wide an array of factors favorable to democracy as any society. Cultures are multi-stranded and provide fibers that permit political crafters to weave many different patterns. In fact, philosophy professor William Theodore de Bary finds that neo-Confucianism not only had legal constitutionalist tendencies but also had a uniquely strong human rights potential. Add to this Kenneth Minoque's understanding of Christian theology as at best incoherent on human rights, and one is compelled to conclude that culture is not what decides whether a polity democratizes.

In the same way that culture does not stop democratization, so, too, political reforms of the economy in the post-Mao era show that economic forces are not unchangeable structures that preclude democracy. Post-Mao reforms have weakened the collectivist system of Leninist socialism that indeed produced anti-democratic, feudal-like dependencies. This policy change remakes a prior but mutable obstacle to democracy. As Barrington Moore long ago showed, democratization is not easy without commercialized agriculture. Plantation slavery, latifundia peonage, and socialist collectives need to be, can be, and have been transformed to facilitate democratic consolidation. That, too, is a political task.

Still, China's command-economy state enterprises tied to a soft budget state apparatus could, as with mercantilist monopolies and company towns elsewhere, build institutional interests and labor dependencies that work against democratization. Political will, work, and savvy are required to change changeable socioeconomic factors. But reform policies in post-Mao China have already so greatly decreased the weight of such antidemocratic forces that enough space already exists for securing a democratic breakthrough. There is no intrinsic, permanent, or systematic structural dynamic that precludes these institutions from being made market-oriented, with their employees freed from ensnarement by these totalistic units. The workers can be empowered as citizens. The problems for democratizers lie in the political sphere.

Once one realizes that neither culture nor socioeconomic structures block democratization in China, one still faces the conventional wisdom that China lacks practical experience with democracy and so would produce a disaster if it prematurely tried democracy,[2] as did the French after their 1789 revolution.

The people of China do indeed fear chaos. In politics, a strong preference for continuing orderly prosperity over risking malignant chaos is quite normal. The argument that continuity is the most likely succession crisis outcome is, on the surface, persuasive. China's reform policies have permitted so many Chinese to benefit from extraordinary economic growth that the ideological attacks on some negative side effects of reform—whether from fundamentalists or democrats—will almost certainly be rejected by all sectors of China, from the military high command to the villager down on the farm. Chinese leaders would have to be suicidal to opt to turn against continuing the successful policies of the Deng Xiaoping era. In addition, Chinese fear that a failed democratic thrust could hasten national disintegration and civil war. In fact, it could. The rulers aim their propaganda of dictatorial harmony at this widespread cacophony of anxiety. The dictators in China survive at the end of the twentieth century in no small part because people prefer a known "bad" to an unknown potential disaster of bloody chaos that, in politics, is the worst of the worst. Ruling conservatives point to instances, ranging from Africa after independence to Eastern Europe after the fall of the Berlin Wall, where attempts at democracy turned into national disasters.

It is indeed true that democracy is no guarantee that elected rulers will successfully resolve economic quandaries or any other dilemmas. Democracy is only an opportunity. People can squander it. Democratic societies and governments all too frequently have indeed made messes and discredited the process. This is a general phenomenon, not something relegated to one part of the planet, although a focus on Africa or Latin America often persuades "us" that only "they" have this problem.

The American democratic republic set up under the Articles of Confederation after independence was won in 1781, in fact, is often understood the same way, as a failed opportunity. So is the subsequent Constitution that came into play in 1789. The people and the process could not resolve regional division or peaceably end the evil of enslavement, leading to a Civil War that killed more people than all other American wars combined. The republic was almost lost more than once. Nothing guarantees success in making a democracy work. These American disasters occurred despite long experience in America with colonial legislatures. There are no foolproof guarantees.

Some may therefore conclude that the Chinese, supposedly with no democratic experience, are yet more likely—unintentionally—to produce a disaster should they attempt premature democratization. Indeed, China's dictatorial rulers in the post-Mao era legitimate their unaccountable power by claiming that democratization in China is quite likely to lead to economic failure, social chaos, monstrous bloodletting, and civil strife. The alternative is supposed to be stable dictatorship with growth, a long period of socioeconomic development under despotism that, as with Spain or Chile, one day in some distant future allows for a peaceful rupture and transition to democracy while maintaining the basis of the new prosperity uninterrupted.

The data in this book, however, challenge the logic of this neoconservative defense of despotism as natural and popular. The legitimacy and identity crises shaking China are changing the political agenda.

To discover that democracy is not a panacea for economic ills and has often even failed to hold a nation together is not the same as misleadingly asserting that Chinese cannot make democracy work because they supposedly have no experience with or understanding of democracy. Actually, Chinese do have a long and intimate experience with democracy. Around the turn into the twentieth century, as documented in the scholarship of John Fincher and others, a great movement for constitutional governance was led in China's provinces by its enlightened gentry. In addition, Don Price shows that the media spokesmen of this movement for constitutional liberty had a clearer understanding of what democracy was about than even their counterparts in Britain. But the imperial Manchu rulers of China would not concede power, while the democratic opponents of the Manchu *ancien régime* found it easiest to woo mass support against the Manchu monarchy by appealing to emotions of communalist exclusion, that is, to anti-Manchu sentiment. A struggle ensued in which political elites and political challengers, rather than look for a process of compromise and peaceful reconciliation that would advance constitutional democracy, instead used hate-filled communalist slogans as part of appeals to exclusivist emotions. Historian Frederic Wakeman explains that

> by 1899 the Dowager Empress was so aware of increasing anti-Manchuism in the South and so desperate to identify the throne with the masses, that the Boxers appeared to her the very symbol of acceptably righteous popular zeal. And in 1906, when she sponsored constitutional reform, Tz'u-hsi was similarly hoping to bypass provinced officials (now approaching the fiscal and military independence of the later warlords) to link directly up with the people—mainly local gentry. . . . For, in spite of the constitutional principles involved, she thought only to share *hsin* (feeling), not *chuan* (authority, power) with the people. This was a crucial miscalculation. (Wakeman 1973, 48)

A desire by the ruling group to monopolize power precluded democratic evolution through constitutional monarchy. Such evolution has occurred in nations as different as Sweden, Japan, and Britain. Many Chinese at the end of the twentieth century experience the entire century as a total waste, seeing the post-Mao dictatorship as repeating the politics of the late Qing Empress Dowager and the Boxers. It is hard to argue that a politics based in antagonistic communalisms, which have also been intensifying in late-twentieth-century China, will facilitate an easy compromise of peaceful progress between elites and challengers. Instead, intransigence by a northern regime against a supposedly subversive south could again condemn Chinese to a painful political destiny without the blessings of political liberty.

Most nations experience numerous breakthroughs or openings to democracy. Few people successfully and swiftly consolidate and institutionalize the original breakthrough, not in America, not in China. A few years after the Empress Dowager died, the overthrow of the Manchu Dynasty in 1911 gave China an opportunity again to institutionalize democracy, this time in a Republic of China. National elections were held that were at least as free and fair as most first elections ever tend to be. The Nationalist Party headed by Song Jiaoren won. Song would become premier. But then the acting president and head of northern armies, Yuan Shikai, had Prime Minister Song assassinated, and so murdered constitutional democracy one more time.

The Chinese people could act democratically, but old-guard elites refused to recognize that reality. There are diverse explanations as to why Yuan and Song could not reach a *modus vivendi,* but one important one includes the impact of foreign influence in the era of high imperialism.

As with the lost constitutional democracy in Persia of 1905, imperialist powers did not believe that non-European people could make democracy work. Even the great John Stuart Mill in his justly famous essay *On Liberty*, which praises the worth of liberty for all law-abiding, rational adults, will not grant liberty to colonized peoples, "those backward states of society in which the race itself may be considered as in its nonage" (chapter 1, paragraph 10). Racist, imperialist forces helped create a climate of opinion within President Yuan's camp and its followers that legitimated the assassination of Song, a military coup, and an attempt to restore monarchy backed by large foreign loans. Imperialists self-servingly contended and pretended that infant-like races could not do as the supposedly mature Europeans did.

This did not turn China's political class against democracy. It did not even, as Don Price's scholarship establishes, persuade them that China needed a temporary dictatorship until the threat of imperialism was defeated. Instead, with Japan experienced as an enemy made militarily aggressive by its dictatorial politics, dictatorship seemed inhuman. Only democracy was moral. Liberal values seemed even more attractive, an ethical and efficacious way to achieve the political liberty and prosperous life of such countries as Britain. China's constitutionalists lost because, as any student of Confucius's own career could understand, the times were unpropitious. Armed forces and imperialist supporters were united in their opposition to democracy. Strikingly, the immoral victory of tyranny, however, made democracy, progress in liberty, and autonomous dignity yet more valued.

The momentous May Fourth Movement beginning during Europe's Great War, what Chinese called the European Civil War, what Europeans called a World War, re-energized a Chinese national commitment to democracy. This is manifest even in the political ideas held then by the future head of China's Communist movement, Mao Zedong.

Mao found in the May Fourth era that "Those who have a spirit of independence are heroes" (Schram 1992, 10). "There is no higher value than that of the individual. . . . Thus there is no greater crime than to suppress the individual or to violate particularity" (ibid., 208). "As the spirit develops, the ideals become diverse" (ibid., 222). "Killing . . . is inhumane" (ibid., 228). "I advocate two principles. The first is individualism" (ibid., 251). "Throughout our entire lives, all of our activities obey the ego. . . . [E]ach self exists for itself; . . . only the self can be honored" (ibid., 273). "I do not agree with the idea that the life of the individual derives from the life of the nation. . . . The individual comes before the nation. The life of the nation . . . is formed of the combined lives of individuals" (ibid., 281). "Self-realization means to develop fully both our physical and spiritual capabilities to the highest" (ibid., 285). "Even before its full flowering, religion was a force that restrained naked violence and protected the young and the weak" (ibid., 296). "A people without its individuals loses its powers" (ibid., 308).

"[I]f this had been a western society, and Miss Zhao's father had slapped her in the face when she refused to get into the sedan chair [for an arranged marriage], she [instead of committing suicide] could have taken him to court and sued him, or she could have resisted in some way to protect herself" (ibid., 428). "The power of the human need for love is greater than that of any other need" (ibid., 445). "Today's politics is representative politics, based on elections" (ibid., 451). "The people of [Mao's home province of] Hunan feel bitterly angered . . . because freedom of speech has been completely swept into the dust" (ibid., 479). "The realization of civil rights and human rights in every country . . . has come only after active struggles." (ibid., 511). "Our 30 million [Hunan] people must all have freedom of speech, publication, assembly and association. These are our greatest hopes" (ibid., 530). "We shall always adopt an open-minded attitude toward all views." (ibid., 537). "[T]he big China that has existed for four thousand years has no foundation. . . . It is the individual citizens who comprise the foundation." (ibid., 546).

In the late 1920s and into the 1930s, as democratic efforts were militarily overwhelmed by warlord politics and some came to argue that China first and foremost needed centralized military strength to defeat Chinese warlords, unify China's armed strength, and stand up to foreign invaders, a debate occurred over democracy versus dictatorship as the best way ahead (Gu Xin n.d.). Even in this perilous time, so strong was the Chinese commitment to democracy that proponents of constitutional governance still were not overwhelmed.

It was not until the mid-1930s when the Japanese military expanded across Chinese territory that the view grew in popularity that everything else, even the cause of individual freedom, had to be sacrificed to win national freedom. Wartime, crisis, and emergency, of course, lead to a weakening or suspension of democratic commitments in all republican systems. Lincoln's suspension of habeas corpus in the American Civil War, however, no more proves Americans antidemocratic than did priorities of Chinese in the anti-Japan war. But Mao Zedong's forces, committed to establishing Leninist dictatorship in perpetuity, cleverly used that momentary unidimensional mood of the anti-Japanese war to try to legitimate the notion that only they knew how to liberate China and that bourgeois democratic forces could never consolidate Chinese independence. Yet when the war ended, the Communists found they had to respond to public opinion preferring the institutionalization of democracy.

China still had another opportunity to build a constitutional government after the defeat of the Japanese aggressors, especially in early 1946, the era of the New Democracy. In retrospect, real power was decided by a clash of armies between 1945 and 1949. Nonetheless, many observers in the mid-1940s found Chinese culture so individualistic or familistic that it seemed inconceivable that Chinese could ever welcome a prolongation of the pains of dictatorship. The dictatorship of Chiang Kai-shek (Jiang Jieshi) could not legitimate dictatorship. Mao in fact sold his anti-Chiang policies not as a superior dictatorship, but as a New Democracy. Mao suggested coalition government. Educated people who joined China's Communist Party struggle at the end of World War II often believed they were joining a truly democratic movement. They valued democracy. They imagined themselves as liberating Chinese from landlordism, superstition, imperialism, bureaucratic comprador capitalism, and militarism to build a people's democratic state. As naive as they may subsequently seem to have been, they were real in their commitment to democracy. They eventually felt betrayed when Mao's new government crushed liberties.

China's Leninist Party apparatus after 1949 institutionalized Leninist-Stalinist despotism, appealed to popular Jacobin-Leninist purposes (patriotism, antispeculation), and attacked supporters of liberal democracy as spies and traitors, as friends of imperialism and enemies of the people of China. The cruel 1957–58 antirightist movement labeled as rightists millions of democracy-oriented Chinese and their family members who had spoken for civil liberties, protected rights, and the due process of law in the 1956–57 Hundred Flowers Movement. It was only in 1957–58 that it began to be obvious to many Chinese democrats that the People's Republic would be a cruel despotism that rested on Mao's charismatic legitimacy as a savior and founder, and therefore a legitimate first despotic legislator. There was no love affair with the authoritarianism of the Communist Party dictatorship. Mao's charismatic authority made possible the stability of Leninist despotism.

In fact, the corrupt, selfish tyranny of the Leninist order became so broadly hated that when Mao in 1966 initiated the so-called Cultural Revolution, invited Chinese to topple power holders who were greedy and brutal, the outpouring of popular support (i.e., opposition to Communist authoritarian power), was so massive and the desire for real democracy so great that Mao eventually decided to call in the military to crush the democratic thrust of young rebels throughout China and ignore the purported commitment to a truer democracy, as in a Paris Commune of democratic elections that the Cultural Revolution seemed momentarily to have embraced. In response to the crushing of this democratic upsurge, the alienated, democratic, educated youth of China began to rethink their commitment to democracy in terms of principled opposition to Mao's despotism.

The ruling elite split. The youth who spearheaded the democratic attacks on Mao's monstrous dictatorship tended to come from ruling families. Among the well-known consequences of this political turn against Mao's tyrannical order are the 1974 Li Yizhe big-character poster for democracy and legal rights; the 1978–79 Democracy Wall Movement for democracy, legal rights, and scientific progress; and the post-Mao 1980–81 spread of popular democratic journals throughout the nation that ran a spectrum from Wang Xizhe's democratic Marxism in the south to Wei Jingsheng's liberal democracy in the north. In summary, Chinese politics witnessed manifestations of a continuous commitment to democratization as the path to dignity and development throughout the twentieth century. Many Chinese can therefore find that they have lots of expensively purchased experience with democracy, from real elections in classes at school in the People's Republic to figuring out what is needed to stop phony People's Republic elections run by the ruling dictatorial party. Given the Chinese lives sacrificed in a century of struggle for democracy, it is difficult to lend any credibility to the notion that Chinese lack the qualifications to make democracy work. Their democratic tuition has not come cheap.

What further qualifications for democracy are ever needed? The great American historian John Hope Franklin, writing on the post–Civil War United States, conceded that

> most of the ex-slaves were without the qualifications to participate effectively in a democracy—although in this respect, he noted tellingly, they were little different from the enfranchised recent immigrants of the northern cities. (Friedrickson 1993, 33)

There is little evidence for the claim that American democracy is the fruit of a uniquely democratic American political culture and much to the contrary (Smith 1993).

Is democracy ever premised on some precularily democratic political culture? The eminent Italian political theorist of democracy, Noberto Bobbio, doubts it of Italy. "I do not know how many Italians are really true lovers of liberty. Perhaps there are few" (Anderson 1992, 126). Likewise, John Stuart Mill did not find that the existing English democracy rested on an English political culture friendly to freedom. Mill instead found the English to be intolerant sectarians who are "far from setting any value on individuality," but seek rather "to make everyone conform," "to maim by compression like a Chinese lady's foot, every part of human nature which stands out," which was not surprising, since the British system grew out of seventeenth-century "fanatical moral intolerance." According to H. Von Trietschke, French culture, too, was antidemocratic such that Napoleon's dictatorship "satisfied the inner compulsion of the French to be slaves" (Bobbio 1987, 147). The idea that democracy results from a unique European cultural appreciation of individualism is a contemporary concoction.

From Albania to Mongolia, other successfully democratizing former Leninist societies were far less prepared for democracy than China in 1989. The difference was that a dominant faction in the ruling party in Tirana and Ulan Bator, but not in Beijing, decided on peaceful accommodation with democratic forces on behalf of democratization. The unanswerable question for China is whether this obduracy within its ruling party will so alienate society that the subsequent outcome will not be an eventual, peaceful, Spanish-like transition to democracy but a coming apart of the nation as in so many other post-Leninist societies.

Most analysts downplay how illegitimate China's post-Mao economic reformers are despite extraordinary economic growth. Few Chinese, however, credit the regime for the growth. Instead, Chinese tend to see the successes coming from avoiding the corrupt, parasitic, selfish rulers who suck the blood of the people to enrich their own personal networks of support—forces of spying and coercion, bloated and incompetent bureaucracies, kin and allies, and money-losing, inefficient state enterprises.

A government official in Hebei province's Raoyang county told me that it was my responsibility to tell foreigners that China is quite stable and foreign fears that chaos is rife are misplaced. Actually, I believe this official, as so many other Chinese, is fixated on the growing potential for social strife, fearful that today's tenuous political stability just might not last. Surely, when the national government in Beijing deploys plainclothes security officers all over college campuses in the early months of 1994, that does not betoken assured confidence in tranquility as a social given. This is not a government confident enough to dare tell its people the full story of the mass murder of Taiwan tourists in southern China in April 1984. There is a ghost haunting China.

The front page of the March 1993 issue of the Chinese journal *Classified News* asked, "Will China Split Up?" The answer was given in interview form featuring a Japanese international relations specialist and He Xin, a much-hated Chinese academician popularly thought of as a total opportunist who associates with the most reactionary elements. As is his wont, Mr. He ridiculed foreigners as ignoramuses, this time for focusing on the issue of China's likelihood of going down the Yugoslav–Soviet Union path of division.

Mr. He paid no attention to the question of the Japanese scholar as to whether China's economic liberalization would lead to political liberalization and a system of legal due process that would be conducive to long-term, stable foreign investment, a particularly crucial issue for China since its extraordinarily speedy post-Mao economic growth is so strongly tied to foreign investment, foreign trade, and foreign technology. China's trade-dependency ratio is 35 percent, which is much higher than Japan's. Instead, Mr. He argued that China under a Communist Party dictatorship would remain stable. That was enough. He declared that no Chinese speaks out for a breakup of China, which I find indeed still is true.

Mr. He further argued that China could not break up, which is a very different matter. One leaves the realism of subjective intention to focus on objective forces. What was objectively decisive for Mr. He was that China's people were all the same race, blood, and culture. Actually, the concept of race is the worst opium evil that nineteenth-century Europe exported. It has no scientific reality. There is no Chinese race. I won't even comment on the fascist concept of a pure group of one blood type. As for a common culture, as this book has detailed, in the last decades of the twentieth century, Chinese actually have focused on the cultural factors that divide them. The resurgence of lineage in China, however, is popularly experienced as the rise of blood ties. The regime's vicious anti-American propaganda combines with a vision of the nouveau riche on the coast as people who go to nightclubs and take concubines and enjoy karaoke—things that solid moral Chinese do not do—to make people who are angry about the growing income gap see the newly rich as virtually another race. China is boiling with a brew that could result in a nasty, militaristic, and even expansionist Chinese fascism. Mr. He promotes race consciousness but obscures the pains that infuse it.

Refusing to discuss actual tensions in China, including centrifugal social forces, Mr. He went on, in an amazingly counterfactual way, to compare China and the Soviet Union, to show that China could not follow the Soviet Union in the direction of division. He falsely claimed that while China was a place with millenia, or at least many centuries, of good and close relations among the majority Han and all other peoples, in contrast the Russians in the west of the Soviet Union were close to Europeans and separated throughout history from all the other peoples in the Soviet Union. In addition, the Russian Bolsheviks only used political methods to control the other peoples. In sum, the breakup of the Soviet Union was a historically ordained, inevitable, and obvious trend.

Actually, little could be further from the truth. Anyone with even a little real knowledge of the Soviet Union or China knows that Mr. He's description is patently absurd. In fact, it was bad relations among communities in China—that is, anti-Manchu sentiment—that facilitated China's 1911 republican revolution. Mao-era cruel policies that attacked regional cultures greatly alienated all minorities from the center in the People's Republic.

Meanwhile, under Stalin Russians spread to the Pacific Ocean, Russifying Siberia and Russia's Far East. A division of production was created in the Soviet Union so that all regions depended economically on Russia. Large numbers of Russians migrated to all areas of the Soviet Union. Local people were promoted to positions of regional power. As a result of these policies, most analysts concluded for the Soviet Union until 1990, as Mr. He does in 1993 for China, that a division of the country into regional communalisms was absolutely impossible. Mr. He does not ask why they all were wrong, why all these supposedly decisive factors turned out to be insufficient to hold a reforming Soviet Union together.

Since the Soviet Union did break apart, it is important to note that Mao did less for national integration than Stalin. Mao, in contrast to Stalin, implemented policies that strengthened regional economic independence. Thus there is reason to take seriously Mr. He's passing comment that "the Chinese people do not slight the existence of the danger of a break-up" of China (p. 9). This might have led to an analysis of regionalism.

Mr. He pays little attention, however, to the contention of the Japanese scholar indicating that increasingly the center in China is forced to rely on secret meetings of regional representatives to decide issues like taxes and that such meetings and issues are of great significance in shaping China's future political system (pp. 8, 11). I would only add that this center–region tension holds other possibilities in addition to a breakup or fascism, everything from representation and federalism to new types of center–region relationship that maintain central power, including, most importantly, a project of hegemony for southern consciousness.

Mr. He's only response to the Japanese scholar's focus on regional power is that in China the Communist Party government rests on big state-owned enterprises (SOE), whereas in Japan, South Korea, and Taiwan private enterprises and other social forces grew and developed. That is, Mr. He claims that China right now lacks a basis for political liberalization that would empower civil society, as has occurred elsewhere in East Asia. He overlooks the fact that China's economic growth rests in large part on the extraordinary growth of rural so-called *xiang-zhen qiye*, village and township enterprises.

A hidden factor in China's rural-driven flexibility and reform success and Russia's urban-based rigidity and relative reform failure is a matter of relative size and place. In contrast to Russia's gargantuan urban SOEs, China's small, Mao-era, rural collective industries could cheaply and quickly transit out of command-economy monopolies and into market-oriented applications. For rural China, only a few jobs were at risk each time. Only minimal capital was needed for each retooling. Privileged access to cheap money and other vital resources, which in the Mao era meant renting a position that guaranteed unearned success, could now, at local levels, leverage state-supported competitive advantages—as in Japan and Korea—that won genuine market-oriented competitions, but only for China, for micro-sized firms (the village and township enterprises, a designation from a 1985 renaming in the countryside of all units), as in Taiwan. Suddenly, unexpectedly, China had an economic dynamo that combined the leveraging advantages of a Japanese-style development state with the adaptability advantages of a north Italy–style, superflexible exporter, which is what Taiwan has been. Still, Mr. He is right that in China, unlike Taiwan, this economic dynamism is not part of a robust civil society.

Mr. He does not explain why China lacks a vital civil society. The answer is well known. What Leninists call socialism is actually a form of statism that fears and represses most forms of social self-organization. But is it helpful to stability in China that social groups are not allowed to organize and express their interests? The result of Leninist Stalinism is a society-wide feeling of powerlessness and a popular blaming of all that is bad on the center. But is this combination a recipe for prolonged stability, or could it be a formula for an eventual explosion? The latter prospect is a pervasive fear of Chinese people. They fear an outburst of bloody hatred.

From the countryside, which has lost its basic medical care program and which is excruciatingly conscious of a growing income gap, village theft and fighting intensify. More than fifty million villagers have fled, seeking better jobs. This combination deeply worries the central authorities, who see it as an augur of possible grain shortages—official claims of a 1993 record grain year are literally incredible—combined with hunger, hate, and unemployment that could be social dynamite on a short fuse. Hence the center seeks both to persuade people that there is no grain shortage and to scapegoat foreigners and worshipers of foreigners for China's problems. The Chinese government sees a great danger of chaos aborning. This possibility is not a foreign invention.

How can Mr. He ignore the danger? Some of its causes were pointed out long ago by Tocqueville. A system that destroys or delegitimates all intermediary groups fosters the possibility of a war of all against all when the center falls. With China's center illegitimate and its supposed base, according to Mr. He, the SOEs, despised, what is there to hold society together should there be a political crisis? Chinese understand the danger. They increasingly rely on family and accept the present evil in dread of the yet worse horror that may lie just around the bend. Should one uniformly praise a Leninist system that invariably creates this threat, or praise partial reformers who refuse to face up to the need for political reform to avoid the extreme evil or who wish it away with shortsighted policies that enhance prospects for a fascist outcome? If China avoids the horror of evil chaos, it will not be because of the wisdom of leaders who, in seeking short-term stability, do nothing to counter the terror that Tocqueville so ably explicated.

The SOEs that Mr. He embraces as a basis for stability are thought of by most Chinese as parasitic money-losers concentrated in the northeast that unfairly exploit the rest of the nation. They do not provide a long-term basis for an acceptable political system.

Workers at such enterprises fear that privatization and marketization will cost them their jobs. The government in Beijing fears labor discontent if it imposes profit-making criteria. Consequently, Beijing has moved at a snail's pace on closing down bankrupt SOEs.

Some analysts believe that the rest of the Chinese economy is doing so well that China can afford to maintain social stability by subsidizing these enterprises. Meanwhile, very gradually, these optimistic analysts find more and more SOEs are beginning to make themselves internationally competitive and economically profitable.

This long-term process and possibility, while real, could easily be derailed in the short run by a host of not unlikely political changes, from an increase in regional power that produces a decision against further subsidization of the SOEs of the northeast to a financial panic over budget gaps and inflationary pressures that leads to a similar decision. Put simply, the success of the economic reforms remains in a bit of doubt because of continuing political uncertainty.

On the other hand, so open is China's future that some prospects seem positive and benign. A Chinese government analyst of SOEs suggested that it was likely that reformed SOEs would join with the forces of the more open south and other more economically dynamic regions to smash the regressive SOE areas of the northeast, thereby peacefully transiting out of a Leninist system. That, however, is not a happy dream for entrenched Leninists.

The Chinese central government is, of course, aware of these problems and possibilities. Indeed, since key facts and figures are maintained as state secrets, the outsider cannot help but be somewhat uninformed on what is most crucial. It seems that the center by the mid-1980s began to regret its singular stress on allowing the far south to open to the outside first. The original intention was to keep bad foreign influences isolated far away from the Chinese heartland. But the center greatly underestimated the expansive force of the reform thrust from opening to the outside. The center soon did not like the fact that a more open and pluralistic far south was changing China in the south's image.

By the mid-1980s, therefore, the center began to facilitate growth in Shanghai. The goals of favoring Shanghai included allowing a city with 75 percent heavy industry, and consequently great dependent ties on the center, to grow, to influence the provinces up the Yangtze River and to block the spread of scary southern influences. In addition, Shanghai would receive priority privileges in financial matters so that its historic role as an international financial center would be restored. If my reading of kremlinological clues is correct, the importance of Hong Kong in the south for China would fall in this governmental design, a decline quickened by an eventual movement of many Chinese exports and imports through Shanghai rather than Hong Kong.

Shanghai would also take the lead in reforming state enterprises. Like Wuhan,

Shanghai, through joint ventures and other mechanisms, has made great strides in transforming a few of its SOEs into profitable businesses. Government propaganda often suggests that all SOEs are about to become internationally competitive and thus end their drain on the budget and their upward pressure on inflationary forces. But it seems that in fact the northeast has not followed suit. Instead, the northeast seems ever more isolated, dependent, and parasitic; and Shanghai, as Canton, seems ever more dynamic, independent, and open to the outside. It is not clear how this regional politics will play out, no matter how intelligent and clever are central leaders. It is obvious, however, that the center, like the provinces, is playing a game of regional politics.

In the northern port city of Tianjin, intellectuals in 1994 proudly boasted of southern (Jiangnan) origins. Government officials insisted that port regions produce open and progressive people. They often declared that Tianjin's best time was 1950–51, not only a moment just before the state campaigns decimated Tianjin business, but also a time when Tianjin was China's busiest port, far ahead of Shanghai in the south. People even insisted that the nationally idolized Three Kingdoms–era advisor Zhuge Liang should be thought of in terms of his southern descendants.

In 1994 the center began a tax-reform process by setting meetings with all the provinces, but one at a time. The center's goal was to establish a tax formula in which each province would experience its share as fair and the center would take and control sufficiently much so that all regions would again be dependent on the disbursement of funds from the center. In short, the political struggle over the relation of center and region has become central to Chinese politics and decisive for China's future.

The alternatives are not merely continuity or a breakup of the nation. This data reminds us that unity with southern hegemony is one possible solution. Regional communalism actually holds many possibilities.

On an April–May 1994 visit to north China, however, I found manifestations of divisive regionalism mixed with communalism ubiquitous. In a television interview in Tianjin, I was asked only questions about Tianjin, beginning with how many times I had visited Tianjin and ending with a request for my speculation on whether Tianjin could surpass Shanghai and Canton. The city is organizing its economy as an integral part of Northeast Asia. The region is what matters.

A retired official from Subei explained how politico-economic tensions in the Jiangnan area embody regional communalisms. In Shanghai, before the Mao era, the Jiangnan people who ran the city looked down on the miserably poor outsiders from Subei who migrated in and took any job, even the worst, to survive. The army loyal to Mao that liberated Shanghai in 1949 was naturally full of Subei people, since the Red armies recruited best in the poorest rural areas. Subei people took over all of Jiangnan. Local people who subsequently experienced the cruelty, waste, and tragedy of the Mao era often experience it as having come from Subei people. In the post-Mao era of reform and growth, Jiangnan's economy has taken off. Local people are making it economically despite a corrupt and incompetent Communist Party government. The popular Jiangnan experience is that their community would be doing better if they could just get rid of the Subei rulers who have been useless and thieving. The split between state and society is experienced as communalist.

Driving through the north China rural hinterland in a car with a Tianjin license plate, more signs of regional communalism attacked the eye and the pocketbook. A bridge was blocked. Detour was necessary. The car wound through village dirt lanes. Suddenly a lane was blockaded by a truck and an overturned tractor. Young toughs manned the barrier. One claimed to be a Party secretary. Tribute had to be paid for the car to get through. But that did not get us out of the maze. Still we wound through deserted village lanes. Twice more in two subsequent villages young toughs blocked the roads and made demands. It grew a bit scary. It was not clear one would ever return to the main road. The driver explained that all the drivers in Tianjin and Beijing know the Hebei peasants are out to get them. The Tianjin and Beijing license plates are targets for venting their ire. We experienced this violence again further down the road when we ran into a Daoist funeral. As the mourners marched past our Tianjin license-plate car, they banged nastily on the sides of the car and shook the vehicle. Later, on a drive to Beijing in a Hebei license-plate car, I told the story of the highway holdups in Hebei to that driver. He harrumphed and commented that he drives regularly through neighboring Shandong, Henan, and Shanxi and has had similar experiences in all these provinces, although, he added, people in counties who have to pay to build bridges do have a right to tax outsiders who use them. Still the comminglings of violence and parochial communalism seem pervasive.

Even when I reached my hinterland destination, signs of the new regionalism were everywhere. As always in this superloyal rural place, painted slogans were commonplace. But this time they all promoted this particular locale only. People for the first time insisted that I try to speak the local patois instead of Beijing dialect.

The communalist tendency is more than hometown boosterism. The regionalist communalism reflects deep and sharp angers and is embedded in ever more entrenched economic realities. Everyone is conscious that social stability is fragile and that cruel and explosive hates lie just beneath a thin veneer of civility.

A spate of brutal and crippling beatings of price inspectors was all the gossip. People also told each other about the retired workers whose fixed pensions could not keep up with inflation and who had surrounded a host of government buildings. Also on various college campuses throughout China, students demonstrated against bad food. All social groups seemed angrily discontented.

Chinese people are so frightened and fixated on their fragile social order that they see totally unrelated issues in its reflection. Sophisticated urban Party people declared that America's goal in long tying China's most-favored-nation

(MFN) trade status to human rights was to cause social disorder in China, subvert China's successful reforms, and reduce China to the chaos of Russia. To be sure, this propaganda line from the center could change tomorrow. What is interesting and dangerous is how even many informed people, who one would think should know far better, instead respond positively and emotionally to the Party line because of their deep anxieties about the society fracturing into violent and hate-filled regional communalisms.

A national chauvinism could also win out. As never before, in my 1994 trip I was asked by a diverse range of people to explain America's evils, its supposedly unique prevalence of homosexuality in the military, an amoral welcoming of endless extramarital affairs, and an inhuman egoistic selfishness that slights the responsibilities of the young to the old. Government propaganda seems to have struck a receptive chord in north China, facilitating a reactionary blood-based belief that foreign blood pollutes. And yet the north at the end of the twentieth century is also changing rapidly and giving birth to a host of better possibilities.

The imagined north of hidebound reactionary traditions is dying and being reborn in far more hopeful potentials. In the countryside, as in the city, I found in 1994 that when educated folk thought of themselves as acting in the tradition of Confucius, they no longer comprehended Confucius as the progenitor of an authoritarian patriarchy but instead focused on Mencius as a protodemocrat and on a Confucian heritage that highlighted the sixteenth-century thinker Huang Zongxi, whose progressive protoconstitutional ideas were two centuries ahead of Europe's Enlightenment. The droves of Chinese college students who select popular electives on the ancient culture find their teachers explicating Confucianism as a protodemocratic ethos.

Among the general populace, the focus was less on an ideational heritage of protodemocratic possibilities and more on a sharp contrast between a stable China—the fixation of my friend in Raoyang—and chaos elsewhere. While the West was polluted by intolerant, violent communalisms, by Hitler's genocidal war on Jews, by fratricidal conflict in Northern Ireland between Catholics and Protestants, in contrast, Chinese people are imagining themselves as more culturally democratic, as historically tolerant. This is taken to be China's deep cultural secret for historically avoiding religious warfare and for maintaining social stability.

An unintended but widespread consequence of the Chinese government's endless daily barrage of its citizens with bad news about civil turmoil in every part of the world, meant to persuade the Chinese people that they are fortunate to have the stability provided by their wonderful post-Mao government, is that the people have sought a different explanation, since they do not think of the corrupt, useless officials they deal with daily as wonderful. Instead they have begun to imagine Chinese culture as wonderful, a development missed by Chinese intellectuals who still attack Chinese culture as feudal. Instead Chinese are reconceiving themselves as uniquely tolerant and open. This China is represented by the openness of the Tang and the commercialization of the Southern Song and a supposed lack of religious hates and strife in Chinese history. People even are beginning to boast about the independent ways of their children. Thus it is easy to see why the campaign starting in 1984 to promote Confucius has achieved so little in its attempt at relegitimating Confucian Leninism. China's Confucius is not a Leninist. Instead, increasingly, popularly, China's Confucian culture is imagined as particularly compatible with democratic stability.

The data in this book have shown, in addition, how a Chinese democratic potential has come to be identified with a more open southern national project, an end to northern parasitism. Only in 1992 would Beijing retract a Mao-era policy of grain first that forced southerners to grow rice instead of maize, causing "the south . . . poor efficiency from feeding hogs rice" (Liu 1992, 61). In general, southerners told each other about how the government in the north stole from them. In 1991, a story spread of how a southern military unit reported to Beijing that it now earned so much money that it no longer needed central government subventions. The north's response to southern success was to send down a team that arrested and executed the successful southerners and then monopolized the southern enterprises and the profits. The rulers in the northern city of Beijing are imagined in negative stereotypes.

In fact, of course, Shenzen, the leading Special Economic Zone in the south, is actually dynamized by northerners, often children of former Party elites who suffered from Maoist fundamentalism. Well-educated, open to the world, this northern contingent speaks Mandarin, not Cantonese. These people, however, tend to be a set of individuals whose family histories during the Mao era set them in opposition to the reactionary, Confucian, post-Mao old guard in Beijing. It is more natural for them to ally with the southern national project, to cooperate with the workers from Guangdong who are building Shenzhen brick by brick and who speak Cantonese. The south need not be just a region; it can be a potentially nationwide consciousness of purpose. Outward-facing people in the north reject the northern reactionary appeal to Confucianism as a way to "foster the unity of a great national ethnic family with the [Confucian Han] Chinese at the head" (Zhang Xinhua 1990, 104).

Of course, northerners are far from uniformly enthralled by the rise of a southern national project. Many insist that Cantonese have no culture. The Shenzhen elite wards off Cantonese communalism. Some northerners will say that they would even feel more at home in Japan than in south China now. There is a tendency of some to curse any innovation that is disliked as southern. Thus, on registering at a hotel and being informed of a rule change that requires the last day's rental to be paid on registering, a northerner might explode about another damned southern innovation. Within both this anger at and injured condescension toward the south lie possibilities of division or conflict or defeat of the southern project. The outcome of China's politico-cultural struggle remains up for grabs. The outcome of the struggle over democracy in part depends on the debate over national identity.

The appeal to Confucianism was linked by conservative rulers to the desirability of the new Asian prosperity in contrast to Western democracies, portrayed as economically stagnant and socially immoral. Confucian authoritarianism, in contrast, was propagandized as "the historical guiding principle for the Chinese people's political structure . . . different from any western model." In contrast to the purported selfishness, greed, and polarization of Western liberal democracies, Confucianism, it was argued, held "the essence of humanism and democracy" because it "aided in the establishment of benevolent and moral government." These "positive ingredients [were] usable by socialism," a source of "success in launching the East Asian economies." The West's slogans of freedom were senseless. "Compared to the West, China's [Confucian] cultural thinking . . . just might be ahead" (Zhang Xinhua 1990). The conservative Confucian national identity is the subject of a discourse about Asia's global rise.

The official Chinese media propounds the conservative cultural chauvinist view of anti-Westernism that asserts that liberal America is a fraud, a society actually pervaded by "the feminization of poverty, rape, the degradation of women in most pornography, and widespread unemployment and underemployment of women" (Moghadam 1989, 93). But women in China tend to know that they suffer all these evils and that the rulers cause them. A prodemocracy poster that condemned the regime was copied and spread in 1989. It declared, "If hoodlums can successfully hold up . . . an entire passenger train . . . [if] the population's out of control, what does this all mean?. . . [R]ivers are polluted . . . marriage is a commodity . . . AIDS spreads unchecked; . . . where is China going?" (Gunn 1990, 251). The rulers seem to have failed in their attempt to blame China's social problems on Western pollution. The conservative rulers are held responsible for evils for which they try to scapegoat the West.

What is amazing is how little impact the chauvinist appeal has had, since throughout history there have been many in all cultures who have opted for security and food over freedom. The people of Israel, fleeing bondage, complained to Moses, "Why did you bring me from Egypt—to kill me and my children and my livestock with thirst?" (Exodus 17:3). Dathan and Abiram complained to the liberator, "You brought us up from a land flowing with milk and honey to kill us in the wilderness" (Numbers 16:13). People who privilege other values above freedom flourish in all cultures.

Chinese, however, reject the northern reactionary message of hiding behind walls. As one high school student wrote about the script for the television series *He Shang*, which identified China's better national future with basic reform and openness to the world, "When our teacher read aloud the passage in which the Great Wall is depicted as a huge monument of national tragedy, we all applauded with excitement" (Chen Xiaomei 1992, 703).

China's Confucian conservatives appealed to fundamentalist misogyny to discredit the forces of freedom. The "authorities authorized a march by the Xian Muslim community to protest the publication in Shanghai of *Sexual Customs*, which they found insulting to Islam. With banners calling for death to the 'Chinese Rushdies' who had authored the book, and shouting slogans praising the Communist Party . . . about 20,000 Muslims marched . . . [in] strictly gender-segregated groups" (Esherick 1990, 220–21).

Yet this appeal to repressive conservative values over personal fulfillment has won few takers. Chinese women could see and act as proposed by Nawal El Saadawi.

> Freedom has a price. . . . [A] woman always pays a heavy price. . . . [S]ince she has to pay [a price], why not the price of freedom? . . . [T]he price paid in slavery even if accompanied by some security, and the peace of mind that comes from acceptance, is made higher than the price paid for freedom. . . . For a woman to be able to regain her personality, her humanity, her intrinsic and real self is much more worthwhile (Saadawi 1981, 209).

The superficially frail woman, Chai Ling, symbolized the principled hunger strike of courageous 1989 supporters of democracy. The commitment could draw on the historic ethic that death was superior to life without virtue. "If women risked all, how could men hold back" seemed to be the popular attitude that led society to focus on the sacrifice of women. Although there was but one woman among the hunger strikers in Shenyang, "Onlookers were said to be especially struck by the woman's participation" (Gunn 1990, 249). The cause of freedom for women and China were experienced as one.

In China's south, Chinese University of Hong Kong history professor Honming Yip reports, single women have been going overseas for over a century to work and return foreign currency remittances to their lineages back home. These families therefore had more resources with which to succeed. Their lifestyle could set a standard. These lineages maintained a dignified place for their single unmarried female members who went overseas and who eventually returned to live in spinster houses and to have influence in family affairs. They kept spirit tablets for deceased spinsters and publicly displayed the products of their handicraft work. They showed that young women had independent value aside from being brides married into other lineages. The south has been the nurturer of international openness and economic progress tied to the worth of independent young females.

Although northern court culture was previously propagated as Chinese culture, in fact, fine porcelain, rice, landscape gardening, landscape painting, and progress in both printing and economic wealth all flowed from the south. Increasingly, even northerners see southerners as uniquely capable of leading China into the twenty-first century. One such northerner commented to a foreign visitor as their plane landed at Canton, "Now we enter a world where the people seem to have capitalist genes," meaning the capacity to gain prosperity for the people of China.

My experience in Raoyang county in Hebei suggests that many northerners may now believe southerners deserve their prosperity. They do not share the center's goal of limiting the spread of influence from the south. Instead, they welcome and even seek out southern inputs. A picture of Jiangnan has even been painted at the entrance to Raoyang city's largest market.

After the great north China flood of August 1963, northerners were impressed by the relief items sent from the south, such that the south seemed amazingly prosperous. In 1967–68 young people who went south in the Cultural Revolution experienced the south as a land with a surfeit of water, an amazingly green landscape. There was a virtual contrast between southern oasis and northern desert. By the 1990s, as the north at last tried to upgrade its collective enterprises, it discovered it lacked the "smarts" of the south. It has spent great sums to import technicians from the south to help upgrade northern production. The dirt-poor village of Gengkou in Raoyang pays 900 yuan a month to a retired Jiangsu specialist and considers it a bargain. In fact, Gengkou's yarn-spinning know-how began in 1962 when a worker was forced back home from the south at the end of three famine years. The popular experience is that the south is ahead because the south has what it takes to get ahead. The north–south gap and southern predominance seem fair.

This attitude is most manifest among a new generation of Party secretaries, hitherto unrecognized members of a lost generation. They are a set of most intelligent individuals in the northern countryside whose real education ended between 1966 and 1968 because of the Cultural Revolution. Some found a way to continue their education in the early 1970s; most did not. But all experienced the Cultural Revolution as a disaster, a waste of time, life, and talent. It did not merely destroy their personal opportunities to rise out of the poor countryside, it wasted skill and knowledge—especially of teachers they respected. Forced back into their home villages, they rose quickly in the post-Mao reform era, some in politics, others in business. They believe in technology, growth, education, openness. They hate the Cultural Revolution. For them the south has pioneered a path onto which they must lead or drag their less enlightened or more conservative northern neighbors. They are talented, hard-working, and very open-minded. To them, the north must learn from the south to rise as the south has done. National hegemony for the southern project of wealth creation makes good sense, I believe, to ever more people in the north. A change in national identity betokens an important national possibility that is usually totally ignored.

Harry Harding, writing in a special issue on "Greater China" in a leading China studies journal, found that the "most crucial question" was "the content of modern Chinese identity" (Harding 1993, 674). The problem he finds is a combination of a competition among many places to be the center of the future China and a growth in power in regional identities such that people are "less interested in national history, in high national culture and in the use of *guoyu*," the Beijing dialect taken as the national language (ibid., 676).

In one sense, of course, China's national identity crisis is nothing special. In the economic and political realignment in the global move from a centralized, modern industrial society looking to European peoples to a postmodern information society looking to Asia, many peoples are reimagining their national identity.

In addition, Chinese are forced to confront the need to build a new nationalism as China reforms away from the Mao-like command economy to replace a now meaningless anti-imperialism. All Leninist states that reform confront this identity crisis. What makes China special is that these double sources of a deep national identity crisis are complicated by so many other factors, such as the need to modernize and the painful imperative to come to terms with the prior target of its former anti-imperialist nationalism, Japan, the Asian leader in postmodern information technologies.

Finally, China's national identity crisis is infused with and distorted by the emotional particulars of the original Mao-era anti-imperialist nationalism that made poor, heroic, north China hinterland (*shanbei*) peasants into heroes, people who martyred themselves against Japanese invaders. These peasants at the end of the twentieth century are not imagined as embodying China's better future. In fact, at Shenzhen's park of folk cultures, these *shanbei* peasants display their primitive arts along with China's so-called minorities. The north China martyrs of yesterday now are the backward, those who must learn from the coastal peoples who had and have the most contact with foreigners, previously defined as imperialist devils, sources of pollution and evil, something once to be avoided and kept out of the rest of China.

In sum, even though few northern Chinese can even understand the notion "national identity crisis," in fact, this book explores earth-shaking phenomena whose manifestations are confronted every day all over China. The data is overwhelming. The crisis is real. The question I put to this issue of national identity in the chapters of this book is whether the changes waiting in the wings have the capacity to enter stage center in socialist China and then play a role that enhances the likelihood of a democratic denouncement to the present, still open-ended, political script.

I would emphasize forces disrupting a notion of Greater China centered in Beijing. First, overseas Chinese in North America, Australia, Europe, and increasingly Southeast Asia are ever more identified as ethnic citizens of their particular country and not as Chinese overseas. That is, they are American Chinese (*Meiguo huaren*), not overseas Chinese in America (*Meiguo huaqiao*). Second, language politics is beginning to disrupt any notion of a single Chinese language center such as Beijing, since China is in fact a land of numerous unintelligible tongues. Although no one predicted it, Taiwanese identity is increasingly tied to the shared language of most multigenerational dwellers on Taiwan, *minnanhua*. This makes for a search for links with other *minnan* speakers wherever they are, in Southeast Asia, the South Sea Islands, Hainan Island, the Wenzhou region of Zhejiang, or Fujian province.

If one looked to the uniquely dynamic Wenzhou area of Zhejiang province on China's east coast in search of reasons for the economic dynamism, one found a region where virtually no one speaks the Beijing dialect, which strongly resisted Mao-era collectivization. It was a front-line region that received little state investment and was kept so miserably poor in the Mao era that its residents survived by black-market activities. Its unlicensed peddlers and underground factories were poised to grab the opportunity of post-Mao mobility and marketization. They are big investors on rapidly growing Hainan Island, and they are tied in to investment, capital, and trade with Wenzhou speakers who earlier migrated to Southeast Asia and Europe. They are also increasingly seen as descendants of non-Han people who opposed mainstream Confucianism.

There is ever less meaning to Beijing or a northern Han ethnos as a possible center. Cultural China as a definition of one homogeneous cultural Greater China is increasingly rendered incoherent. Indeed, inside the city of Beijing, numerous regional or language communities have established neighborhoods that are identified by their place of origin. Likewise, the city of Beijing is surrounded by villages that have sold residences to people from all over China who have come to work in Beijing. The periphery or peripheries are already in Beijing. The center almost no longer exists. The center experiences itself as overrun by the periphery.

In some sense, the old guard in Beijing is anxiously aware of this potential loss of its centrality and thus reacts so strongly to threats to its centrality that it often unintentionally intensifies its own undermining. At times, the regime has appealed to anti-immigrant, antirural feeling in Beijing. At times, it has tried to crack down on or keep down the in-flow from the periphery. Such policies were soon softened or abandoned when they hurt the economy. Michael Yahuda suggests that just such a response of narrow chauvinism and economic irrationality by Beijing to minimal democratization in Hong Kong could eventually produce "a collapse of confidence in Hong Kong" that "could even threaten . . . the survival of the Communist party. " (Yahuda 1993, 692).

Thomas Gold, a sociologist who studies popular culture, finds that the rise and spread of culture from Hong Kong and Taiwan into Canton and throughout China "is redefining the essence of what it means to be a 'modern' Chinese" (Gold 1993, 907). People imitate the "Hong Kong accent." Loaned words from Hong Kong are replacing Mandarin neologisms (ibid., 912).

In line with Harding's idea of many contenders to be a new center, Shanghai people (*Wu yue* culture) contend that the cultures of Taiwan and Hong Kong are really embodiments of the culture of Shanghaiese in exile (ibid., 909). In either case, the Beijing accent of the north feels "ideological and shrill" (ibid., 913), while southern tones sound "soft" and "seductive" (ibid., 914). The Chinese writer Ah Cheng similarly finds that mainland Chinese love the "soft, gentle tones" of Taiwan writing and music "because it's been so long since they've heard it." It's like "breathing" again, a return to "normality." Consequently, Ah

Cheng concludes, "the greatest hope for Chinese culture lies" in Hong Kong and Taiwan (Ah 1994, 116). Beijing no longer can give popular meaning to a desirable Chinese identity.

The cultural inventions of the northern rulers meant to hold back the southern tide "failed ignominiously." These northern emanations "were perceived as relics" of a system of "corruption and sybaritism" "hopelessly out of touch," yet still offering a "tiresome trumpeting of asceticism, sacrifice, struggle" (Gold 1993, 920). A history professor on Taiwan makes the same point more gently: "[I]n the mainland the emphasis was placed on officially sanctioned high ideals. . . . [T]here was an urgent need to compensate in the areas of daily concern like familial or romantic love" (Chen Shumei 1994, 112). Hence the cult of freedom for young women has had a larger significance for freedom for all Chinese.

Gold finds that the southern cultural tidal wave "is corrosive and potentially destabilizing." It leads him to see as "a central issue," "Does the south . . . wish to embark on a new Northern Expedition, or merely protect its autonomy?" (Gold 1993, 925).

Language politics in China as a core of identity politics can mean more than Cantonese versus Mandarin or joining the two in bilingualism. Given how many language centers are competing, it would be wrong to underestimate the strength of fissiparous forces. In contrast, Steven Levine finds it more probable that China's Communist Party will resolve its "identity crisis" (Levine 1993, 981) not, as has happened elsewhere in the Leninist world, by yielding "the political arena to gladiators of a nationalist" or, I would add, many competing ethno-nationalizing politics, but by Beijing's own "adoption of a nationalist identity," which "has been happening recently" (ibid., 982). This book has argued not that the probability highlighted by Levine is impossible, but that given the ignominious fate of the campaign to cherish Confucius and the unpopularity of the new authoritarian nationalism wished by Beijing, it is at least as likely that an anti-Confucian (or democratic Confucian), southern-based identity will become the core of the new Chinese nationalist identity as a way of fending off disunity and division, the evil that Chinese most fear.

The better national future for China is experienced as being spawned from its south. When China's National People's Congress met in Beijing in March 1992, former Guangdong governor Ye Xuanping was not there for the opening session. It was announced that he was ill. But the evening news showed this quite healthy and very popular southern leader of reform in Canton, accompanied by Deng Pufeng, a son of Deng Xiaoping, presiding at an olympiad for the handicapped that was also attended by much of the other reform leadership of the Party, none of whom chose to be with the proletarian dictatorial apparatus in the north, preferring the humanitarian southern agenda. At least that is what hopeful Chinese perceived and excitedly told each other. One certainly could not look to the north for hope that the nation would be saved.

It was not only in the coastal south that people shared stories that proved that the rulers were not patriots, that the regime acted in self-serving ways that inevitably ended up revealing its hypocrisy in such extreme ways as to deeply antagonize local peoples everywhere. For example, during the Cultural Revolution, in Sichuan Province in west China, folk were kept from climbing the holy Buddhist mountain known as Emei. But then China's Buddhist ally, Prince Sihanouk of Cambodia, asked to visit the holy mountain. Immediately, local people were conscripted into forced labor brigades to build a road up the mountain to carry Sihanouk in a comfortable car. Palpably, the regime that claimed to be patriotically serving its people revealed itself as more concerned with the good opinion of foreigners than of the people of China. More and more, the regime would seem to be selling out the people to foreigners, as with foreign aid to foreign ingrates in Albania, Vietnam, Indonesia, Cuba, and Mozambique, all of which in the 1960s or 1970s spurned China, thereby proving that the rulers had wasted the treasure of the people in wooing unworthy foreigners who would not even support China. At a vulgar popular level, this notion of having been abandoned by the rulers who preferred undeserving alien others to the Chinese people was expressed in racist, antiblack, or anti-African terms. Ever more, in an endless variety of popular terms, the regime, even in its own nationalist terms, was illegitimate.

Chinese increasingly take for granted that most politically conscious compatriots agree that the rulers are virtual traitors who sell out even to the Japanese, who never even were forced to pay an indemnity for their aggression, rape, Nazi-like medical experiments, and mass murder in China. Political strategist Yan Jiaqi declared after the June 4, 1989, massacre and a swift re-embrace of Tokyo and Beijing that included soft and commercial loans, "I solemnly declare that a new Chinese government will not bear responsibility for the repayment of loans provided by the Japanese government to prolong the life of the Communist dictatorship" (Yan 1992, 264). Zhang Jie already presumed the same view of history and evaluation in her 1986 short story, "What's Wrong With Them?" It is explained to an enterprising Chinese clothing importer from Hong Kong who went broke that he was bankrupted by the selfish collusion of corrupt and unpatriotic Chinese officials with sharp Japanese. "You didn't realize that . . . tons of highly profitable Japanese clothes were being shipped in duty free from Japan—it hadn't occurred to our Customs that such things would be imported—clothes stripped from the dead or picked out of garbage heaps. These, though second hand, were smarter than those from the street markets of Sha Tai Kok" (Zhang Jie 1987, 142).

There is a beginning of a redefinition of Mao's movement as not merely traitorous to the Chinese but as not even Chinese. While most northerners are unaware that Deng Xiaoping is Hakka, southerners who are anti-Communist joke about it. In fact, the Communist base areas in the south in the 1920s and the 1930s were largely in Hakka areas. The "Long March moved from Hakka village to Hakka village" (Erbaugh 1992, 937). "A Hakka-based underground railway supported an intelligence network in the Soviets" (ibid., 953). Almost no other socioeconomic characteristic correlates higher with top CCP leadership than Hakka origin.

Yet the Hakka were ridiculed and damned by their southern neighbors as if they were a debased breed. In 1994 I heard southerners mock the Long March as the Hakka road. Southern peasants fled and allied with southern Chinese landlords against the Hakka Communists, as Mao himself acknowledged. Mao's movement in the south was seen there as meeting Hakka purposes, not Chinese purposes. Although the Mao government classified the Hakka as Han, many southerners see a clear communalist distinction between themselves and the Hakka. Much of the Long March army leadership that fled from the south to the north and came to run the People's Republic was Hakka. Chinese journals declared at the outset of 1993 that recent research had discovered that even Mao's ancestors were Hakka who came south only in the Ming Dynasty. With the death of the Long March ruling elite in the reform era, "Hakka power is now on the wane" (ibid., 961). Reactionary post-Mao leaders Wang Zhen and Chen Xitong, however, are Hakka. A democratized China could redefine the Communist movement in its most reactionary and fundamentalist guise as Hakka. Communalist passions could easily explode in China.

Analysts err, however, when they see nationality as real and primordial. A nation is an imagined and then a constituted community. It is not an essence. For southerners who in the 1980s backed Guangdong province reform leader Ye Xuanping, whose father Ye Jianying had been one of the early Hakka Red Army leaders, Ye was southern, not Hakka. If a patriot within the southern worldview embraced Zhou Enlai, then one stressed Zhou's Jiangnan ties, not his northern origins. People will of course experience Jiangnan and Subei as a real divide and see the Mao-era disaster for Shanghai as a result of its Subei (i.e., northern) rulership. They speak of fundamentalist Wang Hongwen as Subei, although he was not. His wife was. These mutable experiences remind us that Mao's anti-Japanese, anti-imperialist, pro-self-reliance nationalism was also the product of a historical moment and not of an eternal Chinese essence.

What the data in this book show is how easy it would be for a new nationalism to dismiss the entire era of Communist rule in China as alien, or Hakka, or backward hinterland northern peasant, or some similar negating or stigmatizing category. Already a minority of southerners at the start of the 1990s have seen it that way. They seemingly have commented about a Deng Xiaoping they do not like as a Hakka who visits Hunan province to speak that Hakka language to those people, that is, the reactionaries tied to the Mao Ziyong faction (with the name pronounced in Cantonese so it means "useless") who have kept the people of Hunan poor. It is possible that, as in Russia, consciousness could change rapidly if the Leninist system crumbled; and as Lenin, Trotsky, Dzerzhinsky, Stalin et al. were in Russian consciousness reimagined so that none was Russian (Lenin was said to be Mongol and depicted in paintings as such), so the Chinese Communist movement could be reimagined as an alien excrescence, a foreign imposition, a horror that suppressed all that was good in Chinese culture. After all, Marxism-Leninism and the Soviet Russian state system were foreign imports.

Chinese who hold to the anti-imperialist northern narrative are shrinking in number. It is possible to imagine people in the hinterland west, exploited by Beijings's low and imposed prices for their primary products, preferring to join the south, imagining themselves as at one with the south historically. Back in Tang Dynasty times, after all, the capital in the northwest welcomed Turks, Uighurs, Tocharians, Sogdians, Syrians, Tartars, and Tibetans. Almost half the 8,000 students at the National Academy were from Korea, Japan, Tibet, and Central Asia. In the thirteenth century the chief architect of Beijing was a Muslim. (In 1994 I heard local officials who previously hid the fact they were Muslim instead brag about it.) When the Ming Dynasty moved the capital to Beijing, its neighboring garrison town of Tianjin became a lively commercial center. Increasingly, museums in the north and west embody this "southern" identity of openness and pluralism.

In short, the Chinese future is yet to be created by rapidly changing Chinese. A new and rising Chinese national consciousness tied to market openness certainly makes ever more likely confidence in, political action toward, and future success for a newly legitimate national project at odds with Mao's discredited monist and nativist project.

Yet northern chauvinism persists and regime reactionaries appeal to that nativism whose anti-imperialism opposes the south's pollution by trade, by missionary activity, and by cultural exchange. The regime has tried to associate those pollutants with AIDS, prostitution, and an immoral subversion of the sacred Chinese family. It is extraordinary how poorly this propaganda line has done. Ever fewer nationalistic Chinese identify their nationalism with this northern viewpoint that imagines the future in terms of an ancient northern authoritarian Confucius. The relation of north and south has been transformed and revalued. So has patriotism and the China–Japan relationship. The consequences are manifest in popular gossip, in youth socialization, in mass culture, and in elite consciousness. When a leading Chinese intellectual in the 1990s publicly defined China's options as Daoism or Confucianism and then opted for Daoism (Yue 1993, 12), this is not an academic disquisition on fine points of ancient philosophy; it is a choice of democracy over dictatorship, the southern project over the northern one, even while the northern despotism supposedly monopolizes the mass media. Such effect is ubiquitous.

The new narrative is shared by defenders, critics, and opponents of the regime. Its revisioning of China appears in cultural productions from specialized archeology to the mass media. In the movie *Farewell My Concubine,* the character of the Chu ruler of the south declares as the Communist's Red Army marches into Beijing, as he had of all other cruel armed enemies of the south, Chu, the better China: "The Han army has invaded our land." Han is the enemy. This extraordinary, yet largely hidden, re-evaluation pervades life and increasingly shapes how people are socialized to see Chinese dynamics at the end of the twentieth century. The south is not a place. It is a national consciousness, the road of people who work hard and prosper, in contrast to northerners who talk and talk but cannot really work.

A Taiwanese returning from the mainland recounts such gossip of the lazy and alien north surviving on a welfare dole from the south. "Most of the places immediately south of the Yangtze River are lands of abundance. . . . [O]ther places are different. My younger sister . . . told me that Wushih [Wuxi] City [in the south] hands over 2 billion JMP [U.S. $384 million] to the central authorities . . . [which is] equivalent . . . to the annual . . . state subsidies for Inner Mongolia. Without such subsidies, people in Inner Mongolia would starve" (*Free* 1991, 5).

People loyal to the northern regime tend rather to find that subsidies have made possible the rise of the south. Southerners, however, now imagine themselves as historical victims of the north, noting, for example, that while the center paid to double-track northern railroads, only in the post-Mao era could southern people achieve the same result, and then only by paying all the costs themselves. There is little gratitude to the northern rulers for post-Mao improvements.

With post-Mao reform, the structure of wealth in China has been rapidly changing. Political scientists agree that issues of wealth redistribution are most politically explosive. The post-Mao reforms make for extraordinary redistribution and tremendous struggles over tax revenues and budget spending. These are virtually never mentioned in the Chinese press. Increasingly, the center has to negotiate with the regions to obtain tax revenues. The center is experienced as exploiting the regions. For example, when Beijing takes a World Bank loan at a certain interest rate for hard currency, it then reloans the money to a province, charging the province a higher interest rate. The province reloans the money at a yet higher interest rate to a local region. But, in addition, Beijing keeps devaluing the national currency, the *renminbi*, to keep exports competitive. This means that regions have to repay Beijing much more *renminbi* than they originally bargained for. Often that is impossible. In Inner Mongolia, Chinese friends tell me, this led to a default. Beijing refused to send in any more budget funds. Inner Mongolia then threatened to withhold its taxes from the center. Mediation, decided in favor of Inner Mongolia, followed. While the center tries to protect its dwindling powers, power and wealth seem increasingly in the hands of the regions.

The above case also highlights how China is not merely following the supposed East Asian recipe for growth with stable legitimacy, referred to as East Asian capitalism or the Asian model or development-state policies or soft authoritarianism or the Japanese way. To be sure, as have Japan, South Korea, Hong Kong, and Taiwan, China also has pursued exports aggressively, pricing its currency low to keep its exports competitive. But Beijing lacks the political reach or central financial institutions to control foreign currencies or discipline its capital so that only winners are rewarded, as Tokyo and Singapore and Seoul did.

In addition, Beijing is not a strong, technocratically competent, bureaucratic state. China's MOFERT simply cannot do what MITI did, even though it was set up to emulate MITI. The equity in the system in Japan, Taiwan, Korea, Hong Kong, and Singapore that came from merit recruitment of the educated for the higher civil service is impossible in China's Leninist system, which is based on promoting solely the politically loyal. Consequently, political and regional tensions down to the village level are very sharp in China.

Most importantly, not only is Beijing administering a corrupt and inefficient bureaucracy, in contrast to the rest of East Asia, but Chinese people will not delay mass consumption for a generation while the center reinvests earnings. Japanese, because of defeat in World War II, South Koreans, because of a deeply felt threat from the north, and Taiwanese, because of a similar threat from the mainland, could readily be persuaded that delayed gratification was a legitimate national imperative. In contrast, Chinese on the mainland, having been victimized by false promises for the entire Mao era, want a better life now. What Chinese see, however, are glaring inequities, since nothing restrains the garish spending behavior of the newly rich.

The East Asian development model is premised on extraordinary overall income equity, which creates an experience that all the people are sacrificing together. But in China, given the unaccountable power of the state apparatus and pervasive corruption of the command economy Party system, people see a growing and illegitimate polarization. They feel no fairness in the system.

While this list of fundamental differences between post-Mao Chinese development and growth elsewhere in East Asia could readily be expanded, one cannot gainsay the post-Mao era fact of both extraordinary growth and a tremendous reduction of misery among even the poorest of the poor. Deng-era achievements are very large and palpably real. One reason for this is land reform. In China after World War II, as in Japan, Korea, and Taiwan (Hong Kong and Singapore are city-states without a significant peasant population), a truly equalizing land reform was carried out. Because peasant households, as Chayanov shows, are the most competitive producers in early industrialization, post-Mao rural reforms that have restored much of the growth potential of the original land reform (see Friedman, Pickowicz, Selden 1991) have liberated tremendous economic energies.

Rather than copying the East Asian model, for which China lacks the state capacity, China has taken advantage of opportunities uniquely available at the end of the twentieth century, including a United States effort to get Tokyo and the newly industrialized economies (NIEs) of East Asia to raise the price of their currencies to make American exports more competitive; an industrialized nations' policy removing general system of preference (GSP) benefits from newly rich countries such as the NIEs; a quota system in the industrialized democracies on textiles; and a combination of high wages, accumulated capital, global market know-how, and suitable technologies throughout East Asia that can prove beneficial for China. In addition, China has learned from Taiwan's Gaoxiong Free Export Zone. The result has been open policies in China that have won an extraordinary in-flow of resources from East Asia and provided a magnificent opportunity for earning foreign exchange that can then be spent on importing whatever China needs to raise its standard of living. Also, the higher quality and advanced productivity of foreign enterprise in China is copied and carried all over the country. From clothing to construction, the gains are enormous.

In addition, Beijing has carried out a basic political reform that empowers regions and enterprises in foreign trade. This has permitted local flexibility, free from the suffocating grip of the centralized bureaucracy. But it also has moved power from the center to the regions, away from a despotic center. (The center is not beloved in any of the industrial democracies in the postmodern era.) Consequently, conservatives at the state center in China opt for recentralization. This cannot help but intensify the experienced division of center versus region and north versus south as the past versus the future, Confucianism versus Daoism, monolithism versus pluralism, and so on.

In short, Beijing is in a most precarious position even though everything is stable and no one seeks instability. The contradictions in the situation do not guarantee that everything will fall apart. But a corrupt and inefficient bureaucracy in a state where growing income inequalities are experienced as unjust in the extreme and only superchauvinism can hope to legitimate the ruling group does not seem a formula for permanent peaceful progress. The conventional wisdom that presumes continuity in the post-Deng era does not seem omniscient. Usually, it does not even consider the central issue of national identity.

Can an analyst estimate if the global democratic surge that began at the start of the last quarter of the twentieth century is, as was the spread of democracy in the wake of World War I—a war whose aims were said to include saving the world for democracy—merely a small crest soon to be wiped out by a strong countering wave of authoritarian forces, as Weimar democracy gave way to Nazi tyranny and as Taisho democracy fell to Japanese imperial militarism? Analysts with their political fingers on the pulse beat of China, such as Huan Guocang, doubt the conventional wisdom that authoritarianism will continue in China. Looking at an illegitimate ruling party, alienated youth, outraged minorities, Dr. Huan finds it "questionable whether the military will support the highly unpopular and ineffective hardline leaders in the forthcoming succession crisis" (Huan 1992, 101).

One popular way to be a Chinese nationalist at the end of the twentieth century is to appeal to the Chinese in the diaspora. Beijing is not looked to for truth. Privately and publicly Chinese speculate about replacing the corrupt, over-centralized People's Republic with a liberal, more decentralized, and locally accountable pluralistic republic that has little in common with Mao's walled-in, overly centralized, exclusionist regime. Chinese in private talk of a confederation that could appeal even to a democratic Taiwan.

It is easy to imagine a reform-oriented regional Party leader—not from the south—legitimating the new and more open national consciousness after becoming first among equals in a succession crisis in which the old guard, their heirs, and other authoritarians all seem too much like outmoded and discredited forces, such as the reactionary Manchu Empress Dowager was at the end of the nineteenth century. Chinese could enjoy yet another opportunity to consolidate one more democratic breakthrough.

The great force of constitutional democracy at the end of the Qing and beginning of the Republic in 1911 might have won power. And so might the Democracy Movement of spring 1989. The results turned on contingent factors. These defeats of democracy are not proof that China uniquely lacks a democratic culture. As Greek philosophers recognized, even in the era of democratic ancient Athens, no people (or culture) is born democratic. Neither Plato nor Socrates considered the full citizens of Athens as suited for democracy. In the West, as elsewhere, culture tends to be authoritarian. All peoples consequently have to craft democratic institutions that negate the thrust of inherited antidemocratic forces and cultures. This political crafting has been shown as possible in Muslim Albania and Muslim Turkey, in Buddhist Sri Lanka, among the heirs of Japanese Shintoism or Israeli Judaism, among people from Catholic Latin America to animists in the South Sea Islands, and even to the heirs of Genghis Khan in Mongolia. Given democracy's gains in so many Confucian East Asian places, including South Korea, given that Chinese Confucianism is so much weaker than robust Korean Confucianism, it is difficult to see any impediments to democracy in China, outside of the political arena, that cannot be readily dealt with.

Had China's senior Communist leaders chosen to compromise with the democrats in spring 1989, as apparently was the wish of the group led by Premier Zhao Ziyang and the desire even of many senior military leaders, then China could have democratized peacefully. Weaker democratic mass movements in other Communist nations met such a prodemocratic reception from their Party leaders, thereby permitting an evolutionary breakthrough toward democracy. In contrast, China's Deng Xiaoping proved an obdurate despot. The defeat of democracy in China was not caused by some imaginary, deep Chinese cultural obstacle. Although he was the paramount leader, Deng is not an embodiment of a unique Chinese essence.

However, it is not surprising that so many Chinese thinkers blamed the culture for China's democratic failure. A similar erroneous diagnosis prevailed in France in the mid-nineteenth century after the breakthroughs to liberal constitutionalism in 1789, 1830, and 1848 were all crushed and reversed. The French analysis of a unique French cultural resistance to democracy in the mid-nineteenth century, however, was wrong.[3] By 1871 the Third Republic inaugurated a long era of peaceful democratic evolution in France (see Friedman 1994). Deep cultural arguments are invariably circular and therefore superficially persuasive at their moment of origin, when they unconsciously appeal to common prejudices of the era, but only of that moment. These cultural explanations invariably are eventually exploded and shown to be ridiculous rationalizations of readily comprehensible political defeats. So it should be with China's struggle to build a democratic nation.[4]

Chinese want change. They experience regime propaganda as a lie. They have to survive daily by leading a two-faced life. And they know it. What it means to be a Chinese person is being redefined. This quest for simple truth, Hannah Arendt and Vaclav Havel have eloquently shown, eventually subverts Leninist tyranny. The democratic transition, Lech Walesa has explained, comes as "shedding the invisible veneer of a lie" and establishing a "communion of people who did not wish to participate in a lie" (Blum 1989, 289, 294). The dynamics of that transition, this book shows, are already in place in China. The northern mythos is the lie. Southern consciousness offers the new communion. That Chinese are cynical and apolitical, as East Germans were in 1988, does not mean they will not act politically in the future. Just because cynicism in East Germany was misunderstood in 1988 is no reason to err yet again. Rather, the late-twentieth-century unwillingness among Chinese to accept any political line should be understood as more than cynicism or a crisis of faith. It also is part of a healthy skepticism that makes possible an open and free polity.

The conventional wisdom expressed in an article by Spector and Medeiros, however, is that China is special. Somehow it is not like the others. "Unlike the Soviet Union, China is not an empire waiting to break apart." But in fact, China was an empire until 1911. And the post-1949 People's Republic, no more than the defunct Soviet Union, did not find a way to integrate the diverse identities of Mongol, Turkic, or Tibetan, of Jiangnan, Minnan, or Chaozhou into a new national identity. Political scientist Lucien Pye in fact has long insisted that China remains an empire in search of a nation. This book offers much data on the fragility, if not the failure, of the Mao-era nation-building project at the ideational and identity levels. Language/regional political splits are live possibilities on the mainland of China. Taiwan language politics is redefining political identity on Taiwan, too. Seemingly primordial identities are sensitive and can erupt.

The specialists at the Congressional Research Service of the Library of Congress reflected this hegemonic predilection for ignoring all data on regionalism by concluding a December 20, 1993, report on *China in Transition*,

> Provincial authorities have been given greater control. . . . Provincial governments also evade central government decisions. . . . The power of the provincial leaders also may be reflected in their growing role in the central elite. . . . The decentralization of political power in China . . . poses serious difficulties for Beijing. (Congressional Research Service 1993)

As usual, the realists then ignore their data and treat continuity as inevitable. "Yet . . . prospects for the political fragmentation of China remain remote." (ibid., 10).

The Spector–Medeiros conventional wisdom remains, therefore, that "most observers are optimistic that the integrity of the Chinese state will not be threatened during the post-Deng transition" because the military "is dedicated to a unified, powerful China that can take its rightful place on the world stage."

Putting aside the guess on the state of the Chinese military, which in fact is increasingly regionalized, one cannot slight the importance of the economy. Power in the world entering the twenty-first century is mainly defined by global economic competitiveness, such that many successful regions, from Lombardy to the Czech Republic to the Baltic states, have become actors in the splitting of a prior state, experienced as inappropriately overcentralized and overmilitarized, as the Chinese state is also experienced by its residents. Not to believe that powerful forces of reimagined national identity can remake Chinese politics and even enhance the prospects for democracy requires believing that only Chinese do not act as do all other human beings.

This does not mean that China will disintegrate or that the crafting of a democratic Chinese confederation will prove an easy inevitability. Chinese still speak of themselves as one people, still fear chaos and disunity, still offer no audience for splitism. Yet one should also pay attention to other surging forces that are discussed in this book. These developments suggest that a host of worse and better alternatives to continuity are realistic political possibilities. Success or failure rests on political action in China. The future agenda is not yet set. Since politics is a contingent arena premised on mutable and unpredictable factors such as leadership, timing, the historic moment, coalition building, and agenda setting, there is no way to predict confidently tomorrow's future. The Ottoman Empire lived long after it served no useful purpose.

But when so many forces of change have piled up, surely politically stagnant continuity is not invariably the likeliest outcome. Most people will, however, still nod to the pseudorealist notion that tomorrow will be more or less like today, that continuity and Beijing-based national integrity are almost sure things. They could be right. I certainly do not claim to have the powers of a fortune teller.

A new, perhaps southern, national consciousness may not succeed in imposing itself on or in China's people. But it seems that in Canton the cry is ever louder that we are not Han; we are the people of Tang. Northerners are riffraff, barbarians, Mongols, or worse. The true Chinese culture is in the south. Beijing-imposed centralized monism no longer seems to be China. Even the southern region of Guangdong is a plurality of communities: Cantonese, Chaozhou, Dan, Hakka, and many more. One conclusion seems obvious, given the data presented in this book. It is absurd to treat peaceful, northern authoritarian continuity as inevitable. The hitherto little-commented-upon change of national identity in socialist China discussed in this volume has opened up new, real, and viable prospects, some with democratic potential.

Notes

1. For the view that Confucianism blocks democratization, see Huntington (1968 and 1993).
2. For a sophisticated and persuasive response to this defense of dictatorship, see McCormick (1994).
3. The similarity to the twentieth-century Chinese debate of the nineteenth-century French discourse on cultural obstacles to democracy is explored in Friedman (1994) and chapter 1.
4. It would be impossible within the new Chinese nationalism that privileges the south to imagine China's past as did the historian John King Fairbank. He argued that "Early Chinese civilization grew up in North China rather far from the ocean." In contrast to the rice-farming Chinese south, Fairbank contended, "the dry farming of North China and Europe was . . . more amenable to diversity of cropping . . . and large economies of scale. . . . All this made for a higher degree of change in social structure and polity" (Fairbank 1986, 3, 4, 5).

References

Ah Cheng. 1994. "Towards Normality." *Sinorama* (March), pp. 114–16.
Anderson, Perry. 1992. *A Zone of Engagement*. (London: Verso).
Blum, Lawrence, and Victor Seidler. 1989. *A Truer Liberty* (New York: Routledge).
Bobbio, Noberto. 1987 (1984). *The Future of Democracy*. (Minneapolis: University of Minnesota Press).
Chen, Shumei. 1994. "From Mao Zedong to Chiung Yao." *Sinorama* (March), pp. 106–13.
Chen, Xiaomei. 1992. "Occidentalism as Counterdiscourse." *Critical Inquiry* (Summer), pp. 686–712.
Congressional Research Service. Library of Congress. 1993. *China in Transition*. Washington, DC: Government Printing Office.
de Bary, William Theodore. 1985. "Confucian Liberalism and Western Parochialism." *Philosophy East and West* 35.4 (October), pp. 399–412.
———. 1988. "Neo-Confucianism and Human Rights." In Leroy Rouner, ed., *Human Rights and the World's Religions*. (South Bend, IN: University of Notre Dame Press), pp. 183–98.
Des Forges, Robert. 1993. "Democracy in Chinese History." In Des Forges, ed., *Chinese Democracy and the Crisis of 1989* (Albany: State University of New York Press), pp. 21–52.
Erbaugh, Mary. 1992. "The Secret History of the Hakkas." *The China Quarterly*.
Esherick, Joseph. 1990. "Xi'an Spring." *The Australian Journal of Chinese Studies* No. 24 (July).
Fairbank, John King. 1986. *The Great Chinese Revolution* (New York: Harper and Row).
Fincher, John. 1981. *Chinese Democracy: The Self-Government Movements in Local, Provincial, and National Politics, 1905—1914* (New York: St. Martin's Press).
Fredrickson, George. 1993. "Pioneer." *The New York Review of Books* (September 23), p. 33.
Free China Journal. 1991. (February 14), p. 5.
Friedman, Edward, Paul Pickowicz, and Mark Selden. 1991. *Chinese Village, Socialist State* (New Haven: Yale University Press).
Friedman, Edward. 1994. *The Politics of Democratization* (Boulder, CO: Westview).

Gold, Thomas. 1993. "Go With Your Feelings." *The China Quarterly,* No. 136 (December), pp. 907–25.

Gu Xin. n.d. Unpublished manuscript. "Democracy versus Dictatorship."

Gunn, Anne. 1990. "Tell the World About Us." *The Australian Journal of Chinese Studies*, No. 24 (July).

Harding, Harry. 1993. "The Concept of Greater China." *The Chinese Quarterly*, No. 136 (December), pp. 660–86.

Havel, Vaclav. 1986. *Living in Truth* (London: Faber and Faber).

Huan Guocang. 1992. "Whither China?" *The Journal of Contemporary China* 1.1 (Fall).

Huntington, Samuel. 1968. *Political Order in Changing Societies* (New Haven: Yale University Press).

———. 1993. *The Third Wave* (Norman: University of Oklahoma Press).

Levine, Steven. 1993. "China's Fuzzy Transition." *The China Quarterly*, No. 136 (December), pp. 972–83.

Liu Zhongyi. 1992. In *Nongcun Gongzuo Tongxin* [Rural Work Newsletter] (March 5). Translated in JPRS-CAR–92–052, July 17, 1992.

McCormick, Barrett. 1990. *Political Reform in Post-Mao China* (Berkeley: University of California Press).

———. 1994. "Democracy or Dictatorship?" *The Australian Journal of Chinese Affairs*, No. 31 (January), pp. 95–112.

Minoque, Kenneth. 1979. "This History of the Idea of Human Rights." In Walter Laguer and Barry Rubin, eds., *The Human Rights Reader* (New York: New American Library), pp. 3–17.

Moghadam, Val. 1989. "Against Eurocentrism and Nativism." *Socialist Democracy* (Fall–Winter).

Moore, Barrington, Jr. 1966. *Social Origins of Dictatorship and Democracy* (Boston: Beacon Press).

Nathan, Andrew. 1988. *Chinese Democracy* (New York: Knopf).

Price, Don. 1990. "Constitutional Alternatives and Democracy in the Revolution of 1911." In Paul Cohen and Merle Goldman, eds., *Ideas Across Cultures* (Cambridge, MA: Harvard Council on East Asian Studies), pp. 223–60.

Saadawi, Nawal El. 1981. *The Hidden Face of Eve* (Boston: Beacon Press).

Schram, Stuart, ed. 1992. *Mao's Road to Power: Revolutionary Writings*, Vol. I (Armonk, NY: M. E. Sharpe).

Smith, Roger, M. 1993. "Beyond Tocqueville, Myrdal and Hartz." *American Political Science Review* 87:3 (September), pp. 549–66.

Spector, Leonard, and Evan Medeiros. 1993. "China's Perilous Nuclear Puzzle," *Washington Post Weekly* (October 11–17), p. 25.

Wakeman, Frederic, Jr. 1973. *History and Will* (Berkeley: University of California Press).

Wang Xizhe 1985. "Strive for the Class Dictatorship of the Proletariat." In Anita Chan et al., eds., *On Socialist Democracy and the Chinese Legal System* (Armonk, NY: M. E. Sharpe).

Yahuda, Michael. 1993. "The Foreign Relations of Greater China." *The China Quarterly*, No. 136 (December), pp. 687–710.

Yan Jiaqi. 1992. *Toward a Democratic China* (Honolulu: University of Hawaii Press).

Yue Daiyun. 1993. "Standing at a Theoretical Crossroads." *China Exchange News* 21.3–4 (Fall–Winter), pp. 9–12.

Zhang Jie. 1987. "What's Wrong with Him?" *Renditions*, Nos. 27, 28 (Spring and Fall).

Zhang Xinhua. 1990. "On Using Traditional Culture as a Wellspring to Build a New Culture." *Shehui Kexue*, No. 3 (March 18). Translated in JPRS-CAR–90–049, July 11, 1990, pp. 103–6.

Index

Bawang Bie Jie. See Farewell My Concubine
Beauty contests, 152
Beauty parlors, 165
Bei Dao, 80
Beijing (China), 71, 331
Beijing Massacre, 167, 303
Beijing University, 298
Bendix, Richard, 37
Bennett, Jeremy, 288
Bentsen, Lloyd, 188–89
Bismarck, Otto von, 265, 275
Bloody Black River (Hao), 161
Bo Yibo, 282
Bobbio, Norberto, 318
Bolsheviks, 210, 236, 252
Bourgeoisie, 220, 271
Boxers, 38
Brezhnev, Leonid, 127
Bride price, 183*n.25*
Brinton, Crane, 250
Brus, W., 46
Brzezinski, Zbigniew, 236–37
Buddhist Lamaism, 49
Bukharin, N.I., 209
Bukovsky, Vladimir, 276*n.6*
Bulwer-Lytton, Edward, 211
Bureaucracy, 209, 213, 223, 337, 338
Burke, Edmund, 286
Burma. *See* Myanmar

C

Cai Jinhua, 164
Camel Xiangzi (She), 96
Canton, 68, 71, 100, 108–09
Can Xue, 172
Cantonese (language), 109, 144
Capitalism, 25, 46, 52, 87, 266
Carter, Jimmy, 182*n.10*
Catholicism, 237
Censorship, 96, 274, 303, 308

Centralization, 18
Chai Ling, 30, 328
Chan, Anita, 15
Chan, Sylvia, 166
Chaos, 303–05, 312
Chauvinism, 18, 30, 65, 66, 71, 130, 240, 272, 325
  See also Nationalism
Chen Kaige, 168
Chen Kun, 106
Chen Xitong, 334
Chen Xuezhao, 138
Chen Yun, 102
Chen Ziming, 110
Cheng Li, 9
Chiang Kai-shek. *See* Jiang Jieshi
Chile, 188
Chin, Ann-ping, 15
China
  democracy in. *See* Democracy; Democratization
  economy. *See* Economic reforms; Economy
  ethnicity. *See* Ethnic identity
  failed modernity of, 63–74
  foreign policy of. *See* Foreign policy
  and Japan. *See* Japan
  military. *See* Military
  national history in, 7
  national identity. *See* National identity
  nationalism. *See* Nationalism
  north-south split in, 3–19, 33–36, 40, 57, 68, 70–72, 77–86, 108, 145, 326, 329, 341
  revised history for, 82–86
  southern supremacy in, 81–82
  populist movements in, 272–73
  possible disintegration of, 80–81, 318–19
  in post-Leninist world, 58–61
  revolution in. *See* Revolution

China *(continued)*
southern cultural renaissance,
76*n.35*
succession crisis, 306
uniqueness of, 27–28, 340
unique opportunities for,
337–38
*China and Japan in the Global
Setting* (Iriye), 135
China Daily, 155
China in Transition, 340
China Youth Daily, 152
Chinese Communist Party (CCP),
117, 213, 218
Chinese Economic Area, 79, 145
Ching, Julia, 166–67
Chu culture, 102–05, 107, 108,
110, 172
Civic culture, 250, 309, 321
Civil service, 205
Civil War (U.S.), 249, 261*n.11*,
312
Classified News (journal), 318
Class struggle, 268
Clothing, 167
CMEA. *See* Community for
Mutual Economic Assistance
Coastal development, 199
Codrescu, Andrei, 154
Cohen, Myron, 200
Cold War, 242
Collectivization, 123, 197, 267
COMECON. *See* Community for
Mutual Economic Assistance
*The Coming Decline of the
Chinese Empire* (Louis), 77
Command economy, 194, 255
Communalist identity, 45, 78, 80,
85, 323–24
Communications, 78
Communism. *See*
Barracks-Communism;
Leninism; War communism

Communist Party. *See* Chinese
Communist Party
Community, 58
Community for Mutual Economic
Assistance (CMEA;
COMECON), 193
Compensation, war. *See*
Reparations
Competence, 213
Confucianism, 7, 13, 17, 22*n.53*,
41, 59, 69, 72, 73, 110, 145,
149–81, 274, 325, 327–28
campaign for, 151–53
cultural creations against, 167–69
as despotism, 237
and economic reforms, 190–91
and modernization, 276*n.2*
Constitution (U.S.), 249, 312
Continuity, 5–6, 341
Corruption, 192, 265, 296
Coups, 103
Creativity, 98
Cui Guozhen, 298–99
Cultural identities. *See* Ethnic
identity
Cultural Revolution, 105, 127,
162, 209, 268, 289, 317, 329,
333
Culture, 81, 302, 328
claims of uniqueness, 241
oral, 99
pluralism in, 99
Currency devaluation, 336
Cynicism, 299, 340
Czechoslovakia, 12, 127, 252

D

Dai Qing, 158, 159, 171, 173, 180
Dalien (China), 39
De Bary, William Theodore, 311
Decoding. *See* Oppositional
decoding

Edward Friedman teaches about China, democratization and transitions from socialist systems, in the Department of Political Science at the University of Wisconsin, Madison. His most recent book is *The Politics of Democratization* (1994). His co-authored work *Chinese Village, Socialist State* (1991) was chosen by the Association of Asian Studies in 1993 to receive the Joseph Levenson Prize as the best book on modern China.

Dr. Friedman speaks and reads Chinese and has traveled widely in China. His work appears regularly in both major scholarly journals and also in magazines and newspapers of informed opinion. He received an M.A. in East Asian Studies and a Ph.D. in Political Science from Harvard University.